THE
Penguin History
of
AMERICAN
LIFE

Also by Michael Willrich

City of Courts: Socializing Justice in Progressive Era Chicago

POX

AN AMERICAN HISTORY

MICHAEL WILLRICH

THE PENGUIN PRESS

NEW YORK

2011

THE PENGUIN PRESS
Published by the Penguin Group
Penguin Group (USA) Inc., 375 Hudson Street, New York, New York 10014,
U.S.A. · Penguin Group (Canada), 90 Eglinton Avenue East, Suite 700, Toronto,
Ontario, Canada M4P 2Y3 · (a division of Pearson Penguin Canada Inc.) ·
Penguin Books Ltd, 80 Strand, London WC2R 0RL, England · Penguin Ireland,
25 St. Stephen's Green, Dublin 2, Ireland · (a division of Penguin Books Ltd) ·
Penguin Books Australia Ltd, 250 Camberwell Road, Camberwell, Victoria 3124,
Australia · (a division of Pearson Australia Group Pty Ltd) · Penguin Books India
Pvt Ltd, 11 Community Centre, Panchsheel Park, New Delhi – 110 017, India ·
Penguin Group (NZ), 67 Apollo Drive, Rosedale, Auckland 0632, New Zealand
(a division of Pearson New Zealand Ltd) · Penguin Books (South Africa) (Pty)
Ltd, 24 Sturdee Avenue, Rosebank, Johannesburg 2196, South Africa

Penguin Books Ltd, Registered Offices: 80 Strand, London WC2R 0RL, England

First published in 2011 by The Penguin Press,
a member of Penguin Group (USA) Inc.

LIBRARY OF CONGRESS CATALOGING IN PUBLICATION DATA
Willrich, Michael.
Pox : an American history / Michael Willrich.
p. ; cm.—(Penguin history of American life)
Includes bibliographical references and index.
ISBN 978-1-59420-286-5
1. Smallpox—Epidemiology—United States.   2. Smallpox—History—United
States.   3. Epidemics—United States—19th Century—History.
4. Epidemics—United States—20th Century—History.   I. Title.
II. Series: Penguin history of American life.
[DNLM: 1. Smallpox—epidemiology—United States.   2. Smallpox—history—
United States.   3. Disease Outbreaks—United States.   4. History, 19th Century—
United States.   5. History, 20th Century—United States. WC 590]
RA644.S6W55   2011
614.5'210973—dc22   2010034544

Printed in the United States of America
1   3   5   7   9   10   8   6   4   2
Designed by Michelle McMillian

For Wendy

Contents

NEW YORK, 1900

Manhattan's West Sixty-ninth Street no longer runs from West End Avenue to the old New York Central Railroad tracks at the Hudson River's edge. In the space now occupied by aging high-rise condominium towers and their long shadows, there once stood a low-slung street of tenements and houses. At the turn of the twentieth century, it was said to be the most thickly populated block in the most thickly populated city in the United States of America. Someone called it "All Nations Block," and, being a pretty fair description of the place, for a while the name stuck.

A brisk walk from the fashionable hotels of Central Park West, All Nations Block was a rough world of day laborers, bricklayers, blacksmiths, stonemasons, elevator runners, waiters, janitors, domestic servants, bootblacks, tailors, seamstresses, the odd barber or grocer, and, far outnumbering them all, children. Each morning, the children streamed east to Public School No. 94 at Amsterdam Avenue or to the crowded kindergarten run by the Riverside Association at 259 West Sixty-ninth Street. That same footworn building housed the charitable association's public baths; in any given week, four hundred men or more paid a nickel for a towel, a piece of soap, and a shower that had to last. The tenement dwellers of All Nations Block did not choose their neighbors. It was the kind of place where an itinerant black minstrel actor, feeling feverish and far from his southern home, could find a bed for a few nights, in a great warren of rooms whose other occupants were Italian, Irish, Jewish, German, Swedish, Austrian, African American, or simply, so they said, "white."[1]

The men of the West Sixty-eighth Street police station knew the block and its ways well. The policemen came when the neighbors brawled, when jewelry went missing in an apartment by the park, or when the Irish boys of the All Nations Gang got too rough with the Chinese laundryman on West End Avenue. The police came once again on the night of November 28. A forlorn and drunken stonemason named Michael Healy, imagining himself to be under attack in his room ("They're after me," he had shouted, "See those black men!"), had hurled himself through a fourth-floor window and fell, in a cascade of glass, to, or rather through, the ground below. The Irishman made a two-by-two-foot hole in the surface, breaking through to some long-forgotten trench near the building's cellar. A neighborhood boy ran to the Church of the Blessed Sacrament on West Seventieth Street and summoned a priest. When the priest arrived, he crawled right through the hole and into the trench, which was already crowded with police, an ambulance surgeon, and Healy's broken but still breathing body. Before this subterranean congregation, the priest administered last rites. That was the way things went on All Nations Block. It was the night before Thanksgiving, the first of the new century.[2]

New Yorkers of a certain age would remember that Thanksgiving as the day the smallpox struck the West Side. The outbreak had in fact started quietly a few days earlier, on All Nations Block. The city health officers found the children first: twelve-year-old Madeline Lyon, on Tuesday, and on Wednesday, a child just across the street, identified only as a "white boy four years old." For the health officers to diagnose the cases with any confidence, the children must have been suffering for days, with raging fevers, headaches, severe back pain, and, likely, vomiting, followed by the distinctive eruption of pocks on their faces and bodies. Once the rash appeared and the lesions began their two-week metamorphosis, from flat red spots to hard, shotlike bumps to fat pustules to scabs, the patients were highly contagious. The health officers removed the children, stripped their rooms of bedding and clothing, and disinfected the premises.[3]

The health department followed the same procedure with the five other cases that were reported elsewhere in Manhattan within hours of the Lyon case. One was a white domestic servant named Mary Holmes, who worked in an affluent apartment house on West Seventy-sixth Street. The other four were black, evidently from the neighborhood of the West Forties. They were Adeffa Warren, Lizzie Hooker, Susan Crowley, and Crowley's newborn daughter—these last two had been removed in haste from the maternity ward at Bellevue Hospital. Through interviews, health officers had established that the four black patients had come into contact with an unnamed infected "negress," who remained at large. How any of these patients might have been connected to the children on West Sixty-ninth Street, about a mile and a half uptown, remained uncertain. But the authorities were working on the assumption that the outbreak started on All Nations Block.[4]

The officers of the internationally renowned New York City Health Department, medical men given broad powers to police and protect the public health in one of the world's most powerful centers of capital, were not easily shaken by the odd case of smallpox among the wage earners. Now and then an infected passenger got past the U.S. government medical inspectors at Ellis Island or crossed into the city on one of its many railroad tracks, waterways, roads, footpaths, or bridges. Most New Yorkers had undergone vaccination for smallpox at one time or another—on board a steamship crossing the Atlantic, in the public schools, in the workplaces, in the city jails and asylums, or, if they possessed the means, in their own homes under the steady hand of a trusted family physician. When an isolated case of smallpox triggered a broader outbreak, the health officials took it as an unmistakable sign that the population's level of immunity had begun to taper off, as it did every five to ten years. The time had come to sound the call for a general vaccination. "We are not afraid of smallpox," said Dr. F. H. Dillingham of the health department, when the news broke that smallpox had reappeared on Manhattan. "With the present facilities of this department we can stamp out any disease."[5]

On Thanksgiving Day, as the Columbia University football team took the field against the Carlisle Indian School and three thousand homeless people lined up for a hot dinner at the Five Points House of Industry, a vaccination squad from the health department's Bureau of Contagious Diseases moved into West Sixty-ninth Street. The four doctors began a quiet canvass of All Nations Block, starting with the immediate neighbors of the infected children. Health department protocol called for a thorough investigation of each case, in order to trace its origin, followed by the immediate vaccination of all possible contacts. In a place as densely inhabited as All Nations Block, everyone would have to bare their arms for the vaccine.[6]

With a willing patient, the vaccination "operation," as doctors called it, lasted just a minute or two. The doctor took hold of the patient's arm, scoring the skin with a needle or lancet. He then dabbed on the vaccine, either by taking a few droplets of liquid "lymph" from a glass tube or using a small ivory "point" coated with dry vaccine. Either way, the vaccine contained live cowpox or *vaccinia* virus that not long before had oozed from a sore on the underside of an infected calf in a health department stable. In the coming days, the virus would produce a blisterlike vesicle at the vaccination site. In due course, the lesion would heal, leaving a permanent scar: the distinctive vaccination cicatrix. If all went well, the patient would then enjoy immunity from smallpox for five to seven years, sometimes longer. And, of course, as long as a person was immune, she could not pass along smallpox to others.[7]

The health department's plan was to secure All Nations Block first and then follow the same procedure on the surrounding streets. In the coming days, health officers and police would maintain a quarantine on the block and enforce vaccination in the neighborhood schools. The health department would use all the available methods to fight the disease: total isolation of patients, quarantine of their living environment, vaccination of anyone exposed to the disease, disinfection of closed spaces and personal belongings, and close surveillance of the infected district and its residents.[8]

It was a sensible protocol, born of medical science and the city's long experience with the deadliest contagious disease the world had ever known. Historically, smallpox killed 25 to 30 percent of all those whom it infected; most survivors were permanently disfigured with the dreaded pitted scars. Decades after the scientific revolution known as the germ theory of disease, biologists and doctors were still searching in their laboratories for the specific pathogen that caused smallpox. But they felt confident they had a strong understanding of the microbe's behavior: its pathological course in the human body, its epidemiological effects in a population, and the immunological power of vaccination to prevent the virus from attacking an individual or proliferating across an entire community. According to the state-of-the-art scientific knowledge, the "infecting germs" of smallpox spread unseen from one nonimmune person to another, communicated in a cough, a brush of bodies, or across the folds and surfaces of everyday things: an article of clothing, a Pullman porter's whisk broom, a piece of mail, a newspaper, a library book, a bit of currency, a shared cigarette. Because smallpox had an incubation period of ten to fourteen days, during which the infected person presented no noticeable symptoms, health officers strived to retrace the circuits of human contact in order to identify probable carriers and contain the outbreak.[9]

The vaccination corps had not been on the block long before the doctors realized the need for reinforcements, men armed with more than vaccine. As the physicians moved from door to door, rapping loudly and calling for the occupants to come out and be vaccinated, many residents refused to cooperate. The doctors tried to explain the danger, which could not have been easy given the many tongues spoken on the block. But many people would not submit to having their own or their children's arms scraped by the vaccinators without, according to *The New York Times*, "loud wails and even positive resistance." Receiving word of the worsening situation on All Nations Block, the commander of the West Sixty-eighth Street station dispatched a detail of six policemen to assist the doctors in "enforcing the vaccination."[10]

Well into the cool autumn night, All Nations Block echoed with the rapping of nightsticks on doors, the shouting and pleas of the residents within, and, through it all, the rattle of the horse-drawn ambulance wagons as they moved to and from the infected district. By midnight, the vaccination corps had discovered another twenty-two cases on the block, many of them little children, all of them, in the health officers' view, requiring immediate isolation. The ambulance wagons carried the patients five miles over rough city roads to the Willard Parker Hospital, the health department's contagious diseases facility at the foot of East Sixteenth Street on the East River, where the doctors gave them a more full examination. From there they were ferried off Manhattan and many more miles upriver to the city smallpox hospital, the "pesthouse" on North Brother Island, a nineteen-acre wooded island situated between Rikers Island and the Bronx mainland.

Pesthouses, public hospitals used to isolate poor people suffering from infectious diseases, were the most dreaded of American institutions. The trip to North Brother Island was a grim journey into unknown territory. No known cure for smallpox existed. The pesthouse doctors could do little more than treat the patients' symptoms. It was up to the virus, and to each patient's own resources, to determine who among the infected would die in the seclusion of North Brother Island.

The germ theory taught that contagious diseases such as smallpox did not arise spontaneously; they did not spring to life in vaporous miasmas from stagnant water or decomposing filth, as physicians and sanitarians had previously assumed. Doctors now understood smallpox to be caused by invisible life forms—"germs"—that could only survive and proliferate by infecting human carriers. There seemed to be no animal or insect vector for smallpox: no species of mosquito, rodent, or bird that carried the disease from person to person, place to place. If smallpox suddenly appeared in a previously healthy community, there were only two possible explanations: either viral material from a recent case had survived for a time in clothing or bedding or, more likely, someone had brought the pox into the community. On this point medical science reinforced the common reflex of human communities everywhere to blame sudden misfortune on their most marginal inhabitants, outsiders and "others."[11]

"What a potent factor in maintaining the prevalence of small-pox is that unemployed and largely unemployable degenerate, the habitual vagrant or tramp," observed a writer in the London-based *Lancet*, the preeminent English-language medical journal. "The fact that this parasite upon the charity and good nature of the community is in his turn a vehicle for the spread of other parasites, both animal and vegetable, is common knowledge but practically no compulsory steps have been taken to curtail seriously the vagrant's movements or to promote his elementary cleanliness."[12]

Suspicion fell immediately upon one of the infected patients en route to North Brother Island, the black minstrel actor who had just arrived on All Nations Block. A member of the traveling Wright Troupe, the man (whose name is lost to the historical record) had come north only a short time before and had taken a room in one of the houses where the sick children were later discovered. The rumor quickly spread that "this negro" had carried the germs in his body from Pittsburgh and, living in a house filled with playful innocents, infected at least one of them. That child, the theory went, infected classmates in the swimming bath of the Riverside Kindergarten. The theory had an easy plausibility; the white doctors of the health department, no less than the residents of All Nations Block, lived in an American culture of race that scorned black bodies as vessels of moral and physical danger. But perhaps there was more to the theory than a reflexive racism. Smallpox had been epidemic for several years in the American South, where it had spread first and most widely among black laborers in the coal mines, railroad camps, tobacco plantations, and crowded cabin settlements of the rising New South. Given the long incubation period of the disease, it might have been expected that an African American traveler would eventually bring the southern smallpox to New York. On two separate occasions during the preceding three years, smallpox epidemics had struck upstate communities. Each time the New York State Health Department had attributed the outbreaks to a traveling negro minstrel show.[13]

As the city health department grew concerned about the seemingly connected center of contagion, in the neighborhoods of the West Forties near Eighth Avenue, rumors circulated about a second suspect. He, too, was black. Albert Sanders, twenty-two, had suffered through nearly the full course of smallpox without medical attention before he was discovered; no patient found so far had been infected longer than he was. During this time Sanders had managed to mingle with many people. Unlike the minstrel man, Sanders had been in town for a while, and his name had appeared in the papers before. In the brutal West Side race riot of August 15, 1900, as hundreds of whites taunted and beat blacks in the African American neighborhoods along Eighth Avenue, Sanders had been listed among the injured, suffering from scalp wounds and cuts. Evidently the experience had not inspired in him a trust of whites, doctors included.[14]

Once two dozen cases of smallpox had turned up on the West Side, the question of the outbreak's precise origin became almost moot. Whoever had started it—the minstrel man of All Nations Block, the unnamed "negress," Albert Sanders, or someone else—the outbreak would now be difficult to contain.

By December 6, one week after Thanksgiving, the New York papers were calling the outbreak a full-blown smallpox epidemic, the worst in Manhattan since 1892. Three of the patients on North Brother Island had already succumbed to the disease: the servant Mary Holmes; twenty-year-old Elizabeth Oliver; and the Crowley infant, whose mother, it seemed, had not had the heart to name her. The pesthouse now held forty-four smallpox patients, with more arriving almost every day. All hopes of keeping the outbreak quarantined in a small area of the city had vanished when five-year-old Sadie Hemple, until recently a resident of West Sixty-ninth Street and pupil at the Riverside Kindergarten, turned up across the river in Hoboken with a case of smallpox. The virus had incubated in her body while she and her parents moved to their new home, a five-story tenement house where some twenty other children lived. The Hoboken authorities removed Sadie to their own pesthouse, in a place called Snake Hill. New York officials had to concede that the West Side outbreak had "overleaped the bounds" of All Nations Block.[15]

The health department's vaccination corps was now scraping the arms of the poor at the rate of fifteen hundred per day. Resistance to vaccination had abated in some of the infected areas—where the people were, in the words of one city vaccinator, "well scared up." More than five hundred poor people called each day for free vaccinations at the board of health's headquarters on West Fifty-sixth Street, most of them mothers with little children in tow. But with each new outbreak in another of the island's crowded tenement districts, the vaccination corps met fresh resistance. Over time, the corps would ever more closely resemble a military outfit. Across the city, private physicians and druggists bought up "hitherto unheard of quantities" of the health department's vaccine stock. At factories, department stores, and offices, employers told their employees to get vaccinated or not bother showing up. On Wall Street, the managers of the New York Stock Exchange set up their own on-site vaccination station. All employees had to submit to the procedure before they could take their positions in the great scrum of the trading floor.[16]

Among the many political effects of the widening epidemic in New York City was an earnest moral discourse, as the city's chattering classes mulled the significance of the event. The ancient and filthy scourge of smallpox had struck at the very heart—and, it seemed to many, the *very moment*—of modern American civilization.

The New York Times, the moderately progressive voice of elite opinion, published a series of editorials in which it called the epidemic "a matter of grave public concern." The editors cautioned their affluent readers against indifference; the outbreak was no longer safely confined to "the congested tenements of one locality." "Public conveyances and places of public assembly bring all classes together to such an extent that only the recluse can feel quite safe," the *Times* advised, "and not even the recluse if ministered to by servants who visit friends in the infected districts."[17]

Such a recognition of the inescapable interdependence of modern urban life stood as the grand unifying theme of the many disparate progressive reform campaigns of the turn of the century: movements for safer working conditions, social insurance for wage earners and their families, better housing for the poor, new programs to rehabilitate criminals, and innumerable measures to protect the public health. The same ethical and political logic, which held individual liberty subordinate to the collective interests of society, underlay the *Times*'s call for universal vaccination: "This is not only a wise measure of personal precaution, but it is a public duty which every citizen owes to those with whom he comes in daily contact." The *Times* was prepared to take this logic to its furthest conclusion and endorse the most punitive measures for vaccination in the "great and crowded city." But the editors expected that such measures would prove unnecessary. The "anti-vaccination heresies" that had spread so perniciously in England and other foreign countries in recent years would find few followers in the United States, the *Times* insisted. "Here a saving common sense has prevailed in all classes of the population, and smallpox works serious ravages only in remote corners inhabited by out-and-out savages." A progressive appeal to social interdependence, civic obligation, and enlightened common sense did not, in this instance, imply tolerance, empathy, or solidarity. Or good taste: three people had recently died in the city, ravaged by smallpox. Were they "savages"?[18]

These were, of course, the overheated ruminations of editorial writers.

The *Times*'s editors got the high moral tone of the moment just right, and the facts of the historical events unfolding around them all wrong.

In December 1900, the United States was in the throes of an extraordinary five-year wave of smallpox epidemics. It was the worst visitation of smallpox in a generation or more, and the last Americans would experience on a continental scale, as a national event. From Alabama to Alaska, no state or territory was untouched. Smallpox made its way across an increasingly interconnected American landscape: from southern tobacco plantations to western mining camps to immigrant tenement districts in aging east coast cities; from the nation's capital in Washington to Filipino and Puerto Rican villages on the farthest edges of the new American empire. The epidemics did not confine themselves to a few "remote corners" of the country. Many major American cities experienced deadly epidemics. New Orleans reported nearly 1,500 cases and 450 deaths in 1900. In Philadelphia, smallpox infected 2,500 people and killed nearly 400. Boston recorded 1,600 cases and 270 deaths. And by the time the smallpox epidemic that started on All Nations Block was through with New York City in 1902, the health department had recorded 2,100 cases, and 730 men, women, and children lay dead.[19]

No reliable figures exist to quantify the overall damage done by smallpox to American lives, commerce, and property during these epidemic years. The U.S. Public Health and Marine-Hospital Service, the federal disease-control agency, conceded that its smallpox statistics were woefully incomplete. The federal officials dutifully published the data they received from state and local health boards, but in many states those agencies were just coming into their own. Many smallpox-infected communities lacked the will or the wherewithal to accurately report cases of infectious disease.

Still, the admittedly spotty statistics of the federal health service suggest the broad chronological arc of the epidemics. At the beginning of 1898, smallpox was largely absent in the United States, apart from a few trouble spots, mostly in the South, including Birmingham, Alabama, and a hard-bitten Appalachian coal town called Middlesboro, Kentucky. As Surgeon General Walter Wyman of the Public Health and Marine-Hospital Service recalled, "[I]t was during the winter of 1898–99 that the disease began to assume great proportions." In 1899, the service reported more than 12,000 cases, from all over the South, followed by 15,000 cases, now in the midwestern states, too, in 1900. In 1901, the number of new cases surged to nearly 39,000. According to the *Medical News*, by then the distribution of smallpox in the United States had become "alarmingly general." In 1902—the year Wyman would remember as "the high-water mark" of the epidemics—the service counted 59,000 new cases. The agency tallied another 42,590 new cases in 1903. By the end of that year, the surgeon general assured the nation that "the disease has spent its force and will now continue to decrease until it practically disappears." In fact, smallpox did taper off dramatically in 1904, but the disease did not disappear. Smallpox would continue to trouble American communities until the last reported U.S. case occurred in 1949. All told, during the five-year wave of epidemics around the turn of the century, the federal service counted 164,283 American cases of smallpox. The actual number of cases may have exceeded five times that figure.[20]

But for American public health officials, the truly stunning statistic from those epidemics was the body count. It was shockingly *low*. According to the federal health service reports, only 5,627 people died. Again, the mortality figure was impressionistic at best; the Census Bureau independently reported nearly 4,000 smallpox fatalities in 1900 alone (more than five times the health service's figure for that year). Still, all agreed that the death toll was astonishingly, inexplicably, blessedly small. If smallpox had measured up to its historical virulence, the epidemics of 1898–1903 would have killed at least 50,000 Americans.[21]

Although in some places smallpox proved as destructive as ever, in the vast majority of American epidemics after 1898, the disease seemed to have lost its lethal force. Vaccinal protection could not explain the phenomenon: when the smallpox came, most Americans had not been vaccinated in years. It seemed a new "mild type" of smallpox had appeared on the epidemiological landscape, the likes of which the "civilized" nations of Europe, England, and the United States had never seen. No one could say how long the new pox would remain mild. Many medical authorities expected the disease to revert to classic, malignant smallpox at any moment. For American health officials, the low mortality rate posed the greatest medical mystery—and the toughest political challenge—of the turn-of-the-century smallpox epidemics.[22]

The sudden appearance of a new mild form of smallpox altered the political calculus of compulsory vaccination—a measure that had been none too popular in late nineteenth-century America. To this day, medical experts consider smallpox vaccine, which contains a bovine virus called *vaccinia*, "the least safe vaccine available." Serious complications, including postvaccinial encephalitis and death, are rare: scientists expect one million vaccinations to cause three to five serious reactions. But milder reactions— rashes, fatigue, headache, fever, painfully tender arms—are common. In 1900, vaccination carried significantly greater dangers. The government compelled vaccination, but did little to ensure that American vaccine makers produced safe, effective vaccine. Newspaper stories, medical texts, and popular rumors linked vaccination to syphilis, tetanus, and the ubiquitous "sore arms" that caused countless American breadwinners to lose days or even weeks of work. Because the new pox killed less than 1 percent of the people whom it infected, many laypeople and even doctors refused to believe it was smallpox at all. In the absence of a recognizably horrific case of smallpox, many failed to see the benefit of vaccination. Many saw vaccination as the greater risk to life and limb. And their resistance to compulsory vaccination would help persuade the federal government to impose new regulatory controls on the American vaccine industry.[23]

But reasonable health concerns do not alone explain the widespread opposition to compulsory vaccination at the turn of the twentieth century. Antivaccinationism was an international phenomenon, but everywhere it reflected the social divisions and political tensions of its time and place. The roots of American antivaccination sentiment ran deep and wide. Race stymied smallpox control, as white taxpayers, particularly in the South, balked at paying for vaccine to protect blacks; meanwhile, African Americans rightly mistrusted government vaccinators whose chief aim was to protect the white community. Christian Scientists viewed compulsory vaccination as a violation of religious freedom. Physicians who practiced popular forms of alternative medicine decried government vaccination orders as yet another example of creeping "state medicine." Parents resented school vaccination mandates for encroaching on their domestic authority and for violating their children's innocent bodies. Antivaccination propagandists traced compulsory vaccination to a corrupt conspiracy between health officials, lawmakers, and vaccine manufacturers. On the broadest level, though, the vaccination question revealed a sharp uneasiness toward the authority of medicine and the power of the state at the height of the Progressive Era, a period of time when both institutions were reaching more ambitiously than ever before into American life.[24]

Contrary to the *Times*'s assertion, then, an unquestioning submission to vaccination was anything but the "common sense" of the American people during these smallpox outbreaks—even in the many places where local and state governments made such submission compulsory by law. Ordinary Americans responded to government vaccination orders in a variety of ways, ranging from ready compliance to violent riots. They organized antivaccination societies, conducted legislative campaigns (some of them successful) to repeal state vaccination laws, and flooded the courts with lawsuits challenging compulsory vaccination as a violation of their constitutional rights. More often, people resisted public health authority in more private, mundane ways: by concealing sick family members at home, forging vaccination certificates, or simply dodging their legal duty to be vaccinated. In the aftermath of this nationwide fight against smallpox, the United States would remain, in the words of one of the nation's preeminent public health experts, "the least vaccinated of any civilized country."[25]

The aim of this book is to explain why this was so. To trace the origins and broader significance of smallpox and the "vaccination question" in Progressive Era America, I have found it necessary to stray far from the familiar narrative conventions of the epidemic tale. This is not a story of rising body counts and medical heroics—though the changing lethal power of the smallpox virus, the emergence of the modern vaccine industry, and the strenuous work of public health officials are all central to this narrative. Nor is the story told in these pages a comforting tale of human solidarity springing up in unexpected places: the tragic disaster that forces the people of a community to overcome their differences and work together to survive and rebuild. The smallpox outbreaks of the turn of the century did occasion such moments, and they are remembered here. But the history of these

American epidemics is, inescapably, a history of violence, social conflict, and political contention. And that made all the difference.[26]

America's turn-of-the-century war against smallpox sparked one of the most important civil liberties struggles of the twentieth century. To readers versed in the scholarly literature about American civil liberties, this claim may sound curious (or even spurious). According to the conventional textbook narrative, the modern era of civil liberties properly begins with the famous free speech cases of the post–World War I era, when the U.S. Supreme Court established new First Amendment protections for political dissent. But contemporaries of the period, including no less a giant of the American legal realm than Justice Oliver Wendell Holmes, Jr., of the United States Supreme Court, recognized that the celebrated free speech battles reprised constitutional questions that the vaccination struggle had raised for Americans two decades earlier. As Justice Holmes wrote in a 1918 letter to Judge Learned Hand, "Free speech stands no differently than freedom from vaccination."[27]

In a burst of litigation arising from the smallpox epidemics, the critics of compulsion had carried the vaccination question all the way to the U.S. Supreme Court in 1905. They raised a broad set of questions about the nature of institutional power and the bounds of personal liberty in a modern urban-industrial nation. Their demands went far beyond the right to speak out against the government. The critics of compulsory vaccination insisted that the liberty protected by the Constitution also encompassed the right of a free people to take care of their own bodies and children according to their own medical beliefs and consciences. It was a bold but deeply problematic claim. And it brought the opponents of compulsory vaccination into direct conflict with the agents of an emerging interventionist state, whose progressive purpose was to use the best scientific knowledge available to regulate the economy and the population in the interests of the social welfare.[28]

This, then, is the story of a largely forgotten American smallpox epidemic that killed relatively few people but left a surprisingly deep impression on society, government, and the law. The story begins where the epidemics did, in the fields and work camps of the New South.

ONE

BEGINNINGS

"To begin at the beginning, and I think it was the beginning," Dr. Henry F. Long wrote in his 1898 report to the North Carolina Board of Health, "the first small-pox experience we, of Iredell, had, was when the negro Perkins made his way from Neal's camp, on the M & M Railroad, to Charlotte."[1]

Henry Long was the superintendent of health of Iredell County, an area of low ridges and valleys known for its loamy soil and its many creeks. Most of the citizens were North Carolina natives, like their mothers and fathers before them. Long himself carried on the medical practice established by his father in Statesville, an old town of wide, elm-lined streets that served as the county seat. In the past twenty years, the hum of industry had altered the rhythm of life in the Piedmont. Farming families and respectable townspeople like the Longs had had to accustom themselves to growing numbers of wage earners and outsiders. Apart from farming wheat, the people now spent their days making furniture, processing tobacco, tending textile machines, working on the railroads, and, as ever, raising families. Until the winter of 1898, most folks in Iredell County had never seen a case of smallpox. Then that, too, changed.[2]

Harvey Perkins was fifty-seven years old that February, when he left his home in Pelzer, South Carolina, and traveled some one hundred and fifty miles north and east to seek work on the Mocksville & Mooresville extension of the Southern Railway. He arrived, the fever already upon him, at Neal's Camp, one of the turn-of-the-century South's ubiquitous railroad construction camps. He spent the night in a hut with two other laborers. As

Long explained, patients in the preeruptive stage of smallpox already battled their unseen foe: "The pulse is strong, full and bounding. . . . The patient is restless and distressed and when sleep is possible has frightful dreams." When morning broke, Perkins noticed the first spots on his face. Guessing at their significance, and fearing that his new bosses would confine him in quarantine, he left camp without a word and slipped into the woods.[3]

All Harvey Perkins wanted was to get home to Pelzer, maybe by picking up a train in Charlotte, forty miles south of Neal's Camp. By the time Perkins walked the twelve miles to Mooresville, in southern Iredell County, the eruption was visible to anyone who cared to look him in the face. But a sick old black man did not usually attract much notice, especially from white people. Perkins spent the night. He resumed his journey the next day. He was just two miles from Charlotte when his strength finally gave out and he "fell by the wayside." A pair of bicyclists found him in the woods, his face and body covered with pocks. Perkins warned them not to come near. Local authorities transported him to the city pesthouse, a makeshift isolation hospital on the outskirts of Charlotte in Mecklenburg County, where Perkins discovered he was not alone. Dr. Long had not, in fact, begun at the beginning.[4]

Smallpox had been stalking North Carolina's southern border for months, maybe longer. Health officials in the lower South thought the disease confined to the African American sections of a few cities and to the dispersed settlements of black farmers, laborers, and families. Since the end of slavery, the white medical profession had paid African Americans little notice and offered little aid. Within the past year or so, smallpox had broken out, seemingly without warning, in parts of Florida, Alabama, Georgia, South Carolina, Tennessee, Kentucky, and Virginia. Some white physicians and laypeople dismissed the disease as a peculiar negro malady: "Nigger itch," they called it. But Dr. Long and other seasoned public health officials knew better. "So far the disease has been almost exclusively confined to negroes," said the Kentucky Board of Health, in a circular titled "Warning Against Smallpox," "but this exemption of the white race cannot long be hoped for if it continues to spread."[5]

In late January, the North Carolina Board of Health issued a smallpox bulletin. The "justly dreaded disease" had crossed the state line. Wilmington, the state's largest city, had the dubious honor of reporting the first case, in "a negro train hand of the Atlantic Coast Line whose run was into South Carolina." Soon after, Charlotte health authorities discovered a case in a black railroad hand named William Jackson. He had recently returned from a run to Greenville, South Carolina, the very place Perkins had caught his train north. By the time Perkins arrived at the Charlotte pesthouse, there were three other people detained there. Within twenty-four hours, there would be four more. All of them were African American. Three of them were broken out with pocks, including William Jackson's four-year-old son Frank. Jackson himself was already dead. The remaining five inmates showed no symptoms, but since they had come into contact with the others they would be detained for two weeks.[6]

Charlotte was in a state of turmoil. The physicians who examined the pesthouse patients disagreed about whether the cases were smallpox at all. At the request of the state authorities, Surgeon General Walter Wyman of the United States Marine-Hospital Service, the federal government's civilian health corps, dispatched an officer to Charlotte. For Dr. Charles P. Wertenbaker, a surgeon in command of the service's station in Wilmington, diagnosing smallpox was fast becoming a specialty. In the quasi-military argot of the corps, Wertenbaker held the rank of "passed assistant surgeon," meaning he was a midlevel officer who had passed the service's famously rigorous examination for promotion. He told the mayor of Charlotte that all four patients had smallpox. The quarantined inmates would almost certainly develop the disease, too. Instead of segregating suspects from patients, pesthouse officials had put suspects to work nursing the sick.[7]

To Wertenbaker's eye, Perkins presented a "typical" case, in the "fifth day of the eruption." But in an old man smallpox was especially cruel. Perkins died in the pesthouse ten days later. He was buried in a nearby woods, more than a hundred miles from home.[8]

The citizens of Charlotte had dodged a bullet, Wertenbaker announced in a bulletin issued by the state board of health to drum up support for vaccination. Had Perkins been stronger, "he would have come into the city; he might have stood next to any one in a crowd and infected him, he might have come in contact with one of your servants, and in this way sent the disease into your homes."[9]

Dr. Henry F. Long learned the truth of these words. From the "seeds" of smallpox Perkins sowed at Mooresville arose the largest outbreak North Carolina had seen in years. An itinerant black preacher named A. B. Smoot unknowingly carried the disease from Mooresville to Statesville. More than sixty cases were eventually reported in Iredell County. It was anybody's guess how many more people suffered, as Perkins had aimed to, in the privacy of their own homes. Dr. Long set up a hospital and detention camp in the woods outside Statesville. He hired the recovered Reverend Smoot to drive the ambulance wagon. When Long tried to organize a county-wide vaccination campaign, he ran up against fierce opposition, most of it "from the whites." The city council gave Long power to vaccinate the citizens, with or without their consent. One state health official reflected, "The unreasoning prejudice of ignorance is extremely difficult to meet, and sometimes requires a resort to methods that are very obnoxious to Americans."[10]

As the summer heat climbed into the Piedmont, the Iredell County epidemic of 1898 ran its course. But as Long put the finishing touches on his report, the fetid odor of smallpox, "insupportable and tenacious," continued to haunt him. He was not going to escape that smell anytime soon. The North Carolina Board of Health, facing a widening epidemic in counties across the state, was about to create a full-time position for him: State Smallpox Inspector.[11]

The age of AIDS did not invent the notion of "Patient Zero." Epidemics are dramatic events of cultural as well as scientific meaning, and the hunt for an outbreak's first case has ever served needs and purposes other than those of medicine. One Alabama health officer reached all the way back to Genesis 3:15—the story of the serpent in the garden—to launch his narrative of the Greene County smallpox epidemic of 1883. The epidemic, he said, had begun with the arrival on an evening train from Birmingham of one Eliza Burke, the "colored woman 'who brought death and all our woe.'"[12]

Narrative accounts of smallpox outbreaks—whether recounted aloud to neighbors, scratched into a letter, or prepared, like Dr. Long's history, for a government report—rarely failed to include a few words about the first case. These sketches of suddenly infamous men and women cast flashes of light on obscure figures, most of them otherwise untraceable. The way these stories were told reveals at least as much about their tellers: their forensic certitude, their fixed ideas about race and place, and their faith that buried somewhere in the human wreckage of an epidemic lay the stuff of larger moral reckonings. The desire to begin at the beginning, with a cognizable first case, was particularly strong at a time when the actual agents of so much misery and loss—the unseen, unseeable particles of the variola virus—were so imperfectly understood.[13]

After the fashion of Harvey Perkins, or the minstrel actor who stayed over on All Nations Block, the alleged source of infection was typically an outsider or a marginal local figure whose work or wanderings brought him in promiscuous contact with strangers. Consider three first cases reported by county physicians to the Kentucky Board of Health during the outbreaks of 1898 and 1899: smallpox invaded Boyd County in the body of a deckhand who worked on a "steamboat plying between Pittsburgh and St. Louis"; the disease was spread around Clay County by "a young girl of bad reputation"; and it struck Lincoln County in the person of a peripatetic real estate salesman named Joseph Sowders, a white man whose taste for the "biled juice of the cereal corn" had landed him in a smallpox-ridden Catholic mission in Columbus, Ohio, before he stumbled home to Lincoln. When smallpox struck Los Angeles in the winter of 1899, infecting thirty-five people and killing seven, officials blamed unnamed "tramps or trainmen from Arizona." In port cities from New York to San Francisco, anyone arriving by boat, especially in steerage, loomed as a potential threat. North and south of the Mason-Dixon line, itinerant African Americans were the most prime of suspects: laborers "traveling afoot," performers in "Uncle Tom's Cabin" shows, missionary preachers, Pullman porters, coal miners, roustabouts, even, in the case of Columbia, South Carolina, a "runaway student" from a black college.[14]

Other reports attributed the spread of smallpox not to a single individual but to the undifferentiated inhabitants of entire encampments of people on the move: railroad camps, mining camps, logging camps, Army camps, convict labor camps, African American revival meetings, fairs, lodging houses, and any other short-lived settlement where strangers crowded in an unfathomable mass. "The camp as a focus of disease is more potent than all others," wrote Dr. James N. Hyde, a smallpox expert at Chicago's Rush Medical School. In such places, Hyde argued, people who had become adapted to the particular microbial environment of their distant homes were thrown together, "under subjection," unable to choose where or with whom they slept. "The chances of thus begetting disease are enormously multiplied."[15]

The United States was not just a nation of farms, small towns, and industrial cities. For the country's poorest working people, America was a vast archipelago of camps. Nothing did more than smallpox to reveal this rarely mentioned fact about American society at the turn of the twentieth century.

During his tenure as state smallpox inspector, Dr. Long developed his own theory about the origin of the great wave of epidemics that struck the southern states beginning sometime in 1897: it all started in a single labor camp in Mexico. A few years before the southern epidemics, Long explained, a railroad contractor from Birmingham had taken a crew of African American railroad workers across the border to do a job. They contracted smallpox in the camp there and brought the disease back home with them. From Birmingham smallpox had slowly made its way, in the bodies of itinerant black workers, to the east and north, unnoticed or at least unremarked by the white public health authorities. Maybe the narrative of the North Carolina outbreaks properly began there.[16]

Epidemiological uncertainty made moral certainty easier. A common, cautionary theme pervades this accumulating archive of smallpox narratives: "The pestilence that walketh in darkness" travels unseen in the bodies of the strangers and outliers who move among us. And it is fearful indeed.[17]

At the end of the nineteenth century, smallpox still reigned as the most infamous and loathsome of infectious diseases. Since the 1870s, serious epidemics of smallpox had grown relatively uncommon in the United States, but that did not lessen the fears attached to the disease. Nor did the fact that Americans of the period were far more likely to fall ill or die from diphtheria, influenza, scarlet fever, typhoid fever, or consumption. Smallpox occupied a special place in the hall of human horrors. As J. N. McCormack, secretary of the Kentucky Board of Health, put it, "One case of small-pox in a tramp will create far more alarm in any community in Kentucky than a hundred cases of typhoid fever and a dozen deaths in the leading families."[18]

The 1898 outbreaks coincided with the centennial commemorations of the invention of vaccination. In 1798, the English physician Edward Jenner had published his first paper on his experiments with smallpox vaccination (which he had conducted in 1796). Newspaper articles, magazine stories, and public speeches across the United States regaled Americans about the horrors of smallpox and the scientific triumph of Jennerian vaccination. In a speech to the "plain people" of Winston, North Carolina, "Colonel" A. W. Shaffer of the state board of health proclaimed that smallpox had been a "vile destroyer" since before "the first century of the Christian era." "Great kings and royal princes, stately women of high degree and matchless beauty, and babes at the mother's breast fell alike before its destroying blast and were disfigured and deformed for life, or thrust into the same hole with the filthy carcasses of their meanest subjects."[19]

Shaffer did not exaggerate. The variola virus had been entangled with human history, to devastating effect, for millennia. No one knows when or how the virus first infected human beings. The earliest unequivocal descriptions of smallpox date to the fourth century A.D. in China, but scientists have long believed that the pustules found on the cheeks of Egyptian mummies from the twelfth century B.C. were caused by smallpox. Smallpox may have emerged as early as six thousand years ago—when the introduction of irrigated agriculture enabled human civilizations to grow large and dense enough to sustain the disease. By the time of Christ, smallpox was probably commonplace in the thickly populated valleys of the Nile and Ganges rivers, spreading from there across southwestern Asia. An inveterate camp follower, variola hitchhiked in the bodies of traders, soldiers, and other migrants. It spread east along the Burma and Silk roads and into China. In the eighth century, Islamic armies carried it through North Africa into the Iberian Peninsula. By the end of the tenth century, its expanding territory included much of southwestern Asia and the Mediterranean littoral of Africa and Europe. Many places had yet to be touched by the disease. But during the next six hundred years, smallpox became endemic in much of Europe, from whence it spread to most inhabited regions of the world. By the end of the eighteenth century, when Jenner first introduced vaccination in England, 400,000 Europeans were dying each year from smallpox.[20]

If the early history of smallpox remains mysterious, the origin of the variola virus itself is murkier still. The most plausible theory holds that the virus originated in a rodent, made the species leap to humans, adapted to its new host, and never went back. This much is certain: the variola virus has a special affinity for humans. Variola is one species in a larger genus of disease agents—the *orthopoxviruses*—that infect diverse members of the animal world. There is cowpox, monkeypox, raccoonpox, camelpox, and so on. Many of those poxviruses infect multiple species. Cowpox, for example, has naturally occurred in cows, gerbils, rats, large cats, rhinoceroses, elephants, and humans. But the natural host range for variola is decidedly more narrow. It only infects people.[21]

The bond between variola and humans is not merely a virological curiosity. It is a fact of epidemiological and even world-historical significance. It is perhaps the essential fact about a virus that killed at least three hundred million people during the twentieth century alone—more than all of the century's wars. There is no animal reservoir or vector for smallpox. It cannot be transmitted by mosquitoes (as with malaria) or lice (typhus) or rat fleas (bubonic plague) or domestic animals (anthrax). Nor, for that matter, can smallpox infect people through their sewage-tainted water supplies (as does cholera) or contaminated food (typhoid fever). Smallpox can spread only from one person to another, normally through face-to-face contact.[22]

Smallpox is, as George W. Stoner observed in his *Handbook for the Ship's Medicine Chest* (1900), a "self-limited disease." An attack followed a distinctive clinical course for which there could be but two outcomes: smallpox either killed its victim or left the survivor immune for life. Although particles of the virus could persist for long periods in scabs on the bodies of the dead, variola did not remain in a living body after convalescence. There was no chronic recurrence, as in many herpes viruses. Smallpox survivors did not become symptomatic and infectious time and time again. They could never again get or spread the disease. This, rather than an appreciation for the poetry of the situation, was why Dr. Long hired Reverend Smoot to drive the pesthouse wagon.[23]

Human beings appear to be universally susceptible to the variola virus. Unless they have been made immune by a previous infection with variola or another orthopoxvirus—such as cowpox or vaccinia, the principal viruses used in vaccination—they will almost certainly develop smallpox if the virus particles enter their respiratory tracts.

Together these facts about the variola virus begin to explain the epidemiology of smallpox—its behavior in human communities. When the virus entered a population, smallpox tended to be passed around until most people had been infected. In small, relatively isolated populations, such as most towns of colonial North America, the virus would soon die out. The virus particles did not normally survive for long outside the human body, and when the ranks of vulnerable humans were exhausted, variola had no place to replicate. For smallpox to become *endemic* in a given population (prevalent for a long period at a relatively low level), there had to be a steady influx of susceptible bodies, whether through significant levels of in-migration or by natural reproduction. This is why in societies where endemic smallpox existed, such as European or English cities in the eighteenth century, smallpox was known as a disease of children. Most children born in London had smallpox before their seventh birthdays; the disease was a rite of passage. In English towns, nine out of ten fatal smallpox cases occurred in children under five. It was endemic smallpox that the nineteenth-century British historian Lord Thomas Macaulay famously called "the most terrible of all the ministers of death." "The smallpox was always present," he wrote, "filling the churchyard with corpses, tormenting with constant fear all whom it had not yet stricken, leaving on those whose lives it spared the hideous traces of its power, turning the babe into a changeling at which the mother shuddered, and making the eyes and cheeks of the betrothed maiden objects of horror to the lover."[24]

Of course, the "speckled monster" earned its worldwide infamy by its horrific epidemics. Major smallpox epidemics arose in two distinct epidemiological situations. In a so-called virgin soil population, one that had never been afflicted with smallpox or had been spared the virus for many years, a single epidemic could be devastating. In 1241, the people of Iceland had such an encounter with variola: some twenty thousand of the island's seventy thousand people died. The experience of indigenous populations of the Americas with epidemics of smallpox after the arrival of the Europeans in 1492 is well known if not easily fathomed. Many factors may have contributed to the extraordinarily high susceptibility of sixteenth-century American Indians to smallpox, including malnutrition, dislocation, and poverty—problems caused or exacerbated by the violent process of European colonization. But the likelihood that American Indians and their ancestors had no previous contact with the disease helps explain mortality rates that ran from 50 to 80 percent. Variola was the deadliest killer in a terrible onslaught of alien microorganisms that, by some historical estimates, may have decimated as much as 90 percent of the precontact population of the Americas.[25]

A different sort of epidemic occurred in well-populated places where smallpox was more or less always present, such as parts of late eighteenth-century Europe and England. The number of susceptible individuals in a community gradually built up over time, creating fodder for an "epidemic year," when smallpox became suddenly widespread and lethal. In this situation, where a majority of the adult population, including most of the breadwinners, was immune from previous infection, an epidemic could cause untold misery without seriously threatening the population's subsistence.[26]

As with many infectious diseases, the incidence of smallpox rose and fell with the seasons. Climate, social factors, and the traits of the virus itself conspired to make smallpox a disease of the winter and spring. Variola remained viable longer at cooler temperatures. And the tendency of humans to crowd together indoors during the winter months made the virus's journey from person to person a short one.

Turn-of-the-century medical experts, well versed in the germ theory, assumed that some life form, invisible to the naked eye, caused smallpox. But they could only guess at its nature. "The contagious principle, probably a microbe, has not been discovered," declared an authoritative 1899 pamphlet, prepared by Marine-Hospital Service scientists for Surgeon General Wyman. Since the introduction of the germ theory, European and American scientists had hunted for the disease agent under their microscopes. A few reported seeing traces of smallpox "germs." Orthopoxviruses are among the largest known viruses, but they are still extremely small. According to one modern writer, it would take three million of them, laid out in rows, to pave over a standard typographic period. An actual sighting would not be possible until the invention of the electron microscope in the 1930s. In 1947 Canadian and American scientists finally viewed the particles, or virions, of variola.[27]

Since that time, variola virions have often been called bricks, because of their shape: a three-dimensional rectangle with slightly rounded edges. The name fits for other reasons as well. Each virion is made up of a combination of a hundred different proteins, which interlock in a structure so durable that it enables the virions to survive for a time in the open air. The knobby protein exterior of each brick protects the genetic jewel within: a molecule of double-stranded DNA. By attaching itself to and then penetrating a susceptible cell, usually in the mucous membranes of the throat or lungs, a single virion has the power to trigger an unstoppable process of genetic replication that can turn a healthy person into a corpse.[28]

For all of its mysteries, the clinical features of smallpox were fairly well understood in January 1899, when Surgeon General Wyman issued his "Précis upon the Diagnosis and Treatment of Smallpox." The timing was significant. The disease was invading communities, mostly in the South, where neither the laypeople nor the physicians had seen a bona fide case of smallpox in many years, if ever. The "Précis" was, in no small measure, a political document. Wyman aimed to remind people of the necessity of vaccination, to shore up confidence in the nation's vaccine supply, to clarify the national government's limited responsibilities, and to spur the fiscally conservative local and state governments to take action.[29]

Wyman's officers in the Marine-Hospital Service disseminated the "Précis" widely, especially in the South. The report reflected state-of-the-art American medical knowledge about smallpox. Wyman's description of the clinical course of smallpox squares with descriptions of the disease found in medical treatises and journals from the period, as well as the accounts of local cases written by physicians such as Dr. Henry Long. The vast scientific literature on smallpox produced since that time has generally confirmed that clinical picture, while shedding new light on the virological and pathological processes that underlay the disease. Unlike the vast majority of physicians alive today, these turn-of-the-century experts had firsthand experience with smallpox. For them smallpox was not a frozen stockpile preserved, like ancient DNA sealed in amber, in a carefully guarded government laboratory vault and read about in medical journals. For them smallpox was still a part of the known world.[30]

Perhaps the most significant misunderstanding about smallpox shared by the authors of the "Précis" and many of their scientific contemporaries had to do with the mechanics of disease transmission. They understood correctly that smallpox could be spread by the passage of "the microbe" from one person's respiratory system to another's. In fact, a person suffering from smallpox shed virions in each droplet of saliva. A single breath, cough, laugh, sigh, or spoken word was enough to launch the virions into the air. When one or more particles touched down upon the mucous membrane of another person's mouth, nose, throat, or lungs, the process of viral replication began within hours.

Where the "Précis" went wrong was in its insistence that such face-to-face contacts constituted a lesser threat than did the scabs and crusts of dried pus that fell from the skin of a convalescent patient. "The contagion is tenacious," the "Précis" stated, "and may be conveyed by persons and by fomites, such as hair, clothing, paper, letters, furniture, etc., or it may be spread through the air by means of the wind blowing the dust containing the virus." This belief in the infectious power of "fomites," contaminated objects of countless variety, led to the conclusion that smallpox was what nineteenth-century sanitarians called a "filth disease"—dangerous to all but spread chiefly by the lower orders. As the "Précis" put it, smallpox was "more common among the colored races, probably on account of their condition of living in small, crowded rooms, with slight regard for cleanliness."[31]

The "Précis" got the infective nature of variola about half-right. The crowded sleeping quarters that the world's poorest people called home—be it a sharecropping family's one-room cabin or a bamboo hut—were prime variola territory. It surprised no one when, two weeks after Harvey Perkins shared a hut with two other workers at Neal's Camp, reports

reached Charlotte that two cases of smallpox had broken out in the encampment. There were obvious obstacles to maintaining personal hygiene
and health under such circumstances. Still, scientists now believe that "filth"
had little to do with the spread of smallpox. Laboratory tests have shown
that the virions in smallpox scabs can, under optimal conditions, retain
their infectivity for years. But the virions are so tightly bound within the
hard fibrin mesh of the scab that it takes heavy grinding to release them.
For this reason, many experts have concluded that fomites were "relatively
unimportant" transmitters of infection, compared with the spread of virions in sneezes and coughs. This does not mean that infection by fomites
never occurred—contaminated bed linen, in particular, readily transmitted
infection—but the long-standing association of smallpox with the filthy
poor was grounded more in class and racial bias than in medical reality.[32]

Once the first virion penetrated the first cell in a person's respiratory
tract, the incubation period began. During this period, most people
presented no symptoms—perhaps a little malaise or gastric discomfort.
Meanwhile, the variola bricks silently but explosively replicated and spread
in the host's lymph nodes, spleen, and bone marrow. Over time, the virions
piling up in the patient's cells would number in the quadrillions. The incubation normally lasted from ten to fourteen days. The "Précis" gave twelve
days as the norm. Such medical facts determined the politics of smallpox
control. Conservative health officials enforced two weeks as the term a
smallpox "suspect," showing no symptoms, could be held against her will
in a quarantined house or detention camp.[33]

When the symptoms finally came, they struck with such unexpected
force that the "Précis" called the onset the "Invasion." The patient felt a sudden chill, followed by severe pain in the loins and lower back, a splitting
headache, and a high fever, in some cases surging to 106 degrees F. The
pulse raced. Many patients vomited. The tongue grew thick with a brown
coating; the appetite vanished, but the thirst was unquenchable. Some
adults grew delirious. Some children were rocked by convulsions.[34]

In this early phase, as Dr. Long learned while attending to patients in
the Iredell County pesthouse, smallpox remained inscrutable even to the

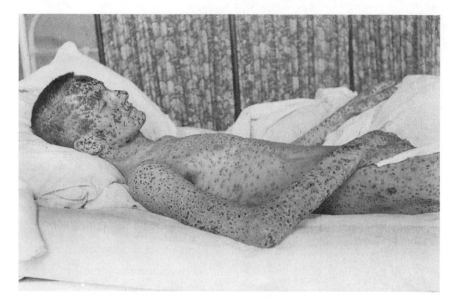

Smallpox patient from the Cleveland epidemic of 1901–03. This photograph was taken by Dr. Homer J. Hartzell, who headed the city's smallpox hospital. COURTESY OF THE DITTRICK MEDICAL HISTORY CENTER, CASE WESTERN RESERVE UNIVERSITY

trained medical eye. It could be typhoid fever, malaria, la grippe, or dengue. For the patient, these feverish days felt like a bad case of the flu, and some managed to carry on with their work. President Abraham Lincoln is believed to have been fighting the preeruptive fever of smallpox when he delivered the Gettysburg Address on November 19, 1863. One listener described the president's appearance as "sad, mournful, almost haggard." The rash appeared two days later.[35]

In a typical case, the fever fell by the second or third day. The constitutional symptoms abated. The patient felt better. So much so, a nineteenth-century nurse's manual noted, that he might "suppose himself convalescent." Unknown to the patient, the lesions had already begun rising, about twenty-four hours earlier, on the mucous surfaces of the mouth, the back of the throat, and more generally throughout the alimentary and respiratory tracts. Modern virologists call this eruption the "enanthem." The enanthem turned the patient into a veritable mist machine of infection. The lesions evolved rapidly and broke down within two or three days, releasing virions in vast quantities into the saliva. For the next week or more, the patient's every breath might launch a fusillade of invisible infective particles into the air. Although the patient could remain infectious for weeks, twentieth-century studies concluded that smallpox sufferers were most likely to infect others during the first week of their skin rash.[36]

From the perspective of the patient, and the turn-of-the-century physician, the true horror—and the real danger—of smallpox resided on the outside of the body, in a rash so spectacular and explosive it was universally called "the eruption." It was the eruption that ancient commentators had described, and that peoples around the globe had painted, with pointillist precision, on the images and figurines of smallpox sufferers. It was the eruption that had caused a medieval bishop to give the disease its Latin name, *variola*, meaning "spotted." (In England, the disease was known simply as "the pox" until the late fifteenth century, when the term "smallpox" was adopted to distinguish it from syphilis, the "great pox," or the French pox.) For physicians working at the turn of the twentieth century, it was still the eruption, above all else, that defined and signified smallpox.[37]

The eruption appeared on the skin just as the fever broke, caused by the infection of the epidermal cells. The rash appeared first as small red dots (called macules) on the forehead and scalp, and often around the mouth and the wrists. Patients often got a "worried face," a disturbing contraction of the facial muscles that some experienced doctors recognized as a diagnostic sign of smallpox. Within twenty-four hours the lesions spread over the body. They appeared so rapidly that even the most attentive patients found it difficult to track the order of their appearance. In the worst cases it would become difficult to distinguish the rash from the skin, but smallpox was, in its way, an orderly disease. It distributed itself in a characteristic centrifugal pattern that distinguished it from other skin diseases: it was most dense on the face, hands, and feet, though it also covered broad areas of the chest, back, trunk, arms, legs, and genitals.[38]

Over the next two weeks, the lesions followed a well-known clinical course. Wyman's "Précis" ticked off the stages: "macule, papule, vesicle, and pustule, ending in desiccation and desquamation." By the second day of the rash, a small raised bump (the papule) formed atop each red macule, rising just above the skin as the papule filled with fluid. Physicians described the papules as "shotty," because they could be rolled between thumb and forefinger, as if shot from the blast of a hunter's gun had become embedded under the skin.[39]

In a few more days, the papules evolved into vesicles, blisters with navel-like depressions in their centers. (Physicians called the vesicles at this stage "umbilicated.") The depressions gradually rounded out as the vesicles became filled with a pressurized fluid that started opalescent and gradually turned opaque. When that process was completed, after a few days, the lesions were called pustules. The puffy pustules had a yellowish gray color encircled by a red border. They reached their full size, like blood-engorged dog ticks, by the tenth day of the eruption. In the most common form of smallpox cases, the rash remained "discrete": normal skin could still be seen between the lesions. But in more severe, "confluent" cases, there were so many pustules that they fused together, especially on the face. Dr. Long found it "almost impossible to paint a pen-picture" of the "terrible faces" of confluent patients.[40]

Throughout the eruption, the patient suffered. As if to trumpet the ascendance of the pustules, the fever returned, as did many of the symptoms that had attended the fever the first time around. By this time, the patient's face was normally swollen and disfigured, the hands puffy and aching, the skin inflamed. Ulcers burned the mouth and throat, growing so large in some cases that the patient had the sensation of suffocating.

Stoner's *Handbook for the Ship's Medicine Chest* offered a concise description of the final clinical stages of smallpox, which occurred by the end of the eruption's second week. First came the desiccation: "The pustules break, matter oozes out, crusts form, first on the face and then over other parts of the body following the order of the appearance of the eruption." The secondary fever gradually abated. Then came the desquamation, or scaling off: "The crusts rapidly dry and fall off, leaving red spots on the skin." This could take two or more incredibly itchy weeks. Given the reigning scientific beliefs, all scabs and crusts had to be carefully collected and incinerated.[41]

From the onset of fever to the separation of the scabs, smallpox typically lasted three to four weeks—though sometimes much longer. Throughout, there was not much an attending nurse or physician could do but try to ease the suffering. "As regards treatment, there is little to say," wrote Dr.

Long. Cold compresses and cool drinks for the fevers. Morphine for the back pain. Vaseline ointments for the exfoliating scabs. A few ounces of whiskey sometimes bought the patient a moment's peace. Dr. Llewellyn Eliot, who ran the District of Columbia Smallpox Hospital during the winter epidemic of 1894–5, said he tried every treatment regimen he could think of: "the expectant, the bitartrate of potash, the salicylic acid, the antiseptic, and, finally, the do-nothing." Still, good nursing care could make all the difference. As late as the 1970s, studies showed that in developing countries, where hospital facilities were typically "poor" and "grossly overcrowded" (a fair description of most American smallpox hospitals circa 1900), smallpox patients cared for by devoted family members, in their own homes and villages, had a higher chance of survival.[42]

In a run-of-the-mill case of smallpox, as it had been known from time immemorial until the twentieth century, the sufferer had about a one-in-four chance of dying from the disease: a case-fatality rate, in epidemiological parlance, of 25 percent. Beneath this historical average lay wide variation, caused by differences in viral strains and the particular susceptibilities and immune responses of different individuals and groups. In cases of discrete smallpox, the case-fatality rate could be as low as 10 percent; in confluent cases, it could run to 60 percent or higher. Age also affected the prognosis. Mortality was highest in infants, lowest for young children, and from there it tended to rise with age. Smallpox was especially severe in pregnant women. It often caused miscarriages or stillbirths, and fetuses could be infected in utero.[43]

Some outbreaks were so sudden and severe as to defy comprehension. In March 1900, the *Atlanta Constitution* reported that the small community of Jonesville, Mississippi, was "honeycombed with smallpox of the most virulent and loathsome form." The case-fatality rate was 75 percent. Nearly one hundred people died. Entire families perished. It all happened so fast that city officials could do little more than order coffins.[44]

When death came, it usually occurred around the tenth or eleventh day of the disease. Scientists still do not know exactly how smallpox killed. By the tenth day, the variola bricks had piled up in cells throughout the body, including many of the vital organs. Still, the disease did not normally destroy the organs. The slow, painful death from smallpox was usually caused by severe viral toxemia—a generalized poisoning of the body. In the final moments, most patients suffered respiratory failure.[45]

It could be worse. Discrete and confluent smallpox were subtypes of "variola vera," or true smallpox. ("Ordinary type" is the preferred term today.) In a small percentage of cases, smallpox presented in far more severe forms. If a particularly virulent strain of the virus met with an extremely weak immune response at the cellular level, as sometimes occurred in children, the lesions remained flat, turned black or purple, and were said to feel "soft and velvety to the touch." The patient's body looked charred. This form of smallpox (now called "flat type") was almost invariably fatal. Rarer still, and almost always fatal, were the various forms of "hemorrhagic" or "black smallpox," in which the virus caused explosive bleeding. Through it all, patients suffering from hemorrhagic smallpox were said to exhibit "a peculiar state of apprehension and mental alertness." They seemed to know exactly what was happening to them.[46]

The best thing to be said about smallpox was this: when the disease was done with a person, it was done. The virions did not persist in the body. Smallpox survivors were forever immune. In most cases of variola vera, though, the skin never fully recovered. From 65 to 80 percent of patients bore deep scars on their faces, the pitted "pockmarks" that made smallpox unforgettable.

During the Cleveland smallpox epidemic of 1901–3, in which 266 people died, Dr. William T. Corlett, a professor of dermatology and syphilology at Western Reserve University medical school, kept a photographic record of patients in the smallpox hospital. After poring over Dr. Corlett's photos of patients—their cobblestoned faces, their blistered nakedness, the distant stares of those who can open their eyes—it should come as a relief to find one of a fully recovered man. It does not. He could be thirty. Or forty-five. He wears a heavy woolen suit, with a gold watch pin at the top buttonhole of his vest. He stands erect, chin up, his body squared off to the camera. But his face is just a few degrees askew, as if he can't quite look the camera in the eye. His forehead, cheeks, nose, and chin are a dermatological rubble. The survivor's proud, clamped mouth carries the weight of the photograph. But the unforgiving eyes command the viewer's attention.[47]

The scars of smallpox might fade with time, but they never went away.

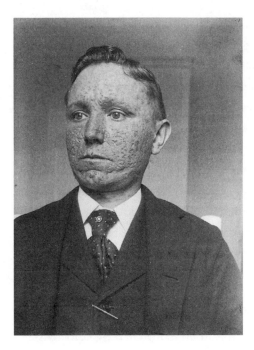

Dr. William T. Corlett of Cleveland's Western Reserve University took this photograph of a recovered smallpox patient. The scars were permanent. COURTESY OF THE DITTRICK MEDICAL HISTORY CENTER, CASE WESTERN RESERVE UNIVERSITY

In the patent medicine marketplace of early twentieth-century America, unscrupulous purveyors touted newfangled procedures and ointments which, they promised, would make pockmarks disappear. In the same newspapers where the patent hucksters hawked their wares, the police blotters printed notices about wanted criminals. On any given day, the reader might be advised to keep an eye out for any number of physical markers in the hustle of the urban crowd—one suspect's height, another's build, yet another's race. But one trait in particular—the smallpox marks tattooed indelibly on the suspect's face—told the vigilant reader that the fugitive had a history of escaping tight situations.[48]

Not all "germs" are alike. Bacteria, which are much larger than viruses, are single-celled microorganisms, capable of reproducing on their own and metabolizing nutrition. Since the advent of penicillin in the 1940s, scientists and pharmaceutical companies have developed a widening range of antibiotics that work by killing or inhibiting the life-sustaining activities of various disease-causing microorganisms. Viruses are impervious to antibiotics. They are difficult to kill because they are not exactly alive. A virion is essentially an inert package of genetic information, encased in proteins. It can only replicate when it penetrates a vulnerable host cell. At that point, the virion sheds some of its protective layer and begins to convert the cell into a virion factory. The best way to help a human body beat a virus like variola is to teach the cells to recognize the virions and to respond quickly with a powerful immune response. For some viral diseases physicians artificially immunize patients by exposing their bodies to an inactivated ("killed") or attenuated ("live" but weakened) form of the virus; for other diseases, a related virus does the trick. When preventive immunization works, the body reacts to an invasion of virus with an immune response that will prevent infection, or at least reduce the damage the virions can do.

We know all of this because of the exponential growth of scientific knowledge that has occurred since the introduction of the germ theory of disease during the second half of the nineteenth century. In the 1860s and 1870s, laboratory pioneers such as the French chemist Louis Pasteur and the German physician Robert Koch marshaled increasing evidence behind an idea that we now take for granted. Overthrowing long-held medical beliefs, the new theory proposed that contagious and infectious diseases arose neither from the grossly deficient "constitutions" of their sufferers nor from atmospheric "miasmas" arising from stagnant water; rather, specific diseases were caused by particular microorganisms. From the late 1870s into the early twentieth century, laboratory scientists identified one pathogenic "microbe" after another (including the bacteria that caused cholera, consumption, gonorrhea, and typhoid). As scientific knowledge of bacteria, viruses, and other "germs" accumulated, so did understanding of the mechanisms and pathways by which those germs circulated across populations: contaminated food and water, casual contacts, insect vectors, and so on. From these new understandings of the etiology of infectious diseases arose new strategies for policing them. To the ancient practices of isolation and quarantine were added antispitting ordinances, food and milk regulations, and a growing arsenal of vaccines, antitoxins, and serums. In the United States, where many physicians had been slow to embrace the germ theory (and laypeople had been slower still), health officials of the local, state, and federal governments approached the twentieth century with a greatly enlarged sense of their duties and powers.[49]

The history of smallpox vaccination has a special but curious relationship to this scientific revolution. Smallpox was the granddaddy of infectious diseases: the deadliest scourge in recorded history and the one upon which the field of immunology was founded. Smallpox *variolation* (using live variola virus) and *vaccination* (using the live viruses of cowpox or vaccinia) were the oldest practices of preventive immunization. In fact, they were practiced long before the germ theory took shape. Both techniques had been developed without the benefit of microscopes and laboratory smears, through experiments based upon everyday observations about the disease. Pasteur himself saluted this lineage when he proposed, in 1881, that the term "vaccination" be universalized to apply to preventive inoculation with other infectious agents.[50]

Variolation was practiced in China and India as early as the tenth century. It probably originated in the commonplace observation that people with pockmarks never contracted smallpox. The practice entailed introducing a small amount of material from the pustules or scabs of a smallpox patient into the body of a healthy person. In China, the common method was nasal insufflation: scabs were ground into a fine powder and then snorted. In India, the pus material was inserted into the skin. Variolation normally produced a mild attack of smallpox, followed by long-lasting immunity. The practice spread far and wide from its Asian (and perhaps African) origins. By the early eighteenth century, variolation spread into Europe from the Balkans and from Turkey into England. Called "inoculating the smallpox" or simply "inoculation" by the English, it grew increasingly common in Britain and the colonies—especially when epidemics threatened. In the terrible Boston epidemic of 1720–21, Reverend Cotton Mather and Dr. Zabdiel Boylston caused a public firestorm by promoting inoculation. In 1777, as North American smallpox epidemics took more than 100,000 lives, General George Washington ordered the compulsory variolation of all new recruits into the Continental Army. The wide adoption of variolation during the eighteenth century is perhaps all the evidence one needs of the severity of smallpox, for the practice carried serious risks.

The artificially induced attack was not always mild: as many as one in fifty died. Even worse, during the infection the inoculated person could infect others with full-blown smallpox.[51]

Vaccination descended directly from variolation, and it came about in much the same way. In the late eighteenth century, it was a commonplace observation among the country people of smallpox-ridden parts of England and Europe that milk hands and milkmaids rarely had pockmarks. An English country doctor named Edward Jenner, who had himself suffered a harsh bout of smallpox following his childhood inoculation, had trouble persuading dairy workers to take the pox. The workers, Jenner later explained, had the "vague opinion" that they had been protected by their exposure to diseased cows. Some of the workers had pocklike ulcers on their hands, gotten by milking cows whose teats were broken out with cowpox. From one such ulcer, on the hand of a milkmaid named Sarah Nelmes, Jenner extracted the pus that he inserted, just beneath the surface of the skin, on the arm of a young servant named James Phipps on May 14, 1796. Jenner later repeated the experiment on several other children. After several months, he inoculated the children with smallpox. In every case, it failed to take. The children's bodies resisted the variola virus. Vaccination, which takes its name from the Latin word for cow, was born. The new technique had neither of the limitations of variolation: it did not give people smallpox, and it did not cause them to spread it either.[52]

When Jenner published his first results in a 1798 paper, his claims bred skepticism and controversy among medical men and laypeople. An English political cartoon from the period depicts a gaggle of country bumpkins lined up to get jabbed in the arm by the bewigged Dr. Jenner. The right half of the frame is a riotous scene filled with men and women who have already taken the vaccine. Horns, hooves, and entire cows spring forth from their arms, faces, and rear ends. The cartoon is titled, "Cow Pock—or—the Wonderful Effects of the New Inoculation!" Despite opposition, vaccination spread far and wide with remarkable speed. Jenner estimated that within three years, 100,000 people had been vaccinated in England. By that time, Professor Benjamin Waterhouse of Harvard University had brought vaccination to the United States.[53]

More than half a century before the germ theory, then, the fundamentals of preventive immunization were in place. And yet at the turn of the twentieth century, smallpox remained full of mystery. The causative agent had not been identified, the process of human transmission was imperfectly understood, and the exact nature and biological effects of the vaccine strains in circulation were largely matters of conjecture and debate. What scientists and physicians could say for certain, based upon a century of medical experience, was that vaccination worked. Wyman's "Précis" summed up the medical consensus: "The most efficient means for preventing the spread of smallpox is by vaccination. The protection, provided the [vaccine] virus is pure, is believed to be as complete against contagion as is that of smallpox against a second attack." Unlike a bout with actual smallpox, the authors cautioned, vaccination conferred only a temporary immunity, perhaps five years or more. Accordingly, the "Précis" advised that communities encourage revaccination, whenever smallpox became prevalent, to "continue this protection indefinitely."[54]

In the best scenario, vaccination prevented a person exposed to smallpox from getting the disease at all. Even when a previously vaccinated person did contract the disease, the vaccination accelerated the clinical course of smallpox, producing a milder form of the disease called "varioloid." The patient remained infectious until recovered: "The most virulent form of smallpox may rise from exposure to varioloid," the "Précis" warned. But fatalities were rare and pockmarks uncommon. Physicians found that if they vaccinated a person infected with smallpox during the first five or six days of the incubation period, the patient would normally suffer a mild case of the disease.[55]

Despite the power of this revolutionary scientific technology, England and America did not rush to embrace compulsion. Some European governments established compulsory vaccination of infants in the first decades of the early nineteenth century: Bavaria in 1807, Denmark in 1810, Norway in 1811, Bohemia and Russia in 1812, Sweden in 1816, and Hanover in 1821. But England, the birthplace of Jennerian vaccination, did not enact its first compulsory measure until 1853. It applied only to children.[56]

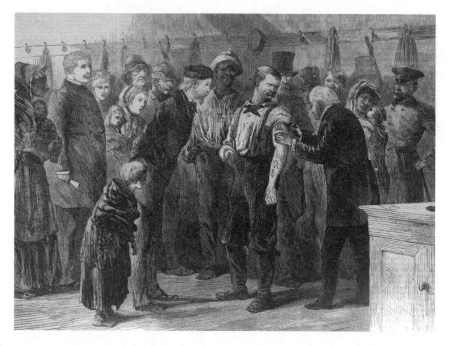

Sol Ettinge, "Vaccinating the Poor." The engraving pictures a New York City police station house during the 1872 smallpox epidemic. From Harper's Weekly, *March 16, 1872.* COURTESY ROBERT D. FARBER UNIVERSITY ARCHIVES AND SPECIAL COLLECTIONS DEPARTMENT, BRANDEIS UNIVERSITY

Until the mid-nineteenth century, the thorny legal question regarding vaccination in the United States concerned the right of local communities to use tax money to provide free vaccination for the poor. Things began to shift after England adopted compulsion. In 1855, Massachusetts became the first American state to require public schoolchildren to get vaccinated. Between the end of the Civil War and the turn of the twentieth century, public officials and lawmakers gradually built a legal regime of compulsory vaccination in America. By the 1890s, that regime included federal inspection of immigrants at the nation's borders, some form of compulsory vaccination for public schoolchildren in most states, and general vaccination orders issued by county courts, city councils, and local boards of health during epidemics.[57]

For Surgeon General Wyman, the case for compulsion was simple: it worked. He reminded Americans of the lesson of the Franco-Prussian War of 1870–71. As the French and Prussian armies collided, the war unleashed a pandemic of smallpox that killed more than half a million people in Europe, including some 143,000 German civilians. Both France and Prussia had poorly vaccinated civilian populations. But the armies differed dramatically. The thoroughly vaccinated Prussian army, 800,000 men strong, suffered only 8,463 cases of smallpox and just 457 deaths (a case-fatality rate of 5.4 percent). The smaller, sparsely vaccinated French army counted 125,000 cases and 23,375 deaths (18.7 percent). After the war, many European countries enacted new legislation compelling vaccination (and in some places subsequent revaccination) as a basic duty of citizenship.[58]

As epidemics broke out in the United States during the next few years, American state and local governments responded with measures of their own. Again, the German example proved irresistible. By an 1874 law, the unified German state required all citizens to submit to vaccination and revaccination. In 1899 the disease took only 116 lives in Germany, a nation of 50 million people. For Wyman, the success of vaccination imposed a clear moral responsibility upon American citizens and their governments. "Smallpox is a disease so easily prevented by vaccination that the smallpox patient of to-day is scarcely deserving of sympathy," he wrote in December 1899, as the wave of epidemics that had begun in the South moved across the country.[59]

But vaccination carried its own well-known health risks, and compulsory measures clashed with medical beliefs, religious tenets, the rights of parents, and dearly held notions of personal liberty. As nations tightened their smallpox vaccination laws in the late nineteenth century, those efforts ran up against strong, even violent, antivaccination movements, in the metropoles and in their overseas colonies. Antivaccination riots rocked Leicester, Montreal, and Rio de Janeiro. Since the 1870s American antivaccination leagues had challenged compulsory measures in the statehouses; after 1890, they began turning to the courts as well. Across the United States, citizens resisted public health authority by burning down pesthouses built in their neighborhoods, running away from vaccinators, fighting with police, forging vaccination certificates, or, perhaps most commonly, by quietly taking care of their sick loved ones in their own homes, instead of surrendering them to the authorities.[60]

American supporters of compulsory vaccination—including public health officials, the rising professional class of physicians, and the editorial writers for major newspapers such as *The New York Times*—often dismissed the opposition as an insignificant coterie of "imbecile cranks" who had fallen under the spell of foreign ideas. But the opposition was far more broad and complicated than that. It did not arise solely from a transatlantic critique of modern state medicine. Nor did it spring, fully formed, from American traditions of rugged individualism and constitutional liberty. The turn-of-the-century epidemics in particular would reveal that opposition to government-mandated smallpox vaccination grew up in the same soil from which had sprung compulsion itself: the conflict-laden realm of everyday social and political life in local communities.[61]

The variola virus itself played no small role in the vaccination controversies that embroiled communities across the United States. As reports of outbreaks reached Washington from communities across the South during 1898 and 1899, many local physicians, public health officers, and political leaders commented that smallpox did not seem its old self. And the more people smallpox struck, the bigger the "kick" the public put up against vaccination.[62]

Dr. Henry F. Long was one of the first southern medical men to report on this unprecedented new situation. Harvey Perkins had died as expected. But something peculiar happened to the sixty-two others who landed in Dr. Long's pesthouse during the months after Perkins made his long walk through the woods of Iredell County: every last one of them survived.

TWO

THE MILD TYPE

A peculiar new form of smallpox invaded communities across the American South during the last three years of the nineteenth century. The mysterious disease brought little of the horror people expected from smallpox. For every hundred people infected, only one or two died. Physicians and laypeople often mistook the symptoms for chicken pox, measles, or some other eruptive disease. The eruption passed through the normal stages, but the pustules typically remained superficial and discrete. Miraculously, most people recovered without pockmarks. At first the new pox reportedly spread almost exclusively among African Americans. Because of its unprecedented mildness and its reputation for infecting "none but negroes," the new smallpox was allowed to gain a beachhead in the southeastern United States. Local governments were slow to respond until someone died or the disease crossed the color line. In this way, isolated cases became outbreaks, outbreaks became full-scale epidemics, and a disease whose ultimate capacity for destruction no one could foretell made its way from place to place.[1]

As the disease spread back and forth along the rivers, roads, and rails of the southern states, a growing inventory of popular sobriquets traveled with it. "Cuban itch," some called it, or "Porto Rico scratch," "Manila scab," "Filipino itch," "Mexican bump," "Nigger itch," "Italian itch," "Hungarian itch," "Camp itch," "Army itch," "Elephant itch," "Kangaroo itch," "Cedar itch," "Bean pox," or simply "Bumps." These invented diagnostic names, which some physicians adopted, expressed the lack of alarm with which ordinary people greeted this highly contagious, obviously itchy, and occasionally fatal eruptive disease. They'd seen worse.[2]

Like the rumors that everywhere circulated about the new disease, the made-up names traced its origins, in a matter-of-fact way, to particularly salient features of the social and political landscape of end-of-the-century America. Americans continued the practice, already old when smallpox first exploded across Europe, of ascribing the foul scourge to rival powers, the wandering poor, and other scapegoats. Surely, the Americans said, the "itch" came from the exotic colonial frontiers opened by the war with Spain. Or from the rowdy work camps that had sprung up across the southern countryside, wherever logs needed cutting, tracks laying, or coal hauling. Or from the bodies of a formerly enslaved people, now moving about the region in search of work and a greater measure of freedom. Or from the new immigrants who steamed across the Atlantic from unfamiliar parts of southern and eastern Europe. But behind all of these names, and the tales of origin they told, lay an old foe. "In nine out of ten cases," said Passed Assistant Surgeon C. P. Wertenbaker of the U.S. Marine-Hospital Service, "these prove to be smallpox."[3]

The full scope of these southern outbreaks may never be known. Many localities—and even some state governments, such as Arkansas's and Georgia's—had no public health board, much less any system for tracking the incidence of infectious diseases. Even where active health boards existed, the diagnostic confusion caused by the new "mild type" of smallpox ensured that many cases went unreported. The people most vulnerable to smallpox, unvaccinated African Americans and poor whites, were the members of southern society least likely to receive professional medical care—or to volunteer information about kinfolk and neighbors to police and health officials. When health authorities declared an epidemic, the public record thickened, because that declaration obliged local governments to seek out and isolate all infected people and their known contacts. But the efforts of state health boards and the federal Marine-Hospital Service to keep tabs on smallpox invariably came up short. The vast majority of Southerners who contracted smallpox during these years probably went uncounted.[4]

Still, a visitation of this magnitude did not go unrecorded. Local newspapers, state health boards, and the federal Marine-Hospital Service tried to survey the damage to people, commerce, and local reputations. Smallpox struck every southern state from 1896 to 1900, affecting hundreds of local communities. The first reported outbreak of the mild type began in Pensacola, in the Florida Panhandle, on November 20, 1896: 54 people caught the disease, and no one died. The first major epidemic began in the summer of 1897, some 250 miles north of Pensacola, in the manufacturing center of Birmingham and the surrounding coal camps of Jefferson County. Within a year, Alabama reported 3,638 cases with 51 deaths (a case-fatality rate of just 1.4 percent). Meanwhile, smallpox broke out in every state in the old Confederacy, as well as West Virginia, Kentucky, and a few northern and western states. A Kentucky Board of Health bulletin observed, early in 1898, that the disease showed "an unusual tendency everywhere to break over official control and assume an epidemic form." By the end of 1901, the board had counted 394 separate outbreaks; only 9 of the state's 119 counties escaped infection. All told, Kentucky reported 11,279 cases with 184 deaths (1.63 percent). From January 1898 to May 1903, North Carolina reported 11,735 cases and 331 deaths (2.82 percent). In other states the story was much the same. Almost everywhere, health officials wondered at the exceptional mildness of smallpox—and the fact that they seemed unable to get rid of it.[5]

Leading health officials, including Surgeon General Walter Wyman of the U.S. Marine-Hospital Service, warned local governments and the public that they could not afford to take mild smallpox lightly. Smallpox was smallpox. Mild or not, the disease still caused suffering and occasional death, and epidemics slowed local industry and commerce. No one knew what made the mild type mild, and no one could predict how long it would remain so. Given the scientific knowledge available to them, responsible health officials proceeded under the reasonable assumption that smallpox could regain its full lethal force at any moment. Trying to convey this concern to a skeptical and predominantly rural public, North Carolina health officials warned that mild smallpox might be planting the "seeds" for a truly horrific epidemic.[6]

The wisdom of such predictions seemed confirmed by localized outbreaks that claimed many lives. The experience of New Orleans, the South's largest city, was worrisome. The mild smallpox reached the city, reportedly in the body of a "negro steamboat laborer," in February 1899. (The theory of origin would have shocked no one: almost every epidemic to reach New Orleans since its foundation had been traced to a sailor or riverman.) That year, the New Orleans Board of Health reported 283 cases and only 6 deaths (2.1 percent). But the following year, during what city health officials described as "an almost incessant battle" with smallpox, New Orleans recorded 1,468 cases and 448 deaths (30.5 percent). Mississippi weathered deadly winter epidemics in 1900 and 1901. In just the first six weeks of 1901, the state reported 2,066 cases and 456 deaths (a 22 percent fatality rate)—a greater toll, noted the *Atlanta Constitution*, than the dreaded yellow fever had taken there in any year since the great epidemic of 1878. Outside the South, lethal outbreaks occurred around the turn of the century in New York, Philadelphia, Boston, Cleveland, and other cities. In Boston and Cleveland, these epidemics, in which hundreds died, came fast on the heels of outbreaks of mild smallpox.[7]

The slow accumulation of epidemiological experience would eventually persuade public health officials that mild type smallpox was a distinct disease entity. In 1913, Charles V. Chapin of the Providence Health Department, one of the preeminent American health officials of the early twentieth century, published the first major scientific article on the history of mild type smallpox in the United States. Basing his article on the evidence from public health reports, Chapin suggested that the mild type "seems to be a true mutation" with a marked tendency to "breed true." That is, mild type smallpox begot more of the same. Mild smallpox could still give rise, in susceptible individuals, to horrifying confluent smallpox; it could even kill. Infants, the elderly, and people with preexisting health problems were especially vulnerable. But, said Chapin, "tho it is possible that a few outbreaks of the severe type may have developed from the mild type, there is no conclusive evidence that they have been numerous, or extensive." Twenty years later, Chapin stated his claim in stronger terms. Citing the belief of "practically all epidemiologists and health officers who have had experience with smallpox in the United States," he wrote, "there is no proof that, during the more than thirty years the mild type has been with us, it has *ever* given rise to a permanent strain of the severe type." That remains the consensus of smallpox scientists today.[8]

Experts now believe that *two* strains of mild smallpox appeared for the first time at the tail end of the nineteenth century. One probably arose in the southeastern part of North America (the Pensacola strain), the other a bit earlier in southern Africa. Laboratory studies would eventually show that the two regional varieties of smallpox had different DNA, but their clinical and epidemiological characteristics were so similar that scientists created one term to cover both: *variola minor*. Classical smallpox was given a new name: *variola major*. Until the advent of genetic testing, the only sure way to tell variola minor from variola major was to count bodies. Variola minor was defined in the scientific community as that form of the virus that killed between 0.1 percent and 2 percent of its victims.[9]

Since the 1910s, the North American strain of variola minor has been referred to by its Brazilian name, *alastrim*, a Portuguese word that means "burns like tinder, scatters, spreads from place to place." The name encapsulates its global history. Since many of its victims remained ambulatory, and because so much of the U.S. population at the turn of the century moved around the country in pursuit of work and profit, alastrim spread with unusual speed over great distances. From its likely southern origin, it traversed the United States from 1896 to 1902, slipped into Latin America, England, and Europe, then made its way around the world. In other words, the disease so many Americans called "Cuban itch" was almost certainly a U.S. export.[10]

Variola major did not go away. The classical form of the virus apparently caused those deadly epidemics in New Orleans, New York, Boston, and elsewhere in 1900 and afterward. The virus in its deadliest form continued to infect and kill millions of people around the globe until the 1970s. In the United States, however, the incidence of variola major declined sharply after 1905. (The last major epidemic struck Ohio, Michigan, and western Pennsylvania in 1924–25.) After the turn-of-the-century epidemics, then, the mild type became the only form of smallpox most American communities would ever know.[11]

Government officials must often act in tight situations with imperfect knowledge. It's part of the job description. Health officials in the late nineteenth-century South were fighting, in real time, against a mysterious disease whose capacity for taking human life no one could predict. In their eyes, there was only one sure way to permanently reduce the dangerous threat of smallpox: universal vaccination. Experience quickly confirmed that Jennerian vaccination worked just as well against the new smallpox as it did against the old—which was all the proof most health officials needed that the two diseases were, in fact, one and the same.

Because of the diagnostic confusion that followed "the mild type" wherever it went, public health officials found themselves fighting a hard public campaign on many fronts. They had to persuade town and county officials, who held the purse strings, to appropriate scarce funds for smallpox control. They had to convince skeptical physicians that this new disease was smallpox at all. They had to protect their own communities from infection by neighboring towns where lax or inept officials let epidemics spiral out of control. And they had to get the people vaccinated. This last task would prove the most intractable. Public health officials used every available tactic to secure universal vaccination among citizens who detested the procedure and feared its results. Those political tactics included education, intimidation, and, with the aid of local police, criminal sanctions. Especially when they confronted opposition from African Americans, the authorities readily resorted to violent force.

Public health imperatives alone did not determine the impact of smallpox in the South. Particular features of the region's social and political landscape eased the spread of the mild smallpox and made its eradication extraordinarily difficult. Faced with an escalating public health disaster of regional scope, many local and state governments would turn for assistance to an unlikely ally: the federal government.

Smallpox burned across the South, without respect for such man-made boundaries as county lines and state borders. Even the color line, which for a while seemed to hopeful whites to hold the virus at bay, proved an ephemeral barrier. As indifferent as smallpox was to such political and ideological boundaries, they did shape how Southerners and their governments experienced and battled the disease. The smallpox epidemics of the end of the century constituted an event of regional and, ultimately, national significance. But in a more fundamental sense, they happened locally. And mild smallpox proved at least as adept as the most devastating variola major of the past at revealing the true boundaries and character of a community.

One place in particular—Middlesboro, Kentucky—showed the nation in the winter of 1898 just how much damage even the mild type of small-pox could do under the right social and political conditions. An Appala-chian mountain city of 3,500 souls, Middlesboro occupied a shallow valley at the northern end of the fabled Cumberland Gap, just a few miles from the spot where the borders of Kentucky, Tennessee, and Virginia met. The "Magic City," as local boosters called it, was just ten years old. Already it stood as a stark monument to the creative destruction of industrial capital-ism. Before the epidemic there ended, the city would stand for failings of a decidedly more personal nature.[12]

Middlesboro was "west" before it was "south." In the late eighteenth and early nineteenth centuries, thousands of westering Americans passed through Cumberland Gap, the natural passageway in the Appalachian range made famous by Daniel Boone, on their way to the Kentucky blue-grass and the North American interior. But few stopped long in the three-mile-wide geomorphic basin known as Yellow Creek Valley. Railroad construction bypassed the area in the early nineteenth century, and the traf-fic through the Gap reversed itself; the historic gateway to the West became a muddy conduit for men driving hogs to market in Tennessee and North Carolina. During the Civil War, Union and Confederate forces fought for control of the Gap. The mountain people of neutral Kentucky would not soon forget how troops from both sides had stripped their hills and homes. After the war, Yellow Creek Valley and its hillside grew isolated again, home to sixty farm families who lived close to the land and seemingly beyond the reach of the industrializing society of the United States.[13]

In 1886, a Scottish-born Canadian named Alexander Arthur prospected the area for a railroad company and found the place rich in hardwoods, iron ore, and coal. A distant relative of former president Chester A. Arthur, Alexander Arthur fit the type of the mutton-chop-wearing, fast-talking capitalist who earned the Gilded Age its name. With capital from New York and North Carolina, he started buying up options to the land. He then approached investors in London and sold them on the idea that Yellow Creek Valley had the makings of a great iron and steel manufacturing center, a place where surplus British capital could be brought to bear upon untapped American natural resources to generate extraordinary wealth. Arthur had arrived in London at an opportune moment, the very peak of British investment in U.S. enterprises. The economic potential of such boomtowns had already been demonstrated elsewhere in the "New South," most notably in the coalfields and steel mills of Birmingham, Alabama, established in 1871. With Arthur running the U.S. side of the operation, the London investors incorporated in 1887 under English law as the American Association, Ltd. The association secured title from the mountain people to eighty thousand acres of land. A separate Arthur entity, the Middlesborough Town Company, launched construction of the physical city, named after the iron center in northern England. A local postmaster, as if to announce the presence of federal authority in this new community, lopped off the last three letters. Arthur's secretary later told the tale of Middlesboro's birth in terms not far from the mark: "[A]lmost a hundred years after England lost her colonies, 'conquistadores' from Albion came out to a still crude and unsettled quarter of the United States for the purpose of further colonization."[14]

By 1890, twenty million dollars' worth of British capital and the muscle of thousands of American and European workers had turned Yellow Creek Valley into a boomtown of five thousand people. Railroad workers dug a tunnel under the Gap, connecting Middlesboro to Tennessee and the markets and ports of the southeastern United States. A rail beltway circled the town, with spurs shooting off to the hillside collieries that various companies operated under leases from the Association. The Appalachian skies grew thick with the smoke and smells of ironworks, blast furnaces, tanneries, sawmills, brickyards, and breweries. The early encampment of tents gave way to a well-ordered grid of wide streets filled with streetcars, stores, saloons, hotels, banks, schools, churches, sturdy wooden houses for the workers, and stone Victorians for their bosses. Middlesboro even boasted an opera house and one of America's first golf courses. And the American Association and its distant investors controlled it all.[15]

The bust came as swiftly as the boom. In the spring of 1890, a fire leveled the Middlesboro business district. The buildings were quickly rebuilt, but at great expense to the Association and the local government it controlled. Later that year, the Bank of Baring Brothers in London declared bankruptcy, taking many of Middlesboro's British investors down with it. As the town's sources of capital dried up, the realization dawned that the area's reserves of commercial grade iron ore were thinner than expected. Then came the American financial panic of 1893. All four of the town's banks failed. Merchants closed their stores. Employers laid off workers. People drained out of the place. The Association mortgaged seventy thousand acres of land to a New York bank for $1.5 million and then, in October 1893, declared bankruptcy. And yet, Middlesboro survived. With its rail connections, its coal reserves, its furnaces, and its hungry labor force, the city still had the stuff of a scaled-down industrial city where profits could be made. In 1894, a federal court ordered a public auction of the mortgaged acres. A new company, incorporated under U.S. law, snapped up the land for a mere $15,000. The company's name had a familiar ring: American Association, Inc. Its roster of investors looked familiar, too. They were mostly the same London capitalists who once called themselves American Association, Ltd.[16]

Middlesboro shed its most grandiose aspirations (along with most of its wealthier residents) and settled down to the hardscrabble life of an Appalachian company town. The place more closely resembled a remote settlement of impoverished wage earners than a conventional urban or rural place. The local government carried a heavy debt; without a penny in the treasury, the city routinely paid its schoolteachers and other employees in devalued city scrip. The rest of Middlesboro's breadwinners, with the exception of the factory superintendents and a small professional class, scratched out a living where they could, doing day labor and working for the mines, works, and factories that still operated. European immigrants had helped build Middlesboro, but almost everyone who stayed was a southern-born American. More than one fifth of the city's 3,500 residents were African American.

Middlesboro heeded southern racial norms, with segregated schools and much of the black population consigned to work in the meanest jobs and to live in the thickly settled sections known as "Alabama Row" and "Over the Rhine." (The latter name recalled a defunct German brewery that had once perfumed the area with the sweet stench of hops.) In the fall of 1897, the everyday life of Middlesboro was tied more closely than ever to the furnaces and the mines that fed them. In mid-November, the local newspapers buzzed with the first really good news that anyone had heard in a long time. The Ducktown iron mines over Cumberland Mountain were set to reopen. Soon trains would carry ten cars a day loaded with ore to Middlesboro. The furnaces would run at full blast again: "Prosperity is certainly coming to this section," the *Middlesboro Weekly Herald* promised.[17]

Prosperity never came. Smallpox did.

It started in the Over the Rhine section. In late October, an African American miner named Scott had left the smallpox-infested coal camps around Birmingham and traveled more than three hundred miles for a new job in the Mingo Mines, located just across the border from Middlesboro in Tennessee. He found housing in the Over the Rhine section. Scott was a member of a fast-growing occupation. The number of black miners and quarrymen in the United States doubled during the 1890s. Like the vast majority of African Americans (roughly 90 percent), most of them lived in the southern states. And like roughly one third of all African American breadwinners at the end of the nineteenth century, they worked at least part of the year in nonagricultural occupations, often in rural industries such as mining, turpentine production, and lumbering. The age of Carnegie generated enormous demand for coal. And the rapidly expanding southern railroad network brought southern coal reserves within easier reach of the national market. In southern Appalachia, the coal-rich region stretching from central Alabama to West Virginia, one third of all miners were African American. The work was dirty and dangerous, the jobs mostly nonunion, the bosses white. Typically the first let go when business slowed, a black miner like Scott had to be ready to move.[18]

Although he had no way of knowing it, he carried a bit of Birmingham with him when he did. A Marine-Hospital Service surgeon stationed in Birmingham during the smallpox epidemics of 1897–98 described black miners as "the great disseminators of infection. Essentially itinerant, they travel from mining camp to mining camp, from town to town, carrying the disease with them." About a week after his arrival at Mingo, Scott came down with a fever and chills. A week later came the eruption. Someone called for a doctor.[19]

On November 14, a white Middlesboro physician named Dr. F. P. Kenyon examined Scott. He found the miner lying ill in a building in Over the Rhine. Located across the tracks and the lazy Yellow Creek from the heart of Middlesboro, the section was notorious for its rowdy saloons and bawdy houses where whites and blacks mixed. The building where Scott lay had once housed John Hughes's saloon, remembered locally, in the words of a white newspaperman, as "the scene of many a bloody coon scrap." Dr. Kenyon recognized Scott's condition, but just to make sure he called in a second physician, who confirmed his diagnosis: a "well developed case of smallpox."[20]

That simple act of naming Scott's condition brought the miner and the physicians into the orbit of the law. A Kentucky statute required all physicians and heads of household to report any contagious and infectious diseases to their local board of health. In most communities in this predominantly rural state, "local" meant the county. But under state law, a city of Middlesboro's size (more than 2,500 residents) was supposed to have a board of health and a health officer of its own. Middlesboro had no hospital in 1898, let alone a functioning board of health. But two of the three members of the Bell County Board of Health, Dr. T. H. Curd and Dr. L. L. Robertson, lived in the city, and they, too, confirmed the diagnosis, estimating that roughly fifteen people had come into contact with Scott. That night, residents clustered in the streets to discuss the rumored outbreak, the latest insult in a long run of bad luck. Some said it was time to leave Middlesboro for good. Meeting in an emergency session, the city council ordered the police to enforce a quarantine against the Over the Rhine district. Priding itself on its healthy mountain air, Middlesboro had no pesthouse. Scott and several African American residents known to have been exposed to him were placed under guard in the old Hughes saloon.[21]

Politically, the city council's strategy for thwarting a smallpox epidemic had two things going for it: it didn't inconvenience the white citizenry much, and it was cheap. Kentucky law held local governments liable for the cost of managing an epidemic. In a legal case arising from the Bardstown smallpox outbreak of 1883, a Kentucky court noted that this obligation went further than "the ordinary social duty to care for the helpless." "If the poor man is neglected he may starve or freeze, but the calamity is personal, and his grave hides it; but if, having an infectious disease, which poisons the air, he is left where he lies, the entire community is menaced." Whether this fiscal responsibility properly fell on Middlesboro, Bell County, or both would become a heated issue. For now, the city council decided that local police, already on the payroll, would enforce the quarantine. A more aggressive approach—a targeted quarantine and a well-run pesthouse coupled with compulsory vaccination of the entire population—would have been much more expensive. A pesthouse cost money: fees for the physician, wages for the guards, and food for the indigent patients. A general vaccination order posed other problems.[22]

Vaccination was not popular in Kentucky. Although state board of health rules required that public schoolchildren submit to vaccination, the board estimated that at least one third of the state's white residents and a larger part of its African Americans had never been vaccinated. In Middlesboro, according to one estimate, nine tenths of the population had never undergone the procedure. And when a local government ordered a general vaccination, it was liable under state law for the cost of providing vaccination free to the poor. In a place as impoverished as Middlesboro, that meant paying a lot of doctor's fees and buying a lot of vaccine.[23]

Another factor weighed into the political calculus. A good many Middlesboro residents, including the editors of the local newspapers, greeted the news of a smallpox outbreak with skepticism. The *Weekly Herald* described Scott's illness as "a malady something like smallpox." Scott had a relatively mild case, and it may have looked just like chicken pox to the few people who got a look at him. Economic self-interest and civic pride strengthened medical doubts. To call the "malady" smallpox would threaten the reputation and livelihood of Middlesboro. The city council of neighboring Pineville, the county seat, had already ordered a quarantine against Middlesboro, forbidding anyone from the mountain city to enter the town. The Middlesboro newspapers, which agreed on little else, warned citizens not to spread "wild exaggerated reports" that might lead other towns to choke off the flow of people and goods to and from Middlesboro. In Middlesboro's straits, the spread of rumors seemed more dangerous than the spread of smallpox itself.[24]

And then the smallpox "scare" ended. Scott recovered. No new cases had come to light. On December 9, the city council declared victory and lifted the quarantine. And so, as life returned to normal in Middlesboro, the population remained almost entirely unvaccinated.[25]

Weeks passed before the white officials of Middlesboro realized their quarantine had failed. A smallpox outbreak often begins slowly. Due to variola's long incubation period, two weeks may pass between the initial discovery of a single smallpox case and the appearance of the next cluster, or "generation," of cases. The medical logic of the quarantine is that by waiting out the incubation period, keeping potential carriers—"suspects"—apart from everyone else, officials can contain an outbreak and eventually snuff it out. But for those who must live on the other side of the quarantine line, the medical rationale is not always its most salient feature. When Pineville had announced its quarantine against the entire city of Middlesboro, city leaders had cried foul. The historical record mentions no such public outcry from the African American residents of Middlesboro's own quarantined district, who were confined to a territory ostensibly justified by the public health but drawn explicitly by race. But the unanticipated consequence of this policy was that African Americans in the district did not notify the white authorities when more people in their community broke out with smallpox.[26]

This failure or outright refusal to cooperate with the local white power structure had its own unintended political effect. For when the authorities realized that smallpox had spread in the Over the Rhine section, the discovery merely reinforced their belief in the legitimacy of their quarantine. The *Middlesboro Weekly Record* ran a series of satirical dialect pieces that purported to represent the "niggahs'" point of view on the smallpox situation. In one piece, an old "aunt" tells a reporter that the only way to stop "dem low down niggahs from spreading smallpox is for de perlice" to "scrub that 'ol Alabama dirt . . . off 'n 'em."[27]

In late December, a second case was reported in the Over the Rhine district, followed by several others. At first the city council did nothing, reluctant to spend money it did not have in the absence of public alarm.

Although the Bell County Board of Health called upon the county government to provide funds, the county Fiscal Court, in charge of such appropriations, said it viewed this as a Middlesboro matter. Among the people
of Middlesboro, rumors still circulated that the disease was not smallpox.
A winter surge of chicken pox added to the diagnostic confusion: many
people had trouble distinguishing one disease from the other. Some Middlesboro blacks were calling the mild smallpox "Elephant Itch," a name that,
according to some accounts, old-timers, former slaves, had long used for
smallpox. Another name, "African Itch" (the polite, newspaper euphemism
for "Nigger Itch"), expressed the belief of many local whites that this disease, whatever it was, wouldn't trouble them as long as they kept their
distance from blacks. For well over a month, the disease did in fact remain
confined entirely to African Americans. And when the city government finally got around to setting up a pesthouse, in mid-January, all of the patients and suspects detained there were black. In early February, the *Weekly
Record* made a plea for calm: "Up to the present, no white people have been
attacked and there is positively no occasion for alarm."[28]

One nearby community after another instituted shotgun quarantines
against Middlesboro. Given the city's border location, the epidemic inflamed interstate politics. Lee County, Virginia, quarantined against Middlesboro. A Tazewell, Tennessee, newspaper called the Middlesboro
authorities "criminally negligent." Officials in Claiborne County, Tennessee,
home to Tazewell and the Mingo Mines, promised to enforce their quarantine against Middlesboro "if there is any virtue in a Winchester." The
Middlesboro council denounced these actions as "unwarranted, uncalled-
for, unprofessional, ungentlemanly, and unworthy." The quarantines cost
local businesses thousands of dollars.[29]

A series of events in mid-February finally spurred the local officials
to take serious measures to stop the epidemic. The first was the long-
anticipated arrival, on February 12, of Dr. J. N. McCormack, secretary of
the Kentucky Board of Health. Students of American government use the
term "federalism" to describe the distinctively decentralized operation of
political power in the United States before the New Deal. The states, especially in the South, had their own form of federalism: localism. Controlling
infectious diseases—like policing the streets, running public schools, and

administering poor relief—was the indisputable province of local authority. And where that authority rested, so did liability for the cost of disease
control. The Kentucky Board of Health, a body of prominent physicians
with a small staff of inspectors and the power to issue statewide regulations,
only intervened in local affairs when local officials let local matters get
totally out of hand. Which is exactly what McCormack's presence in Middlesboro signified.[30]

Joseph Nathaniel McCormack of Bowling Green knew the Kentucky
health laws as well as anyone. He'd written most of them himself. The fifty-
year-old Kentucky native held medical degrees from the Miami Medical
College in Cincinnati and the University of Louisville. He had served on the
state board since 1879, holding the position of secretary for most of that
time. He would remain as the state's top health officer until his death, in
1912, when the Kentucky political leadership passed that office on to his
son, Arthur Thomas McCormack. Joseph's Kentucky pride did not extend
to its communities' fierce independence in matters vital to the health of the
entire state. He devoted much of his life to the quixotic project of building
a unified state health system.[31]

Arriving in Middlesboro, McCormack inspected the pesthouse, examined all of the known cases in the city, about twenty in all, and interviewed
the health officers. What McCormack saw convinced him, as he said later,
that "the parsimony and incapacity of the city and county officials" had
laid "the foundation of an epidemic." Standing before a special session
of the city council, McCormack testified that every case he had examined
was smallpox. He "recommended" that the council order compulsory
vaccination.[32]

Up to this point, the half-dozen private physicians and company doctors
working in Middlesboro had vaccinated a few hundred people, but most
residents remained unprotected. The councilmen had a strong incentive to
carry out the secretary's recommendation. If they did not, the state board
would exercise its full quarantine power against the city. The state board had
the power to forbid anyone to enter or leave the city and to prevent any
transportation company from delivering freight (coal, iron ore, food) without the board's written permission. The board could bring Middlesboro's
already beleaguered economy to a standstill. Before adjourning that after-

noon, the council passed a compulsory vaccination ordinance and ordered the edict published on posters and distributed about the city.[33]

That same afternoon, a man named Will Sheffly died in the pesthouse—the outbreak's first fatality. The next day smallpox crossed the color line. The first white patient was Charles Dudley Ball, a saloon-keeper, gambling den operator, and deputy sheriff whose brother happened to be the chief of police. Charley Ball was not allowed to suffer the indignity of being the lone white man in the pesthouse. The authorities moved him to a deserted house on the outskirts of town. During the next forty-eight hours, eight more people with smallpox were discovered, four of them whites. Even more than Dr. McCormack's visit, the infection of white Middlesboro residents, apparently by their black neighbors, gave the city vaccination campaign a sense of urgency among the city's white leadership.[34]

The compulsory vaccination of Middlesboro began peacefully, as the overwhelmed city and county physicians attended first to the many residents, white and black, who came forward voluntarily. But after the initial rush subsided, the vaccinators began the slower work of house-to-house vaccination in the neighborhoods, where they met resistance with threats of arrest, jail, and fines. The vaccination order was part of a raft of emergency ordinances enacted by the council. The councilmen closed the schools, churches, and saloons. They forbade the public to assemble in the streets and children to go out at all unless accompanied by a parent or guardian. Inmates of the city jail were put to work cleaning up the city—an act of urban renewal that shows the hold upon medical thinking of the old notion of smallpox as a filth disease, an association that even the ascendance of the microbe in medical science did not dispel. Meanwhile, the postmaster, still the lone agent of federal authority in Middlesboro, set up a fumigating apparatus for all outgoing mail; punching holes in letters and packages, he sealed them in a box for five hours with burning sulfur. Citizens could purchase their own personal disinfection devices from enterprising local merchants. S. R. Sneed Co. touted the Pasteurine Pocket Disinfectant and Deodorizer—"A deadly foe to Contagion."[35]

Given how long they had waited to take action, the city officials should have known the epidemic would get worse before it got better. More people with smallpox surfaced almost every day. By the end of February there were fifty-two known cases among African Americans and poor whites from various parts of the city. Several people suffered from confluent smallpox, and a second patient died. To make matters worse, Middlesboro officials were still haggling with Bell County over which government would pay for all of the guards, doctors, and food. The Bell County Fiscal Court continued to reject requests for aid, reasoning that so far the epidemic was confined to Middlesboro, and Middlesboro should take care of its own mess. As a result, the smallpox control effort slowed to a virtual standstill.[36]

On February 28, three months after Scott brought smallpox to Middlesboro, the Kentucky Board of Health stepped in. Secretary McCormack sent his son, Dr. A. T. McCormack, the state's chief sanitary inspector, to run the operation. The younger McCormack, who was just twenty-five, brought along two deputy state inspectors, Dr. Austin Bell and Dr. B. W. Smock, and on his father's request, the Bell County health officer, Dr. Samuel Blair, moved into the town, too. Most of the manpower—police, inspectors, guards, and vaccinators—were provided by the city government. The state board made clear at the outset that although it was taking control of the epidemic, it would not be paying the bills.[37]

A. T. McCormack quarantined the entire population of Middlesboro, posting armed guards day and night on the eight roads leading out of town. He took over a deserted row of buildings called "Brown's Row" and established a new pesthouse and detention camp there, under the charge of Dr. Blair. The city was divided into eight districts; inspectors and vaccinators canvassed each one. As they found people with symptoms, they moved them immediately to the pesthouse. The inspectors disinfected the homes of "the infected" by burning sulfur in the closed rooms. When they found a house too leaky to hold the sulfur gas, they burned it to the ground. "Suspects" were placed under quarantine in their own houses and were visited daily by one of the health officers.[38]

McCormack put Dr. Bell in charge of the vaccination corps. The medical men entered the neighborhoods with health inspectors and police in tow. The men returned to the same homes later, to make sure the vaccine took. For some residents, the vaccine took *too* well. In February and March, the newspapers ran four stories about citizens who became sick or temporarily disabled following vaccination. The arm of one mail clerk, according to one newspaper report, "swelled to three times its normal size."[39]

African Americans in the Over the Rhine district learned how a smallpox epidemic could transform years of official indifference and neglect into coercion and violence. Racial tensions had risen during the winter, as white officials and newspapers blamed black townsfolk for the events that brought shame on the community. The *Weekly Record* called for a public law, like the Louisiana separate coach law the U.S. Supreme Court had upheld in *Plessy v. Ferguson* (1896), to "keep the colored people in a separate section of the town. If it cannot be done by process of law, it can be accomplished by public sentiment."[40]

The thin line between process of law and white public sentiment vanished when Dr. Bell's vaccination corps moved back into the Over the Rhine section in early March. Entering crowded wooden houses and shanties, they confronted the consequences of black distrust of white health authority. The inspectors found twenty or more adults and children suffering from smallpox, who had hidden (or been concealed by their parents) from the authorities. As the inspectors removed the patients from their homes and hauled them to the pesthouse, the physicians examined the arms of the other residents, finding many that had never been touched by a vaccinator's lancet. As they attempted to enforce the vaccination order, the physicians were met, according to the *Weekly Record*, with "the greatest opposition." That was what the police were for. This time there would be no arrests or fines. All who resisted were handcuffed and vaccinated at gunpoint.[41]

McCormack and his men brought a new measure of expertise, discipline, and violence to Middlesboro. In the ten days after the state took control of the epidemic, the health authorities handled 169 cases of smallpox. Thirty-four of the patients were white, the rest black. The youngest was an infant just one day old when the eruption appeared simultaneously on mother and child. Miraculously, the baby survived. By March 10, many of the patients had recovered, and no further deaths had occurred. Dr. Bell's vaccination corps had scraped the arms of 1,968 people—the exactness of the count offered as a testament to the state officers' efficiency. Earlier reports had put the number vaccinated by the city officials somewhere around a thousand. And others had been vaccinated by their own physicians. But the epidemic was not over. There were still seventy people packed into the pesthouse on Brown's Row. And they were running out of food.[42]

One thing McCormack and his deputies had not brought to Middlesboro was money. The state board didn't have much in the first place; its annual appropriation was just $2,500, and half of that went to pay J. N. McCormack's modest salary. The state was counting on city and county officials to pay for the guards and the pesthouse supplies. But squeezing money from the local governments proved even harder than getting people vaccinated. The Bell County Fiscal Court still refused to contribute a penny, and the scrip (called "warrants") that the city had been using to cover expenses had become so devalued as to be all but worthless. As a consequence, the guards were virtually working without pay. When A. T. McCormack wired the news to his father, the secretary resorted to the only weapon at his disposal: the threat of a total quarantine against Middlesboro. J. N. McCormack wired Mayor John Glasgow Fitzpatrick: "Unless city or county can arrange [to pay the expenses], will be forced to release you and local Board from duty, stop all trains and advise adjoining counties to protect themselves."[43]

Secretary McCormack underestimated the political acumen of the local officials. Shortly after receiving his telegram, Mayor Fitzpatrick, a lawyer and businessman connected to local mining interests, sent a telegram of his own. He wired Middlesboro's congressional representative in Washington, a favorite son of Yellow Creek Valley named David Grant Colson. A Republican, Colson had served as mayor of Middlesboro for four years before taking his seat in Congress. He understood the situation there better than anyone else in Washington. Fitzpatrick wrote: "County refuses aid; city has no funds. Can Federal aid be had?"

It was a good question. The United States in 1898 had no federal welfare state as such. But since 1790, Congress had on roughly one hundred occasions used its spending powers under the Constitution's "general welfare" clause to appropriate relief for the hapless victims of wars, floods, fires, famines, cyclones, grasshopper invasions, and other disasters. Yellow fever epidemics and Mississippi floods had aroused Congress to send aid to southern communities on more than one occasion since the Civil War. But long-standing practice dictated that such appropriations be reserved for cases in which blameless people had been overwhelmed by circumstances beyond their control. The Middlesboro smallpox epidemic did not meet that test. The misguided parsimony of public officials, rather than an act of God or some other uncontrollable force, had caused the "disaster" in the mountain city. And how would Congress have responded to the Middlesboro leaders' racial theory of the epidemic? Were African Americans a force beyond their control? Was this "African" epidemic an act of God? Congress never had an opportunity to ponder such questions. Rather than make the hard case for congressional relief, Colson contacted Walter Wyman.[44]

Colson may have been aware that Wyman's federal health bureau, the U.S. Marine-Hospital Service, had for the past two months been working with local authorities in Birmingham, Alabama, to control a smallpox epidemic there. In his message to the surgeon general, the congressman narrated the Middlesboro epidemic as an emergency. "The situation is a very grave one," he wrote. "Neither the municipal, county or state authorities are able to control the epidemic." But Colson astutely crafted his case for Marine-Hospital Service intervention in the political language of federalism. "All Southwest Kentucky, East Tennessee, and Southwest Virginia are involved, or *liable to be*." Middlesboro's location on the border made an uncontrolled epidemic there a danger to other states. This fact alone made direct federal intervention plausible. For good measure, Colson enclosed a note from Rep. Walter P. Brownlow, a fellow Republican whose district lay in northeastern Tennessee, just across the border from Middlesboro. "I fully concur in the above," Brownlow said. "Small-pox is spreading in my district. I ask for immediate action."[45]

Passed Assistant Surgeon C. P. Wertenbaker was working at his station in Wilmington, North Carolina, later that day when the telegram came in. "Proceed to Middlesboro, Ky," Wyman ordered. "Report on situation there and neighborhood with recommendations." The surgeon general added a word of caution to his officer before he embarked upon his five-hundred-mile journey from the Carolina coast to the heart of Appalachia: "Local authorities should meet expenses, [federal] government expenditures are interstate only." Wertenbaker caught the next train west.[46]

. . .

It was dark by the time the surgeon reached the mountain city, the high wooded ridge of Cumberland Mountain a presence more felt than seen in the cool March night. A clock had only just tolled eight, but the broad streets were virtually empty, the saloons shuttered, the trains dead on their tracks. Out on the public roads, men toting lanterns and shotguns guarded the quarantine line. No one in, no one out. The guards at the train station, though, had made an exception for Wertenbaker. They'd been expecting him.

In his crisp blue uniform, Charles Poindexter Wertenbaker was the very model of a Marine-Hospital Service physician during Walter Wyman's long tenure as surgeon general (1891–1911). A university-trained medical man with the discipline of a soldier and the bearing of an officer, Wertenbaker knew how to handle a microscope, a pen, and a gun. Wertenbaker was thirty-seven years old. An inch or two shy of tall, he had fair skin, light eyes, and a thick mustache that in his younger days he had waxed into a fashionable pair of handlebars. He had spent ten years in the Service, working the federal outposts in a succession of American ports: Norfolk, Galveston, Chicago, and Lewes, Delaware. He took over at Wilmington just days before the smallpox arrived there, reportedly in the body of an African American railroad hand. Now, three months later, he was still figuring out the politics of smallpox control. For him, Middlesboro would be an object lesson.[47]

When daylight broke on March 14, Wertenbaker toured Middlesboro on foot with A. T. McCormack. As they walked, Wertenbaker noted the Old World character and surprising sturdiness of the Appalachian boomtown: the broad streets with their English names, the imposing bank buildings and substantial storefronts of the business district, the Victorian mansions of the finer neighborhoods. Even the wood-framed houses constructed for the workers looked built to last. On many of those houses hung the telltale placards or yellow flags. McCormack told him that four hundred residents, roughly one ninth of the population, were now under domestic quarantine—prisoners in their own homes. Another seventy-two people were in the pesthouse. So far, McCormack told Wertenbaker, his men had vaccinated nearly two thousand people. At this point, anyone who had not been vaccinated probably aimed to keep it that way. In any event, as Wertenbaker reported to Wyman later that day, "forcible vaccination is still progressing."[48]

McCormack did not hide his resentment at Wertenbaker's presence in Middlesboro. McCormack was a young man, but he was no country doctor. He had a medical degree from Columbia University. The Kentucky Board of Health was, in a sense, the McCormack family business. He was his father's most trusted man in the field. He did not intend to let the Middlesboro debacle tarnish the board's honor and reputation. The physician assured Wertenbaker that he had wasted his time in coming all the way to Middlesboro. The state had everything "under control."[49]

Next the men arrived at the pesthouse. The crowded structures, located in a thickly settled part of the city, housed seventy-two men, women, and children. As he moved through rooms thick with the sickening sweet smell of smallpox, Wertenbaker kept a running tally. Forty-nine of the inmates had already broken out with clear cases. The rest showed some early symptoms or were being detained as "suspects." According to the standard Service practice, the suspects should have been kept apart from the patients, to avoid unnecessarily spreading the disease. Most of the inmates were African American; seeing Middlesboro from the perspective of smallpox, Wertenbaker mistakenly concluded that half of the city population was black. From his experience in North Carolina during the past few months, Wertenbaker couldn't have been surprised that smallpox and Jim Crow had conspired in Middlesboro, too. But something else did surprise him. The inmates were not just sick, or in imminent danger of becoming so. As he wired Wyman later that day, "the patients are without food."[50]

Months of haggling between city and county authorities had come to this. Without the backing of the Bell County Fiscal Court, the city scrip was worthless. A few days earlier, the grocer who had already supplied the pesthouse with $500 worth of food refused to provide any more until he was "satisfied of reimbursement." While Wertenbaker traveled to Middlesboro, the last of the food had run out. Some guards now refused to work until they were properly paid. The strategy of the McCormacks, father and son, was to exploit the public embarrassment of the pesthouse crisis and the threat of a county-wide quarantine in order to finally squeeze an appro-

priation from the county government. It must have seemed a sensible strategy to the McCormacks; thanks to the wire reports coming out of the city,
newspapers as far away as Grand Forks, North Dakota, and New York City
were running stories on the "starving" pesthouse inmates of Middlesboro,
Kentucky. But locals knew better than to underestimate the fiscal parsimony
of Judge James Neal of the Bell County Fiscal Court, whom the *Middlesboro
Weekly Record* described as "a little, one-horse, whipper-snapper of a judge
with a brain about as big as a mustard seed and a soul infinitely smaller."
And so while government officials engaged in a standoff over funds, the
pesthouse inmates went hungry. If more guards abandoned their posts,
could anyone expect the inmates to stay in the pesthouse?[51]

That afternoon Wertenbaker and McCormack addressed a roomful of
indignant local businessmen and political leaders at the Middlesborough
Hotel. Speaking for the state board, McCormack told the assembly that
national government aid was unnecessary, the epidemic was already under
control, and the county "could and would be made to pay." Wertenbaker
told the men that he could not take control of the epidemic unless the
state board of health appealed to the surgeon general for assistance. Upon
hearing this, several of the locals constituted themselves as a Citizens' Committee. They drafted a telegram to Governor W. O. Bradley and J. M.
Mathews, president of the state board of health, asking them to call on the
national government. The decision to appeal to Mathews, the political ap-
pointee who presided over the board, rather than J. N. McCormack, who
actually ran it, no doubt stoked the indignation of both McCormacks.[52]

The Citizens' Committee's telegram was but the opening salvo in a war
of the wires—a clash of rhetorical performances that would last three days
and reverberate for months afterward. The entire discussion centered on
cash, control, and, in an indirect way, the Constitution. The McCormacks
blamed the episode on Wertenbaker, whom they came to see as an arrogant
interloper who had usurped their authority by promising the citizens of
Middlesboro a bag full of United States currency. As A. T. McCormack recalled bitterly, "A number of citizens who had given us little or no aid
during our hard work consulted and reconsulted with the Service surgeon,
and, inspired by either his talk or their dreams of government pelf, they
kept the wires hot with messages appealing for government assistance."[53]

J. M. Mathews wired back to the Citizens' Committee that, after consulting with the governor, he would happily authorize Dr. Wertenbaker to take charge—"if the Federal Government will defray expenses. There is no money in our treasury and no law to appropriate any for this purpose." Having no doubt received a copy of Mathews's telegram, Secretary McCormack then wired to Chief Inspector McCormack and told him to gather his men and leave Middlesboro at once. Once J. N. McCormack recalled the state officers, Wertenbaker was eager to take control, wiring the surgeon general that the state withdrawal left Middlesboro "absolutely unprotected." "If authority in Mathews' telegram is sufficient, I recommend that I be authorized to take charge to-night. . . . Please authorize necessary immediate expenditures for provisions, guards, etc."[54]

Walter Wyman was furious. He ordered Wertenbaker to notify both McCormacks that he had not been authorized to take control, and the state officers should not be recalled. "The [federal] government's interest is in protecting other states," he said, "and nowhere is the whole expense borne by the government. Every municipality should have enough pride in itself to suppress this ordinary contagious disease."[55]

But the men who had controlled the Middlesboro epidemic for the past two weeks had already caught the night train out of town. The Bell County Board of Health was back in charge—without any funds. A. T. McCormack and his men had barely left town before Judge Neal announced, again, that the county would not appropriate a dime.[56]

The same message arrived soon from Frankfort, as the governor and Kentucky lawmakers abdicated responsibility for the Middlesboro debacle. After receiving the Citizens' Committee's telegram on March 14, Governor Bradley had wired his fellow Republican, Representative Colson, to intercede with the surgeon general. His confusion about the legal authority of the federal government in such a situation was evidently total. "Act of Congress not in library," Governor Bradley said. "I do not know what the law allows. Am told Surgeon-General of the United States may be appealed to take charge immediately. If such can be done, request him in my name to take charge." The next day, Bradley appealed to the state legislature for an emergency appropriation, but the lawmakers adjourned without granting his request.[57]

Meanwhile, Mayor Fitzpatrick wired Surgeon General Wyman with a direct appeal. The mayor framed the Middlesboro situation as a relief crisis. "Middlesboro has 3,500 people dependent for support on wages of working people," Fitzpatrick said. "People poor; business suspended; request for immediate assistance." The mayor's language was telling. He appealed not in the name of the city government, which he headed, but in the name of the deserving wage earners of Middlesboro and their families. He was trying, belatedly, to craft a narrative about a blameless community deserving of federal aid. Significantly, he left race out of his story.[58]

For Walter Wyman, the request from Governor Bradley was enough. On March 16, Wyman wired J. M. Mathews and told him the Marine-Hospital Service was prepared to "furnish medical officers, attendants, guards, inspectors, and attend to vaccination and disinfection." The local authorities would still be expected to "care for poor not sick" and to furnish the pesthouse with food "so far as possible." Wyman did not want to open up a massive federal relief effort in Middlesboro. It was J. N. McCormack who wired back to accept Wyman's offer, so long as the Service intended to "aid and co-operate under our regulations." Wyman agreed to this face-saving language. But he added a condition of his own: "All expenditures . . . must be supervised and accounted for by our own officer." A reasonable condition, to be sure. But also a brisk slap in the Kentuckian's face.[59]

All of these niceties did not disguise the new political reality in Middlesboro. As the *Lexington Morning Herald* reported, "Uncle Sam is in charge of small-pox now."[60]

There was one recent precedent for a federal takeover of a local smallpox epidemic. On January 8, 1898, two months prior to Wertenbaker's arrival in Middlesboro, another Marine-Hospital Service surgeon named George M. Magruder had taken control of the smallpox epidemic in Birmingham and Jefferson County, Alabama. This was the same epidemic the miner named Scott thought he had left behind as he made his way north to the Mingo Mines. Built on a swampy valley floor, the manufacturing and mining boomtown with its highly transient population was a public health disaster waiting to happen—and never waiting very long. The area had weathered one epidemic after another since its founding in 1871, including serious bouts of Asian cholera in 1873 and typhoid in 1881. Alabama laws, enacted during the 1870s, established a state board of health and authorized the creation of county health departments. But at the moment smallpox broke out, not a single full-time county health organization existed in the entire state.[61]

Smallpox had been raging since July 1897 in Jefferson County, an area of a thousand square miles and 110,000 people. Half of the residents lived in Birmingham, the rest in mining camps, small towns, and manufacturing settlements outside the city. By the time Magruder arrived on the scene, more than 400 cases of smallpox had been reported in the area, with 15 deaths. As it would be in Middlesboro, the disease was confined almost exclusively to the African American population. The *Atlanta Constitution* assured its readers, "There is no danger of a spread of the disease among the white people."[62]

So far the disease had proved exceptionally mild, but also exceptionally expensive. The city and county governments spent the huge sum of $30,000 fighting the epidemic. They set up quarantine camps, enforced vaccination, and furnished 75,000 tubes and points of free vaccine. City officials strictly enforced vaccination: at least seven people were arrested in the first weeks of the epidemic for refusing to be vaccinated. But outside Birmingham, enforcement was spottier, and by December 1897, more than twenty towns and camps reported smallpox. In January, the local authorities called on the Marine-Hospital Service for aid. Surgeon General Wyman extended to Birmingham and Jefferson County the same offer he would later make to Middlesboro: the U.S. government would take general control of the quarantine camps, provide free vaccine, and organize a corps of men to inspect and vaccinate the population. But the city and county must "bear all other expenses." The local authorities readily accepted.[63]

From his headquarters in Birmingham, Magruder organized a corps of thirty inspectors, recruiting local physicians and medical students. He assigned each to a territory within the city, in which they inspected all homes and their occupants. Magruder advised the inspectors to extend courtesy to everyone—the "refined and rough, reasonable and unreasonable, crank and sage." But under no circumstances would the Service honor certificates of vaccination. "In all large towns," he explained, one could find "some physi-cians who will give false certificates for a small fee." Magruder's instructions show his awareness of the urban tradition of resistance to compulsory vac-cination, abetted by local doctors who were supposed to be the front line of public health. He told his inspectors to check every person's arm for a fresh vaccine scar—the only real proof of a successful recent vaccination. The inspectors were to make a thorough search of every room they visited, "es-pecially in negro quarters," looking for concealed people with smallpox. Ambulance wagons carried the sick to one of the quarantine camps. All suspects found living in a house with a smallpox sufferer were vaccinated at once and sent to the detention camp to be kept under watch for sixteen days. At the camps, Magruder introduced an innovation of which he was particularly proud. He surrounded each camp with a high fence of barbed wire. Thirty feet inside of this line he marked out a "dead line," beyond which no "patient" was allowed to tread. At night the entire area was illu-minated with gasoline torches, "enabling a small number of guards to ef-fectually prevent the escape of convalescents." Even with the doctors moving to and fro, to the detainees the federal quarantine facilities must have in-vited comparisons to Alabama's notorious convict labor camps.[64]

The mining camps outside of the city posed a special problem. Magruder believed the disease was spread chiefly by itinerant African American coal miners, who avoided vaccination whenever they could. Since they lived in unincorporated camps, none of the local compulsory vaccination ordi-nances applied to them. When superintendents of mining companies tried to enforce vaccination, "the men would leave in such numbers as to cause serious embarrassment from lack of laborers." The men just picked up and moved to another camp where vaccination was not enforced. As a conse-quence, those mining superintendents who had tried compulsory vaccina-tion on their premises gave up the effort.[65]

Magruder had an idea. He called together the owners and superinten-dents of the mining companies. These men ran mines and furnaces that employed thousands of workers, including many with families. Magruder persuaded the company men to cooperate—with each other and the federal government. They posted notices at their mines and furnaces, stating that no one would be allowed to work who refused to have himself and his family vaccinated. The notices listed all the area companies that had entered into the agreement. Once employers tightened control over their work-force, Magruder reported, the phenomenon of vaccination-induced walk-outs "almost entirely ceased." The surgeon's plan merged government and private authority in an ingenious solution to a seemingly intractable prob-lem of industrial management and public health. Magruder's account makes one wonder if the cooperative agreement he engineered among the employers might have laid the foundation for future agreements to control the organization and conditions of labor in their industries.[66]

Other southern communities watched the Marine-Hospital Service's work in Jefferson County with great interest. In short order, the mayor of nearby Talladega, Alabama, where smallpox had spread in the cotton mills, asked the Service to step in there, too. During the three months after the Marine-Hospital Service took over at Birmingham, the Service's corps of inspectors had paid more than 41,000 visits to private residences, many of them the poorly constructed houses and cabins of African American work-ers and their families, where they had found a great many concealed cases. The corps had vaccinated nearly 39,000 people. The Service had treated 352 patients in its three quarantine camps, with only nine deaths. Among the 225 patients at the Birmingham Quarantine Hospital, all but six were Afri-can American; more than two thirds were male; nearly half were in their twenties; and nearly half had never been vaccinated.[67]

By March 10 (the very date that Representative Colson asked Surgeon General Wyman to intervene at Middlesboro), George Magruder an-nounced that the epidemics in Birmingham, Jefferson County, and Talla-dega had ceased—at least "for the present." Magruder had no illusions about the permanency of his achievement in Alabama. Barbed wire, gas torches, armed guards, and men with lancets could only accomplish so much in this industrial frontier, where "large numbers of the unvaccinated persons are daily coming in." And there were several towns and mining camps where the inspectors had met with such intense local opposition that Magruder had withdrawn them, leaving behind large unvaccinated communities. As he prepared to pull up stakes from Birmingham, Magruder had to concede that despite all his efforts, and the support he had received from employers and citizens' groups in Birmingham, there were still enough unvaccinated people in the area to "keep the disease alive for some time." He was right. In 1899 alone, 9,150 cases of smallpox were reported in the state of Alabama. Significantly, 5,265 of those cases were white—a number roughly proportional to the percentage of whites in the state population. In Alabama as elsewhere, the early promise of a special dispensation for whites did not last.[68]

On March 17, C. P. Wertenbaker officially took over smallpox control at Middlesboro, Kentucky. He set up his headquarters, complete with a telephone, in a suite of offices in the business district. He hired five inspectors and twenty-five guards outfitted with Springfield rifles. He had four physicians on his medical staff, including Dr. Blair from Bell County, who would head up the inspector corps. A crew of nurses, cooks, attendants, and ambulance drivers rounded out the operation. Wertenbaker kept the mountain city under strict quarantine. Armed men guarded the public roads and the train depot, allowing no one to enter or leave the city without a pass signed by Wertenbaker. Within a week, one local newspaper reported, the federal surgeon had the smallpox control operation "running smooth as oil."[69]

For all of the similarities between the Jefferson County, Alabama, and Middlesboro, Kentucky, epidemics, the crisis Wertenbaker inherited from A. T. McCormack was far less intractable. The field of action was small by comparison—ten square miles against one thousand, a population of 3,500 against 110,000. And the Middlesboro population had been forcibly contained; unlike Jefferson County, which had laborers coming and going throughout the epidemic, Middlesboro had been under armed quarantine for weeks. Thanks to the efforts already made by local authorities and the state, the vast majority of the population had been vaccinated. In fact, if one believed everything printed in the state reports and the local newspapers, the total number of vaccinated people *exceeded* the actual population of Middlesboro.

Wertenbaker's inspectors, under the charge of Dr. Blair, set out immediately into the streets and neighborhoods of Middlesboro. Wertenbaker divided the city into five districts, assigning one inspector to each to make a house-to-house canvass. A local newspaper boasted awkwardly that the Service's inspection showed that "outside of small-pox this is the healthiest town on the globe." They examined everyone, vaccinating the few unscarred people they found. Anyone who refused the vaccination order was promptly turned over to the city authorities, who gave the violator the option of being vaccinated or taken to jail. As Wertenbaker reported to Wyman, it was something of a moot question, because if the uncooperative person chose jail, "they are vaccinated as soon as they enter, under a law requiring all inmates of jails to be vaccinated." The violence of compulsory vaccination at gunpoint in the Over the Rhine district had given way to something different, more orderly but still highly coercive.[70]

Wertenbaker took steps to separate the smallpox patients from the smallpox suspects. He turned a row of twelve houses near the old Brown's Row pesthouse, where patients and suspects had been confined, into a detention camp for suspects. He placed the camp under the charge of Dr. W. N. Shoemaker of Birmingham, who had become acquainted with Service methods from the epidemic there, and a staff of attendants and guards. For a smallpox hospital, Wertenbaker rented the old Biggerstaff boardinghouse, a two-story building on the city's western outskirts, and fitted it out with beds and supplies. Someone christened it the South Boston Hospital, after the nearby South Boston Iron Works, once a major supplier of cannons and armaments to the U.S. government. Wertenbaker's men moved the ninety-one people who had been languishing in the Brown's Row pesthouse into the hospital and placed them under the charge of Dr. W. C. Duke, a physician from Memphis who had been trained in Service work. It was a simple facility, but Duke had the assistance of nurses and attendants, and no patient would go hungry for lack of provisions.

In all smallpox epidemics, good nursing care—including the provision of such basic human needs as warmth, proper food, water, and clean sheets—had a major influence on mortality rates. A poorly run or ill-provisioned pesthouse (and many turn-of-the-century pesthouses were both) could be far worse for a patient's chances of recovery than care at home with family, which is one reason why so many families hid their sick from the health authorities. During the Service's operation at Middlesboro, the hospital treated 103 patients. About three quarters of them were African

American, and the males outnumbered the females 64 to 39. The patients' ages provided a very rough measure of the vaccination status of the general population before the epidemic. All but six of them were under forty. Dr. Duke's staff treated twenty-two children under ten years old, including seven younger than a year. All of the patients in the hospital, including the infants, survived. Even in an epidemic of mild smallpox, that was no small achievement.[71]

Given the strong contemporary belief that smallpox could be spread by contaminated objects, or fomites, a critical component of any state-of-the-art smallpox eradication effort was disinfection. Wertenbaker's Disinfecting Division, under Acting Assistant Surgeon Ira W. Porter and his crew, traveled the city equipped with two large autoclaves for sterilizing objects, another disinfecting apparatus for burning sulfur, and a third for hosing rooms down with bichloride. In all, the division disinfected nearly one hundred houses. All clothing and bedding was destroyed. Houses too ramshackle to be disinfected were burned.[72]

From the date the Service took over, only seven new cases developed in Middlesboro. Each day the Smallpox Hospital released more recovered patients. First they underwent a regimen of baths, while hospital staff washed their clothes in bichloride of mercury. The last smallpox case surfaced on April 6. Wertenbaker had returned to Wilmington the previous day, leaving the cleanup operation in Middlesboro in the hands of a Service officer named Hill Hastings. By April 14, only two cases of smallpox remained in Middlesboro. Hastings had them transferred to the Bell County pesthouse. (It was the very least Bell County could do.) On April 15, on Surgeon General Wyman's orders, Hastings and his men broke up the Marine-Hospital Service's camp at Middlesboro. Five months after it began, the Middlesboro epidemic finally came to an end.[73]

For J. N. and A. T. McCormack of the Kentucky Board of Health, the Middlesboro epidemic had been a disaster—a disaster that threatened to overtake the entire state, one ill-governed community at a time. Political fecklessness and pound-foolishness had allowed Kentucky's first encounter with mild type smallpox to spiral out of control. On March 25, Secretary

McCormack issued a state bulletin, warning that the Middlesboro epidemic would be repeated everywhere if local authorities did not take its two main lessons to heart.

The first lesson was legal: under Kentucky laws, the expense of smallpox control had to be quickly met by the affected counties and cities. The price of inaction in Middlesboro amounted to thousands of dollars in government funds, "very many thousands in loss of business," and the sheer "mortification of clamoring for outside aid." In the future, McCormack said, the state board would not hesitate to order a quarantine against cities and counties that failed to do their duties.[74]

The second lesson was racial: Kentucky communities could no longer ignore the spread of smallpox among African Americans. "The exemption of the white race" from the new smallpox was coming to an end. In a chilling statement, McCormack advised that "visiting and strange negroes be hunted, vaccinated, and kept under observation." As the Kentucky epidemic spread, McCormack redoubled his efforts to control the movement of African Americans. At the October 1898 meeting of the board, he warned that the unrestricted travel of unvaccinated colored persons constituted "a menace to the health and lives of the people of this state." The secretary proposed a resolution, which the board swiftly adopted. The new regulation made it unlawful for any person exposed to smallpox—and any African American, *period*—"to leave Cincinnati, Louisville, Memphis, Evansville, or any other point or place where small-pox now or may hereafter prevail," for any point in Kentucky by train, steamboat, or other conveyance without a certificate of vaccination issued by a public health officer. A vaccination certificate had become a kind of internal passport, required of all blacks, as well as those whites who had actually been exposed to smallpox, for travel into, or within, the state of Kentucky. The most basic freedom of all— freedom to move—which African Americans had exercised in extraordinary numbers in the late nineteenth-century South, redefining the national map in the process, was now made dependent upon their vaccination status.[75]

In the aftermath of the local outbreak that launched a four-year-long epidemic in the state of Kentucky, costing county and municipal governments more than $300,000, the officials of Middlesboro and Bell County seemed no more inclined than before to assume the legal obligations that came with local autonomy. Dr. Samuel Blair of the Bell County Board of Health sued the county to recover payment for his services at Middlesboro. A local jury ruled in his favor, and he received a judgment of $250. But Bell County appealed. The county suggested that because two members of its own board of health (Drs. Robertson and Curd) were taxpayers in Middlesboro, they had "fraudulently acted with the intention to charge the county and relieve the city from the burden." An appellate court ruled in favor of the county, declaring that a city of Middlesboro's size was not only empowered to fight contagious disease but also liable for the costs.[76]

Remarkably, in all of the paper left behind during this five-month episode, there is not a single word of any effort by local officials to seek relief from the men of capital who had created Middlesboro and still owned its coal and its future. An ocean away, the American Association, Inc., did not lift a hand to aid the citizens of Middlesboro during their hour of need. Some Middlesboro citizens, though, seemed able to find a joke in everything. When reports reached the mountain city that a smallpox epidemic of more than five hundred cases had struck Middlesborough, England, one local newspaper asked if the disease had been carried there by "a negro from Kentucky."[77]

Back in Washington, Surgeon General Wyman saw the events in Middlesboro as a cautionary tale. The epidemic had cost the federal government a great deal of effort and $3,500 in cash. In his 1898 annual report, Wyman issued a terse statement titled "Principles Governing the Extension of Aid to Local Authorities in the Matter of Smallpox." The surgeon general railed against the shortsightedness of local and state officials who, he believed, had allowed smallpox to rage out of control in Kentucky and elsewhere in the southern states. The spread of smallpox, Wyman thundered, "is so easily prevented under proper management that it is a disgrace to the sanitary authorities of any State, municipality, or locality whenever this disease is permitted to get beyond their control."[78]

Henceforward, Wyman declared, the role of the Marine-Hospital Service in local smallpox control would be strictly limited, in keeping with the constitutional principles of American federalism. Local governments were the first line of defense against epidemic disease, supported, when things got out of control, by state institutions. The Marine-Hospital Service's surgeons in the field, Wyman explained, would not lightly assume responsibilities that were so clearly local. They would merely furnish "expert assistance" to local and state authorities, settling differences of opinion about whether a particular infectious disease was smallpox. The surgeons would also offer "advice" regarding smallpox suppression. But the Service would take full control of an epidemic only when doing so was "necessary to prevent the spread from one State to another." Monetary aid would be withheld "except under the most urgent circumstances."[79]

Stern language. Given the nature of the southern outbreaks, however, the surgeon general surely understood that his "Principles" enabled the exercise of federal power as much as they restrained it. The spread of "mild type" smallpox placed an elite corps of federal officers—the medical men of the U.S. Marine-Hospital Service—in the almost unheard-of position of exercising police power in local communities. For the right to name a local outbreak of "Elephant itch" or "Cuban itch" a bona fide epidemic of smallpox was the very act that set the machinery of disease control in motion. Once that happened, the federal "advisor" who diagnosed the disease was well placed to take charge of operations on the ground. And when did smallpox ever respect national borders or state lines? As smallpox made its way across the southern states at the end of the nineteenth century, with little regard for political boundaries or man-made laws, the hundreds of urgent requests from local communities for federal assistance would put the old constitutional principles to the test. All of which is how C. P. Wertenbaker and the medical men of the U.S. Marine-Hospital Service became the vanguard of federal power in the American South.

THREE

WHEREVER
WERTENBAKER WENT

Though he never went to war, C. P. Wertenbaker lived his entire life in uniform. As a boy, he donned the outsized epaulets and tasseled shako cap of the Warrenton Rifles, a company of the Virginia Volunteers that was legendary in Charlie Wertenbaker's world for its stand at Fairfax Court House on June 1, 1861. (The Rifles' commander, Captain John Q. Marr, lost his life that day, the first Confederate officer to fall in the Civil War.) While a medical student at the University of Virginia, and during his half-dozen years as a practicing physician, Wertenbaker turned out for militia duty in the resplendent garb and sergeant's insignia of the Volunteers' Third Infantry. At twenty-eight, he put on yet another uniform, the one he would wear with honor for the rest of his career. The simple navy-blue field suit of a commissioned officer in the U.S. Marine-Hospital Service, meant to suggest military-issue without quite being military-issue, consisted of dress pants and a fly-front coat, the only adornments a pair of gold Service insignia—a fouled anchor and caduceus—on the coat's upright collar. For ceremonial occasions, he sported the Service's full dress uniform, a double-breasted suit with two rows of big brass buttons, golden epaulets, white gloves, and, at his side, a sword etched with the Great Seal of the United States of America. It was this national uniform, rather than the state regalia of his younger self, in which Wertenbaker would one day choose to be buried.[1]

But the most memorable outfit Wertenbaker ever wore, and the one most truly his own, was the one he contrived for his southern "smallpox work" in the late 1890s. Before he stepped, uninvited and unannounced, across the threshold of a sharecropper's cabin or a mill worker's wood-framed house, he pulled on a pair of crisp, sterile overalls and a coat that reeked of formalin disinfectant. He wound cloth around the top of his head, looking like a soldier with a head wound. And over his mouth and nose he tied a respirator that he fashioned from a yard of cheesecloth and a piece of thick cotton. It was not until Wertenbaker completed his inspection—after he had posed his last question, examined the last squirming child, and scraped his lancet against the very last arm—that the subjects of his attentions finally got a good look at him. Their eyes followed the U.S. government man as he stepped outside, doffed his cap and respirator, and set them aflame.[2]

The road that carried C. P. Wertenbaker from his privileged childhood on Virginia's upper Piedmont Plateau to the humblest homes of laborers in the Deep South ran through Richmond, New York, Norfolk, Galveston, Chicago, Washington, and a great many points in between. The Marine-Hospital Service surgeon had at least one thing in common with the railroad workers, rivermen, agricultural laborers, miners, drummers, minstrel performers, and machine tenders who ferried smallpox across the South in their bodies and on their clothes: he never stayed put for long. For many laborers in the end-of-the-century South, the ability to pick up and go was the only form of mobility their lives offered. To aging former slaves and their children, freedom of movement was a cherished right, one exercised, sometimes, for the sake of exercising it, to demonstrate to an exploitative boss or landlord that their bodies and labor could not, in fact, be owned. For the Service surgeon, member of an elite cadre of some two hundred mobile federal medical men, transience was part of the job description.[3]

And, as Wertenbaker would learn, it was more than that. The surgeons' readiness to move, the very portability of their federal medical expertise, made them a force for the integration and bureaucratic standardization of public health in the United States. Wertenbaker and his colleagues were the vanguard of a modern, national public health system. That such a system

*C. P. Wertenbaker as a young
surgeon with the U.S. Marine-
Hospital Service in 1888.*
COURTESY OF THE ALBERT
AND SHIRLEY SMALL SPECIAL
COLLECTIONS LIBRARY AT THE
UNIVERSITY OF VIRGINIA

would not reach fruition in their lifetimes does not diminish the significance of their work.

A half century before the establishment of the federal Communicable Disease Center (now the Centers for Disease Control and Prevention) in Atlanta in 1946, public health was still an explicitly coercive form of social regulation, or "police power." As one early twentieth-century authority observed, "The famous Roosevelt doctrine to 'speak softly, but carry a big stick' is particularly applicable to public health work." For the most part, local and state governments still wielded that authority, or neglected to, with little interference from Washington. But the mobility of the Service surgeons—premised upon the fact that smallpox and other infectious diseases did not respect borders—enabled the U.S. government to deploy scientific expertise and project an extraordinary measure of national authority across a vast region, a far-flung nation, and into new colonial possessions in the Caribbean and the Pacific. For a growing number of people across America and many other parts of the world, a medical man in a navy suit was the first representative of the U.S. government they ever encountered. In 1891, Congress had assigned the Service a new role as sentinels at the nation's borders and overseas ports, to ensure that immigrants did not carry foreign diseases onto American soil. Though virtually forgotten today, the intervention of Service officers like Wertenbaker at the scenes of local outbreaks—often deep in the American interior—may have been just as important as border control to the long process by which the U.S. government learned to govern its territory and people like a modern nation-state.[4]

The smallpox years of 1898 to 1900 were the busiest in the history of the Marine-Hospital Service to date, and those years were also the most mobile of Wertenbaker's career. The surgeon's sorties to smallpox-stricken locales across the American South afforded him an exceptionally broad regional perspective on the tangle of factors—the institutional constraints and conflicts, the clash of interests and beliefs, and the unpredictable behavior of a once-familiar disease and the individuals affected by it—that made smallpox control such an intractable political problem in southern communities. Middlesboro, Wertenbaker learned, had been just the beginning, an extreme example of the social dissension and political failure he would find everywhere. His experiences in the field would turn him into something of an extreme case himself, a strong advocate for greater national control in this traditionally local realm of law and governance, public health.[5]

Like most Americans born before the Civil War, Charles Poindexter Wertenbaker's first loyalties were to family, community, state, and God. Born in Charlottesville, Virginia, on April 1, 1860, Wertenbaker descended from a long line of soldiers, scholars, and scribes, whose generations of service to the Old Dominion he traced back to a distant ancestor, a colonel who sat on the Bacon's Rebellion court-martial in 1676. A great-great-grandfather on his mother's side had received one hundred acres of Virginia soil for his service in the Revolutionary War, a fact Wertenbaker used to establish his right to membership in the Sons of the American Revolution. His grandfather, William Wertenbaker, fought while still in his teens in the War of 1812 and was appointed by Thomas Jefferson in 1825 to be the first librarian of the University of Virginia, a position he held for more than half a century. In his application to the Sons of the American Revolution, C. P. Wertenbaker failed to mention that his father, a cigar manufacturer named C. C. (Charles Christian) Wertenbaker, had spent his prime in a very different war. He fought with General Robert E. Lee's Army of Northern Virginia during the bloody 1862 invasion of Maryland and was wounded himself two years later. C. C. Wertenbaker stood with his regiment when it surrendered, with the rest of General Lee's forces, at Appomattox Court House on April 9, 1865, eight days after Charlie's fifth birthday.[6]

Charlie Wertenbaker grew up in relative privilege, in a household with three or four servants, white and black. But illness and death were as familiar to his childhood landscape as the green lawns and white columns of Mr. Jefferson's university. Charlie was the eldest of the eleven children born to C. C. and Mary Ella Wertenbaker. Seven of his siblings died in infancy or childhood; his mother died before he turned thirteen. Such family tragedies were common in nineteenth-century domestic life, with influenza, tuberculosis, and other infectious diseases causing most of the misery. But the relentless rhythm of loss in the Wertenbaker home would have been unusual even in the tenement districts of the disease-ridden northern cities. The mortality in the Wertenbaker family exceeded that found among nineteenth-century American slave children, more than half of whom died before reaching the age of five.[7]

This legacy of loss may partly explain why, when Charlie Wertenbaker came of age, he not only signed on with the Virginia Volunteers, in the family tradition, but enrolled in the medical department at the University of Virginia. At the time, a career in medicine promised neither high status nor great wealth. Still, it was a respectable calling, and by the 1870s educated people were beginning to think of medicine as a powerful science, capable of preventing the spread of infectious diseases, not just treating the symptoms that ravaged the human body. Wertenbaker earned his doctor of medicine degree in 1882. After graduation, he moved to the rebuilt capital city of Richmond, where he worked as an intern at the Retreat for the Sick under the eminent surgeon Hunter McGuire, erstwhile medical director of General Thomas J. (Stonewall) Jackson's Second Corps (and future president of the American Medical Association). From 1884 to 1888, Wertenbaker moved north to work in hospitals in and around New York City. He entered the U.S. Marine-Hospital Service, as an assistant surgeon, in August 1888.[8]

The federal bureau, with its Washington headquarters and its uniforms of blue, must have seemed to some of his militia buddies a curious career choice for the eldest son of a proud old Confederate. But given the straitened southern economy after the Civil War, many young university-trained physicians from the region competed for positions in the federal government, particularly in the medical services of the Army and Navy and in the Marine-Hospital Service. Southern men would predominate at the Service's entrance exams until the 1930s. Wertenbaker's alma mater was known in the corps as "The University."[9]

From its humble origins in 1798 as a federal fund to support sick and disabled seamen, the Marine-Hospital Service had grown after 1870 into an increasingly centralized and professional federal bureaucracy. Overseen by the secretary of the treasury, the Service modeled itself after the medical corps of the Army and Navy. It adopted a system of rigorous examinations, commissioned ranks (rising from assistant surgeon to passed assistant surgeon to surgeon), merit-based pay grades, and uniforms for the surgeons assigned to its many hospitals and relief stations at ports along the nation's coasts and major inland waterways.[10]

The presence of the national government in the South had receded after the collapse of Reconstruction and the removal of the last federal troops from the South Carolina statehouse in 1877. But in the control of epidemic disease, the political current flowed in the opposite direction. As Congress expanded the Service's scope of action, and the bureau's cadre of mobile medical officers moved into areas of governance hitherto dominated by the state and local authorities, the South proved the greatest recipient— sometimes solicited, sometimes not—of federal aid. The National Quarantine Act of 1878, enacted during the devastating yellow fever epidemic that killed twenty thousand people in the Mississippi and Ohio river valleys, empowered the Service's officers to enforce quarantine regulations in the region, a major expansion of federal authority in the realm of internal police power. The yellow fever work made the institution and its officers more familiar to Americans in the South than in any other region.[11]

The scale and scope of the Service's activities continued to grow after

Wertenbaker joined it, and not only in the South. In 1890, Congress gave the bureau permanent authority to administer interstate quarantine regulations. The following year Congress put the Service in charge of medical inspection of immigrants at the nation's major border crossings and ports, including Ellis Island. Among the many things the U.S. medical men demanded of arriving immigrants was proof of a recent successful vaccination against smallpox—preferably in the form of a fresh vaccination wound on the upper arm. After war broke out with Spain in 1898, the Service followed the flag, administering quarantine at the coastal ports of Puerto Rico, Cuba, and the Philippines. By the time Congress renamed the institution in 1902, calling it the U.S. Public Health and Marine-Hospital Service, the bureau had already achieved that position in fact, with its hospitals, stations, state-of-the-art National Hygienic Laboratory, and traveling surgeons. In the eyes of Surgeon General Walter Wyman, who presided over this institutional growth, the United States finally had "a sanitary structure worthy of this nation."[12]

The manly martial and scientific culture of the Service offered Wertenbaker a way of living in the world that he must have found both familiar and exotic. Wyman, a St. Louis native who bore a passing resemblance to Theodore Roosevelt, recognized that enforcing maritime quarantines and traveling to epidemic zones was lonely and dangerous work. And though the surgeon general could be an overzealous enforcer of bureaucratic edicts, he cultivated camaraderie in the ranks. This esprit de corps rested upon a soldierly discipline and the faith that, as one officer put it, "scientific investigation at the bench and in the field would yield eventually the knowledge to deal with the diseases of man."[13]

Wertenbaker's Service career, from 1888 to 1916, coincided with the meteoric rise of scientific medicine. Professionals in medicine, the biological sciences, and public health were dramatically reducing Americans' rates of mortality and morbidity from infectious diseases. Wyman encouraged his surgeons to think of themselves as men of science working at the front lines of this historic campaign. He dispatched them to medical conferences. He published their field reports in the Service's journal. And when his surgeons fell in the line of duty, he honored them in words redolent of the values of the institution they had served. Yellow fever killed Assistant

Surgeon John William Branham, a young husband and father, in Brunswick, Georgia, in 1893. The surgeon general praised him for his "education and medical attainments, . . . manliness of deportment and gentlemanly bearing."[14]

As Wertenbaker rose in the Service and built a small family of his own, he kept that eulogy in his personal files, not far from his two life insurance policies. He must have wondered if he, too, would one day be remembered as an honored citizen-soldier in Walter Wyman's war against disease.[15]

C. P. Wertenbaker could not have foreseen that he would spend several years of his life fighting smallpox. Until 1898, the Service's work consisted chiefly of running its 22 hospitals and 107 relief stations for American seamen on the coasts and interior ports, manning immigrant inspection stations, and administering maritime quarantines when yellow fever threatened. Suppressing a smallpox epidemic was a different proposition from inspecting vessels and passengers at port. Fighting smallpox involved close control of entire local populations, on their own turf. To do the job right meant compelling men, women, and children to undergo an unpleasant and unpopular medical procedure, vaccination. With the exception of the major entry points for immigrants into the American nation, such intervention was still viewed as a matter of police power, like punishing criminals and regulating noxious trades.

According to the conventional understanding of the Constitution's Tenth Amendment, police power—the right to interfere with individual liberty and property rights in order to serve the public welfare—was reserved chiefly to the states. During the constitutional firestorm of Reconstruction, the U.S. Supreme Court had breathed new life into that old understanding, almost as if the Civil War and the Fourteenth Amendment had left the federal system unaltered. The immediate losers in the Court's jurisprudence were African Americans, whose civil rights Congress proved increasingly powerless (and unwilling) to protect. But the decisions reverberated in other areas as well. In the *Slaughter-House Cases* (1873), the Court's majority reinvigorated the long-standing constitutional position that gave the state and local governments primary and, as far as the federal courts were concerned, well-nigh unlimited authority to restrain liberty and property in the name of the public health.[16]

In practice, the boundaries of local, state, and federal power frequently blurred. From time to time Wertenbaker did encounter smallpox in his work for the Service. On assignment in Chicago, he served as the federal sanitary inspector at the World's Columbian Exposition of 1893. With Asiatic cholera spreading across Europe and visitors and performers arriving in Chicago from all corners of the globe, American officials braced themselves for an outbreak at the Exposition. Instead, smallpox struck the White City that summer and spread across the real-life Second City during the fall and winter, taking hold in the West Side tenement sweatshops and killing more than a thousand people. Wertenbaker assisted overwhelmed city health officials by searching for concealed cases on the hundreds of boats that had taken up winter quarters along the icy Chicago River. He surely heard about, if he did not witness for himself, the small riots that broke out as city vaccinators worked their way through the tenements. State Factory Inspector Florence Kelley, a Hull House social settlement veteran who knew the West Side well, would never forget "the feeling against vaccination in the tenements." One young surgeon on the vaccination squad had been "disabled for life" when an agitated tailor shattered his elbow with a bullet.[17]

If Wertenbaker ever doubted the effectiveness of vaccination, as some physicians did, his work in Chicago and elsewhere gave him reason to believe. Vaccination as practiced in much of the United States during the 1890s was an unpleasant and risky medical procedure. Even under the best of circumstances newly vaccinated people often felt ill and achy for days. But in the vast majority of people, vaccination worked. As chief of the Service's Delaware Breakwater Station in August 1896, Wertenbaker inspected the steamship *Earnwell*, just in from Colón, Panama. Three men on board had broken out with pox. Two of them had undergone vaccination before their voyage; they experienced mild attacks. The first mate had evidently escaped vaccination, and he suffered terribly from a severe confluent case. Wertenbaker could do little more than watch the seaman die from a preventable disease.[18]

In January 1898, Wertenbaker took command of the Marine-Hospital Service station at Wilmington, North Carolina, his first southern assignment in seven years. A bustling port located thirty miles up the Cape Fear River from the Atlantic Ocean, Wilmington was the state's largest city. Roughly half of the city's 21,000 inhabitants were African American. Most black residents worked in manual and domestic labor, but Wilmington had a sizable African American middle class of skilled tradesmen, physicians, lawyers, and—ever since a fusion campaign of Republicans and Populists won control of the government in 1894—several municipal officials. Wertenbaker arrived in the city at a moment of rising political tension. In the course of 1898, white Democrats would become increasingly well organized and violent in their determination to seize control of the government and bring an end to "Negro domination."[19]

As a white southern Democrat himself, Wertenbaker must have had an opinion about these developments, but he did not express it in writing. The Virginian took Jim Crow for granted. He chose to continue the station's practice of maintaining separate "white" and "colored" hospital wards. Apart from a white steward, the entire staff was black. Wertenbaker introduced a new level of discipline at the station, including weekly inspections, for which the surgeon turned out in his full dress uniform, sword and all. Wertenbaker moved into the station officer's residence, on the first floor of the two-story main hospital building, with his wife, Alice Girardeau Wertenbaker, who descended from a prominent South Carolina family, and their infant daughter, Alicia. Alice would make a respectable household for the young family, and she and little Alicia toured the coastal area in the Service's "station wagon," a horse-drawn affair operated by a black driver in livery. Charles Wertenbaker himself never had a chance to settle in.[20]

During Wertenbaker's two and a half years at Wilmington, his telegraphic orders from Surgeon General Wyman sent him, over rail lines and dirt roads, to disease-stricken locales in Virginia, North Carolina, South Carolina, Georgia, Alabama, Kentucky, and Tennessee. Wertenbaker called this phase of his long career in the Service "my smallpox work." And if, at times, that work seemed as cursed as smallpox itself, he could take some satisfaction in the fact that no one did it better.

He established himself as the Service's foremost smallpox expert in the field, known to governors, mayors, and state and local health officials as a master diagnostician of the new "mild type" of smallpox, and a man with a proven strategy for stamping out the disease. Such was Wertenbaker's stature in the field that he received temporary appointments to the staffs of the governors of Virginia, Georgia, and Nebraska. In 1899, Wertenbaker sent Wyman a long memo entitled "Plan of Organization for the Suppression of Smallpox." The surgeon general published it as a supplement to the Service's "Précis upon the Diagnosis and Treatment of Smallpox." If the "Précis" presented the latest scientific knowledge of the disease, the "Plan" offered a comprehensive strategy—part medical intervention, part military operation—for suppressing local outbreaks. The highest demand for both pamphlets came from the southern states, and though the tactics Wertenbaker outlined should have worked just as well anywhere, they were distinctly the product of his own experience fighting smallpox in southern cities, towns, plantations, and work camps.[21]

Wertenbaker had been on the job at Wilmington for only a few days when North Carolina's first reported case of mild type smallpox arrived in the city. On January 12, 1898, a local physician informed Mayor S. P. Wright that Stephen Johnson, an African American brakeman who worked the Atlantic Coast Line between Wilmington and Florence, South Carolina, had contracted smallpox. City health officials hung a yellow quarantine placard outside the Johnson home on Hanover Street and quarantined three neighboring houses, vaccinating all the residents. Mayor Wright posted two policemen on the block to prevent residents from leaving. Wertenbaker had no jurisdiction in the matter. But he offered his assistance to the local government, ordered a hundred points of vaccine, and told Wyman he would vaccinate "all persons applying." During the next three weeks, Wertenbaker watched Wilmington turn into a battleground over public health.[22]

On the first day of the outbreak, Wertenbaker accompanied Dr. William D. McMillan, the city superintendent of health, as he searched for a suitable site to establish a pesthouse. McMillan planned to remove Johnson from his thickly settled neighborhood as soon as possible. The doctors chose a three-room house on Meares Street, amid the sandy lots in the far southeastern section of the city. The place seemed ideal. It occupied a block by itself, the nearest house being three hundred yards away, and the caretaker said his tenant would be happy to move out so he could rent it to the city. But the area was not as deserted as it looked. Unlike Johnson's neighborhood, inhabited almost exclusively by African Americans, the blocks around the Meares Street house were overwhelmingly white. When the *Wilmington Messenger* announced the opening of the pesthouse, twenty or thirty armed white men assembled at the property, warning that they "meant business" if an ambulance wagon showed up carrying Stephen Johnson. Under pressure from his neighbors, the tenant decided to stay put.[23]

Dr. McMillan reset his sights on the northeastern corner of the city. He found a house on Nixon Street, located between the railroad tracks and one of Wilmington's largest African American sections. The house had recently served as a barracks for a gang of convict laborers employed grading a link line for the Wilmington and New Bern Railroad. As soon as African American neighbors got wind of McMillan's plan, they did just what the white residents of Meares Street had done. They formed a mob. But theirs was larger. Three hundred men, women, and children turned out at the property when Mayor Wright and Dr. McMillan paid it a visit. The crowd threatened to burn the house if the authorities brought Johnson there. That evening, Nixon Street teemed with men carrying pistols, shotguns, and, as one policeman commented, "some old time war muskets with muzzles big enough for rats to run into." According to one witness, the many women in the crowd were even "more vehement" than the men. White men joined the crowd and "took a hand in the defiance." Men and women blocked every avenue to the house; a hundred men stood guard along the railroad tracks to prevent the authorities from delivering Johnson by that route. No ambulance or train carrying Johnson materialized that night. But the crowd burned the house to the ground anyway. A smaller two-room house stood on the same property. The next day, a rumor spread that officials planned to move Johnson there. That evening a crowd set the second house on fire.[24]

The authorities decided to let Stephen Johnson recover or die in his own home. (He survived.) A few days later Wilmington officials discovered a second man with smallpox, an African American stevedore named James Harge. Determined to remove him from his home, they settled on a remote site three miles from the city.[25]

The Wilmington board of aldermen did not rush to order vaccination in the city. They debated the question for nearly two weeks. Several aldermen, including A. J. Walker, one of the body's African American members, opposed the idea. Finally, on January 24, the board adopted an order requiring all residents to show proof of recent vaccination. Violators were subject to a $5 fine or ten days in jail. (Mayor Wright had called for stiffer penalties.) The mayor appointed five city vaccinators, including two African American physicians who were assigned to the black neighborhoods.[26]

On January 27, some five hundred citizens of Wilmington, including about fifty African American men, assembled at city hall to protest the vaccination ordinance. They carried a protest document that had been drawn up earlier that day outside of J. T. Smith's store on Front and Castle streets. The men took their stand as breadwinners, acting, as their petition announced, "[o]n behalf of ourselves, our wives and our children, and the thousands of our citizens and their families, who provide their livelihood by manual labor." Two cases of smallpox did not justify a measure that threatened the arms and livelihoods of Wilmington's wage earners. "[C]ompulsory vaccination will inflict an unnecessary hardship," the petition said, "especially upon the poor who have to labor for their living." The petitioners vowed to "resist to the uttermost with all our influence and manhood the enforcement of this iniquitous law." The group's leaders included an African American doctor named Bill Moore, who claimed that the document represented "the sentiment of two-thirds of the people of Wilmington." According to the *Wilmington Messenger*, the physician's statement was "greeted with applause by white and black." In an impressive display of biracial local democracy, the committee appointed a jury-sized delegation of six white men and six black men. Together they presented the petition to the mayor and board of aldermen.[27]

The aldermen did not rescind the ordinance. They did not have to. The city vaccinators met with such widespread resistance in Wilmington's neighborhoods and workplaces that the board of health suspended the entire campaign just a few days after it had begun. All of the vaccinators had found the work dispiriting. The city's strategy of sending black doctors into African American neighborhoods had not overcome the residents' concerns about vaccination. One African American woman drove a black physician from her doorstep with an axe. An African American man brandished a gun to defend his threshold from a city vaccinator and two policemen, all of them black. White vaccinators hadn't fared much better in white working-class neighborhoods. As the city hall protest had shown, compulsory vaccination was perceived as dangerous and unjust by many people, regardless of race.[28]

By the time the city vaccinators ceased their unfinished work, Johnson and Harge had begun to recover. No further smallpox cases had come to light.

The Wilmington smallpox skirmishes of 1898 would be overshadowed in the city's memory by the bloody race riots that came just ten months later during the November elections. The riots left more than ten blacks dead in the streets of Wilmington, caused thousands to leave the city, and put Democrats in control of the city government. Soon after that tragic episode, the North Carolina Board of Health issued its annual report. Citing the Wilmington smallpox outbreak as a cautionary tale, the board lamented that the city government's efforts to stamp out the disease had been "so violently resisted by the negroes as to cause the abandonment of the attempt." Absent from the report was any mention of the white and black pesthouse mobs, or the biracial coalition of Wilmington men, some five hundred strong, who had together taken a stand at city hall as workingmen and breadwinners opposed to compulsory vaccination.[29]

For C. P. Wertenbaker, the pesthouse fires and antivaccination protests marked the beginning of an education in the contentious politics of southern smallpox control. Wherever Wertenbaker went, he saw smallpox engender intense conflict between "the public health" as a political ideal and "the public" as a fractious social reality. The public health implied a unity of purpose and interests—within the medical profession, between physicians and the state, and between state and society—that Wertenbaker rarely encountered. Instead, he found governments that wouldn't govern and citizens who wouldn't let them when they tried.

He witnessed this conflict in Wilmington in January 1898. He saw it that February in Charlotte, where white cotton mill workers, fearing vaccine poisoning, refused to comply with the city government's vaccination order. He saw it again in March in Middlesboro, Kentucky, where local officials rebelled against their own legal duties as keepers of the public health. When Wertenbaker returned to Wilmington in April, Wyman forwarded to him a letter that J. W. Babcock of the Columbia, South Carolina, Board of Health had sent to Senator Benjamin R. ("Pitchfork Ben") Tillman. As smallpox raged in the capital city, the board had ordered a general vaccination. "My private opinion," Babcock told the senator, "is that we shall not get much cooperation from the white people, and none at all from the negroes." Babcock asked Tillman to secure "the services of a competent officer of the Marine-Hospital Service, who would come here to advise and act with the Board in stamping out the disease." Dispatched to Columbia, Wertenbaker reported that he found "much the same condition of affairs" as he had "in so many other places." There was so much difference of opinion about the disease among doctors and so much concern about vaccination among the working people that health officials had "great difficulty in inducing the people to take necessary precautions."[30]

Wertenbaker's experiences in the field would make him into an advocate for reform in the field of public health administration. He pushed for better, safer vaccines. He promoted official candor and public education as the best remedies for the pervasive "prejudice" against vaccination. And though Wertenbaker never discarded the racial beliefs of his time and place, he would, in an era of overwhelming white indifference to African American health, call for the government to mobilize rural blacks to organize their own fight against infectious disease. Ultimately, Wertenbaker's smallpox sorties led him to conclude that there was only one way to stamp out infectious disease in the South—by increasing the scale and scope of federal police power.[31]

If late nineteenth-century American jurists were certain about anything it was this: the states could take any action necessary to protect their citizens from the "present danger" of a deadly infectious disease. Since the dawn of the republic, state and local governments had wielded powers both plenary and plentiful to defend the people from outbreaks of smallpox, yellow fever, cholera, and other pestilences. Individual liberty and property rights melted away before the state's power—indeed its inherent legal duty—to defend the population from peril. Under the broad authority of the police power, state and local governments confined suspected disease carriers against their will, established armed quarantines on land and at sea, seized private homes for smallpox pesthouses, removed infected persons by force from their homes, and enacted, in the approving words of the U.S. Supreme Court, "health laws of every description." Considering the case of a merchant from Burlington, North Carolina, who had refused to submit to his town's vaccination during the epidemic winter of 1899, Justice Walter McKenzie Clark of the state supreme court drew a ready analogy between public health and the sovereign's power of self-defense. "[I]t is every day common sense," he said, "that if a people can draft or conscript its citizens to defend its borders from invasion, it can protect itself from the deadly pestilence that walketh by noonday, by such measures as medical science has found most efficacious for that purpose." Like war, it seemed, epidemic disease was the health of the state.[32]

But in the cities, towns, and rural hamlets that C. P. Wertenbaker visited across the South, convalescent people with infectious smallpox scabs on their faces and limbs moved freely about the streets, ran country stores, and went to work in the fields and mills. Meanwhile, local physicians engaged each other in front porch debates about the nature and provenance of this mysterious eruptive disease. When alarmed public health officials called for strong measures, local government agents often hesitated to act, not wanting to interfere with business or upset the electorate. When officials finally did act, as Wertenbaker wrote in a report to Surgeon General Wyman, time and again the people "revolted."[33]

Health officials met with resistance to every form of action they took. African Americans were said to be particularly quick to hide sick relatives and friends from health inspectors and the police, but whites did it, too. Shotgun quarantines on the public roads proved to be a weak defense against rural folk who knew their way through the woods. "We had just as well undertake to quarantine against red foxes and jack rabbits," said one Kentucky health official. Pesthouses that had been hastily built were just as swiftly torched or torn asunder by crowds of people, white and black, who refused to let their neighborhoods be turned into smallpox dumping grounds. "We were totally unprepared to take care of a contagious disease," recalled Dr. J. M. Manning, superintendent of health of Durham, North Carolina. Dr. Manning rode with the mayor across Durham, looking for a suitable place to pitch an isolation tent, but they were "met with shot-guns" wherever they stopped. Where officials did manage to establish pesthouses, they had to find a way to keep people in them. Even with armed guards and gasoline torches, most pesthouses and detention camps could not hold people who had the will and energy (as patients with mild smallpox often did) to escape. Local newspapers that a generation earlier had published notices of runaway slaves now ran stories about African American pesthouse fugitives who had broken loose from their confinement and fled into the night.[34]

No public health measure inspired more ill will than compulsory vaccination. Some of the opposition came from the top of the political order—from state lawmakers, who almost everywhere maintained that if compulsory vaccination were to exist at all it must be by local mandate. Even in the midst of the regional epidemic, efforts to enact uniform statewide vaccination legislation failed in several states, including Alabama (despite strong support from the medical profession), Florida (where rural representatives killed a bill favored by their urban colleagues), and North Carolina (where a bill drafted by the state board of health was "treated with absolute contempt"). Even in those few states that did enact new vaccination laws—such as Mississippi, a yellow fever state with an exceptionally well-funded board of health—lawmakers merely authorized local governments to compel vaccination and impose penalties. Compulsory vaccination of public schoolchildren could be attempted under state legislation or local authority, but in a region with almost no compulsory school attendance laws, such measures had limited reach. As Secretary Richard H. Lewis of the North Carolina Board of Health commented, "One practical difficulty on educational lines now is to get the children to go to school at all."[35]

In the absence of state statutes, during smallpox epidemics local governments often ordered vaccination under their own general police powers, performing their legal duty to protect their populations from immediate danger. The orders usually resembled the one issued by the Wilmington aldermen: they required everyone in the community to show proof of a recent successful vaccination. The penalties ranged dramatically—with fines from \$5 to \$100, jail terms from ten to forty days. Some judges ordered violators to work on the public roads. In one North Carolina town, a man who refused to be vaccinated and threatened to spread smallpox among his "political enemies" had "three buggy whips worn out on him." By contrast, some state and local measures created exemptions for specific classes of people. The city of Nashville made exceptions for people aged seventy or over, for women more than five months pregnant, and for individuals who, "in the opinion of the vaccinating physicians, are too ill to submit to the procedure." Wertenbaker took a dim view of such exemptions. Only two classes of people should be allowed to neglect this duty, he wrote in his "Plan": those who have had smallpox already and "those who are dead."[36]

Local or not, compulsory vaccination orders engendered strife. Much the same drama played out across the South, from High Point, North Carolina—where Wertenbaker arrived to find that the furniture factory employees had "closed their houses, and gone into the country to avoid being vaccinated"—to Sherman Heights, Tennessee, where a crowd of citizens drove off county vaccinators with stones, curtain poles, and guns. Some people loudly protested the measures as violations of their personal liberty. Others tried to shrug off the health officers' authority. The health officer of Russell County, Alabama, complained bitterly to a Service surgeon that when he tried to enforce vaccination without the aid of police "the negroes laughed at him."[37]

In carrying out a policy that frequently targeted blacks, officials did not hesitate to use physical force. The sort of actions that Wertenbaker had heard about in Middlesboro (where African Americans were handcuffed and vaccinated at gunpoint) were echoed in official actions elsewhere. The phrase "equal protection of the laws" had little meaning in southern public health. Authorities in smallpox-ridden Thomson, Georgia, made sure that "all the colored population that could be caught were vaccinated" before they pressed the issue with whites. When they met "bitter opposition on the part of the white element," the authorities decided to ask for an "outside opinion" before "forcing the matter." They appealed for the aid of a Service surgeon. Racist pride was probably enough to stop white Thomson officials from asking Uncle Sam to help them handle "their" colored people.[38]

Beleaguered southern health officials had a concise explanation for popular resistance to their authority: the people were "ignorant." After the rebellious citizens of Laurel County, Kentucky, caused the local health board to withdraw its vaccination order, one officer sent a plea to Secretary J. N. McCormack: "you alone know how much unjust, unreasonable and criminal censure these ignorant people are heaping upon us." Other health officials pointed out that the common people had no monopoly on ignorance. Physicians, judges, and county officials were clueless, too. When the opposition came from white farmers or mountain people, some officials inclined toward more charitable, if no less condescending, theories. "Our people are unaccustomed to the restraints and duties incident to the proper management of them according to the principles of modern hygiene," Secretary Lewis of the North Carolina board gently explained. Meanwhile, African Americans who pushed back against white health authority were disparaged as not just "ignorant" but "criminally careless."[39]

As the southern smallpox epidemic wore on, Wertenbaker and some of his state and local peers developed a set of deeper explanations for why both smallpox and popular antipathy to public health authority had gotten so out of hand. Knowledge remained the crucial piece in these explanatory schemes. But Wertenbaker and others realized that a community's understanding of disease depended on something more personal than a public health circular or a family doctor's advice. Medical beliefs rested upon shared experience and memory. On this score, smallpox posed a special problem.

Outside the urban centers and port cities such as Charleston and New Orleans, most communities had not seen smallpox in a generation. People old enough to remember the Civil War recalled the epidemics that had raged in both armies. C. C. Wertenbaker probably told his son about the pox that burned through the Army of Northern Virginia during the Maryland campaign. Union and Confederate soldiers wrote in their diaries and letters of the wonders and horrors of arm-to-arm vaccination: the common practice of inoculating men with pus taken from another soldier's vaccination sore or, worse, from an actual smallpox lesion. Some troops expressed gratitude for the protection their vaccinations afforded, while many more recounted stories of terrible fevers, poisoned arms, amputations, and death.

During the battle of Chancellorsville in May 1863, five thousand Confederate soldiers were deemed unfit for duty after being vaccinated with material taken from the arm of a soldier who, as luck would have it, had syphilis.[40]

The civilian population did not have it much better. "Colonel" A. W. Shaffer of North Carolina recalled the desperate measures taken by local communities when vaccine ran out. "Everything having the semblance of a scab or pus passed for vaccine; anything with two hands and a blade or point, for a vaccinator; and every filthy sore at the point of abrasion, for a successful vaccination." So shocking had been the side effects that Shaffer blamed them for the outpouring of antivaccination sentiment in his state some thirty-five years later. "No wonder that the memory of that harvest of vile diseases still burns in the hearts and perverts the brains of the fathers and mothers of this later generation!"[41]

If Shaffer was right, the horrors of wartime vaccination burned more brightly in the memories of the people than did smallpox itself. Many places had not seen a single case since the war's end. Like other rural Southerners, the people of Monroe County, Kentucky, had come to think of smallpox, in the words of a local physician, as "a disease confined to cities . . . a disease to be read about in the newspapers." North Carolinians could boast of the "blessed fact that epidemics of infectious disease of any magnitude have been extremely rare in our State." But the downside of this "wonderful immunity" was that in the Tar Heel State, as in more plague-prone areas of the South, a generation had come of age with no clear memory of how the symptoms of smallpox compared with those of the common childhood eruptive diseases such as chicken pox or measles. It did not seem to matter how much publicity heralded the spread of smallpox across the region. Each new outbreak seemed to catch the infected community by total surprise, like the unexpected return of some obnoxious but long-forgotten relation.[42]

Southern physicians suffered from the same memory deficit. "Many physicians have never seen a case of smallpox, and are unfamiliar with the methods necessary for its suppression," Wertenbaker wrote in May 1898 after visiting Columbia, South Carolina—which was, after all, a state capital, not a one-horse town. Old-timers in the profession remembered smallpox all too well: Dr. M. H. Young recalled treating hundreds of cases during his service as a surgeon in the Fourth Kentucky Volunteer Infantry during the war. But a generation of younger men had entered the field who had never laid a compress on a smallpox-rubbled face, never inhaled the sickening odor of an infected person's room, or, for that matter, never received much college instruction on the subject.[43]

Vaccination, meanwhile, had fallen by the wayside. The procedure, though simple, took time and care to perform correctly, and it normally garnered the physician a nominal fee. In the decades since the war, the once standard practice of arm-to-arm vaccination had been largely abandoned in favor of bovine vaccine, cowpox or vaccinia lymph harvested from cows and dried onto ivory points. The shift from so-called humanized virus to bovine points was hailed by most scientific authorities as a great innovation that reduced the transmission of human diseases, such as syphilis. But for a small-town physician, the changing technology imposed a new burden. If he chose to offer vaccination as part of his regular practice, he had to keep a stock of fresh vaccine on hand. In the absence of either much risk of smallpox, or much reward for performing the procedure, many physicians decided vaccination was not worth the bother. The practice had become, in the words of Secretary McCormack, "one of the 'lost arts' to the majority of country physicians." To laypeople, it became an exotic and dodgy procedure, best left alone.[44]

And so, when the disease returned in the late 1890s, Southerners in general—and African Americans and poor whites in particular—were caught almost uniformly unprotected. Service surgeon Joseph J. Kinyoun, a North Carolina native and the first director of the National Hygienic Laboratory, warned that "Small-pox is more of a menace to the Southern people than to the northern people," because in the South vaccination was "practiced but little, and only in places of large population." In North Carolina, scarcely 10 percent of the population had ever been vaccinated. In Georgia, a Service surgeon placed vaccination levels closer to 25 percent, but that was after smallpox had been back for a few years. At the outset of the Middlesboro epidemic in the winter of 1898, Kentucky officials estimated that "only" two thirds of the state's residents had ever undergone the procedure. But as local reports came in from across the state, the officials had to revise that figure. Two thirds of Kentuckians had *never* taken the vaccine. Among African Americans, vaccination status varied with age. Many of the older former slaves had been vaccinated; their masters' self-interest, if not their vaunted paternalism, had seen to that. But the overwhelming majority of younger blacks, raised in an era of almost total neglect from the white-dominated medical profession, had never been inoculated.[45]

In his travels, C. P. Wertenbaker learned that ignorance, like knowledge, was a product of history. Medical knowledge—in both its popular and professional forms—still depended upon firsthand experience with illness. As far as smallpox was concerned, the wellspring of experience had (blessedly) dried up in the decades after the Civil War.

Any epidemic of smallpox would have caught most southern communities off guard. But the epidemiological profile of these end-of-the-century epidemics made them particularly difficult to manage. Smallpox struck African Americans first. And the disease took an exceptionally mild form. These two facts shaped how the scientific claims and political demands of public health officials would be received by the South's many publics.

Addressing a white Mississippi audience in the early twentieth century, Booker T. Washington told his listeners, as he so often did, that "the destiny of the southern white race" was "largely dependent on the Negro." The eminent African American educator drew upon recent history to make his point. "You can't have smallpox in the Negro's home and nowhere else," he said. "You need to see that the cabin is clean or disease will invade the mansion. Disease draws no colour line."[46]

Several years earlier, C. P. Wertenbaker stood outside a grocery store in Richland, Georgia, a whistle-stop town of nine hundred souls not far from the Alabama border. As people came and went from the store, a crowd of children, white and black, loafed outside. One African American boy caught Wertenbaker's eye. Judging by the scabs on his face, Wertenbaker figured the boy to be in the convalescent stage of smallpox known in the medical literature as "desquamation." Smallpox experts considered desquamation, when the scabs crumbled and fell from the face and body, to be the most contagious phase of the disease. The boy, Wertenbaker recalled, was "scattering infection everywhere he went." No one paid the boy any mind.[47]

It was never easy to get rural people to take mild smallpox seriously, but when the disease appeared to infect "none but negroes" the task proved far more difficult. Federal, state, and local health officials, reporting from points across the South, uniformly identified the African American population as the reservoir for this disease. Newspapers, too, traced local outbreaks to particular African American individuals, families, or settlements. Even after the disease made its appearance among whites, the great majority of reported cases were in black people. In Tennessee and North Carolina, African Americans accounted for three quarters of all reported cases, far exceeding their proportion in the population. In particular locales, officials recorded far greater disparities. In Greenwood, Mississippi, a town of three thousand inhabitants where blacks outnumbered whites by a narrow margin, more than five hundred people contracted smallpox in the winter of 1900; just twenty-three of them were white.[48]

Wertenbaker observed that many white Southerners, including some physicians, called mild smallpox "nigger itch" and claimed that whites could not catch it. Often, the first whites to contract the disease aroused contempt. When a group of young white men in Stanford, Kentucky, broke out with the "itch," their neighbors had a ready explanation: the boys had made "indiscreet visits" to the "Deep Well Woods," an African American settlement on the outskirts of town. The first white patients identified in health board reports were usually marginal figures such as tramps, half-witted women, and promiscuous girls—fixtures of the era's eugenics-inspired literature on southern "white trash." That some rural whites covered their faces before allowing health board photographers to take their pictures attests to the shame they felt at being caught with this "loathsome negro disease."[49]

Southern health officials admitted that a large percentage of smallpox cases went unreported in their states. How, then, could they speak with such certainty about the racial origins of these epidemics? Those in a position to produce official accounts of epidemics have often blamed their occurrence on subordinate social groups. But this is not to say that all such

Smallpox patient at the Tampa pesthouse, 1900.
Courtesy of the State
Archives of Florida

narratives are works of pure fiction. To dismiss the official accounts out of hand—or to read them only as elite ideology—is to forgo all hope of recovering the social experience of disease. The wonderfully idiosyncratic epistolary form that public health reports took in this era inspires at least some confidence in their contents. State reports consisted mainly of letters and telegrams, peppered with chatty detail, sent in by local health officers. Even assuming broad agreement regarding matters of race and class, it would have taken a racial conspiracy of an implausible scale to make all of these reports tell a common story of the epidemic's prevalence among African Americans and poor whites, if there were not some basis for this in fact. With an infectious disease such as smallpox, which spread most easily among people without regular access to medical care and who lived in close proximity to one another, the poorest members of society were exceptionally vulnerable. Inadequate nutrition made poor people susceptible to all sorts of diseases. Public health officials made a revealing leap, however, when they concluded from such epidemiological facts that "irresponsible negroes" (or "ignorant" whites) were morally culpable for the spread of smallpox.[50]

In his personal papers and public writings, C. P. Wertenbaker was serious, dispassionate, and reserved—a gentleman scholar of the Service stripe.

In his field reports to Washington, he dutifully noted whites' belief that they had a natural immunity to the disease they called "nigger itch," but he considered this popular belief a sign of ignorance and a bane to scientific smallpox work. He did not normally indulge in expansive statements of racial ideology, "scientific" or otherwise. But in one letter, which he sent to a Mississippi health official in 1910, the federal surgeon revealed some of his assumptions about the state, and fate, of African American health. "There is no question in my mind," Wertenbaker wrote, "but that the negro constituted the gravest menace to the country in which they lived, from a sanitary standpoint." "The negro is like a child," he continued, "incapable of carrying on any effectual sanitary work unless guided and directed by the white people. . . . Unless there is a marked change in sanitary conditions among the negroes, I believe that within the next 100 years the negro will be almost as scarce in this country as the Indian now is. I believe that the extinction of the race is imminent."[51]

With those few lines Wertenbaker revealed a cast of mind entirely conventional among white medical authorities of his time and place. Such theories had a long lineage. In the antebellum period, southern medical writers had used just such claims to defend the institution of slavery. Observing that African American slaves were less prone than whites to contract malaria and yellow fever (because, we now know, of an inherited genetic resistance to the mosquito-borne viruses that caused those diseases), slaveholders lauded their chattels' natural fitness for back-breaking labor in the coastal rice and cotton fields. Ideologues claimed the intelligence and moral dispositions of African Americans were so deficient that slaves needed their white masters' protection and restraint. In the post–Civil War era, white medical experts ridiculed the freed people's claims to equal citizenship. During the 1890s and 1900s, physicians interpreted African Americans' high mortality and morbidity rates as evidence of black people's supposed biological inferiority, insisting that they brought disease upon themselves by sexual vices and intemperance. Using the flawed late nineteenth-century census returns to bolster their case, white experts claimed that the health of African Americans had plummeted since emancipation. This proved, the authorities claimed, that blacks had benefited from slavery and were so ill suited to freedom that they were now destined for extinction. Such medical racism led leading life insurance companies to refuse policies to African Americans.[52]

In *The Philadelphia Negro* (1899), his pathbreaking work of urban sociology, the young African American scholar W. E. B. Du Bois calmly showed that the prevailing theories of African American health rested on sloppy science and wishful thinking. Since little reliable data existed regarding African American health during slavery, Du Bois pointed out, claims that the health of the race had undergone a dramatic decline since emancipation were, at best, unsubstantiated. Of the myth that blacks were doomed for extinction, Du Bois wrote that it represented "the bugbear of the untrained, or the wish of the timid." But such medical falsehoods had devastating consequences. They inured the nation to the real—and substantially preventable—health problems of poor African Americans in the North and South. The average life expectancy for blacks was thirty-two, compared to nearly fifty for whites. Infant mortality rates were shockingly high. Black men and women were disproportionately struck by many chronic and infectious diseases, including heart disease and consumption (pulmonary tuberculosis), a major killer in the African American population. "In the history of civilized peoples," Du Bois wrote, rarely had so much "human suffering" been viewed with "such peculiar indifference."[53]

That indifference was not just a cultural phenomenon. It was a systemic feature of the white-dominated medical profession, especially in the South. Reputable physicians refused to treat African Americans. As southern cities built new public hospitals in the late nineteenth century, most excluded blacks or relegated them to inferior Jim Crow wards. Such demeaning treatment, Du Bois observed, intensified the "superstitious" fear of hospitals and medicine that he considered "prevalent among the lower classes of all people, but especially among Negroes." As a consequence, most poor blacks did not seek medical aid from a white physician until they were desperately ill. "Many a Negro would almost rather die than trust himself to a hospital."[54]

The best hope for African American health care lay with the black medical profession. By 1900 more than 1,700 black physicians practiced in the United States, up from about 900 a decade earlier. African American medical schools, nursing schools, and hospitals opened during the same period.

Industrial schools such as Booker T. Washington's Tuskegee Institute instructed poor blacks in the use of toothbrushes and everyday hygiene. As significant as these developments were, they could not quickly correct a pattern of institutional neglect so long in the making. As late as 1910, the entire state of South Carolina had only 66 professional black physicians, or one physician for every 12,000 black people. The ratio for white people was about 1 to 800. African American professional medicine existed mainly in urban areas. In the rural South, where most African Americans lived, black physicians were scarce. When rural blacks took ill, they still relied, as they had during slavery, on the informal medical knowledge of friends and relatives, root doctors, and practitioners of magical medicine. In a period of explosive growth in the American medical profession, it remained all too common for African Americans to take ill, suffer, and die without receiving any medical attention.[55]

Even in an era of such systemic neglect, the realization that smallpox was spreading among African Americans across the South was bound to cause alarm among white public health officials. White officials understood from their own observations in the field that smallpox spread like wildfire through unvaccinated populations, regardless of their color. Since the majority of Southerners, white and black, had never been vaccinated, officials made some effort to explain the early prevalence of the disease among blacks.

White medical commentators marveled at African Americans' sociability: their "gregarious habits," their fondness for going on "excursions" and mingling "promiscuously," their "close association and intermixing." And the commentators were not just talking about sex. Many fretted about "religious negroes," who seemed ever to be gathering in one meeting or another. During an outbreak, African American churches were usually among the first places quarantined—right after the black schools. Even the playfulness of African American children was deemed a threat to the public health. In the autumn of 1899, as sharecroppers in Concordia Parish, Louisiana, brought in the harvest, piling the seed cotton high in their cabins, one white official worried that children would pollute the cotton with smallpox: "On this inviting heap the darky children romp by day and sleep by night with that habitual disregard of cleanliness characteristic of the race." The writer knew he could count on his readers' imagination to complete the scenario. With the infected cotton bound for market, and from there to the mills, and from the mills to the homes of unsuspecting white consumers, who could say how far smallpox would travel from those sharecroppers' shacks?[56]

Racial anxieties permeate the official record of the southern epidemics. But the record also contains clues about the deeper causes of the prevalence of smallpox among African Americans. While poor nutrition and overcrowded living conditions made black people especially susceptible to smallpox, institutionalized racism fostered African Americans' longstanding distrust of white doctors. Neglected and mistreated by the medical profession, the vast majority of southern blacks had never been examined by a physician, let alone been vaccinated, and would just as soon keep it that way. African Americans were understandably reluctant to report cases of smallpox in their homes or neighborhoods to white authorities. As the *Atlanta Constitution* noted during the Birmingham epidemic, "[T]he negroes there have a great dread of the pesthouse and use every effort to avoid having their friends and relatives taken there." In other places, the physical or cultural distance from white medical authority was so great that such subterfuge was unnecessary. Traveling through Georgia in 1899, Wertenbaker kept stumbling upon African American settlements or sections of towns with names like "Hell's Half Acre," where smallpox had spread for four or five months, sometimes longer, without attracting the least notice from whites. "The disease became epidemic before it was known," he said.[57]

The close living conditions of African American laborers, even in the most rural of settings, aided the spread of smallpox. Especially efficient carriers, it seemed, were itinerant laborers in the fast-growing rural nonagricultural sector, including men who worked at turpentine stills, in phosphate and coal mines, and on the railroads. Unvaccinated African Americans who slept in crowded cabins, shared tents in mining camps, or huddled for warmth in railroad boxcars were extraordinarily vulnerable to airborne germs. Transient black workers, forbidden by law, custom, and their own poverty from sleeping in a white-owned tavern or inn, frequently stayed overnight in the home of a black family, where they shared rooms and often beds with children and other family members. In February 1899, a white Carrollton, Kentucky, physician named F. H. Gaines examined a transient African American man with a "suspicious eruption on his forehead and wrists." Dr. Gaines diagnosed the eruption as smallpox. He learned from his patient that he had been put off the Madison and Cincinnati packet three days earlier and had spent the next three nights with three separate black families. When the man realized Gaines intended to take him to a pesthouse, he made a quick escape. Two weeks later, smallpox erupted in all three families.[58]

A truism holds that in the Jim Crow South, whites and blacks lived side by side, while in the "promised land" of the urban North de facto racial segregation prevailed in the housing market. But the history of the southern smallpox epidemics suggests just how much social distance actually existed between the races in southern places. Jim Crow laws, which proliferated in the 1890s, stripped most African Americans of the suffrage, forced them into separate compartments on trains and streetcars, and relegated black children to the most poorly funded schools. For all of their flaws, the public health reports reveal some of the collective impact of this emerging regime of white supremacy, even as they attest to the vitality of black social institutions. Reports traced smallpox clusters to African American boardinghouses, schools, churches, restaurants, opera houses, and a few houses of ill fame—including one in Richmond, Kentucky, whose keeper served well-attended court-day dinners to the community.[59]

Booker T. Washington had it right. Infectious disease drew no color line. People did—with their customs, practices, institutions, and laws. The color line, in any event, rarely held. Even when local authorities tried to keep smallpox at bay by ordering quarantines of African American sections—as officials did in 1900 in Wertenbaker's native Albemarle County—smallpox crossed that line. When whites did catch smallpox, a disease that had in some places gone unnoticed for months suddenly attracted public attention. The formerly invisible disease became visible.[60]

Which is not to say it became intelligible. For at that point, as Wertenbaker observed time and again, another problem presented itself. The public refused to believe mild type smallpox was the real thing.

. . .

The smallpox came to Stithton, Kentucky, on a winter's day in 1899, when the Barker boy rode home from Louisville on a bicycle. A peculiar rash speckled the young cyclist's face, and the town physician who examined him feared the worst. He instructed the boy to ride home and stay there, and then rang the Hardin County health officer. Accompanied by several excited physicians, Dr. C. Z. Aud took a ride out to the Barker place. Aud looked the boy over, ran his fingers over the papules, and in the presence of his attentive colleagues and the boy's father, diagnosed smallpox. Mr. Barker did not gasp with alarm, he did not plead for a second opinion, he did not ask what could be done to save the boy. He just let the Hardin County health officer know that his opinion wasn't worth all that much at the Barker place. "I was not very politely told by the old man," Aud recalled, "that he had had small-pox himself, and knew a great deal more about it than I did, and he would not submit to vaccination." Barker's two daughters refused to bare their arms, either. Mrs. Barker said she had already been vaccinated. So Aud and his entourage left. When he got back to his office, Aud learned that Mr. Barker had already called a lawyer to see if he could "get damages from a doctor for saying his son had small-pox when it was a lie." To Barker, Aud's diagnosis amounted to libel. Time would tell that Barker did not know so much about smallpox. Two weeks later, he and his daughters broke out in pox.[61]

Though most rural Southerners had never come near a case of smallpox, they expected to know it when they saw it. And when their expectations were not met, they did not, as a rule, defer to the professional expertise of public health officers. Dr. J. R. Burchell of Clay County, Kentucky, found himself the object of "many a cursing" when he warned his neighbors that smallpox was spreading among them. "One gentleman's idea of smallpox," this health officer reported, "was that when a man had small-pox he was in a hell of a bad fix, and as no one had been in that condition, therefore there had been no small-pox." It proved a difficult position with which to argue. Public health officers at points across the South agreed that one of the greatest obstacles to smallpox control was the doubt that existed in people's minds as to the true nature of this new disease. Frequent bouts with naysayers led some officers to wish, in published government health reports, for the appearance of a "fool-killer": a fatal case of smallpox. As one North Carolina official put it, the best cure for a doubting public was "a good first-class case of small-pox."[62]

That even a second-class case of smallpox could arouse so little public concern speaks to the amount of physical suffering that Americans raised in the nineteenth century expected to endure during their lives. Even in ordinary times, southern newspapers advertised patent medicines promising relief from all kinds of fevers and "itching skin diseases." It took something stronger than mild smallpox to make people welcome government doctors into their lives. Even in a "mild" outbreak, Wertenbaker might see as many as a dozen grotesque confluent cases and one or two deaths. In December 1900, one of Wertenbaker's Service colleagues, Assistant Surgeon John D. Long, inspected a gang of African American railroad workers in a Washington train station. The men had just finished digging a tunnel for the new West Virginia Short Line Railroad and were making their way south. For months, a disease—variously called "Cuban itch," "nigger itch," or "black measles"—had been spreading among white and black workers in the Short Line construction camps. As Long questioned the men, he jotted down their symptoms: "headache, fever, general weakness, vomiting, and pain in the neck and back," followed by a rash that went through the usual stages of "vesiculation, pustulation, and desquamation." Most of the men had been unable to work (or collect wages) for up to two weeks. The camps they had left behind had seen at least 140 cases of smallpox, with 4 deaths. That was "mild" smallpox.[63]

Clusters of severe cases occurred during otherwise mild epidemics often enough to keep Wertenbaker in an almost constant state of apprehension. In each fatal outbreak he envisioned smallpox regaining its historical virulence. From a public health perspective, though, the most dangerous thing about mild type smallpox was that it did not lay people low enough. Some people recovered without ever taking to their beds. Particularly in the convalescent stage of the disease—when patients would ordinarily be confined under close quarantine—people with mild type smallpox often felt well enough to go about their business. Children with infectious scabs on their faces and hands played in the streets. Contagious men and women worked in the fields and factories, ran grocery stores, and mingled in the crowd on court day. Secretary Lewis of the North Carolina Board of Health complained that a man with mild smallpox was "exactly in the right condition for visiting around among the neighbors, or loafing at the railway station, or above all, attending a gathering of any kind—political preferred." The eruption might be so insignificant as to attract no notice. Nevertheless, it was "the genuine article," Lewis warned, "and capable of causing in the unvaccinated the most virulent and fatal form of the disease."[61]

The turn of the century is remembered today as the advent of the modern expert, when university-trained professionals in medicine, the sciences, and law acquired a new authority in American life. But southern health officials often found the public, business interests, and even their own local governments unwilling to accept their warnings or yield them the diagnostic ground. Like Mr. Barker of Stithton, many citizens saw no reason to elevate the medical opinion of a health official above their own.

Like other Americans of the period, blacks were accustomed to experiencing any number of fevers and skin eruptions during their lives. Their first inclination in naming a new disease was to compare it with others they had known. After inspecting a confluent black patient in a room crowded with "eight or ten negroes" in Princeton, Kentucky, a physician found his diagnosis of smallpox challenged by an "old negro" who said he had survived smallpox himself. "Dat nigger nebber had no small-pox," the man declared, insisting that the "little bumps on him" were caused by "big-pox" (syphilis).[65]

As local health authorities raised the pressure—making proclamations, ordering quarantines, calling for compulsory vaccination—critics raised their protests. Some citizens denounced the government officials as capricious and corrupt. Others relied, as rural blacks had since slavery, on the power of rumor. As Wertenbaker frequently witnessed in the field, nothing outran a rumor. Communities of cotton mill workers, who notwithstanding their claims to white privilege were among the most exploited and marginalized of southern laboring people, were deeply distrustful of medical authority. In Charlotte, Danville, and other places in the throes of industrial change, Wertenbaker found the expert claims of health authorities undone by rumors circulating among the mill workers that no smallpox existed.[66]

Much of the diagnostic dissension came from the medical profession itself. Some local doctors readily conceded their "inexperience" and "distress" at the spread of this bizarre eruptive disease, and they welcomed the expertise of county and state health officials. But others openly dissented against the medical claims of the local officers of the board of health, who were after all physicians like themselves who had been given their extraordinary powers by virtue of a political appointment. Public health officers called their uncooperative peers "kicking doctors" (invoking the ultimate rural symbol of stubbornness: a kicking mule). State health officers openly mocked their local opponents in the medical profession, describing in published reports their encounters with many a "low grade" physician who was "as positive as he was ignorant." When Inspector B. W. Smock arrived in Jackson County, Kentucky, a community in central Appalachia, a local physician informed him that (as Smock described the conversation) "they had a 'breaking-out disease' that was mighty 'ketching' up in what is known as Horse Lick Creek." The local doctor reckoned it was measles. But Smock retorted that this disease was nothing less than "seven-day-in-a-week, stay-with-you-forever small-pox." City-based state health officials such as Smock wrote up their travels into the heart of Appalachia as if they were conducting anthropological fieldwork. They marveled at the practices of local institutions, recorded (or mocked) local dialects, and cataloged medical folkways. For these state experts, the unruly subjects of their inquiry were not just the (by their lights) primitive mountain folk but also their "ignorant" physicians.[67]

Local physicians took exception to the increasing interference of government-appointed health officials in their practices. But more than interests were involved. Mild type smallpox simply did not conform to physicians' expectations. The disease differed in several respects from the classical smallpox described in their medical textbooks, which given the long quiescence of the disease in the South were for many physicians the only source of knowledge on smallpox available. Compared with textbook smallpox, the pocks of the new disease were few and superficial (and usually not confluent). Physicians examining patients for smallpox expected them to have a secondary fever, but mild type smallpox frequently brought none. And smallpox was supposed to be a winter disease. The mild type could prevail during an Alabama summer.[68]

Wertenbaker had learned in Middlesboro how difficult it could be to pry smallpox funds from a parsimonious and skeptical county government. To get anything done, health officers needed the support of their local government institutions: vaccination orders (where state law did not give that authority to health boards), money for vaccine and vaccinators' fees, cash to pay the pesthouse guards, and so on. In the larger towns, health officials had to win over the city council. In small towns and rural areas, health officials had to make their cases to county governments—boards of supervisors or, in some states (including Georgia and Kentucky), judicial bodies such as county courts and grand juries. The interests and medical understandings of those government bodies often clashed with those of health officers. For the lay officials, who, as Wertenbaker pointedly observed, were typically merchants, farmers, and other men "unfamiliar with matters pertaining to general sanitation and public health," the smallpox question came down to taxpayer dollars and common sense. Unlike appointed health officials, most aldermen, county supervisors, and judges had to answer to the electorate. If they strayed too far from the common sense of the community, they risked losing their jobs.[69]

Some of the most dramatic clashes between health authorities and lay officials took place in crowded courtrooms, the center stage of local political life at the turn of the century. When the modern expertise of medical science collided with the old-fashioned legal authority of judges and juries, the law won. Having given up on persuading local physicians that the "ketching disease" troubling Jackson County was really smallpox, Inspector Smock made his case to the county court. The state health official delivered a two-hour speech. As a reporter from Louisville described the scene, things seemed to be going well for Smock until a preacher stood up and addressed the assembly. "The Lord has sent this affliction upon us, and the Lord will take it away in His own good time," he said. At that point the county attorney, an elected official in a room full of voters, declared that there was no proof that smallpox existed in the community and he was opposed to any measure that would cost the taxpayers their hard-earned dollars. In a remarkable gesture to rural democracy, the judge decided to take a vote of all those present, asking the courtroom crowd to decide whether the disease was smallpox. "[T]o a man they voted that small-pox did not exist," the journalist reported, "notwithstanding the fact that two men with distinct pustules on their faces were in the crowd."[70]

Like Inspector Smock, C. P. Wertenbaker learned that to fight smallpox in a southern community he had to make his case in the court of public opinion. The politics of smallpox control was a politics of knowledge, as well as interests. Local government officials had many motives for requesting the aid of a Service surgeon. As in Middlesboro, some hoped to persuade "Uncle Sam" to pick up the tab for an epidemic they had allowed to spin out of control. After that debacle, though, Surgeon General Wyman had made clear that the Service would be supplying only expertise, not largesse. More opinions would seem the last thing needed in these local communities, where health officers had run into so much trouble trying to arouse public concern.

But to his surprise, Wertenbaker often found that by the time he arrived in a place, the people were ready to listen to a surgeon from the U.S. Marine-Hospital Service. Evidently, southern suspicion of federal authority had its limits. For Wertenbaker found that the quarreling parties in a community—the "kicking doctors," the health officers, the county officials, and the public—seemed prepared to consider the diagnosis and recommendations of an agent of the U.S. government. Perhaps the Service's years of yellow fever work had left a legacy of trust in the region. Maybe the Service's reputation for medical expertise preceded it. Though local relationships generally mattered a great deal in these communities, it worked to Wertenbaker's benefit that he had neither personal ties to these places nor private interests at stake. Sometimes he arrived to find that the quarreling parties had agreed in advance to accept the federal surgeon's "diagnosis and advice." In any case, he always came prepared to persuade.[71]

And to perform. There was a theatrical, even scripted, quality to Wertenbaker's appearances in southern cities, county seats, and small towns. In an

age of Chautauqua assemblies, traveling circus shows, and political debates in the open air, Wertenbaker's impending arrival was heralded in
advance in the local newspapers and by word of mouth. The public seemed
hungry for information about smallpox and vaccination—or at least eager
for a good show. The medical man gave it to them.[72]

The show began the moment he stepped off a train, packet, or wagon.
Greeted by the local health officers and officials, he asked them to take him
directly to see the smallpox suspects. Before making his inspection, he put
on his smallpox outfit—the overalls, head wrap, and respirator. Typically,
the men, women, and children he examined had already been diagnosed
with chicken pox or "elephant itch" or something else. It rarely took Wertenbaker long to make his own diagnosis, and it was usually smallpox.[73]

Wertenbaker would then call a public meeting. At first he held his meetings in county courthouses, but the audiences soon grew too large and he
moved with them into the public square or streets. The crowds sometimes
numbered a thousand people or more. Entire communities turned out for
the show: farmers and factory workers, businessmen and representatives
of local women's clubs, parents and schoolchildren, whites and blacks.
Wertenbaker announced to the audience that smallpox existed in their
midst and, be it ever so mild, it could kill. He instructed the people in the
clinical features of smallpox, explaining how mild type smallpox differed
from chicken pox, measles, and other common diseases.[74]

Next he would explain the importance of vaccination, and how it
worked. And that's when folks got edgy. Wertenbaker's audiences always
included many people who were strongly opposed to vaccination. It was
during these moments, as he stood in his Service blues preaching the virtues of vaccination to workingmen in overalls and women in homemade
dresses, that Wertenbaker would listen to their complaints and their fears.
He came to appreciate the extent to which antivaccination sentiment grew
from reasonable fears of the procedure. Whether he was speaking in Charlotte or Columbia, Danville or Lumpkin, the surgeon heard the same objection from mill workers, farmers, and other manual laborers: vaccination
caused "sore arms," and that interfered with business.[75]

This common fear of a vaccine-disabled arm was at least as old as the
Civil War epidemics. "I have been in the habit of preaching vaccination for

the last thirty or forty years," one North Carolina physician said in 1898. "I never saw a fiddler vaccinated in my life." The bad batches of "dry point" vaccine flooding the South in 1898 and 1899 turned a lot of people into fiddlers.[76]

Even under the safest conditions—an aseptic procedure, using vaccine free of harmful bacteria—smallpox vaccination typically caused some constitutional disturbance, a fever, and a painful inflammation at the site of the vaccination. That's how a physician knew the vaccine had taken: it "set up a fire." But mass vaccinations during epidemics rarely afforded the safest conditions, and the results of the dry points caused physicians and health officers to voice concern.[77]

In an era when almost everyone earned their living with their hands—farming the land, working wood, laying track, mining coal, tanning hides, rolling tobacco—the prospect of losing a few weeks' wages to a "sore arm" brought on by tainted vaccine was reason enough to dodge the lancet. The belief that this new mild smallpox (if it actually was smallpox) was unlikely do serious harm only strengthened the perceived risk of vaccination. Secretary Lewis of the North Carolina Board of Health noted that opposition to vaccination seemed to be strongest among cotton mill workers. Although he favored compulsory vaccination, Lewis acknowledged the workers' "natural reluctance" to lose the use of their hands. No system of social insurance existed in the 1890s (or for many years thereafter)—no policy of the state or the mill owners that would compensate men, women, and children who worked in the mills for their loss of wages due to bad vaccine. Lewis urged all large employers in the state to promise their workers half pay during any vaccination-induced disability.[78]

In his public speeches and writings, Wertenbaker tried to dispel the worst rumors about vaccination: "Rumors of arms, legs, or life lost as the result of vaccination, have, as a rule, no foundation in fact," he said. But, like Lewis, he developed a real empathy for the predicament of breadwinners. And as he realized how much harm vaccination as it was currently practiced could do, he became an advocate for reform.[79]

He turned into a strong proponent of "glycerinized lymph," a newer form of vaccine in which glycerin was used to kill the bacteria that proliferated in vaccine material (which was, after all, an animal virus harvested on the skin of cows). Glycerinized or "glycerinated" vaccine had been in use for several years, but the old, glycerin-free dry points were more widely distributed in the South during the first years of the epidemics. Wertenbaker was not the first public health officer to suggest that it was the dry points—not vaccination in general—that caused so many sore arms in the South. But the issue became a cause for him. He wrote letters to vaccine manufacturers, complaining about impure products. He sent samples of vaccine, including two dry points and two tubes of glycerinized lymph, to the Service's National Hygienic Laboratory in Washington for testing. Passed Assistant Surgeon Milton J. Rosenau extracted the vaccine material from the samples and heated the material in his laboratory. The tests showed that both of the dry points crawled with bacteria, including virulent *Staphylococcus pyogenes aureus*, with which Rosenau inoculated a mouse. It died. The samples of glycerinized virus were hardly models of purity. They, too, yielded thousands of colonies of bacteria. But at least these proved nonvirulent.[80]

Explaining the superiority of the new glycerinized lymph became a regular feature of Wertenbaker's smallpox lectures. By speaking so candidly about the hazards of the dry point, he won a measure of trust from his audiences. As a regular feature of his performances, he offered to vaccinate volunteers with a tube of glycerinized lymph he carried with him. If all went well, leading citizens would step forward and roll up their sleeves to be scraped before the attentive crowd. On his best days, Wertenbaker told Wyman, "the persons who have been loudest in proclaiming that they will never, never be vaccinated, come up and ask that I vaccinate them at once." Wertenbaker probably exaggerated when he claimed that, as a result of his talks, "the opposition to vaccination almost entirely disappears" and "the people usually readily acquiesce in any measure directed by the authorities." But in their own reports local health officials praised his visits, one calling a Wertenbaker performance "of inestimable benefit." And even when Wertenbaker failed to win over hearts and minds, his talks gave local health officials the leverage they needed to persuade mayors, county supervisors, and judges to appropriate money and take action.[81]

Wertenbaker always concluded his talks by presenting his plan for wiping out smallpox in the community. In the published version of "The Plan," which Wertenbaker gave to his official hosts, he noted such details as the appropriate window shades for the smallpox hospital, pondered the relative merits of formaldehyde versus sulfur disinfectants, and specified the daily routines of numerous physicians, guards, and inspectors. ("By 8 a.m., the officer in charge is at his desk. . . .") He advised (as if such advice were necessary) that in communities "where race feeling is strong," separate smallpox hospitals be set up for whites and blacks. The Marine-Hospital Service surgeons forced local governments to take the health of African Americans seriously, which was in itself a real achievement. But the federal agents showed no interest in upsetting Jim Crow.

Wertenbaker's plan was a model of "military authority": house-to-house inspections by physicians and police, compulsory vaccination of everyone who could not show a recent vaccination scar, the relocation of all suspected disease carriers into detention camps, and treatment of all smallpox patients in an isolation hospital. Wertenbaker leavened this litany of logistics with aphorisms drawn from his experience in the field. "A policeman is of great assistance to an inspector." "Measures, good or bad, half done are worse than useless, as they give a fancied security." "Smallpox cannot be suppressed without the expenditure of money. The more promptly you act the less it will cost." Middlesboro could not have been far from his mind as he wrote those last lines.[82]

Like all measures of health policing since the invention of the quarantine in fourteenth-century Venice, Wertenbaker's "Plan" had a draconian streak. But for all of Wertenbaker's frustration with southern political institutions and officials—who, in his view, had let an eminently manageable pestilence run wild—his smallpox work instilled in him a certain optimism that those officials often lacked about the potential of the people. The people might be ignorant. They might spread false rumors. But in his travels through the southern states, Wertenbaker had learned from them. Above all, he had come to appreciate the ethical and political value of candor. Public health work required a big stick, to be sure, but it achieved little in the long run if the public remained unconvinced. Wertenbaker advised local health authorities to leaven force and discipline with education and persuasion. "If these facts are explained to the people by someone in whom they have confidence," he promised in the "Plan," "much of the opposition to vaccination will disappear."[83]

. . .

As Wertenbaker's faith in the southern people grew, his opinion of their local institutions continued to diminish. In February 1900, after more than two years of smallpox work, Wertenbaker sent Surgeon General Wyman a memorandum. Not only did epidemic smallpox continue to plague many of the southern states, but now reports of new outbreaks of mild type smallpox (and, occasionally, its more terrifying ancestor) were reaching Washington from locales in the Middle West, the urban North, and the far West. The epidemics had become a national problem, making a coordinated federal response imperative.

"As matters now stand," Wertenbaker wrote, "the suppression of the disease is left to individual communities, where action is but rarely taken until after smallpox has made its appearance." Not only were the present methods expensive, but they allowed smallpox to spread endlessly from one community to another. "It is only by a general concerted action, embracing all the infected territory that we can hope to arrest the spread of the disease, and [guarantee] its ultimate suppression," Wertenbaker told Wyman. "The Marine-Hospital Service, being the guardian of the Public Health, seems to be the proper source for the inauguration of such measures." Wertenbaker had always believed that a successful smallpox eradication effort on any scale necessitated having a single "officer in charge." And he let Wyman know that if his proposal for nationalizing smallpox control met with the surgeon general's approval, he, C. P. Wertenbaker, would be willing to be that man.[84]

Wertenbaker surely knew better than to expect any such sudden sweeping change in existing institutions. If the smallpox epidemics of the end of the century had shown anything, it was that democratic institutions and the political communities they governed often moved slowly, especially when official claims to expertise and visions of social control collided with the interests, beliefs, and values of the people. Walter Wyman did not put Wertenbaker's plan in place on the national level, nor did he make Wertenbaker "officer in charge." Seven months later, he transferred Wertenbaker to take command of the Service's station in the huge southern port of New

Orleans—a promotion, to be sure, but not the one Wertenbaker had once asked for.

In 1907, Wertenbaker happily returned with his family to his native Virginia to run the Service station at Norfolk. In the final years of his career, he would become well known to African American educators, ministers, physicians, and nurses for his efforts to organize rural black farmers and church groups into state and local "anti-tuberculosis societies." In classic Wertenbaker fashion, he wrote up a detailed "Plan of Organization" for creating these societies. But the essence of the plan was to mobilize African Americans at the grassroots to fight a deadly infectious disease. By the time of Wertenbaker's death, of kidney disease, in 1916, southern blacks had founded five state leagues and numerous local societies.[85]

C. P. Wertenbaker's grave lies in a well-shaded area of the University of Virginia cemetery, not far from the resting places of the eleven hundred Confederate soldiers buried there during the Civil War. The remains of C. C. Wertenbaker, who outlived Charlie by two years, lie nearby. The words on Charles Poindexter Wertenbaker's tombstone remember a son of the Confederacy who, along with hundreds of other traveling medical men of the United States Marine-Hospital Service, carried the influence of the national government across the South. The inscription reads: "As Soldier, Doctor, and Officer for Twenty Eight Years of the National Health Service His Good Works are Imperishable."[86]

In the years after Wertenbaker left Wilmington, he saw many of the reforms he had advocated come to pass. Local, state, and federal health authorities placed a greater reliance on public education in their work. A new federal system, established in 1902 and run by the U.S. Public Health and Marine-Hospital Service's National Hygienic Laboratory, regulated the manufacture of smallpox vaccine and the proliferating array of new vaccines, sera, and antitoxins on the market. And Congress gave the Service greater authority to standardize and coordinate the control of infectious disease at the local and state levels. No revolution had taken place. But reform surely had come.

At the turn of the century, there existed as yet only a few areas of the American domain where the authority of the nation reigned supreme in the field of public health. Foremost among them were the new colonial possessions acquired by the United States in the Spanish-American War of 1898. In those distant spaces, medical officers of the United States Army exercised powers of a scale and scope that C. P. Wertenbaker could scarcely have imagined.

FOUR

WAR IS HEALTH

Windswept and weather-beaten, the city of Iloilo stood upon unpromising marshland near the southeastern tip of Panay, in the vast Pacific waterworld of the Philippine archipelago. The center of the islands' sugar trade, for decades the old Spanish port had sent forth from its deep harbor steamships bearing that prized commodity, as well as hemp, sapanwood, coffee, mangoes, and mother of pearl. The people of Iloilo were known for their habit of resistance to outside authority, be it the Kingdom of Spain, the Catholic Church, or, now, the United States. In December 1898, Emilio Aguinaldo's Filipino independence movement set up a military stronghold there. By October 1899, when the Twenty-sixth U.S. Volunteers stepped ashore, Aguinaldo's *insurrectos* had already been driven out, but they remained entrenched not far from the city.[1]

The Twenty-sixth was a regiment of New England militiamen. They had recently undergone a crash course in the geography of American expansion. Their journey began two months earlier in Boston. They traveled by train across the continental United States to San Francisco. Encamped in the late summer fog of the Presidio, they learned that smallpox had broken out in a neighboring regiment, which was swiftly quarantined on Angel Island. After a fresh round of vaccinations, the Twenty-sixth crowded aboard the *Grant*, a 454-foot transport ship that carried them across more than seven thousand miles of Pacific Ocean to Manila Bay, with a stopover for coal in Honolulu, the premier port of newly annexed Hawaii. Last, they steamed thirty-six hours from Manila to arrive here, in Iloilo. Their mission was to man the U.S. garrison and establish order.[2]

A *Boston Globe* reporter named J. N. Taylor had traveled with the Twenty-sixth all the way from Massachusetts. "The city was very dirty— oozy with it," he recalled. Of pressing concern to the U.S. command, smallpox raged in the city, killing more residents every day. Prior to the arrival of the Twenty-sixth, smallpox, known by its local name, *buti*, seemed to be accepted as a fact of life. Few of the inhabitants had ever been vaccinated, and they made no effort to isolate the sick.[3]

On the advice of the U.S. health officer on the scene, the soldiers set about enforcing a "progressive policy" of sanitation, "giving Iloilo a bath and a scrubbing." They set up a smallpox hospital outside the city and removed the sick from their families. Soldiers inspected homes, cleaned out decrepit privy vaults, and introduced a new system of dry earth closets. The troops moved with particular force upon an expanse of shacks that stretched a quarter mile from the old Spanish palace to the Jaro bridge. The district housed one thousand of Iloilo's poorest residents, among whom, Taylor noted, "fully 700 were pock-marked." The soldiers leveled the district.[4]

Risking fines or imprisonment, many Ilonggos resisted the American sanitary campaign, which, as Taylor had to admit, did require "a radical change in the sanitary conduct of their homes." The Army's effort to enforce vaccination proved so unpopular that the soldiers found it "necessary to round up the inhabitants with guns to inoculate them."[5]

Within three months of the Twenty-sixth Regiment's arrival, Iloilo seemed to Taylor a city transformed. The offensive odors had abated. Smallpox was disappearing. Even the attitude of the Ilonggos appeared to be softening. Many now called upon the health inspector's office, children in hand, and asked to be vaccinated. Taylor could imagine a time when, with a little more sanitary work (draining the city's swamps was the obvious next project), Iloilo might make a perfectly salubrious home for white men.

"There seems to be no good reason why Iloilo should not be as healthy as Boston," he said.[6]

. . .

W here soldiers go, plagues follow. Since the age of Alexander, the annals of war had known no truer axiom. Mobilizing armies uprooted young men from great cities and remote villages, previously distinct
epidemiological environments, and threw them together in crowded camps
where the air reeked of waste and the water teemed with the unseen agents
of cholera and typhoid. Across the millennia, seasoned generals had fairly
expected diseases to take more lives than spears, swords, or guns. Rarely did
those expectations go unmet. Beneath the staggering death toll of the
American Civil War, in which some 620,000 Union and Confederate soldiers perished, lay the familiar but little understood handiwork of microbial pathogens: nearly twice as many soldiers had died from disease as from
combat.[7]

When army camps grew up near centers of population, microbes circulated indiscriminately between soldiers and civilians. Soldiers on the march
carried smallpox across continents, as the Spanish *conquistadores* had done
in the Americas. The Franco-Prussian War of 1870–71 unleashed a European pandemic of pox that killed more than 500,000 people. Wars disrupted
entire societies, causing famine and poverty, displacing populations, and
destroying fragile systems of sanitation—all of which increased people's
vulnerability to disease. As catastrophic events, wars and the epidemics
they made sometimes became indistinguishable from one another, making
it hard for the soldiers and civilians caught in their crossfire to reckon which
invasion was the defining one. After witnessing the plagues and carnage
of the devastating Crimean War (1853–56), the Russian surgeon Nikolai
Ivanovich Pirogoff concluded, "War is a traumatic epidemic."[8]

And so it took some gall for Rudyard Kipling, well known to Americans
as "the unofficial poet-laureate of the British Empire," to imagine that a
modern imperial army could be a force for public health, rather than an
instrument of apocalypse. In his most famous poem, Kipling wrote:

Take up the White Man's Burden
The savage wars of peace—

Fill full the mouth of Famine
And bid the sickness cease.

Published simultaneously in the London *Times* and the American *McClure's Magazine* in February 1899, "The White Man's Burden" was reprinted in newspapers across the United States. Even Kipling's friend, New York governor Theodore Roosevelt, judged it "poor poetry" in a letter to Senator Henry Cabot Lodge of Massachusetts, though the "Rough Rider" added that Kipling's lines "made good sense from the expansionist viewpoint."[9]

At the moment of the poem's publication, Lodge was exhorting his colleagues in the Senate to ratify the Treaty of Paris, a document that would officially end the Spanish-American War of 1898 and bring the former Spanish colonies of Puerto Rico, Guam, and the Philippines under U.S. rule. (In keeping with the Teller Amendment, enacted on the eve of war, Congress forswore annexation of Cuba; U.S. control of the island would end, officially, in 1902.) But even as the senators made their speeches, a new American war with Emilio Aguinaldo's Philippine Republic was beginning in the suburbs of Manila, a city that, as American anti-imperialists pointed out, lay halfway around the world—five weeks' voyage by steamship—from the U.S. mainland. Kipling appealed to a divided American people, urging them to "take up" their destiny as white colonial rulers in the Philippines. The purpose, he assured them, was noble: to deliver the blessings of Anglo-Saxon civilization, including freedom from want and disease, to that far-off archipelago and its "new-caught sullen peoples, Half-devil and half-child."[10]

A native of British India, Kipling seemed at peace with the glaring ironies of colonial public health, with its frank uniting of idealism and violence. Some of his contemporaries were less untroubled. "It is a bad pedagogy to teach people at the point of a bayonet," objected G. Stanley Hall, the eminent American psychologist and educator. But according to the expansionist viewpoint—informed by the long record of British colonialism and America's own experience with westward expansion—sometimes bayonets were exactly what the situation required.[11]

In a previous story, "The Tomb of His Ancestors," Kipling paid sardonic tribute to the British compulsory vaccination campaigns in nineteenth-century India. An industrious young British military officer, John Chinn,

Vaccinating U.S. troops aboard the Australia, *bound for Manila in 1898. From* Harper's Weekly, *July 16, 1898.*
COURTESY OF THE
NATIONAL LIBRARY
OF MEDICINE

ASSISTANT-SURGEON WHITING HOLDS A VACCINATION BEE.

the latest in his family line to serve the Raj in central India, tricks the Bhil people—who "seemed to be almost as open to civilization as the tigers of [their] own jungles"—to bare their arms to "the vaccine and lancets of a paternal Government." But it was hard work. The Bhils had kidnapped and beaten the first government vaccinator (an Indian) sent to do the job. The clever Englishman succeeded only by playing on the group's superstitions. In "The White Man's Burden," Kipling cautioned the Americans to expect only heartache for their selfless efforts in the Orient:

And when your goal is nearest
(The end for others sought)
Watch sloth and heathen folly
Bring all your hope to nought.

The eyes of the Western world were upon the Americans. But the gazes of the Filipinos would haunt them more: those "silent sullen peoples . . . [s]hall weigh your God and you."[12]

Whether or not they read Kipling, American leaders would come to accept the essential terms of his poem. The moral and political legitimacy of the entire colonial enterprise rested upon the capacity of the colonizers to deliver—not just natural resources, markets, and strategic ports to the metropole, but also freedom from ignorance, famine, and disease to the nation's new subject peoples.

At the turn of the twentieth century, the United States of America, born of a colonial revolt against England, followed in Britannia's wide wake and became, in the words of William Howard Taft, "a colonizing and colony-holding people." Taft was in a good position to know. He served, in close succession, as America's first "civil governor" of the Philippines, secretary of war, and president. In contrast to its long history of conquest and empire-building across North America, the United States had for the first time taken possession of foreign territories without any serious intention of incorporating them into the political nation as states. For Taft and other defenders of overseas expansion, the success of U.S. health interventions in the tropics proved, before all the world, the morally progressive and technologically superior character of American colonialism. Army surgeons and U.S. health officers in Cuba, Puerto Rico, the Philippines, and the Panama Canal zone labored mightily to reduce the incidence of many terrible infectious diseases, including yellow fever, malaria, bubonic plague, beriberi, leprosy, and smallpox.[13]

"We expended many lives and much money in the Spanish War, and in the discharge of the responsibilities that have followed that war," President Taft told a rapt audience at the Medical Club of Philadelphia in 1911. "But they are as nothing compared with the benefits to the human race that have already accrued and will continue to accrue from the discoveries made under the conditions and necessities which the exigencies of that war and the governmental burdens following it presented." Pointing to American "sanitary achievements" in the tropics, expansionists argued that the new possessions, rather than repudiating the values of self-determination expressed in the republic's founding, demonstrated the nation's desire to spread the blessings of liberty and modernity to dark corners of the globe. This belief has remained a touchstone in the ideology of American empire ever since.[14]

None of this, however, had been part of the original war plan. The celebrated American sanitary campaigns originated in a far more limited objective: to protect the health of U.S. troops. A cluster of historical factors raised the stakes involved in meeting even that objective. The Spanish War was the first American war to be fought in the era of the bacteriological revolution. The Medical Department of the U.S. Army was under considerable pressure to show how the scientific advances made in the field of medicine since the Civil War would benefit the soldiers under its care. Alas, the department had already failed the soldiers as they assembled for war. In a grotesque public scandal for the department and the McKinley administration, the mainland encampments had become centers of infection and death.[15]

The intensity with which U.S. military surgeons conducted their sanitary work in the Caribbean and Pacific was heightened, too, by deeply held cultural beliefs that the tropics posed untold hazards for civilized white men. A new discipline—"tropical medicine"—had risen up to address precisely this concern. As *The Baltimore Sun* opined, European and American physicians "look forward to a time when vast regions of the globe, now desert, or inhabited only by inferior races, will afford safe homes for the people of temperate climates." Medical science seemed to hold the key to white settlement and further commercial exploitation of Latin America, Asia, and Africa. But American tropical medicine was still young in 1898, and, after the debacle of the assembly camps, military surgeons viewed their duties in Cuba, Puerto Rico, and the Philippines with deep apprehension.[16]

With great challenges, though, came unparalleled opportunities for the exercise of American health authority. While keeping infectious diseases at bay—including the virulent smallpox that broke out in all three areas after the landing of U.S. troops—the Americans acquired a new mastery of what the brigade surgeon Azel Ames called "the science and art of colonial government." Like the mobile surgeons of the U.S. Marine-Hospital Service, who at that moment were fighting smallpox in the American South, the doctors of the Army Medical Department aspired to use the latest medical knowledge to fight disease. But unlike C. P. Wertenbaker and his colleagues, U.S. military surgeons in the new overseas domain possessed broad national authority and the resources of an army. For the occupying Americans, the vaccination campaigns in particular became a means to gather vital data on the local topography, political institutions, and indigenous peoples—making those exotic tropical places legible to their new rulers.[17]

In the American system of government, guarding the public health was the most elemental action a state could take under its police powers; the almost unlimited legal authority to ward off epidemics had often been compared by the courts to the right of any government to protect its own people from invasion. In the tropical possessions, that old analogy quickly became superfluous. Absent the institutions of popular sovereignty and due process (which the Americans planned to withhold until the indigenous peoples proved themselves fit for a measure of self-government), police power *was* military power. The Army's sanitary campaigns far exceeded the normal bounds of the police power, which by a long American constitutional tradition had always been assumed to originate in sovereign communities of free people. In America's overseas sanitary campaigns, the scale and scope of governmental power were greater, the colonial space was different, and the fact that an institution of the national government, the Army, was undertaking these measures was altogether revolutionary.[18]

By any honest measure, the achievements of U.S. military medicine in the overseas possessions were extraordinary, even when they did not meet the Americans' own ever-rising expectations. Within just a few short years, the Army Medical Department could fairly boast that its surgeons had cleaned up the old Spanish colonial cities and made major discoveries in the etiology and prevention of yellow fever, beriberi, and other terrible diseases. These discoveries took place in Army camps, native villages, and colonial laboratories, using the full intellectual arsenal of the bacteriological revolution. But in the eyes of many Army medical men, it was the fight against smallpox—using the older technology of compulsory vaccination on a hitherto unimaginable scale—that showcased the full humanitarian promise of U.S. military medicine. For the Medical Department's original mission, to protect the troops from disease, unexpectedly gave rise to the first glimmerings of a grander vision. Uninhibited American power might one day eradicate the ancient scourge of smallpox from entire regions of the globe.[19]

. . .

As the first major U.S. military action since the germ theory of disease gained broad acceptance in the medical profession, the war with Spain should have been a milestone in military medicine. And, in important respects, it was. The decades since the Civil War had witnessed the creation of modern health departments in the major U.S. cities, a greater recognition of the importance of aseptic practices in the treatment of wounds, and, in 1895, the discovery of X-rays. During the Civil War, Army surgeons had still probed bullet wounds with unsterilized instruments and unwashed fingers. By 1898, most Army doctors and volunteer nurses knew better. On the battlefield, they wrapped soldiers' wounds in antiseptic dressings. In the field hospital, they used X-rays to locate bullets and assess damage to bones. At the operating table, they followed aseptic techniques. The results (aided by the introduction of small-caliber bullets) were extraordinary. The death rate of wounded U.S. troops during the Spanish War was the lowest in military history: fully 95 percent recovered. And blessedly rare in this war were the heroic amputations that had moved Walt Whitman to poetry during his stint as a hospital volunteer with the Union Army ("the smell of ether, the odor of blood"). As Army Surgeon General George M. Sternberg reported with pride after the Spanish War's end, his surgeons had performed only thirty-four amputations in a wounded list of some sixteen hundred men.[20]

Notwithstanding these achievements, the record of the Army Medical Department during the Spanish War was a public disgrace. "Now that actual fighting is over," wrote Dr. Carroll Dunham in the *American Monthly Review of Reviews*, "it is undeniable that failure adequately to safeguard the health of the American troops is the one blot on an otherwise fair account." In an era of rising expectations about the power of preventive medicine, the department failed to conserve the health of the troops. Only 345 U.S. soldiers died from wounds of combat during the war; 2,565 men died from disease. The ratio of disease fatalities to combat deaths (more than 7 to 1) exceeded those of the Mexican-American War (6.5 to 1) and the Civil War (2 to 1). Tens of thousands of U.S. soldiers spent the Spanish War in the department's ill-equipped hospitals, suffering from preventable infectious diseases. The vast majority of the men who died in this overseas war never left the mainland.[21]

Established in 1818, the U.S. Army Medical Department consisted during peacetime of a small corps of professional officers, reinforced during time of war or emergency by state-appointed surgeons from the volunteer militias and civilian physicians hired on contract. For centuries, medical men had marched with armies, but their status had always been less than heroic. In eighteenth-century Prussia, army doctors still shaved the officers of the line. The very title of "surgeon"—invoking both civilian status and the rough craft of stitching wounds and removing bullets and limbs from wounded soldiers—was viewed as a put-down by some nineteenth-century Army medical officers. The official duties of the U.S. Army surgeon did consist, first and foremost, of evacuating and treating troops wounded on the battlefield. But in the age of modern sanitary science, the duties did not stop there. America's best-known citizen-soldier, Theodore Roosevelt, saluted the profession as a bastion of manly heroism in a feminized age, noting that the surgeons' job required them to be not merely doctors and soldiers but "able administrators." Responsible for the health of thousands of troops in camps and crowded transport trains and ships, the modern Army surgeon was necessarily a public health officer, charged with examining the recruits (rejecting those unfit for duty), vaccinating the line, securing pure food and water, and preaching modern hygiene to line officers and troops.[22]

Under Surgeon General George Miller Sternberg (1893–1902), an internationally recognized epidemiologist who published the first American textbook on bacteriology in 1896, the surgeons of the Army Medical Department aspired to a high degree of professionalism. Like many of the department's senior officers, Sternberg, a Civil War veteran, had honed his medical skills in the late nineteenth-century campaigns against the Indians in the American West. By the 1890s, new candidates for the corps learned their trade in the classroom. They had to take a rigorous entrance exam; in 1897, only 6 out of the 140 applicants passed. The surgeons underwent a five-month program of postgraduate education at the Army Medical School in Washington, where they studied bacteriology, sanitary chemistry, pathology, and military hygiene under a faculty that included such leaders in the discipline as John Shaw Billings and Walter Reed. Reed's academic title—professor of clinical and sanitary microscopy—captured the dramatic changes in military medicine since the Civil War. The microscope and bacteriological culture had taken their places alongside the scalpel and saw as tools of the trade.[23]

On the eve of the war with Spain, the professionalization of the Army Medical Department was still a work in progress. As was the case with practitioners in many other disciplines at the turn of the century, including law and civilian medicine, the military surgeons' claims to the rigor and status of a science outpaced the workaday reality. Under U.S. military law, neither their medical credentials nor their commissioned ranks entitled medical officers to command in the line. The surgeons could only make recommendations regarding camp sanitation to the line officers, who decided whether to implement them. In the past, many line officers had shown little patience with regimental surgeons, insisting that their intrusions interfered with military discipline. During the Civil War, one Union Army colonel had shrugged off his medical officer's complaint that the camp smelled of excrement, insisting the stench was "inseparable from the army. . . . [I]t might properly be called the patriotic odor." (No wonder Whitman recalled that war as "nine hundred and ninety-nine parts diarrhea to one part glory.") By 1898, many line officers and soldiers had grown more respectful of the surgeons' expertise, and the medical corps consequently wielded greater authority over camp conditions. But the national military school still did not offer a course in hygiene. And the advance of scientific medical knowledge since the Civil War had eliminated neither the patriotic odor nor the old tension between line officers and their medical men.[24]

Even within the medical corps, the new knowledge of the microbe did not overthrow older ideas about disease causation that centered on the relationship between bodily constitutions and their geographical environments. Major Reed and two other senior department surgeons, who toured many of the training camps in 1898, found that even "intelligent medical officers" instinctively looked for the sources of camp epidemics in "intangible local conditions inherent in the place." It was as if the old miasmatic theory of disease remained unchallenged. "There is apparent in man a tendency," noted Reed and his colleagues, "to believe in the evil genius of locality." Military surgeons still relied more on their senses than their microscopes, reflexively associating filth and foreign surroundings with pathogens.[25]

When Congress declared war against the Kingdom of Spain, on April 21, 1898, the U.S. Army consisted of just 28,183 men, stationed at eighty posts across the nation. Apart from the late-century campaigns against the Indians, in which many men of the current officer corps had participated, the Army had not fought a war in thirty-three years. By the end of May, the Army mustered in 125,000 Volunteers, men from all walks of life whose military experience was limited to service with their state volunteer militias, units of the National Guard. The regiments bound for Cuba and Puerto Rico assembled throughout the spring and summer in camps in the southeastern states. After Commodore George Dewey's victory in Manila Bay, the Army mobilized an expedition in the western states to steam across the Pacific and take possession of the Philippines. By mid-August, when the fighting with Spain ceased, the Regular Army and the Volunteers had a combined strength of over a quarter million men—the great majority of them inexperienced volunteers.[26]

The War Department and its medical branch were unprepared for this sudden buildup. Like the Army itself, Sternberg's Medical Department was a stripped-down affair during peacetime. The department had no stockpile of supplies and no ready reserve of field-tested surgeons. Many of the older surgeons had been serving at desk jobs and were in no shape to take the field. To the small corps of properly trained field surgeons were hastily added more than one hundred commissioned officers and nearly four hundred medical officers from the state militias. During the summer, the Army would add more than five hundred contract surgeons. The Medical Department suspended its rigorous examination requirement. Lieutenant Colonel John Van Rensselaer Hoff, a seasoned surgeon with the Medical Department, found among the volunteer surgeons "scarcely an officer who possessed the slightest knowledge of medico-military matters."[27]

Some of the civilians, however, were seasoned public health officers who brought that experience to the Medical Department. If military discipline was new to these men, the police power was not. Several of them would play leading roles in staging the overseas campaigns against smallpox. Dr. Azel

Ames, who served as a brigade surgeon with the U.S. Volunteers in Puerto Rico, had founded the board of health in Wakefield, Massachusetts. Dr. George G. Groff, who would serve with Ames as a director of vaccination in Puerto Rico, had a peacetime career as professor of organic science at Bucknell University and president of the Pennsylvania State Board of Health. Like many of the older surgeons of the Regular Army, Dr. Henry F. Hoyt was a veteran of the Indian campaigns—he called himself a "red-haired Indian fighter." But he had also served as commissioner of health for St. Paul, Minnesota, where he enforced smallpox vaccination and established a bacteriological laboratory before receiving his wartime commission as chief surgeon of the Second Division, Eighth Army Corps, bound for Manila.[28]

Smallpox loomed on everyone's mind as the troops and doctors streamed into the national assembly and training camps in Pennsylvania, Virginia, Florida, and Georgia. By the spring of 1898, the new mild type smallpox had spread across much of the South, shaping the War Department's decisions about where to locate the encampments. C. P. Wertenbaker, dispatched to South Carolina just two days after the declaration of war, advised strongly against using smallpox-ridden Columbia as an assembly area.[29]

Since 1834, Army regulations had mandated that all U.S. soldiers submit to vaccination. The Volunteers had their arms scraped as they mustered into service. Army reports and soldiers' letters home recounted the vaccine-induced fevers and inflamed arms that afflicted men in camps and aboard ships headed for the war zones. Lieutenant Colonel Hoff insisted the Army's vaccine was sound, attributing the soldiers' woes to the "hurry and turmoil" of the mobilization and the inexperience of the Volunteers' medical staff. The virtue of compulsion seemed ably demonstrated by the remarkable absence of smallpox in the assembly areas, as tens of thousands of soldiers mobilized for war in the midst of an emerging regional epidemic. Among more than fifty thousand Regular Army troops, only one smallpox fatality occurred on the mainland.[30]

The real horror of the national encampments turned out to be typhoid. The infectious disease had haunted armies since time immemorial, carrying the nickname "camp fever."

By 1898, typhoid fever held few mysteries for Army surgeons. They knew its causative agent (*Bacillus typhosus*), its mode of transmission ("the transference of the excretions of an infected individual to the alimentary canals of others"), and the sanitary measures that would keep it at bay (keeping troops from fouling their own water, food, and personal effects). But the surgeons, particularly those serving with the Volunteers, proved incapable of preventing its spread. The hastily constructed camps provided ideal conditions for an epidemic: poor drainage, a dearth of pure water, and thousands of undisciplined recruits, who, disregarding the entreaties of their medical officers, preferred the nearby woods and streams to the newly dug latrines. Typhoid took hold almost everywhere.[31]

The camp epidemics made a deep impression on the surgeons who would soon accompany the American regiments overseas. Lieutenant Colonel Hoff witnessed the suffering up close; he may even have felt some responsibility for it. Assigned as chief surgeon with the all-Volunteer Third Corps at Camp Thomas, in Chickamauga Park, Georgia, he arrived at the camp in May 1898, after the Regular Army troops had pulled out. By the end of June, Camp Thomas teemed with nearly sixty thousand green recruits and fifteen thousand horses and mules. One line officer remarked how the Volunteers had turned the campground into "a mass of putrefaction." No amount of quicklime could overcome it. For the American public, the typhoid horror stories told by the troops at Camp Thomas recalled the Confederate prisoner of war camp at Andersonville. "Bad Water, Unfit Food, Brutally Stupid Treatment," read one *New York Times* headline. More than ten thousand soldiers contracted typhoid fever at Camp Thomas that summer; 761 of them died. Even more unseemly was Camp Alger, an assembly center just an hour's ride from the Washington offices of the camp's namesake, Secretary of War Russell A. Alger. With its drinking wells driven too close to the regimental sinks, Camp Alger had become a "nursery of typhoid." Soldiers at the Florida encampments—Camp Tampa and Camp Cuba Libre—suffered, too. In all, nearly 21,000 American soldiers caught the disease in the national encampments during the summer of 1898, and 1,590 died. Most of the dead were Volunteers.[32]

Close on the heels of the camp typhoid epidemics came the highly publicized withdrawal from Cuba of the Fifth Corps, overwhelmed by typhoid, yellow fever, and malaria. With the fighting finished on the island by July

17, Colonel Roosevelt warned that 90 percent of the soldiers were inca
pacitated by disease and would, as *The New York Times* put it, "die like sheep
if left in Cuba." The plight of the Fifth Corps—compounded, some said,
by Major General William Shafter's refusal to cooperate with his medical
officers—confirmed the public's worst fears: America was sending its
young men to do battle with tropical diseases more deadly than Spanish
cannon.[33]

The health crises in the assembly camps and the Fifth Corps tarnished
the reputation of the War Department and emboldened critics of the
war. In September 1898, shortly after the cessation of hostilities, President
McKinley appointed a presidential commission, headed up by General
Grenville M. Dodge, to investigate the "charges of criminal neglect of the
soldiers in camp and field and hospital." The Dodge Commission's report,
released to the White House in February 1899 and made public the following year, concluded that the Army Medical Department, for all of the "good
work" it had done during the war, had committed "manifest errors," beginning with its failure to properly investigate the sanitary conditions of the
assembly camps. Modern scientific knowledge and professionalism had not
yet usurped the age-old dominance of disease over combat in the actuarial
tables of warfare.[34]

The tragedy of the assembly camps would continue to haunt and moti-
vate the surgeons of the Army Medical Department as they settled into new
positions with occupying regiments and the U.S. military governments in
Cuba, Puerto Rico, and the Philippines. The shame of the assembly camps
heightened the Medical Department's obsession with the health of the
troops on the ground. It contributed to the intensity with which the Army
prosecuted its sanitation and vaccination campaigns in all three places. And
it gave additional motivation to the scientific work of the Army medical
men as they pursued exciting new lines of research.

In 1901, Walter Reed and a team of colleagues in Cuba, in a bold and
risky series of experiments, confirmed the Cuban physician Carlos Finlay's
theory that yellow fever was spread by the *Stegomyia fasciata* mosquito
(now called the *Aedes aegypti*). Under the command of Major William C.
Gorgas, the Army launched a campaign to destroy the mosquito's breeding
grounds in Havana. By the summer of 1901, the *Stegomyia* had virtually

disappeared from Havana, and so had yellow fever. Reed expressed his relief in a private letter to Gorgas. "Thank God that the Medical Department of the U.S. Army, which got such a 'black eye' during the Spanish-American War, has during the past year accomplished work that will always remain to its eternal credit."[35]

A strong desire to clear the good name of their institution only begins to describe the range of aspirations and interests U.S. military surgeons carried with them or discovered within themselves in the cities, garrisons, and villages of Cuba, Puerto Rico, and the Philippines. Military surgeons went to extraordinary lengths to protect the troops in those tropical places. Over time the surgeons would turn their medical gaze outward, from a narrow professional concern for the health of the troops—the maintenance of a continually shifting cordon sanitaire—to a broader interest in governing the health of the civilian populations of the newly subordinated territories. These agents of the American nation seized upon the vast and (to their eyes) exotic field of medicine, administration, and humanitarian intervention opened up by the Navy's gunboats and the Army's rifles. The worlds they entered would never be the same.

The lingering shame of the national encampments did not diminish the air of sanitary superiority with which American military men and civilians took in the sights, sounds, and smells of their new tropical surroundings. Disembarking from Army transports and commercial steamships, the Americans first encountered the old Spanish port cities. Judging the coastal population centers of Cuba, Puerto Rico, and the Philippines by standards of cleanliness only recently (and all too incompletely) achieved in American cities, the occupiers attributed the unsanitary state of affairs in equal parts to the incompetence of their Spanish predecessors and the indifference of "the natives." "Nauseating odors" assaulted the nostrils of one American visitor to Havana: "dead animals abounded, garbage was encountered everywhere, and open mouths of sewers running in to the ocean and harbor were reeking." Captain L. P. Davison of the Fifth Infantry, newly installed as president of the San Juan Board of Health, described the Puerto Ricans as "a poverty-stricken and extremely dirty and mixed population, living in absolute violation of all civilized rules." In Manila, where residents reportedly thought nothing of relieving themselves at the side of the road or dumping chamber pots from windows, one American official advised his countrymen to walk in the center of the street and always carry an umbrella. To these Americans abroad, filth signified disease. And filth was everywhere.[36]

Wherever they went in these disorienting, humid cities, with their old Spanish churches and crude palm shacks, the Americans noted the traces of a disease they still associated with filth: smallpox. Army surgeons and U.S. health officials likened the epidemiological life of smallpox in these erstwhile Spanish colonies to eighteenth-century Europe, before the invention of vaccination. "[A]s was the case in Europe, so in the Philippines, it seems to be almost a disease of childhood," said one report. "The explanation of this is that all natives who have reached adult age were exposed in their childhood to smallpox, and those who did not contract it may be considered immune." If, as Captain Davison insisted, "Good sanitation is the visible sign of civilization," the unmistakable sign of barbarism and misrule was the pockmarked face of a dark-skinned native.[37]

Like most first impressions, the Americans' commentaries captured only the surface of things. To be sure, the Spanish colonial health systems had been halfhearted during the best of times; as *The Boston Globe*'s Philippine correspondent J. N. Taylor noted with contempt, they paled in comparison to the British sanitary measures in India. But the American occupiers failed to consider that the conditions they encountered might be anything out of the ordinary for these places. In fact, all three areas had suffered through mounting health crises during the late nineteenth century.[38]

Cuba, an island about the size of Pennsylvania that lay less than a hundred miles south of the U.S. mainland, had long been viewed by American health officials as a massive pesthole whose most notable export was yellow fever. The island's 1.8 million inhabitants had experienced an epidemiological crisis during the three-year-long Cuban insurrection against Spain, which lasted from February 1895 to August 1898. The vast majority of the estimated 290,000 Spaniards and Cubans who perished during that war, civilians and soldiers alike, died of starvation and infectious diseases. The most destructive force was the Spanish military policy called "reconcentration," which set a deadly precedent for modern counterinsurgency warfare that the British and the Americans would find irresistible. Aiming to break up rural support for the Cuban Revolutionary Army, the Spanish general Valeriano Weyler ordered the forcible removal of Cuban civilians from the countryside to the urban centers, where the *reconcentrados* lived in close squalor under a form of martial law. Some 400,000 civilians, roughly one quarter of the island's population, were forcibly concentrated into Havana and other cities already overrun with soldiers and refugees.[39]

"Hunger, starvation, and death were on every hand," wrote Clara Barton of her arrival with the Red Cross in Havana in February 1898. In normal times, the population of nineteenth-century Cuba was too dispersed to support endemic smallpox. But the reconcentration of the rural population and the movement of soldiers and civilians across Cuba created a dense network of disease transmission that fostered the epidemic spread of smallpox, yellow fever, and enteric fever. According to *The New York Times*, smallpox was the single biggest killer among the *reconcentrados*. "The people were unable to keep clean, unable to be vaccinated, even if willing, and they died by [the] tens of thousands," one longtime resident of Havana told the *Times*. During the lead-up to war with Spain, American newspapers inflamed the public with reports on Weyler's disease-infested camps. And the escalating events of the U.S. war with Spain in Cuba from April to July 1898—the American blockade of Havana, the naval assault, and a ground war centered around Santiago de Cuba—had further strained the health of Cuba. Neither tropical climate nor simple Spanish incompetence nor the alleged backwardness of the Cubans could have wreaked such epidemiological havoc. Political decisions made these epidemics.[40]

Puerto Rico did not have its own war of independence, and the health situation there in the 1890s was less dire. Still, disease shaped the course of the U.S. invasion. Yellow fever had so disabled the U.S. regiments in Cuba that when Major General Nelson A. Miles landed at Guanica on the southern coast on July 25, 1898, he did so with a small initial force of 3,500 troops shipped in from the states. (U.S. troop strength later grew to more than 14,000 men.) Despite their superior numbers, the Spanish did not put up much of a fight. General Miles ordered three columns of men north to San Juan, but news of the armistice arrived before the soldiers reached their destination. An Army medical officer reported that malaria was "prevalent in all the valleys," noting the "large pendulous abdomens and pale faces of the many little naked children." During the long occupation, thousands of U.S. troops made their garrisons in the midst of local communities, spreading microorganisms wherever they went. By September 1898, one quarter of the troops were on the sick list, suffering from dysentery, malaria, venereal diseases, and a few cases of smallpox.[41]

The last brief battle of the Spanish War took place in the Philippines on August 13, 1898. The surrender of the Spanish garrison to the invading Americans at Manila had been scripted by both sides in advance, enabling the Americans to prevent Aguinaldo's *insurrectos* from entering the city. In the Philippines, the U.S. troops marched into a health crisis that had been building for decades and which their presence and actions worsened.

An archipelago of seven thousand islands, most of them uninhabitable, distributed across a half-million square miles of ocean, the Philippines had been under Spanish rule since 1565. Roughly half of the eight million inhabitants lived on the big northern island of Luzon, home of Manila, a city of a quarter million. The Filipinos had never known Edenic isolation. But prior to the mid-nineteenth century, geographic obstacles and dispersed settlement patterns had reinforced local communities' separateness from one another and from the outside world. Even on a single island, villages were separated by the characteristic landscape of rugged, mountainous terrain rising up from broken coastal plains. Roads were few and travel arduous, particularly during the long rainy season. Local epidemics tended to remain local, running their course among the nonimmune inhabitants. The late nineteenth century brought population growth and an increasing connectedness: a proliferation of towns (pueblos), a stronger market economy, new steamship connections, and a rise in immigration to the coastal cities, mainly from China. As the long isolation of Filipino communities diminished, domestic and imported microbes circulated. By the 1890s, exposure to and mortality from infectious diseases had risen sharply, especially from malaria, dysentery, cholera, tuberculosis, and smallpox.[42]

The arrival of six years of war—first during the Filipino independence struggle against Spain of 1896–98, followed by the Spanish-American War of 1898 and the Philippine-American War of 1899–1902—caused the breakdown of the Spanish health system. Twenty-five thousand Spanish soldiers arrived in 1896. Between 1898 and 1902, roughly 122,000 U.S. troops would come, carrying microbial pathogens from North America and, more important, toting local disease agents from place to place in the islands. The U.S. Army reported nearly one-half million cases of illness in its ranks during the wars, roughly four sick reports per soldier. U.S. soldiers not only engaged the enemy; they fraternized with the civilians, drinking, gambling, having sex, and, all the while, spreading disease.[43]

As the four-month war with Spain gave way, in August 1898, to longer occupations in Cuba, Puerto Rico, and the Philippines, the responsibilities of the Army medical staff did not diminish. In the surgeons' eyes, threats to the good health of the soldiers in the garrisons abounded. Heat exhaustion and sunstroke were perennial fears, leading some in the Philippines medical staff to shed their U.S. military blues and campaign hats for khaki clothes and the white cork helmets favored by the British in India. Army surgeons advised that Filipino or Chinese laborers, presumably accustomed to the oppressive heat, be used for the heaviest manual labor, lest white soldiers succumb to heat exhaustion. Most surgeons and soldiers took it as axiomatic that under tropical conditions a white man's resistance to disease quickly deteriorated, making him especially susceptible to exotic microbes. Even diseases well known to North America seemed more threatening under such conditions. "[I]n this latitude and longitude," reported Dr. Henry Hoyt from the Philippines, smallpox was "very fatal, especially to the white man."[44]

The first American health interventions in Cuba, Puerto Rico, and the Philippines followed the territorial logic of the cordon sanitaire. As the British had done in India, the Americans aimed to create a kind of moving quarantine line, a zone of sanitary and immunological protection around the bodies of their soldiers. In the garrisons, this entailed frequent vaccinations of the troops, strict sanitation, and training the men in hygiene. But since the soldiers necessarily moved across spaces populated by indigenous (and thus "foreign") people, eliminating filth and disease among the most proximate of "the natives" became a military imperative. Those natives with whom the Americans were likely to come into contact, such as the citizens of occupied Santiago, San Juan, or Manila, were the first local communities targeted for sanitary intervention. In the early phase of the occupations, the medical officers expressed no loftier purpose for their work. "From the day of the invasion," said Lieutenant Colonel Hoff, chief surgeon of the U.S. Army's Department of Puerto Rico, "great care was taken to improve the sanitary surroundings of the troops and consequently of the people." Any sanitary benefits that might accrue to the people were incidental. As another Medical Department document put it, "[T]he health of the command depends on the health of the inhabitants."[45]

Army medical officers and their admirers likened their work to that of Heracles in the Augean stables, "the cleanser of foul places and the enemy of evil beasts." In all three of the territories, the Army and its medical staff took actions to sanitize the cities and towns where the Army located its garrisons. From the start, the measures blended police power and military force. "It is perfectly useless," one Army surgeon observed, "for any health officer to attempt to check an epidemic unless he can rule with a rod of steel." To clean up Santiago, Cuba, the U.S. military governor General Leonard Wood, himself a physician, named American businessman George M. Barbour as director of sanitation. "Major" Barbour's sanitary corps impressed local residents into labor, cleaned up the slaughterhouses and markets, shot stray dogs, and horsewhipped inhabitants caught relieving themselves in the streets. Military surgeons still viewed sanitation as the first defense against disease. U.S. troops stumbled into the "dirty little town" of Siboney, Cuba, to find an outbreak of yellow fever. Under the direction of military surgeon Colonel Charles Greenleaf, the soldiers expelled the Spanish and Cuban refugees and conducted a "vigorous" cleanup campaign. Army doctors did not yet understand the role of mosquitoes in spreading yellow fever. When their sanitation measures failed to check the epidemic, the soldiers burned the town to the ground.[46]

From the beginning, Army medical officers claimed for their actions a precedent in the American legal tradition of police power, which allowed for broad governmental intrusions into the everyday lives of American citizens. As Lieutenant Colonel Hoff said of his experience in Puerto Rico, sanitation there "resolved itself down to its simplest form, 'policing.'" How different were the Army's actions really, these officers suggested, from the countless instances when American governments had walked over indi-

vidual liberty and property rights in the name of the public welfare—
whether by driving brothel-keepers and saloon-keepers from town or by
regulating the operations of slaughterhouses, factories, and other noxious
trades? But in the United States, the legitimacy of police regulations had
always been closely tied to the sovereignty of the self-governing communities that enacted them. The very thinness of Hoff's analogy suggests how
far he and his peers were reaching for some foundation, other than military
superiority, for their actions.[47]

Smallpox became epidemic in each of the three major theaters of the
Spanish-American War during the fall of 1898. None of the epidemics involved the new "mild type" of the disease. All involved classic virulent
smallpox (variola major), presumed to be all the more deadly because of
its tropical origin. With thousands of U.S. troops, civilian personnel, and,
increasingly, entrepreneurs and their employees settling into all three
places, the Army surgeons were determined to bring the disease under control. Their first attempts were localized campaigns centered exclusively on
protecting the troops, and those efforts revealed how entrenched in the
thinking of the Army was the old idea of smallpox as a filth disease. In San
Juan, Captain Davison reported, "From the class of people attacked it is
believed that cleanliness of person, proper living and morals are at least
equal to vaccination as a preventive of smallpox." Smallpox became epidemic in the Holguin district of Cuba that November. Under Brigadier
General Leonard Wood, the Second Volunteer infantry and its medical
officers disinfected the towns, burning entire neighborhoods of thatched
huts and vaccinating 30,000 residents. The Army also treated nearly 1,200
people with smallpox. By January, the epidemic had ended. Smallpox,
though, would remain a "constant and increasing danger in Cuba" until
the U.S. military government mandated universal childhood vaccination
on the island in 1901.[48]

In all three tropical theaters, the Army Medical Corps responded to the
first threats of smallpox by cleaning the troops' immediate geographical
environments and vaccinating the bodies of the natives who inhabited
them. Gradually, the military surgeons would turn their attentions outward
to the health of the native population as a whole. As they did, their campaigns would assume a scale and intensity they could not have anticipated

when the war with Spain began. The most formidable efforts took place at the farthest reaches of the new American empire, in Puerto Rico and the Philippines.

Lieutenant Colonel John Van Rensselaer Hoff steamed into the port of San Juan in October 1898. It must have felt good to have the stench of Camp Thomas behind him; unlike most Army medical officers Hoff was struck by the natural beauty of this "fair isle." The port had been churning all month, as ships off-loaded American goods and personnel and the last remaining Spanish soldiers and officials left the island. The incoming chief surgeon of the U.S. Army's new Department of Puerto Rico had nothing but contempt for his predecessors. "Robbed of all superfluities," Hoff declared, "the real reason we are in the Antilles today is because our people had determined to abate a nuisance constantly threatening their health, lives, and prosperity." Of course, there had been "other factors of certain value, strategic, mercantile, humanitarian and sentimental," Hoff conceded. But all these merely underscored the true casus belli: "Spain was maintaining a pesthole at our front door and we could no longer endure it." Forget the *Maine*. In Hoff's decidedly contrarian view, the Spanish-American War was at bottom a police action, taken against a delinquent neighbor that had allowed its properties to overflow with yellow fever and smallpox. Compared with Cuba, Puerto Rico was the lesser threat, but this island, too, "stretched a threatening hand toward our shore." According to the police power tradition, the proper response to a nuisance was to abate it—kick out the bad neighbor and clean up the place.[49]

Fifty years old and full of vigor, Hoff had one of those nineteenth-century careers whose very contemplation induces in the modern mind a sharp sense of historical vertigo. In Hoff's half century, industrial capitalism—with its steamships and telegraph wires and guns—had shrunk the seas, shortened the horizon, and accelerated time itself. Thus it was that Hoff, a Dutch-descended native of the Empire State, could serve during the 1890s in the last of the U.S. Army's frontier Indian Wars, an imperialist venture in its own right, and the first of its modern overseas colonial wars. (The career-to-date of Hoff's fellow New Yorker, Theodore Roosevelt, galloped across a similarly improbable canvas: from ranching in the Dakota Badlands to inspecting tenement sweatshops in Manhattan to storming San Juan Hill.)[50]

In an era when few American physicians had much formal training, Hoff, a second-generation Army medical officer, graduated from Union College and earned his medical degree from the College of Physicians and Surgeons in New York. He practiced surgery in western Army forts, lectured in college classrooms, and traveled in Europe, where he studied the medical services of the great European armies. Hoff distinguished himself on those battlefields Gilded Age America had to offer, the brutal and increasingly one-sided engagements with the western Indian tribes. In 1890, he led a detachment of Hospital Corps litter bearers in the Battle of Wounded Knee, the Army's last major engagement with the Sioux, earning the Distinguished Service Cross for his "conspicuous bravery and coolness under fire." A Protestant in a missionary age, he believed his sanitary work in Puerto Rico and later in the Philippines exemplified the duties of race and nation that his countrymen had taken up after the war with Spain. "Driven by fate we, as a nation, have ventured without our shores," he wrote, "[and] accumulated our full share of the white man's burden."[51]

Hoff stepped ashore in San Juan, a city of 32,000 people, to find a big job waiting for him and no organization in place. "Nothing was and everything had to be," he recalled, "not a record, nor a book in which to keep it." In the coming months, Hoff and his medical staff would evolve into a de facto public health service for Puerto Rico. Under his command, the surgeons pursued health campaigns on a scale the U.S. government had never before attempted on the mainland. They enacted new sanitary codes based upon the police regulations of the American states. They studied diseases and taught modern hygiene to an impoverished rural people. By far the most ambitious of these efforts—"the first big sanitary undertaking of our Government in the tropics," Hoff proclaimed—was the quixotic campaign to vaccinate the entire population of the island. It was "an immense task," another Army surgeon agreed, "and possible only through military agency."[52]

To Hoff and his staff, Puerto Rico was terra incognita. The smallest and easternmost island of the Greater Antilles, with a landmass three quarters the size of Connecticut, Puerto Rico lay roughly a thousand miles southeast of the recently incorporated U.S. city of Miami. A range of rugged mountains called the Cordillera Central divided the island's wet Atlantic-facing northern half from its dryer Caribbean southern half. The climate was unmistakably tropical, with a rainy season that stretched from August to December. Getting around was hard. The island possessed few good harbors, most notably at San Juan on the north and Ponce on the South. But for the old Spanish military road that ran between those cities, there was, as one frustrated Army surgeon noted, "not a good road on the island." In the wet season, the bridle paths and streams that connected the villages and barrios along the Cordillera Central flooded and became impassable for weeks.[53]

The Puerto Ricans confounded the Americans. "The laws, language, customs, institutions, and aspirations of the people were all strange, and in many respects, very difficult of comprehension," said one military government report. American eyes puzzled over the island's peculiar settlement patterns. Puerto Rico seemed to them a contradiction in terms: an overpopulated rural country. Fewer than one tenth of the people lived in cities, the rest in barrios, villages, and small farms. The chief industries centered on the land, especially sugar cultivation (along the coast), coffee growing (in the mountains), and cattle raising (along the southern plateaus). To the occupiers, the islanders' problems resembled those the Americans associated with the tenement districts of their own industrial cities. The crowded palm-thatched huts were "entirely without any arrangements for the disposal of excreta." Three quarters of the population lived in "miserable hovels," subsisting upon "the merest apology for food." Although the island had a small professional elite, including well-trained physicians, few Puerto Ricans could read. And the people suffered prodigiously from intestinal diseases as well as endemic tuberculosis, smallpox, and a deadly disease called anaemia.[54]

The multiracial population of the island defied the familiar American racial taxonomies. Major Ames described Puerto Rico uneasily as "the only 'white' island of the Antilles." American racial norms had consolidated in recent years, with the Supreme Court recognizing the southern states' peculiar "one drop" rule (which made a person with even a small amount of African "blood" black in the eyes of the law). Slavery had survived in Puerto Rico until 1873, and black laborers predominated on the sugar plantations. But Americans were uncertain how to classify the rest of the people. Assistant Surgeon General C. H. Alden reckoned that three fifths of the population was "pure white and almost entirely of Spanish descent." But the Puerto Ricans did not subscribe to the American one-drop rule, and U.S. officials complained of "the natural tendency [of] the mulatto to deny the existence of negro blood in his veins."[55]

Under military rule the Puerto Ricans inhabited an unstable political space within, but not of, the United States. During the invasion, General Miles had issued a proclamation to the inhabitants, assuring them that the American troops marching through their villages carried the "banner of freedom." "This is not a war of devastation," declared the old Indian fighter, "but one to give to all within the control of its military and naval forces the advantages and blessings of enlightened civilization." As the Army built roads, opened schools, and cleaned cities, the military government said its duty was to protect and prepare the inhabitants for their "ultimate destiny" as "an autonomous, self-governing, and law-abiding people." But the military governor lacked clear instructions as to whether the people ought to enjoy the guarantees of the U.S. Constitution. Practical political economy soon answered that question. In January 1899, President McKinley ordered the military authorities to collect customs duties on U.S. imports to the island. The commanding general reasonably concluded that the Constitution had not "followed the flag." A divided U.S. Supreme Court later reached much the same conclusion.[56]

Smallpox was present on Puerto Rico in the best of times, but the rapid spread of the disease in late 1898 sent waves of alarm through the command. The influx of tens of thousands of Spanish and American soldiers and the hurried movements of displaced civilians had carried the disease far and wide. The exact scale of the outbreaks is uncertain. According to one report issued by Surgeon General Sternberg, from December 15, 1898, to February 11, 1899, sixteen villages and towns reported more than 550 cases. The volunteer surgeons Major Ames and Major Groff insisted that post surgeons had reported 3,000 cases during November and December alone. Army officials agreed that the epidemic constituted, in Sternberg's words, "a constant menace to the people and to the material interests of the island." "It steadily took on greater proportions," Ames recalled, "no part of the island being free from it, until nearly all the country barrios (precincts) were infested."[57]

Hoff kept a close watch on the emerging epidemic. His first response was to shore up the cordon sanitaire by ensuring that all troops were well vaccinated and keeping their garrisons clean. But with the soldiers living so closely with the native population, the line could not hold. Stateside news-papers ran stories on local boys who contracted smallpox in Puerto Rico; some of the soldiers died from the disease, others carried it back with them to infect American communities. The pressure rose for stronger measures. For Hoff, the turning point came when neighboring islands, including St. Thomas, Puerto Rico's closest neighbor and a significant port of trade, quarantined against the island. Other ports, including New York, were considering the same action. For a colonial administration dependent on customs taxes, the situation was serious. If America's largest port ceased doing business with the place, this tropical possession, funded largely by the flow of goods to and from the United States, would be in deep trouble. "[T]he success of our first effort in military government was hanging in the balance," Hoff recalled. He paid a visit to the U.S. governor general, Guy V. Henry.[58]

According to the official Spanish legend, vaccine had first arrived on Puerto Rico in European bodies aboard European ships. If this were true, vaccine would have made much the same voyage to the New World as the variola virus itself. In 1518, a quarter century after the arrival of the Span-ish, an epidemic of smallpox decimated the indigenous Tainos. Nearly three centuries later, on November 30, 1803, an expedition set sail from Corunna, Spain. Led by Dr. Francisco Xavier de Balmis, the Spanish court physician, its mission was to bring the new technology of Jennerian vaccination to the people of the vast Spanish empire in Latin America and the Pacific. On board were twenty-two foundlings, whose young bodies had never suffered the smallpox. Before setting sail, Balmis inoculated the first child with vac-cine; as the expedition made its way across the seas, the doctor kept the "precious fluid" alive by vaccinating each child in succession, with pus from the vaccine sore of the previous child, in a continuous arm-to-arm relay.

In this way, the Balmis expedition delivered "the beneficence of the King" to the Canary Islands, Puerto Rico, and Caracas, before breaking into two expeditions. One sailed to South America via Havana, the other to Vera Cruz and Mexico. Balmis picked up a fresh group of twenty-six children in Mexico before setting sail from Acapulco for the Philippines.[59]

In at least one respect, the official Spanish story cheated history. Balmis had arrived in Puerto Rico two months too late. With an epidemic of smallpox sweeping the island, a resourceful San Juan doctor named Francisco Oller (a military surgeon, no less) had procured some vaccine lymph from British St. Thomas. By the time of Balmis's arrival, more than 1,500 residents of San Juan had already been vaccinated. The royal doctor promptly denounced Oller as a fraud and his vaccine as worthless.[60]

Under Spanish rule during the nineteenth century, Puerto Ricans grew accustomed to the occasional spectacle of public vaccinations. During smallpox epidemics, the public vaccinator would call the people of a barrio or village to assemble. Using virus secured from the Central Institute of Vaccination at San Juan, the vaccinator would inoculate a calf or two, drive them to the center of each village or barrio at an appointed date, and set about vaccinating the people with fluid taken directly from the animal. In the final years of Spanish rule there still existed much popular opposition to the medical practice, not least because the vaccine orders seemed so arbitrary and the operation itself so often proved ineffective. In the 1890s the Spanish compulsory vaccination measures, according to Colonel Hoff, had been "honored in the breach more than in the observance," especially in the rural areas. The greatest number of vaccinations performed in a single year was fewer than 25,000 (in a population exceeding 900,000 people). American officials may have exaggerated the defects of Spanish "misrule," but Puerto Rico did suffer a high incidence of smallpox during its final decade under Spain. In 1890, smallpox killed 2,362 people—accounting for 9 percent of the island's deaths that year. For the decade, deaths from smallpox averaged 620 per year. A far greater number were left scarred or blinded by the disease. Lacking an effective measure against the disease, many Puerto Ricans regarded smallpox with a fatalism that Army medical officials too readily interpreted as indifference.[61]

The incidence of smallpox on Puerto Rico at the start of 1899 was not dramatically out of proportion with that of the last years of Spanish rule. Smallpox killed an estimated 522 islanders in 1898, somewhat *below* average for recent years. What was new was the presence of a regime determined to bring its full might to bear in fighting the disease.[62]

On January 27, 1899, the American governor general Guy Henry issued General Order No. 7. "The inhabitants of this island must be protected from smallpox," it proclaimed. "Every resident who has not had this disease will be vaccinated, and hereafter all infants must be vaccinated before reaching the age of six months." Hoff took charge. The order parceled the island into five geographical areas of roughly 200,000 inhabitants, each presided over by an Army medical officer designated as a director of vaccination. Each director, including Major Ames and Major Groff, would command a staff of surgeons, inspectors, and Hospital Corpsmen. The directors would report any neglect by Puerto Rican authorities to carry out the order's provisions.[63]

General Order No. 7 called for compulsory public health on a scale never before seen in Puerto Rico or, for that matter, any territory under the direct jurisdiction of the U.S. government. As the Army carried vaccination to the people, the Marine-Hospital Service ran a quarantine at the island's ports, requiring all arriving passengers to show proof of vaccination and all travelers bound for the mainland to undergo the procedure. The vaccination campaign was all the more ambitious given the serious technological, geographical, and political obstacles that stood in the way. Dozens of centers of contagion existed, including barrios high in the mountainous interior whose people had little experience with sanitary authority. Most Puerto Ricans lived under crowded conditions, moving constantly between the countryside and the towns for trade and work. Like other Western physicians in colonial settings, the military doctors complained of the "indifference" of the "natives." Ames noted the difficulty of delivering modern health to "hundreds of thousands of unregistered people, mostly ignorant and scattered, speaking foreign tongues, and unused to sanitary controls." Unbeknownst to him, his complaint echoed those sounded by Kentucky health officials as they struggled to enforce vaccination in Appalachia.[64]

The most pressing challenge at the start of the Puerto Rico campaign was to secure a reliable vaccine supply. Vaccine did not survive long in heat (a problem that would bedevil tropical vaccination programs until the invention of a heat-stable, freeze-dried vaccine in the 1950s). Vaccine tubes shipped from the mainland usually lost their potency by the time they reached Puerto Rico. The British imperial experience in India (as well as the Spanish record in Puerto Rico and the Philippines, assuming the Americans actually consulted it) taught that ineffective vaccines engendered popular resistance to vaccination in general. The solution the Army settled upon—to produce vaccine on the island itself—was, in keeping with colonial administrative imperatives, the cheapest. It was also the most ambitious. Governor General Henry put Major Ames in charge of the operation.[65]

Azel Ames was one of the hundreds of civilian physicians recruited, as he said, in "hot haste" for the war with Spain. Born in Chelsea, Massachusetts, in 1845, Ames had served in the Union Army and graduated from Harvard Medical School. The unifying theme of his career to date was the way it had blended seamlessly—and, on at least one occasion, scandalously—public service and private interest. As a physician in Wakefield, Massachusetts, he founded the town's board of health. His résumé also included stints as a temperance crusader, state factory inspector, and administrator of U.S. government pensions. Ames had gotten himself embroiled in a national scandal in the 1880s, when he was indicted for abusing his position with the Boston board of medical examiners in the U.S. pension office by extorting bribes from claimants. The jury was hung, and Ames was never convicted. In none of his writings about his Puerto Rican experience did Ames mention any previous experience with vaccine production. But vaccine manufacture in the late nineteenth century remained a largely pastoral pursuit. And in Ames's Wakefield it was not unknown for a physician to keep a calf on hand to meet his patients' needs for lymph.[66]

The Puerto Rican vaccine farm was the capstone of Ames's career, pulled off, if he said so himself, on a "grand scale . . . practically in the open air, in a new country, by unskilled hands." Ames based his operations on rented fields at Coamo Baths, an area of "fine cattle country" on the dry coastal highlands near the island's south shore. He supervised the construction of stables, corrals, and a camp large enough to sleep over a hundred men—Army surgeons, a pathologist, cattlemen, guards, cooks, couriers, and teamsters. Fresh meat, ice, and medical supplies from the United States were hauled almost daily up twenty-three miles of rough roads to the camp. Working through a native intermediary, a local cattleman named Simón Moret, Ames leased twelve hundred head of local cattle.[67]

The viability of the entire campaign depended on a few glass tubes of lymph imported from the United States. Army medical officers doubted that vaccine virus originating in a temperate climate could retain its "virility" in the moist heat of the tropics. Ames received his little supply, transported eighteen hundred miles by sea then hauled by pack animal up the dusty military road to the camp. An assistant inoculated forty cows with the lymph. The camp waited for the virus to incubate in the animals' bodies. They waited the requisite six days, and then waited some more. Nothing. Ames would recall these hours as the "worst and most anxious" of his life. He and his assistants furiously searched the calves' undersides for the telltale vesicles, the blister-like sores from which the vaccine lymph could be harvested. But there were none. It appeared that the entire shipment of American lymph was useless and that "the undertaking must be abandoned." After twenty-four sleepless hours, Ames and an Army pathologist, Dr. Timothy Leary, took one last look. This time they discovered that many of the animals had scablike "crusts" and "cones." Removing them, the physicians discovered bases flowing with lymph. The doctors realized their mistake. The animals at Coamo had not been confined in stables, as they would be on an American vaccine farm. The vaccine vesicles had been broken by the underbrush, grass, and the calves' own rough tongues. From the ring-shaped bases on the calves flowed "the finest lymph." The operation was soon producing sixteen thousand good-quality vaccine points a day.[68]

The Army's next challenge was to get Major Ames's vaccine to—and into—the people. For this, the Army relied on the Puerto Ricans. Native runners, on foot and pack animals, negotiated the narrow paths and mountain streams to deliver fresh vaccine to the villages and barrios. The Army vaccination directors determined that the population was so dispersed and difficult to reach that the common American method of house-to-house vaccination would be unfeasible. Instead, they would have to bring the people to the vaccinators. The directors set the schedule and secured the cooperation of the alcaldes, the local officials who served in the island's seventy-one municipalities as "mayor, school commission, county commissioner, and sheriff, all in one."[69]

The original plan envisioned using Army Hospital Corpsmen to vaccinate the people. But the medical officers decided to hire native physicians and their assistants, called *practicantes*, for the job, believing (no doubt correctly) that local vaccinators would be "more acceptable to the people." Each director was allowed to hire ten vaccinators, who would be paid in gold. According to the Army's instructions, the *practicantes* must conduct their business at specified hours, "wear white coats," and "always be neat and clean." The skin of the native physicians might be dark, but American medical authority would remain clothed in white. As the physicians and *practicantes* performed their vaccinations—scraping the arms of men, women, and children with the sharp edge of Dr. Ames's points—native scribes recorded each person's name, address, sex, age, and race. In this way, the vaccination teams produced for the U.S. military government its first record of the population. Major Groff found that a single vaccinator, "if hurried," could vaccinate three hundred people in an eight-hour day. Some Army surgeons never overcame their low regard for the Puerto Ricans. S. H. Wadhams, a Yale Medical School graduate who served as an Army surgeon in Ponce, claimed American vaccinators could do "three to five times as much work as the natives."[70]

The military government found it necessary to continually ratchet up the coercion in its vaccination campaign. No vaccination riots were reported, but physicians working for the military government had to take care. When one was asked why he had failed to vaccinate all the spectators at a cockfight near where he was working, he answered, "I feared a thrashing." On March 18, Governor General Henry raised the pressure. He ordered the alcaldes to "use all their authority to secure prompt compliance on the part of the people." The order, which Major Ames himself drafted, contained an important new provision. No one who failed to produce an official certificate of vaccination "shall be admitted to any school, public or private, shall travel by any public conveyance, visit any theater or any place of public resort, engage in any occupation related to the public, or receive employment."[71]

Through the island vaccination campaign, Americans were indeed learning the art of colonial statecraft. Ames's provision pulled a largely illiterate, rural population into a documented relationship with the U.S. military government. It also imposed a new discipline on local institutions, by holding public and private authorities—schoolteachers, managers, and employers—legally liable for enforcing the measure. The strategy worked. "From hills and valleys, hamlets and municipalities, young and old flocked to the vaccinators," Ames recalled, "like John Chinn's Wuddahs, in Kipling's story of the vaccination of the Satpura Bhils. Often two or three hundred, old and young, would be still waiting, unvaccinated, when darkness closed the day's work. . . . Sometimes the vaccination was continued by lamplight to relieve the pressure." The metaphor of police power could no longer contain such ambitions. Like the Kipling character to whom he now compared himself, Major Ames saw himself as the vanguard of a civilizing mission, carrying into those overgrown hills and valleys the vaccine of a paternal American nation.[72]

Even then, some Puerto Ricans refused to cooperate. In June, the new governor general, George Davis, imposed new penalties for people who refused to be vaccinated: a $10 fine, plus $5 for each subsequent day in violation. Anyone who failed to pay the fine would "suffer ten days' imprisonment and thereafter five days for each additional offense." This penalty was harsh even by the toughest standards of vaccination measures in the United States.[73]

On June 25, 1899, Chief Surgeon Hoff received a telegram from Coamo Springs announcing that the vaccine farm had produced its one-millionth point. A week later he brought the campaign to a halt. The Medical Department's vaccination program had carried vaccination to the people on an unprecedented scale. According to Hoff, the vaccinators had performed nearly 860,000 operations (742,062 vaccinations and 116,955 revaccinations) in a period of five months. And the vaccine produced at Coamo Springs was, by contemporary standards, good, with a reported success rate of 87.5 percent. Colonial administrators always kept the bottom line in view. Hoff noted with satisfaction that the entire vaccination campaign had cost only $43,000.[74]

By the end of June, the "head-fire of vaccination" had stopped variola in its tracks. In the decade before the arrival of the U.S. Army, the annual death rate from the disease had averaged 620 people. From January 1 to April 30, 1900, not a single death from smallpox was reported. And during the two years after completion of the eradication campaign, the annual death rate dropped to just two. Under the new superior board of health established under Colonel Hoff's leadership in June 1899, the vaccination of infants continued. U.S. health officials continued to seek out the elusive people Hoff described as the "'submerged' 200,000 who escaped in the grand attack" of 1899.[75]

The new colonial civil administration installed by the Americans on May 1, 1900, would learn soon enough that the vaccination campaign had not permanently eradicated smallpox. The flow of people and goods from the mainland brought variola minor to the island. Still, American officials and journalists followed Ames's lead in touting the Puerto Rican campaign as a "lesson to the world." Ames hoped it would overthrow the "present belligerent skepticism" toward compulsory vaccination in America and Europe. "Small-pox still holds the first place in the list of preventable, readily-disseminated contagious diseases, common to all parts of the globe," he wrote. And in Puerto Rico, the Army had shown how it could be eradicated. Surely, that colonial knowledge could be used to wipe out smallpox on the U.S. mainland.[76]

The question of exporting the Puerto Rican model—or importing it to the American mainland—hinged on how one felt about public health enforced by a form of martial law. Although the smallpox eradication effort had relied heavily upon local physicians to bring vaccination to the people, it had been a military operation through and through. No government agency on the United States mainland would have dreamed of securing a monopoly on vaccine production—in most parts of the United States, there were no regulations at all on vaccine production. To secure the cooperation of local officials, the Army wielded powers of influence and coercion that neither state nor federal authorities could have matched in a place like Middlesboro, Kentucky. That went double for the capacity to impose vaccination upon an unwilling people. When a Kentucky health inspector named W. M. Gibson visited the smallpox-afflicted mountain folk of Jackson County in August 1898, he sent word to his boss, Secretary J. N. McCormack of the state board of health. Dr. Gibson promised to vaccinate "all who willingly apply." But he told McCormack that if he really wanted to see vaccination enforced in Jackson County, "you will find it necessary to send four battalions of four hundred soldiers each, well armed." Gibson wasn't joking.[77]

That Kentucky fantasy would become a reality in the Philippines. There U.S. health officials would have a good deal more than four battalions marching with them. The situation in the Philippines was different not only from Jackson County, but also from Puerto Rico. In the Philippines, the fighting was far from over when the vaccinators began their work.

If the Puerto Rico vaccination campaign deserved pride of place as America's "first big sanitary undertaking . . . in the tropics," the U.S. government's fight against smallpox in the Philippines took place on an altogether grander scale. The Southeast Asian archipelago was both far more distant and far more expansive than the Caribbean island. The Army had many more men on the ground there. Some 125,000 U.S. Regular Army and Volunteer soldiers had arrived by 1902. And their mission proved far more dangerous, as the "splendid little war" against Spain gave way to a three-and-a-half-year guerrilla war with Aguinaldo's republican forces. The people of the archipelago were eight times more numerous than the Puerto Ricans, and, in the eyes of the American occupiers, they inhabited a lower rung on the racial hierarchy. Lieutenant Colonel Hoff, who participated in both campaigns, sized up the Philippine challenge: "It is no small problem to sanitate eight millions of semi-civilized and savage people, inhabiting scores of islands with the aggregate area of a continent."[78]

At their most open-minded, some U.S. officials envisioned a gradual process of "benevolent assimilation." The indigenous elite would be fitted for eventual self-government while the political participation of the "wild" (and especially the non-Christian) masses would be deferred indefinitely. Typical of U.S. officials, most military surgeons regarded the Filipinos in general as racially inferior and indifferent to filth and disease. Not long after he supervised the hut-torching sanitation campaign in Siboney, Cuba, Colonel Charles R. Greenleaf served as chief surgeon of the Army's division of the Philippines. "The native," he wrote, "does not know how to take care of himself; not only is he ignorant of the first principles which govern the preservation of health, but he has never had anybody sufficiently interested in him to instruct him in these principles." Above all else, the presence of endemic smallpox in the islands showed the Filipinos' desperate need for a wise government to take them in hand.[79]

No doubt American military doctors believed their dispatches presented realistic accounts of the beliefs and practices of a backward "Oriental" people. In fact, these dispatches drew upon a common Western language of medical high modernism that had developed in the long nineteenth-century era of nation-state formation and colonial expansion. Within the ever widening world of cross-cultural contact, European and American physicians measured the civilization of subordinate groups along a scale of sanitary evolution. Although in this case U.S. surgeons were talking about Filipinos they encountered in the zones of combat and occupation, the nineteenth-century medical literature teemed with strikingly similar descriptions of the "primitive" health practices of Native Americans on the western reservations, Mexican Americans in the southwestern border-lands, African Americans in the rural South, Puerto Ricans of the Cordillera Central, and the "new" immigrants from Southern and Eastern Europe streaming into America's industrial cities. European and American tropical medicine was embedded in a larger cultural and scientific process—one so homogeneous in its assumptions as to constitute a common project. Self-consciously modernizing nations used medical knowledge to comprehend, categorize, and govern the most marginal peoples within their territories. Tropical medicine was never merely a handmaiden of colonial domination, but it served that purpose exceedingly well.

Of course, for the Filipinos smallpox was not a figment of anyone's colonial imagination. The disease stole children from families. It left thousands blind or scarred. In the absence of effective preventive measures, smallpox was an unavoidable fact of life—like the passing of the seasons. According to American estimates, forty thousand Filipinos died annually from smallpox during the final years of Spanish rule and the early years of the Philippine-American War. Army surgeons working in the provinces reported that between one third and one half of the inhabitants had already suffered smallpox. Greenleaf reckoned that the children of the islands were "practically the only susceptible persons, the adult population being as a rule immune and representing the 'survival of the fittest.'" Although smallpox did the greatest harm to the islands' poorest inhabitants, it did not spare the most elite. In March 1900, Aguinaldo's own infant son died of smallpox while in U.S. captivity in Manila.[80]

The Filipinos were not indifferent to the many diseases that afflicted their families. Popular conceptions of health, disease, and medicine varied from place to place in the archipelago, combining indigenous traditions with Christian teachings and Western medical ideas acquired from the Spanish. Filipinos did not simply reject Western medical ideas; they incorporated those that seemed to work into their own systems of belief. According to commonly held Filipino medical beliefs, diseases could be caused by natural events: smallpox was known to be a disease of the dry months and was expected to wash away with the rains. Or diseases could be brought on by supernatural forces; if smallpox persisted through the rainy season, local healers used rituals to appeal to the spirits. Americans expressed dismay at the Filipinos' practice of treating sickness and death as social events that required the close presence of friends and relatives. The occupiers used strong measures to compel Filipinos to remove the sick from their crowded huts, to promptly bury the dead, or destroy clothing contaminated with smallpox. Some Filipino practices must have fostered the spread of smallpox, but they also powerfully expressed the relationships of family to community and between the natural and supernatural orders.[81]

Many Filipinos had formed specific ideas about the various Western medical practices that the Spaniards had tried (usually halfheartedly) to introduce into their lives. Filipinos could be receptive to Western medical ideas and medicines—at least those that worked. Vaccination had not proven itself worthy of their confidence. In 1897, more than ninety years after Balmis first brought vaccine to the archipelago, the Spanish regime maintained a central vaccination establishment in Manila and employed 120 public vaccinators (*vacunadores*) in the various provinces. But many Filipinos spurned them. Traditional beliefs about the seasonal cycles of smallpox made vaccination seem unnecessary. Filipinos had all too often seen that even after the *vacunadores* did their work, smallpox returned. As Americans discovered, the tropical heat often rendered vaccine inert and thus ineffective. Filipinos had observed that vaccination sometimes spread skin diseases. In fact, the Spanish health authorities' use of the arm-to-arm method for propagating vaccine carried the real risk that syphilis and other infectious diseases might be transmitted from person to person. Reports coming in to the Spanish authorities from the provinces during the 1890s indicated that vaccination had been "completely discredited."[82]

From the outset of the U.S. occupation of Manila, on August 13, 1898, the Army's top brass and medical officers were preoccupied with preserving the health of the troops. That in itself was a tall order. From 1898 to 1902, the Army reported a half-million cases of illness, more than four sick reports for every soldier who served. Every regiment suffered from dysentery, malaria, and venereal diseases. Typhoid fever and smallpox were continuing threats. While the Army's sickness data documented the suffering of white American soldiers, they also showed the power of soldiers to carry infection across the archipelago, transmitting pathogens between local disease environments that had previously been isolated from one another.[83]

As the bustling base of operations for the U.S. command—not to mention for American business interests—Manila topped the Americans' sanitary agenda. The first measures, as Colonel Greenleaf said, were "designed mainly with a view to the preservation of the health of the troops." But the Army approached the cleanup of Manila with the determination of people planning to stay awhile. The commanding general established a board of health for the city, under the leadership of Major Frank S. Bourns, a surgeon with the U.S. Volunteers. The Atlanta physician possessed an exceptional knowledge of the Philippines, having spent four years there on two previous zoological and ornithological expeditions.[84]

By October 1898, Bourns's health board had nearly eighty employees, including a number of European-educated Filipino physicians. A few of the physicians, such as Dr. Trinidad H. Pardo de Tavera, had been members of Aguinaldo's government at Malalos. The board divided Manila into ten sanitary districts, appointing a local physician for each; hired eight municipal midwives; and established special hospitals for smallpox, leprosy, and venereal diseases. Working with the new American department of sanitation, the board cleaned streets, staged house-to-house inspections, and seized and burned the corpses of inhabitants who had died from contagious diseases. Bourns's activities extended beyond purely sanitary matters.[85]

As relations with Aguinaldo's independence movement deteriorated, late in 1898, Bourns began relying on the local physicians and his growing network of personal contacts to acquire, as he modestly put it, "a good deal of information not otherwise obtainable." Bourns's talents were not lost on the Army generals, who assigned him to investigate reports of insurgent activities in the city and suburbs. By the time the first shots were fired in the Philippine-American War in February 1899, Major Bourns had established within the health board what he called a "little spy system, by which we were enabled to keep track, especially in the city, of everything that was going on on the insurgent line." Information-starved U.S. military governments in both Puerto Rico and the Philippines exploited the wealth of local knowledge produced by sanitary campaigns. But Bourns pursued that aspect of a health officer's job with unusual intensity, blending epidemiological surveillance with outright espionage.[86]

The first scattered cases of smallpox had appeared among the U.S. troops in Manila in September. Surgeon General Sternberg reported that the men had been "visiting the huts of the natives, in many of which smallpox of a very malignant character was prevailing." In November, as U.S. forces in the vicinity grew to 21,000 men, more cases appeared among them and also among the 2,000 Spanish prisoners in Manila. The Army's first response was to "protect the command by vaccination." All the Spanish prisoners were vaccinated, and Major General Elwell S. Otis ordered the revaccination of all enlisted men in the islands. After much of the vaccine sent from San Francisco to meet this demand proved inert, Major Bourns reestablished the old Spanish vaccine farm in the city and started harvesting fresh lymph by inoculating local carabao (water buffalo). The situation worsened in December when smallpox infected the Twentieth Kansas Volunteers, killing ten. An investigation traced the origins of the outbreak to a cluster of native inhabitants who lived across the street. By this time, as one U.S. soldier recalled, the rising incidence of smallpox "caused the Army Medical Corps to view the general health and living conditions of the civil population as being pertinent to the well-being of the American command."[87]

Bourns established a corps of city vaccinators, starting with six men, then doubling their number, then increasing them further after the new year as smallpox became epidemic in Manila. On the eve of war, Major General Otis sent Secretary of War Alger a dispatch on the health of the troops: "Smallpox causes apprehension. Entire command vaccinated several times. Twelve physicians engaged several weeks vaccinating natives." Soon the suburbs of Manila were in flames, and terrified residents poured into the congested central city. In the Tondo district, seventy-five Filipinos died of smallpox in March. Bourns's corps aggressively enforced vaccination, meeting "considerable opposition" at first, applying force when necessary. In all, the corps vaccinated eighty thousand residents of Manila that winter. By the end of March, the danger appeared to be over. And by June, Bourns reported, "there were but 4 cases of smallpox in the entire city of Manila."[88]

The Manila epidemic had demonstrated, to the satisfaction of the Army Medical Department, the importance of vaccinating not just the soldiers but the local inhabitants among whom they lived. It had been a costly lesson: from September 1898 through March 1899, the troops in Manila had suffered 236 cases of smallpox. Eighty-five of these were mild cases, reported as varioloid (smallpox modified by previous vaccination). But among the other 151 cases, more than half of the patients (77) had died, seeming to confirm that smallpox in this tropical zone was especially deadly to white men. The presence of *any* smallpox among the U.S. troops in Manila created a public relations problem for a War Department still reeling from the typhoid revelations. American newspapers reported the tragic deaths of young soldiers from the disease and advised parents to disinfect letters received from their boys in the islands. To Surgeon General Sternberg's chagrin, English antivaccinationists seized on the news that smallpox had broken out among the U.S. troops to cast doubt upon the efficacy of compulsory vaccination.[89]

But to Army officials, a strategy of wholesale compulsory vaccination—of the troops and the most proximate natives—had proven its merits. For the people of Manila, the U.S. vaccination campaign far exceeded anything they had experienced under their previous rulers. The Spanish regime's chief vaccinator had reported just 9,136 vaccinations performed in the city during the four years prior to October 1898. During the next five months, the U.S. military government vaccinated 80,000 inhabitants.[90]

The U.S. Army took the war beyond Manila to the provinces, across the central Plain of Luzon and to other islands. By 1900, Aguinaldo's forces adopted guerrilla warfare, which the Americans derided as uncivilized. The Army countered with increasingly violent tactics, including interrogation of suspected insurgents and spies using a form of torture known, in an especially perverse marriage of medical metaphor and military technique, as the "water cure." The Medical Department had its hands full, establishing military hospitals, caring for the wounded, and moving with the line. Controlling infectious diseases remained a high priority. During 1899, the most deadly year of the campaign for the Army, 475 soldiers and officers died from wounds of battle, another 139 died from "other forms of violence," and 709 succumbed to disease, "principally diarrhea and dysentery, smallpox and typhoid." During the same year, nearly two thousand soldiers were sent home due to sickness. Throughout the war, smallpox weighed heavily on the minds of the military surgeons. They vaccinated the troops with great regularity.[91]

Preserving the health of the troops called for measures to sanitize their environment and the peoples who inhabited it. Many of the soldiers were stationed in one of five hundred garrison towns, which soon grew overcrowded with migrants fleeing the war-torn countryside. Stationed indefinitely in garrison towns, the troops mixed promiscuously with the inhabitants, consuming palm wine, gambling, and fraternizing. "The most crying need in the early days of our occupancy of the Provinces was to check the ravages of smallpox," Greenleaf recalled. He advised the U.S. military governor, General Arthur MacArthur, that each garrison should have an army surgeon designated as "health officer," "special orders being given for the vaccination of the population of the towns and neighboring barrios as far as the people could be reached." As one U.S. colonial official reported, the garrison surgeons "had great latitude, and under their direction compulsory vaccination was usually enforced." The surgeons also used "arbitrary military compulsion" to enforce "simple regulations as to cleaning streets, putting dirty premises in order, [and] tying up pigs."[92]

A comprehensive plan for vaccination in the provinces emerged. The idea appears to have originated with a military surgeon named Major Louis M. Maus. Major Maus knew how infection could rip through an army. He began the Spanish War as chief surgeon with the VII Corps in Miami and Jacksonville, bearing witness as more than 5,000 of the soldiers in his care were hospitalized with typhoid fever. Reporting from Bautista, Pangasia, in February 1900, he warned that smallpox prevailed among the people of the towns and was "not rare among our troops as a consequence." It would be impossible, he said, to "stamp out this disease among our soldiers, in spite of the frequent and careful vaccinations among them, until the natives are themselves protected." Not long after this report, the Army issued orders to vaccinate all people within the reach of the division of the Philippines, which at that time included seven provinces north of Manila. Within five months, more than 600,000 Filipinos certified by the medical department as protected from smallpox by vaccination or previous infection.[93]

For the remainder of the war, the Army enforced vaccination wherever it went. Sometimes that meant rounding up the inhabitants with bayonets in order to inoculate them. By 1901, the American vaccine farm in Manila was turning out a million points a year, and more farms were being established in the provinces. The U.S. Marine-Hospital Service established a quarantine station at the entrance to Manila Bay, vaccinating crews and passengers aboard ships approaching the principal harbor of the colonial government. On December 2, 1901, the Philippine legislature put its seal on this emerging American regime, mandating the compulsory vaccination of the entire population of the Philippines. The law ensured that the Army's wartime policy would continue under the colonial regime long after the war's end.[94]

The narrow military imperative of the cordon sanitaire was, during the course of the war, yielding something grander, a more far-reaching system of public health. As it did so, Army surgeons, U.S. officials, and other commentators began to publicize these measures as not merely efficient but humane. As early as 1901, Colonel Greenleaf declared that the Army's sanitary measures were winning hearts and minds. "This object lesson in one of the most important characteristics of the American people, humanity in war, has made a deep impression on the Filipinos, and has been an important factor in winning their allegiance to our Government." The following

year, James LeRoy declared that the surgeons' "little and big services to the
natives . . . not only helped make the name 'Americanos' more acceptable"
but "were also genuine responses to the call of humanity." But as Greenleaf
and LeRoy well knew, willing submission to vaccination remained far from
universal in the pueblos and barrios. Understandably, Filipinos associated
the vaccinators, even those who were native physicians, with the foreign
army they served. The work of vaccinating the natives, conceded Greenleaf,
was "by no means devoid of danger, and several instances occurred where
the vaccinators were captured by insurrectos or kidnapped by the inhabitants and killed."[95]

A fuller articulation of the humanitarian argument did not emerge until
the final, brutal months of the Philippine-American War. The argument
gained momentum at precisely the moment when the American public
learned of the scale of atrocities carried out by the U.S. Army in the Philippines and the devastating effects, upon Filipino civilians, of the Army's
counterinsurgency policy of reconcentration. That policy would forever be
associated with a single forsaken place: Batangas.

In the days before Christmas, 1901—as anti-imperialists in the U.S. Congress denounced the nation's Philippine policy ("We have witnessed the
spectacle of an American Army numbering over 70,000 men engaged in conquering a people struggling for independence," thundered Representative
Samuel W. McCall of Massachusetts)—the peasants of Batangas province
made their way, by winding paths and rough roads, to the pueblos. Market
towns in a prostrated agricultural region with precious little left to sell or
barter, the pueblos were fast taking on a new kind of urban life as Army
"reconcentration zones." Traveling alone, with families, or alongside their
entire uprooted barrios, the Batanguenos stepped past soldiers, through
fences, and around garbage into the teeming camps. They carried rice, chickens, and the pieces of their bamboo and nipa palm huts. On the day after
Christmas, by order of Brigadier General James Franklin Bell of the Third
Separate Brigade, all property remaining beyond the perimeters would be
subject to confiscation or the torch. Any man they found out there without
proper papers would be arrested, or shot if he dared to run away.[96]

Located in southwestern Luzon, just a few hundred miles from the offices of the U.S. colonial government in Manila, Batangas province was one of the last strongholds of the Filipino resistance, the base of operations for insurgent leader General Miguel Malvar. The Army command had organized the Third Separate Brigade for this chief purpose: to "pacify" Batangas and thus bring an end to an increasingly unpopular colonial war.[97]

By the fall of 1901, that war had seemed all but over. Guerrilla bands laid down their arms in one province after another. Then came Balangiga. In a village on the island of Samar, guerrillas and villagers wiped out a U.S. infantry company. American newspapers likened the "Balangiga Massacre" to Little Big Horn. Dispatched on a punitive campaign against Samar, Brigadier General Jacob H. Smith ordered his men to kill everyone over the age of ten and turn the island into a "howling wilderness."[98]

In Batangas, too, the customary distinctions between hostiles and civilians yielded to claims of military necessity. "Practically the entire population has been hostile to us at heart," General Bell explained in a Christmas Eve circular to his officers. "To combat such a population," the war must be made "insupportable." By then Bell's brigade had driven most of the province's 300,000 inhabitants, already weakened by famine and disease, into the zones. American soldiers put the Batanguenos to work grading roads, digging latrines, and gathering rice in the countryside. With the rectitude of a Victorian charity official, Bell insisted "great pains" be taken not to "pauperize the people." He told his men to exact respect in the camps for the American flag, the troops, and "the great nation to which they pertain."[99]

A veteran of the late-century Indian Wars, General Bell did not invent the counterinsurgency tactic of reconcentration: the forcible removal of civilians from hostile areas into militarized towns in order to isolate guerillas from their base of support. The history of U.S.-Indian policy had been, in a sense, one long process of forcible removal. More recently, European armies had resorted to this specific tactic in colonial wars against indigenous, nonwhite populations. The Spanish general Valeriano Weyler's brutal reconcentration campaign in Cuba during 1896–98 had failed to crush the independence movement, but it had caused the deaths of an estimated 100,000 Cubans and tilted American public opinion toward war. In 1900, the young Winston Churchill touted his nation's forced reconcentration of rural South Africans in the Boer War. Still, the severity of the U.S. Army's "concentration camps," as some newspapers referred to them, shocked the American public. General Bell and his superiors defended the camps as a legal and necessary measure to protect the population from bandits and guerrillas. But within the United States the policy strengthened opposition to the war.[100]

Wherever it was undertaken, forced population concentration caused epidemics. In the British concentration camps for Boers and Blacks in South Africa, 42,000 civilians died. Public revelations of the policy's human cost weakened public support for imperialism in England. Like rural people across the Philippine archipelago, the Batanguenos had already suffered mightily in recent years. The effects of the two successive wars—the collapse of the Spanish health system, the movement of troops about the provinces, the destruction of draft animals by rinderpest, and the dislocation and impoverishment of the rural population—intensified the health crisis that had been ongoing for some years. These events elevated the Filipinos' susceptibility to disease while increasing their exposure to pathogens.[101]

The Batangas reconcentration zones seethed with disease and death. One Army officer described the camp he commanded as "some suburb of hell." Vampire bats circled overhead awaiting the day's supply of corpses. Thrown together with thousands of desperate strangers in the filthy zones, the Batanguenos suffered outbreaks of cholera, dysentery, and smallpox. With so many U.S. soldiers living in the camps, something had to be done.[102]

And so as U.S. infantrymen hunted down and killed General Malvar's guerrillas in the coastal flatlands and rolling hills of Batangas, Army doctors enforced vaccination in the camps. The Army hired eighty Filipino vaccinators. According to the official "Directions for Vaccination of Natives," sent in January 1902 to all station commanders in Batangas by Army Chief Surgeon William Stephenson, the vaccinators moved in pairs through the teeming reconcentration camps, each accompanied by an American soldier. As the vaccinating party entered the crowded huts and houses, they drove the inhabitants toward the rear walls. The vaccinators set to work at the doorway, scraping the arms of the men, women, and children as they were led, one by one, into the light. Only those showing recognizable pockmarks were exempt. General Bell himself took a special interest in the minute details of the compulsory vaccination effort. "It can easily be understood by all how serious the difficulty and detrimental to our plan of campaign [it] would be should an epidemic of small-pox break out in any protected zone," he declared in an urgent telegram to his post commanders. "Whenever any opposition is met by vaccinators Commanding Officers will detail sufficient troops to round the people up and compel them to submit to vaccination." While the Third Brigade "pacified" Batangas, the Army's vaccinators performed 300,000 operations—a number roughly equivalent to the entire population of the province—in just two months.[103]

Along with General Smith's Samar expedition, the Batangas military campaign led to Senate hearings on Army misconduct that sullied the Army's reputation for years. Still, General Bell's Third Separate Brigade accomplished its mission. By February 1902, several guerrilla bands had surrendered, some after killing their own leaders. On April 16, General Malvar, his wife seriously ill, surrendered, followed soon after by the remaining insurgents in Batangas and on Samar.

President Theodore Roosevelt chose the anniversary of the Declaration of Independence—July 4, 1902—to declare a formal end to the Philippine "insurrection." More than 4,200 American soldiers died in the war, adding to the toll of 2,910 killed by combat and disease in the Spanish-American War. The death toll among the Filipinos reached a different order of magnitude. In addition to some 20,000 Filipino soldiers, hundreds of thousands of civilians perished from causes attributable in full or in part to the war, including killing by U.S. soldiers, famine, and especially diseases such as typhoid, tuberculosis, bubonic plague, smallpox, and a horrific two-year epidemic of cholera. All of which helps to explain why so many of the Filipinos interviewed for an oral history project during the 1950s would remember the first lethal years of the American colonial regime less for its battles or its atrocities than for its plagues.[104]

In the spring and summer of 1902, the U.S. Senate hearings and newspaper reports confronted the American public with shocking stories of Army misconduct in the Philippine War: interrogations by water torture, summary executions, and scorched-earth tactics. To many, the most disturbing revelation was that the U.S. Army had resorted to methods reminiscent of the "Weylerism" that had helped arouse American support for a war against Spain in the first place. In the end, General Bell survived with his reputation impugned but his career intact. At the height of the postwar debate, a veteran of the Army Hospital Corps named Edward Curran tried to set the record straight. In a letter to *The New York Times*, Curran praised General Bell for the "humane and meritorious concentration" in Batangas, where the corpsman had proudly participated in the strenuous effort to "vaccinate all of these people."[105]

Curran's letter was one small entry in a much larger argument unfolding in American public life, an argument that extolled the exceptional humanity displayed by the U.S. Army and colonial governments during and after the Spanish and Philippine wars. Beginning in 1902 and extending to President Taft's 1911 Philadelphia speech and beyond, an outpouring of official commentary, newspaper and magazine editorials, books, and personal remembrances urged that the sanitary work of the Army Medical Department had shown that characteristic which Chief Surgeon Greenleaf had described as distinctly American—"humanity in war." Arriving in San Francisco in June 1902, Major General Loyd Wheaton offered a humanitarian balance sheet of the Philippine War. "The devastations of war have cost many lives and the loss among the natives has no doubt been large," General Wheaton said, "but when one takes into consideration the hundreds of thousands of lives that have been saved by reason of the sanitary precautions of the American Army and Civil Commission, that loss by war seems infinitesimal." Wheaton referred specifically to the "compulsory vaccination [that] was held in every province, town, and throughout the country. In that way we saved thousands of lives."[106]

The New York Times, a stalwart supporter of American expansion abroad and compulsory vaccination of the urban masses at home, applauded Wheaton's speech. "The anti-imperialist, with his tender regard for the inclinations and preferences of all races except his own, will doubtless object that it is no favor to save the lives of people by forcing them to follow customs and endure Governments distasteful to them," the *Times* noted. "[B]ut with the world as small as it is nowadays, this argument is decidedly weak. . . . The unsanitary have become public enemies, and modern war, with its enormous evils, does spread habits of clean living among 'natives' and the 'un-progressives' whom it leaves alive." As American officials, commentators, and scholars praised the new levels of sanitation, hygiene, and health that the American efforts had brought to the peoples of Cuba, Puerto Rico, and the Philippines—from the old Spanish ports to the rural interiors—a new rhetoric of justification for military action crystallized. U.S. military medicine had preserved the health of the soldiers, protected American commercial interests, and saved the lives of countless natives.[107]

Health administration would remain an integral part of U.S. colonial rule in the Philippine archipelago—and also a principal means of justifying that rule. Americanized Manila stood as a model of the healthful city. In the 1904 fiscal year, the board of health had vaccinated 213,000 people in Manila and an additional 1,007,204 people in the provinces—well over one eighth of the entire population of the archipelago. American-made vaccine, packed for shipment in special boxes of ice, was reaching the people of the interior on horse-drawn *carromatas*, in water-borne *bancas*, and on the backs of Igorot runners. Local officials placed orders for vaccine over the telegraph wires the Americans had installed. Marine-Hospital Service surgeons vaccinated thousands of sailors each year in the harbors and pressed shipping firms to employ only persons holding the Service's blue vaccination cards.[108]

By 1906, the Philippine Commission was boasting of the real possibility of eradication: "The day should not be far distant when smallpox will disappear from the Philippines." The following year, Dr. Victor Heiser, the U.S. director of health, stated the argument in its baldest form. "During the year there has been unquestionably less smallpox in the Philippines than has been the case for a great many years previous. . . . In fact, if any justification were needed for American occupation of these islands, these figures alone would be sufficient, if nothing further had been accomplished for the benefit of the Filipinos." Between the arrival of the U.S. troops in the summer of 1898 and 1915, some *18 million* vaccinations were performed in the Philippines under American rule. The Filipinos, according to U.S. officials, had come to accept vaccination as an effective and necessary measure, suggesting, if true, a dramatic transformation of medical beliefs in a very short time.[109]

With the end of the war, the question of force became the greatest political liability of U.S. colonial health policy. Significantly, in 1904 the Philippine

Commission ordered that public vaccinators would henceforth be "prohib-ited from using force in accomplishing vaccinations." Individuals who re-fused to submit to vaccination would be tried in the courts. All of these ongoing efforts did not succeed in completely wiping out smallpox on the is-lands. The tropical climate continued to render much of the American-produced vaccine useless. But the efforts did dramatically reduce the incidence of smallpox there and laid the groundwork for the Philippines to become, in 1931, the first Asian country in which the disease was eradicated.[110]

At a time of pervasive opposition to compulsory vaccination at home and abroad, U.S. health officials presented the vaccination campaigns in Puerto Rico and the Philippines as evidence of the efficiency of compulsion. Azel Ames touted the Puerto Rico campaign as "A Lesson for the World." Surgeon General Walter Wyman of the U.S. Public Health and Marine-Hospital Ser-vice declared, "No greater proof as to the efficacy of vaccination exists than in the Philippine Islands." For Dr. John E. Snodgrass, assistant to the director of health in Manila, the truth of that proposition could be seen in the scarless faces of the rising generation of Filipinos. "The only argument necessary to explode the theories of the anti-vaccinationists," he proclaimed before the Panama-Pacific International Exposition in 1915, "is to compare the visages of the children of today with those of their parents."[111]

FIVE

THE STABLE AND
THE LABORATORY

Far from the battlefields of the nation's first overseas colonial wars, American health officials on the U.S. mainland encountered rising resistance after 1900 to their own widening war on smallpox. The contentious politics of smallpox control centered on the growing divide between public health authorities and the public itself regarding the risks of vaccination.

Turn-of-the-century Americans lived in a world filled with risk. Each year one out of every fifty workers was killed on the job or disabled for at least four weeks due to a work accident. Railroad and streetcar accidents annually killed and maimed tens of thousands of people. Children worked in mines, stole rides on the back of moving cars, and played stickball in alleys carpeted with horse manure. Apart from a few things recognized by the courts as "imminently dangerous," such as arsenic or nitroglycerin, product liability did not exist. The average American breadwinner carried just enough insurance to cover his own burial.[1]

During the first two decades of the twentieth century, a spate of new progressive social policies would create an enlarged role for the American government in managing the ordinary risks of modern urban-industrial life. The resulting "socialization" of risk, though narrow by the standards of Britain and Germany, was a dramatic departure for American institutions that prized individual freedom and responsibility. European-style social insurance gained traction in the first American workman's compensation laws, enacted in forty-two states between 1911 and 1920. Mothers' pension programs (launched in forty states during the same decade) provided aid to families that lost the wages of the "normal" (male) breadwinner due to his sudden death or disability. In tort law, too, the courts had women and children first in mind as they imposed tougher standards of liability upon railroad corporations. U.S. social politics still had a long way to go before a recognizably modern national welfare state insured its citizens against the financial insecurities of old age, or an American court seriously entertained the argument that an exploding Coke bottle entitled the injured party to compensation from the manufacturer. But the foundation was laid, in the social and political ferment of the Progressive Era, for a government that would one day promise its citizens "freedom from fear."[2]

Arriving just as the American people and their policy makers began to seriously debate these issues, the turn-of-the-century smallpox epidemics raised broad public concerns about the quality and safety of the nation's commercial vaccine supply. The ensuing controversy caused ordinary Americans, private physicians, and public officials to revise old expectations about risk and responsibility and the role of government in managing both.[3]

By the fall of 1901, the wave of American epidemics had carried smallpox to every state and territory in the union. The new mild type smallpox was the culprit in the majority of places, but deadly variola major struck several major American cities, particularly in the Northeast. Compulsory vaccination was the order of the day, enforced at the nation's borders, in cities and towns, at workplaces, and, above all, in the public schools. The public policy was a boon to the vaccine industry, driving up demand for smallpox vaccine. American vaccine makers of the day ranged in size from rising national pharmaceutical firms such as Detroit's Parke, Davis & Company and Philadelphia's H. K. Mulford Company (a U.S. forerunner of today's Merck) to the dozens of small "vaccine farms" that sprouted up around the country. To meet the unprecedented demand for vaccine-coated ivory points or capillary tubes of liquid lymph, the makers flooded the market with products, some inert, some "too fresh," and some seriously tainted. Complaints of vaccine-induced sore arms and feverish bodies filled the newspapers and medical journals. Every family seemed to have its own horror story.

Popular distrust of vaccine surged in the final months of the year, as newspapers across the country reported that batches of tetanus-contaminated diphtheria antitoxin and smallpox vaccine had caused the deaths of thirteen children in St. Louis, four in Cleveland, nine in Camden, and isolated fatalities in Philadelphia, Atlantic City, Bristol (Pennsylvania), and other communities. In all but St. Louis, where antitoxin was the culprit, the reports implicated vaccine. Even *The New York Times*, a relentless champion of compulsory vaccination, expressed horror at the news from Camden, the epicenter of the national vaccine scare. "Vaccination has been far more fatal here than smallpox," the paper told its readers. "Parents are naturally averse to endangering their children to obey the law, claiming that the chances of smallpox seem to be less than those of tetanus."[4]

Pain, sickness, and the occasional death after vaccination were nothing new. But the clustering, close sequence, and staggering toll of these events was unprecedented in America. Newspaper stories of children dying in terrible agony—their jaws locked and bodies convulsing, as helpless parents and physicians bore witness—turned domestic tragedies into galvanizing public events. Allegations of catastrophic vaccine failure triggered extraordinary levels of conflict between angry citizens and defensive officials. In one typical incident, which occurred as the ninth Camden child entered her death throes, the health officials of Plymouth, Pennsylvania, discovered that many parents, ordered to get their children vaccinated for school, were secretly wiping the vaccine from their sons' and daughters' arms.[5]

Jolted from their professional complacency, physicians and public health officials were forced to reconsider the existing distribution of coercion and risk in American public health law. In one sense, compulsory vaccination orders, whether they applied only to schoolchildren or to the public at large, already socialized risk. The orders imposed a legal duty upon individuals (and also parents) to assume the risks of vaccination in order to protect the entire community from the presumably much greater danger of smallpox. Spreading the risk of vaccination across the community made its social benefit (immunity of the herd) seem a great bargain. As any good progressive knew, the inescapable interdependence of modern social life required just such sacrifices for the public welfare and the health of the state. Still, the state did almost nothing to ensure vaccine quality. The bacteriological revolution spawned a proliferating array of "biologics"—vaccines, antitoxins, and sera of endless variety—that were manufactured in unregulated establishments and distributed, by the companies' druggist representatives and traveling detail men, in unregulated markets. The risks of these products lay where they fell—on the person left unprotected by an inert vaccine or poisoned by a tainted one.[6]

The situation illustrates the larger dualism of American law at the turn of the century. Ordinary Americans, particularly working-class people, were caught between the increasingly strong state presence in their everyday social lives and the relatively weak state regulation of the economy. And the government insulated itself from liability. In a leading decision, handed down just three years before the Camden crisis, the Georgia Supreme Court took up the question of whether a municipal government could be sued for injuries caused by bad vaccine used by its public vaccinators. The answer was an unblinking No. Citing "a principle as old as English law, that 'the King can do no wrong,'" the court refused to allow a resident of Rome, who had submitted to vaccination "under protest," to sue the government for using "vaccine matter which was bad, poisonous and injurious, and from which blood poisoning resulted." To allow such a case to proceed, the court warned, "would be to paralyze the arm of the municipal government, and either render it incapable of acting for the public weal, or would render such action so dangerous that the possible evil consequences to it, resulting from the multiplicity of suits, might be as great as the smallpox itself." The arm of the state was protected; the arm of the citizen was not.[7]

Supporters of compulsory vaccination defended the policy in a quasi-scientific rhetoric of risk assessment. From the expert point of view, lay concerns about vaccine safety were steeped in ignorance and fear, which should have evaporated in the face of hard statistical evidence. Officials assured the public that vaccines were safer than ever: "the preparation of glycerinized vaccine lymph has now been brought to such perfection that there should be no fear of untoward results in its use," Surgeon General Walter Wyman said three years before Camden. Even if untoward results did arise, the social benefits of vaccination outweighed the costs. As the *Cleveland Medical Journal* put it, "Better [by] far two score and ten sore arms than a city devastated by a plague that it is within our power to avert."[8]

The vaccine crisis of 1901–2 revealed that cost-benefit analysis was not the only way Americans thought about risk. When the *Times* observed that

Camden parents reasonably concluded that vaccination had become more dangerous than smallpox, turning the public health argument on its head, the paper made a rare concession to vaccination critics. As the *Times* said, the incidents were "furnishing the anti-vaccinationists with the only good argument they have ever had." But most worried parents would not have called themselves "anti-vaccinationists." And much more was involved in the rising popular resistance to vaccination in 1901 than a cool-headed consideration of quantifiable facts.[9]

Perceptions of risk—the intuitive judgments that people make about the hazards of their world—can be stubbornly resistant to the evidence of experts. This is because risk perceptions are mediated by experience, by culture, and by relations of power. Certain factors tend to elevate the sense of risk that a person associates with a specific thing or activity, even in the face of countervailing statistical data. A mysterious phenomenon whose workings defy the comprehension of laypeople causes more dread than a commonplace hazard. A hazard whose adverse effects may be delayed, rather than immediate, heightens perceived risk. Significantly, perceived risk tends to spike when the hazard is not voluntarily undertaken. This is especially true when the social benefits claimed for a potentially hazardous activity are not readily apparent to those ordered to undertake it.[10]

All of which helps to explain why in the fall of 1901 popular perceptions diverged so radically from the official line on vaccine safety. A century after the introduction of Jennerian vaccination, vaccines remained mysterious entities—even to the companies that made them and the physicians who used them. Many American communities had experienced neither a smallpox epidemic nor a general vaccination in over fifteen years, increasing both the public's sense of complacency about the disease and its unfamiliarity with the prophylactic. By force of law, local health boards and school boards ordered citizens to assume the risks of vaccination. Many did, some eagerly, some grudgingly, some only with a billy club against their back. Then the St. Louis and Camden tragedies shocked the nation. Public confidence in the vaccine supply, already shaky, plummeted. Opposition to compulsory vaccination, already strong, surged. Ultimately, these events pierced the veil of official certitude and corporate confidence. Vaccine companies publicly accused each other of peddling poisonous virus. Some health boards suspended vaccination orders. Others launched investigations of vaccine purity and potency. In medical meetings, newspaper columns, and statehouse floors across the country, the debate increasingly turned on a single issue: the right of the state to regulate vaccines. In the fall of 1901, regulation was a controversial idea. A few months later, it was federal law.[11]

A South Jersey industrial city of 76,000 people, Camden lay just across the sewage-choked Delaware River from Philadelphia. Times were good. Camden's population had grown by 30 percent during the 1890s. Decent jobs could be had at the Pennsylvania Railroad and in the city's ironworks, chemical plants, shoe factories, cigar companies, lumber mills, oil cloth factories, and woolen mills. Though the presence of immigrants and other newcomers was more keenly felt than in the past, Camden people remained overwhelmingly white and American-born, a generation or more removed from Europe. Crowded tenements of the sort found in New York and Chicago were scarce. Wage earners lived in low-slung neighborhoods of single-family homes. Like most communities, the people of Camden invested their pride and dreams in the rising generation. In September 1901, eight thousand children took their seats in the city's thirty-two public schools. By mid-November, half of those desks would be empty.[12]

The trouble started on October 7. Eight-year-old Pearl Ludwick took ill with smallpox, followed, in quick succession, by her father, an oil cloth printer, and all seven of her brothers and sisters. Only Pearl's mother was spared the pox; those days must have been among the most trying of her life. Then Pearl's father and eldest brother rose from bed one night and, both delirious with the fever, bumped a table, which knocked over a lamp. The ensuing blaze burned the Ludwick house to the ground—but not before the Ludwicks got out and hundreds of neighbors rushed to the scene. All, of course, were exposed to smallpox. With this improbable chain of events commenced the Camden smallpox epidemic of 1901–2.[13]

New Jersey had seen little smallpox during the past sixteen years, and vaccination had fallen out of practice. But in 1901 smallpox seemed to be causing trouble everywhere in the United States, including Philadelphia.

That summer, anticipating an epidemic year, the New Jersey Board of Health issued a public warning. "An extensive outbreak of small-pox can be prevented with absolute certainty if vaccination of all susceptible persons is secured," the board declared. "[T]he question now arises, Shall general vaccination be done before a great calamity compels resort to this preventive measure, or must there first be startling losses of life to arouse parents, guardians, school boards, the public, and in too many instances the health authorities also, to a realizing sense of their duty to institute precautions against the spread of this pestilential disease?" No matter how you parsed that question, the message was dead serious. But it took the Ludwick family fire to bring its meaning home to Camden.[14]

Camden authorities ordered a municipal pesthouse built, and physicians worked long hours to meet the "rush to get vaccinated." For those families who still needed convincing, the Camden Board of Education announced that it would enforce an 1887 state law that authorized local boards to exclude unvaccinated children. The Camden Board of Health president, Dr. Henry H. Davis, who happened also to be the medical director of the school board, dispatched vaccinators to the city schools. The Camden Medical Society opened a free vaccine station on Federal Street, in the heart of the city. And many residents were vaccinated by private physicians or, on the cheap, by the neighborhood druggist. Within a month, an estimated 27,000 people—more than one third of the city's residents—had undergone vaccination, including five thousand public schoolchildren. And the scraping continued. Across the city, children and adults alike had the sore arms and fresh scars to show for it.[15]

The state board advised physicians to exercise care when performing the procedure. "The operation of vaccination should be conducted with aseptic precautions," the board instructed, "and none but glycerinized lymph from a trustworthy producer should be employed." The board was referring to liquid vaccine that had been treated with glycerin, which acted as a preservative and killed bacteria in the product. Glycerinized vaccine was the state of the art. Whether from a sense of political propriety or fair play to the Philadelphia area's many vaccine companies—including H. M. Alexander's Vaccine Farm, H. K. Mulford Company, and John Wyeth & Brother—the board refrained from endorsing any make of vaccine and offered no advice as to how anyone might distinguish the "trustworthy" from the more dubious products on the market. Trust was a commercial transaction, not a public dispensation.[16]

In early November, word spread in Camden that a sixteen-year-old boy named William Brower had come down with tetanus. Few of life's hazards caused parents more worry than the infectious disease most folks called lockjaw. The New York writer W. J. Lampton called it "one of the strangest and most horrible maladies known to man." In 1900, more than 2,200 Americans died from it. The tetanus bacillus was discovered in 1884 in a Göttingen laboratory. Since then, scientists had found germs in hay dust, crumbling masonry, garden soil, and, especially, horse manure. Turn-of-the-century America—from the farms to the cities—crawled with the stuff. Even so, as Army Surgeon General Sternberg noted in his treatise, *Infection and Immunity*, simply ingesting bacilli-rich filth would not cause infection. Nor was tetanus contagious. The bacilli did not grow in the presence of oxygen. It usually took a traumatic event—a wound of some kind, the narrower and deeper the better—to introduce bacilli into a human body in a way that could cause infection. The classic culprit was a rusty nail—not because of the chemical composition of the rust itself, but because it made the surface of the nail rough enough to hold an abundance of bacilli which the sharp, skinny nail could drive home without much bleeding. Every Fourth of July, hundreds of American boys caught tetanus after cutting their hands with toy pistols.[17]

The symptoms of lockjaw were terrible. William Brower suffered them all. The son of a plumber, the boy had seemed in fine health until he fell suddenly ill around November 1. He suffered a high fever. He felt the telltale stiffness in his face. His jaws tightened like a vise. Excruciating contractions spread from the jaw and neck to all the muscles of the body. His spine arched, as convulsions racked his body. The doctors administered the tetanus antitoxin, a relatively new product with a low rate of success. No one expected the boy to survive. According to the *Philadelphia North American*, William's mother Sarah said, in her grief, "Never, never again shall I have one of my children vaccinated." William had been vaccinated nineteen days earlier. To his parents there seemed no better explanation for his misery. The trusted family physician who had vaccinated William, Dr. William H.

Kensinger, disagreed. "Vaccination doesn't produce tetanus; that I know," he said.[18]

Then came the news that sixteen-year-old Lillian Carty was critically ill with tetanus. The daughter of a railroad clerk, Lillian had been vaccinated twenty-one days earlier by Dr. S. G. Bushey, the city coroner and a prominent member of the Camden Board of Health. Lillian's parents posted a sign at their front door, asking passersby to keep quiet, because the slightest noise agitated her and sent her into convulsions. Antitoxin was administered. No one expected her to survive.[19]

Neither Brower nor Carty was the first child to die. On November 11, Thomas B. Hazelton, age eleven, the son of a shipping clerk, was in the street playing when he started to feel ill, with a pronounced stiffness in his jaw. Someone called for Dr. Bushey, who as the Hazeltons' family physician had vaccinated the boy about three weeks earlier. Never had Bushey seen a patient suffer such "terrible agony." Less than twenty hours after Thomas took to his bed, he was dead. According to the *New York Tribune*, now covering the Camden story, Bushey moved to set the record straight. "[T]he boy's death was not the result of vaccination," the coroner declared. But Thomas's parents had doubts. Mr. Hazelton said he might seek legal advice. He wanted to know whether the vaccine used on his boy was pure and, if it was not, whether the manufacturer could be held responsible for his death.[20]

The next day, November 13, tetanus struck nine-year-old Anna Cochran, the daughter of a teamster. She had been vaccinated about three weeks earlier. The story of little Anna's courage, as convulsions shook her small frame, was, as the New York *Sun* told it, "particularly sad." Just before she died, on November 14, Anna "turned to her parents and whispered through her clenched teeth: 'Don't worry, papa and mamma, I'm going to get well.'"[21]

As parents' initial suspicions swelled into a panic, Dr. Davis of the board of health made a statement to the press. Camden's most prominent physician attributed the tetanus cases to a period of unusually dry and dusty weather. "I am satisfied that none of them have been caused by vaccination," said Davis, "but by the tetanus germs in the air." Local physicians formed a unified public front with Davis and the board, insisting that the vaccine they had used was safe. But a few expressed doubts. Dr. Dowling Benjamin, considered a local authority on tetanus, broke ranks. "This talk of germs being in the air is all absurd," he said. "If that were so there would be more lockjaw than there now is. I think it is highly probable the tetanus germs were in the vaccine tubes before they were sealed."[22]

Local newspapermen turned up three more dead children whose deaths by tetanus had previously gone unreported. Eleven-year-old Anna Warrington, the only child of an illiterate ship carpenter and his wife, had died on November 8, after suffering in "great agony." Six-year-old Frank Cavallo, the child of Italian immigrants (his father was an illiterate rag dealer), had been vaccinated in Philadelphia during a visit to his grandmother; he died three weeks later, on November 9. The other new victim, unnamed, lay buried in the Evergreen Cemetery, believed to have died on November 5. A growing distrust of the authorities strengthened the public's fears. Why hadn't public health officials reported these cases earlier?[23]

On the night of November 15, Lillian Carty gave up her fight. The doctors had done all they could, the newspapers said, administering antitoxin and trying to ease her suffering as her muscles contracted. "Conscious through it all," the *New York Tribune* reported, "she suffered frightfully for two days." Her parents, exhausted from the long ordeal at her bedside, were prostrated in their grief. Remarkably, William Brower was still alive, but in critical condition. The bad news kept coming. The day Lillian died, another child had been diagnosed with tetanus following vaccination. Her name was Mamie Winters. She was eight years old.[24]

Camden was now in a full panic, and regional newspapers had taken notice. With the tetanus outbreak now weighing far more heavily on people's minds than the continuing smallpox epidemic, city health officials and parents searched, in their own ways, for connections between the lockjaw cases. They found few. The children ranged in age from six to sixteen. No two of them lived in the same ward of the city. None had visited the free vaccination station, and no more than two had been vaccinated by the same physician. As the Camden Board of Health saw things, though, there were significant commonalities. Board representatives observed that most of the children were from "lower class" families (a dubious claim, as Hazelton's father was a shipping clerk; Brower's, a plumber; Carty's, a railroad clerk); that the par-

ents were "ignorant" (also unfair, for most of the parents were at least liter-
ate); and that they inhabited a dirty city that had experienced a spell of dusty
weather (demonstrably true). For the lay public, the salient commonalities had nothing to do with social status or the weather. All of the children
had been healthy until they were vaccinated. Roughly three weeks later each
fell ill with lockjaw. Now six of them were dead. Most of the children had
received glycerinated vaccine. To these links, the New York *Sun*, in a November 17 report, added another: most of the vaccine used in Camden had apparently come from a single, trusted Philadelphia firm, H. K. Mulford
Company.[25]

It was probably inevitable that suspicion would fall upon the Mulford
Company vaccine farm and laboratory in Glenolden, Pennsylvania, just
outside Philadelphia. Mulford marketing materials boasted of the company's vaccine sales in eastern Pennsylvania and New Jersey. When the
Camden Board of Health announced its plan for wholesale vaccination,
Mulford and Marietta-based Alexander Vaccine Farm vied to corner the
market. According to the *Sun*, a local chemist who represented Alexander
approached the Camden Medical Society and seemed poised to win the
contract for the vaccine station. Mulford countered by offering the society
a thousand free points. Demand quickly exhausted that gratis supply, and
the society bought more vaccine from Mulford, as did many private physicians. Almost all of the afflicted children had received Mulford virus. Company executives insisted the vaccine was pure. The allegations, they said, had
come from pharmacists who served as agents for their rival companies,
Alexander and Parke, Davis.[26]

The parents of Camden demanded a public investigation of the tetanus
outbreak. James B. Cochran, Anna's father, swore that if the authorities did
not "fix the blame," he would "spend his last dollar doing it himself." Every
family in the city had cause for concern. Parents whose sons and daughters
had dutifully submitted to vaccination were terrified they would be the
next to fall ill. (The children were afraid, too. At Lillian Carty's funeral, her
schoolmates cried for her and worried for themselves.) Parents whose children had not yet been vaccinated feared that submitting now would expose
them to an unacceptable risk of lockjaw.[27]

Camden families launched a school strike, hundreds of parents declaring that their children would not return to the classroom until the school board rescinded its vaccination order. Some parents also talked about litigation, considering whether to sue the vaccine company or seek a court order to open the schools to unvaccinated children. To a knowledgeable lawyer, neither avenue would have looked promising in 1901. One prevailing principle in tort law ("privity of contract") insulated manufacturers from liability for injuries to anyone other than those to whom the makers sold the vaccine directly; while another principle ("contributory negligence") limited a defendant's liability if he could show that the plaintiff had negligently contributed to his own injury (for example, by carelessly letting dirt enter a vaccination wound). Moreover, under New Jersey's wrongful death statute, if the plaintiff's lawyer somehow proved the manufacturer's liability in court, the child's next of kin (normally, the father) would have been entitled only to compensation for his direct pecuniary loss: the child's wages, if any. As for the other legal strategy—seeking a judicial writ to compel school officials to admit their unvaccinated children—two circumstances would have hampered that claim: the school board was acting in accordance with a state law, not merely at its own discretion, and the board had promulgated the order in the midst of an actual smallpox epidemic. In the American legal environment of the era, a school strike was a far more viable option than a lawsuit. But even that option carried a risk: school officials could have had the parents prosecuted for violating the compulsory education law.[28]

Increasingly, people in Camden asked if the compulsory order had really been necessary. On the day Anna Cochran died, the Camden Board of Health had released its monthly report. There had been just fourteen cases of smallpox since October, with only one fatality. The toll from tetanus was much higher. "Camden people are demanding to know where the benefits of vaccination come in," said the Sun. According to the Times, some citizens now saw the health board as an "autocratic" institution, unaccountable to the people.[29]

Events came to a head on November 18, six days after Thomas Hazelton's death. Camden's vaccine crisis was no longer just a local or regional story. It was a national event. Reports of isolated postvaccination tetanus deaths—more schoolchildren—surfaced from Atlantic City and Bristol, Pennsylvania. Philadelphia, too, reported "several cases of tetanus follow-

ing vaccination, but no official action has been taken." As telegraph wires
fed newspapers from Charlotte to San Francisco the latest from Camden,
journalists dusted off other stories from the past year. "The tetanus bacillus
has admittedly found its way into commercial virus to such an extent as to
have given serious trouble in at least five widely separated districts, and
probably in isolated cases wherever vaccination is practiced," said the *Times*.
Cleveland had lost four people to postvaccination tetanus during the past
year. Previously, postvaccination tetanus was a rare complication. One investigator would turn up more than sixty U.S. cases from 1901 alone; most
had occurred in November. All of those local events and stories seemed
connected, like an epidemic, creating a widening sense of collective connectedness and complicity that transcended local political boundaries.[30]

Also on November 18, the St. Louis coroner announced his verdict regarding the first seven deaths from tetanus that had followed the administration of diphtheria antitoxin to children in that city. Citing bacteriological
tests, the coroner said the cause of the deaths was the administration of
antitoxin containing tetanus toxin. The city health department, not a private firm, had prepared the antitoxin—an experiment in public production
that had won the department no small amount of criticism from private
companies and druggists. All of the tainted antitoxin had been produced
from the blood of a single animal, a horse named Jim, "stabled at the Poor-
house Farm." Jim had developed tetanus in October and was put down. But
serum had been drawn from Jim before his symptoms became apparent,
and the serum had not been destroyed. Compounding the public relations
disaster was the revelation that the job of bottling the serum had been entrusted to a janitor. The coroner charged the health department with negligence. American newspapers readily extrapolated from the coroner's
findings to the vaccine cases. "No other suggestion is reasonable," said the
Duluth News-Tribune, "than that the unwelcome bacilli secured a lodging
place in the virus and the antitoxin in the laboratory."[31]

The tetanus scares triggered opposition to vaccination in many American communities. In Rochester, New York, in the midst of its own smallpox outbreak, parents responded to the news from Camden, 350 miles
away, by refusing to allow their children to be vaccinated. Two schools were
"practically closed for want of attendance." In response, the city health of-

ficer, according to the *New York Tribune,* "deprecated the displaying of the Camden news." His peers in many other American communities shared his frustration.[32]

From the beginning of the crisis, Camden health officials and doctors had maintained a united front in defense of vaccination. But with six children dead so far, the schools half-empty, and a national scandal brewing, the board of health called a halt. On the night of November 18, the members passed a resolution ordering physicians to cease vaccination until further notice. The board advised the school board to suspend enforcement of the vaccination law, which that body did the following day. The health board launched a scientific investigation to determine the causes of the tetanus outbreak and, as James Cochran had demanded, fix the blame. The Mulford Company promised its full cooperation.[33]

The board members were not the only medical men determined to settle these same questions. Working on their own, three other men had quietly begun their own investigations—inquiries that would push the limits of medical science. Two of them, Robert Willson and Joseph McFarland, were physicians from neighboring Philadelphia. Willson had recently lost a patient to postvaccination tetanus. McFarland was one of America's leading bacteriologists; his work with diphtheria antitoxin had put Mulford on the map, but he had left the company for academia and a consulting job with Mulford's rival, Parke, Davis. The third investigator, Milton J. Rosenau, was an officer of the federal government, working in a small Washington laboratory, within the U.S. Marine-Hospital Service, that would one day be known as the National Institutes of Health.

All three men believed vaccination was medical science's greatest gift to humanity. All sought an answer to the crisis that had discredited that operation during the most serious visitation of smallpox the nation had seen in years. Their investigations ensured that the Camden Board of Health would not have the last word on the matter.

The Camden tragedy cast unwanted light upon a hitherto little-known sector of the U.S. economy. Part animal husbandry, part laboratory science, the vaccine industry exemplified the distinctive historical in-betweenness of life at the century's turn. On city streets, automobiles and streetcars vied for the road with horse-drawn carriages. In the public sphere, a new scientific rhetoric of social statistics and structures pressed against the older Protestant moralism of individuals and strictures. And in one of the most profitable manufacturing sectors of the U.S. economy, future giants of the nation's pharmaceutical industry—companies such as Wyeth and Parke, Davis—were making names for themselves by harvesting pus from the undersides of barnyard animals. Poised between the stable and the laboratory, the farm and the firm, the vaccine industry embodied a world in transition. Of course, the vaccine makers had no way of knowing what their industry would one day become, but the most innovative among them dared to dream big. They forged close ties with government health departments and universities. And they embraced medical science—not just for the technical innovations that science enabled but for the credibility it offered to an industry built upon incredible promises.[34]

Although vaccination arrived in America in 1800, vaccine manufacturing did not emerge as a commercial industry until the 1870s, with the shift from "humanized" to "bovine" virus. Of course, Edward Jenner had obtained his original vaccine material from a cow, albeit by an indirect method: he took the "lymph" from a pustule on the hand of a milkmaid infected with cowpox. Uncertain about the origin of this disease, the doctor named it "variolae vaccinae," smallpox of the cow. And though Jenner speculated that the disease might have originated in an affliction of horses (and he may have been right), the name vaccine stuck.[35]

Naturally occurring cases of cowpox were rare. Fortunately, Jenner established that vaccine could be serially reproduced in humans. The method entailed taking fluid directly from the vaccination vesicle on the arm of a donor ("vaccinifier"), usually a healthy young child, and applying the virus to the scratched arms of an assembly of recipients. Humanized virus: vaccine without the *vache*. The possibilities were breathtaking, as the Balmis expedition showed the world in 1803–5, transporting vaccine in the arms of orphans to the Spanish colonies of the Americas and the Philippines. In England, the National Vaccine Establishment assumed responsibility in 1808 for maintaining a supply of humanized virus, through serial "arm-to-arm" transfers. The virus could also be preserved and transported by drying the fluid on pieces of thread, quills, or ivory points; or by peeling the crust from a vaccination sore. The lymph-saturated crust could be carried or even sent in the mail; the vaccinator would triturate (crush) and moisten the crust, producing a pasty vaccine material, and then set to work. A North Carolina physician recalled vaccinating his entire town in 1854 with a "very ugly little scab" that he received by post from Wilmington.[36]

Humanized virus worked. When properly collected and used, it took "with great regularity" and produced immunity for years. But there were problems. If the vaccinifier was not as healthy as she appeared, the virus could communicate other human diseases, including erysipelas (an acute skin infection) and syphilis. In Rivalta, Italy, in 1861, sixty-three children were vaccinated with material from the vaccinal sore of a single, seemingly healthy infant. Forty-six of the children fell ill with syphilis, several died, and some passed the disease to their mothers and nurses. The risks of arm-to-arm transfer inflamed antivaccination sentiment almost everywhere it was practiced. Herbert Spencer called it "wholesale syphilization."[37]

A second disadvantage of humanized virus was the challenge, even in a densely populated community, of keeping a fresh supply on hand. For a small town or sparsely settled rural area, keeping up an arm-to-arm relay or a good stock of crusts might prove impossible. Moreover, some physicians believed that humanized virus became attenuated or compromised over time, with the ever increasing distance from the original bovine source. Humanized virus had one other major shortcoming, which only became fully apparent in retrospect. There was never much of a market in it.[38]

The idea of using cows, instead of people, to manufacture cowpox first took hold in Italy. Throughout the century, in Europe and America, some vaccine propagators practiced what came to be called "retrovaccination": inoculating heifers with humanized virus, either to mystically restore some bovine quality to the vaccine or to simply make animals do the work. But the production of the stuff that came to be known as "true animal vaccine" or "bovine virus"—and that would launch a new industry and market— did not catch on in Europe until the 1860s. The idea was to inoculate a heifer with seed virus obtained from a naturally occurring case of cowpox (*not* with humanized virus) and to keep the strain running from calf to calf in a continuous relay, all the while harvesting vaccine for use in humans.[39]

Bovine vaccine had none of the problems that plagued humanized virus. As the Italian practice was adopted by France (1864), Belgium (1865), Japan (1874), and Germany (1884), government officials and private entrepreneurs greeted each newly discovered outbreak of cowpox as a wellspring of vaccine. One of the most famous cases of "spontaneous cowpox" came to light in 1866 in Beaugency, in France's Loire Valley. Although vulnerable to contamination, bovine virus did not spread syphilis. A calf could produce vaccine in far greater quantity than an infant could (while raising fewer qualms). And as doctors, farmers, and druggists soon realized, there was money to be made in bovine vaccine.[40]

Dr. Henry A. Martin of Boston introduced bovine vaccine to the United States in 1870. Using seed lymph from the Beaugency strain, which by that time had already passed through 260 heifers in France, Martin established a vaccine farm in suburban Roxbury. Martin may also deserve credit for initiating the American vaccine makers' practice of tarring rivals' products. An early advertisement said Martin virus should not be "confounded with the feeble, uncertain, and generally quite worthless product of retrovaccination." Martin's family-run establishment operated continuously and with good reputation into the early twentieth century. Others quickly followed in Martin's footsteps, most notably Dr. E. L. Griffin of Fond du Lac, Wisconsin, and Dr. Frank P. Foster of New York. By the mid-1870s, vaccine farms were sprouting up all over the country.[41]

Many of the earliest vaccine producers were men much like Martin and Griffin—reputable local physicians who knew their way around a stable. Some traded on their prominence as members of state or local boards of health. But so low were the barriers to entry—a bit of seed virus, a few cows, and some ivory points—that men on the make from many walks of life entered the business. With equal parts admiration and distaste, the *Brooklyn Eagle* captured the spirit of the new enterprise. "If it be true that what is one man's meat is another man's poison, it is equally true, of course, that what is one man's poison is another man's meat," the *Eagle* said. "The axiom, as amended, is fully verified in this good city of Brooklyn, where men are deriving handsome incomes from that most disgusting and abhorrent of all diseases, small-pox. A new business of vital importance to the community has been started, and hundreds of thousands of men, women and children are walking about with its badge on their arms." In 1871, the New York Department of Health became the first municipal agency in the United States to produce its own vaccine. But elsewhere private makers had the field almost entirely to themselves. And as compulsory vaccination and its handmaiden, compulsory education, spread in the late nineteenth century, the opportunities for profit expanded apace.[42]

To distinguish their products on the open market, vaccine makers appealed to the late nineteenth-century romance of the pastoral and the era's penchant for pedigree. Americans had a fascination with animal breeding and family genealogies, informed by the transatlantic flourishing of hereditarian ideas in the age of Darwin and Galton. Dr. W. E. Griffiths of Brooklyn boasted that his stock derived from a case of spontaneous cowpox discovered in Central New York. Dr. J. W. Compton & Son of Indiana advertised "pure Beaugency cow-pox lymph, non-humanized." In 1885, John Wyeth & Brother, Philadelphia druggists, announced their entry into the field with a full-page advertisement in *Drugs and Medicines of North America*. Calling its new Chester County farm "the model vaccine propagating establishment of the United States," the Wyeth Company obtained its seed virus from the Belgian government. Like many vaccine ads, this one pictured a cow: a healthy looking heifer, bound to a table beneath a lace-curtained window; on the calf's lower belly were several rows of incisions, where the seed had been introduced. Vaccine companies' claims to exalted origins for their products were greeted with jeering from some quarters. Dr. J. W. Hodge insisted, to everyone who would listen, that no vaccine maker had "any definite or exact knowledge as to the real nature, composition or original source of the complex poisonous mixture which they foist upon gullible doctors as 'pure calf lymph.'"[43]

Hodge had a point. In an era when neither smallpox nor cowpox could be seen under the most powerful microscope, the manufacturers' genealogical claims were beyond verification. It was not until 1939 that a British scientist established that most vaccines contained neither smallpox nor cowpox, but a related orthopoxvirus called *vaccinia*. At some time between Jenner's first experiments with cowpox in 1796 and the 1930s, vaccine makers had started working with this different virus, which also occurs naturally in cows. No one knows when the exchange occurred, though the late nineteenth century would seem a good bet. In any event, vaccinia worked. Like cowpox, when introduced in the human system it caused an immune response, usually mild, that conferred a lasting (though not permanent) immunity to smallpox.[44]

The makers' claims to product purity were easier to test than their pedigree claims. In 1895, Walter Reed of the Army Medical Department presented a paper to the District of Columbia Medical Society entitled "What Credence Should Be Given to the Statements of Those Who Claim to Furnish Vaccine Lymph Free of Bacteria?" His answer: none at all. Reed had examined points from several leading U.S. makers. The number of bacteria per point ranged widely, from 43 to 89,000. Most of those germs appeared to be harmless, but others were pathogenic, capable of causing sore arms and infections. Bovine virus was liable to contamination from the common bacteria, such as streptococci and staphylococci, that thrived upon calves' skin or in the stable.[45]

The following year, the Pennsylvania State Board of Health dispatched one of its own bacteriologists, Dr. R. L. Pitfield, to inspect American vaccine farms. Of the fourteen farms Pitfield visited, he could recommend only four. Amidst the wildly various production standards, Pitfield found a common ground of rank commercialism and "a tenacious adherence to original and old and rather preaseptic measures." In one Missouri establishment, a worker used his own fingernail to remove the crust; in another, the heifers were kept in a "dusty and dirty apartment," with urine streaming in from the operating room on the floor above them. Even at the New York City Health Department, one of America's leading scientific establishments, Pitfield found "the accommodations are not as good as they should be." Among the many troubling statements in Dr. Pitfield's detailed report was this one: "In many establishments, tetanus bacilli might find their way to the vesicle and thence to the points and tubes, because dust in large quantities abounds in the incubating stables."[46]

In the late 1890s, American vaccine makers adopted a new production technique that reduced the problem of bacteria-ridden vaccine. For decades,

European makers had added glycerin to their product to keep it from de-composing. In 1891, the Englishman Sydney Monckton Copeman estab-lished that glycerin not only preserved vaccine but gradually killed unwanted bacteria without damaging the virus. Glycerin also acted as a diluent, allow-ing makers to stretch lymph and thus greatly increase the number of vaccine units that could be produced from a single calf. By 1898, glycerinated calf lymph had become the international standard of vaccine, widely preferred by the leading local, state, and federal health officers in the United States.[47]

While some companies (such as the Martin Vaccine Farm and the Washington, D.C.–based National Vaccine Establishment) still dealt chiefly or exclusively in smallpox vaccines, other industry leaders had a much larger footprint in the marketplace. Firms like Parke, Davis and Wyeth Company sold a growing number of biological products as well as com-pounded drugs of almost infinite variety. Even as firms opened branch houses in major U.S. cities and overseas, their vaccine lines required that they keep one foot planted on the farm. H. K. Mulford Company, one of America's most reputable manufacturers of biologics and drugs, still adorned its vaccine ads in 1901 with a healthy heifer standing contentedly by a gentle stream and thought nothing of running those vaccine ads di-rectly beneath another for pint bottles of "Mulford's Pre-Digested Beef." That both products might come from precisely the same source was a fact worth publicizing. Field, laboratory, and slaughterhouse were stages of an industrial life cycle that bound urban life, as ever, to the domestication of rural animals and landscapes.[48]

For the H. K. Mulford Company, "Manufacturing Chemists," a new-comer to the vaccine market in 1898, dealing in biologics meant revers-ing the expected American trajectory. Mulford was born in the city and moved to the country. The company got its start in the late 1880s when twenty-one-year-old Henry K. Mulford bought the "Old Simes" corner drugstore in downtown Philadelphia. At first, Mulford seemed poised to follow the conventional road of the entrepreneur in Philadelphia's robust drug trade, the largest in the United States outside of New York. He intro-duced his own line of medical preparations, including elixirs, lozenges, li-quors, tinctures, antiseptics, and soda fountain syrups. In 1891, with new financial backing, Mulford incorporated and began its swift transformation from retail druggist to nationally prominent manufacturing firm. Henry Mulford and an associate patented their own machine for tableting water-soluble pills, and by 1893 the company, with two Philadelphia laboratories and a branch office in Chicago, was marketing no fewer than eight hundred medical products.[49]

In 1894, the Mulford Company entered the biologics market at its cutting edge, racing to become the first U.S. firm to produce diphtheria antitoxin. Germany's Koch Institute was already preparing the lifesaving antitoxin, which like smallpox vaccine was an animal product. (A horse was inoculated with diphtheria toxin and given time to produce antibodies; later the horse was bled and the antibodies separated from the serum.) The New York City Health Department was developing its own antitoxin. To develop a commercial product, Mulford hired Dr. Joseph McFarland, a bacteriologist who had trained in Heidelberg and Vienna and who was at that time employed by both the University of Pennsylvania and the Philadelphia Board of Health. In a display of the public-private cooperation that drove biologics innovation in the 1890s, the New York City Health Department bacteriologist, Dr. William Park, provided McFarland with the cultures necessary to start his laboratory in a West Philadelphia stable. The University of Pennsylvania's new Laboratory of Hygiene agreed to test lots of McFarland's antitoxin. By 1895, Mulford had placed America's first commercial diphtheria antitoxin on the market. The following year, the company moved its biologics department to newly constructed stables and laboratories in rural Glenolden, eight miles outside Philadelphia. In 1898, the company hired Dr. W. F. Elgin from the National Vaccine Establishment and put him to work making glycerinated vaccine. By 1902, Mulford's annual sales topped $1 million.[50]

Mulford benefited from all of the innovations that had taken place since Martin brought bovine virus to America in 1870. According to Mulford marketing details, the company's stables and laboratories were state-of-the-art operations modeled after "the leading vaccine establishments in Europe and America." The company used suckling female calves, just four to eight weeks old, tested for tuberculosis. "The animals are kept at all times under the most rigid sanitary surroundings in buildings all the materials of which—stone, cement, metal, slate, and porcelain-finish—permit of immediate and thorough disinfection." The calves were fed sterilized milk, their excretions "disinfected and removed as soon as voided." The inoculations and collection of the virus took place in a special operating room set apart from the stables.[51]

Dr. Elgin detailed his procedures in a presentation, complete with lantern slides, to the 1900 meeting of the Conference of State and Provincial Boards of Health of North America. After having its underside shaved, the calf was strapped to an operating table where "the operator," clad in a sterilized gown and wielding an aseptic scalpel, made a series of linear incisions along its lower body. Glycerinated lymph (harvested from a previous calf) was slathered over the entire area and rubbed into the incisions. A worker removed the animal to the sanitary stable, returning the calf to the operating table six days later. Along the incisions had risen a line of vesicles covered with "a slight crust or scab." Using sterilized water, the crust was softened and then removed, "leaving behind rows of pearly white vesicles," which the operator scooped out (using a tool of the trade called "Volkman's spoon") and deposited in a sterilized box. This "pulp" was then placed on glass rollers in a grinding machine and mixed with glycerin. The mixture was stored in large stock tubes and placed in an icebox while the glycerin did its work. Finally, glycerinated lymph was placed in capillary tubes (each containing enough for a single vaccination), hermetically sealed, and prepared for shipping. Mulford followed the practice at the best firms of killing the calves immediately after the collection of vaccine and conducting a postmortem examination to ensure that the animal was in fact healthy; if the exam showed otherwise, the company discarded the vaccine. The postmortem was a costly practice, not universally followed. Some makers still sold their used calves to the local stockyards.[52]

In most European countries, the government controlled vaccine production, either through licensing or through outright government manufacture. Regulating the manufacture of potentially hazardous goods fell well within the ambit of the American police power. But little regulation of vaccines existed. Just seven states had laws providing for some supervision of the vaccine manufactured or used in the state. The Massachusetts statute, the nation's strongest, declared that "All vaccine institutions in the

commonwealth shall be under the supervision of the state board of health";
but even that law specified no penalties for bad practices. Several of the
states governed the use of humanized virus, which had fallen out of favor
in most places anyway. Even these measures showed a narrow conception
of the rightful powers of government in this area. Florida banned humanized virus outright; Maryland made physicians liable for "knowingly or
willfully" using humanized virus that spread disease to a patient; and Michigan required that only bovine product be used in *public* vaccinations.[53]

In the late 1890s, the first glimmerings of a new regulatory approach
appeared when a few state and local governments started inspecting vaccine farms, testing the virus in the laboratory, and publishing the findings.
In an industry that had relied on the endorsements of public health boards
to market their products, this must have been for many makers a most
unwelcome intrusion. In addition to the Pennsylvania Board of Health,
some of the nation's most advanced municipal health departments—
Chicago, Minneapolis, Brooklyn, Charleston, Denver, and St. Louis—began
using their new bacteriological laboratories to test vaccines for potency or
purity. At the most dramatic level of control, the city of New York manufactured its own virus—still in 1901 the only city in the country to do so.
The New York health board rankled commercial makers by selling limited
amounts of its well-regarded virus on the open market.[54]

American vaccine makers were regulated almost exclusively by their
reputations, their commercial "trustworthiness." This encouraged nasty advertising practices. In a 1900 article titled "The Pot Calls the Kettle Black,"
the Indianapolis physician W. B. Clarke observed that vaccine advertisements published in the medical journals had become a scandalous "squabble
literature." "In their greedy commercialism," Clarke wrote, the manufacturers "have fallen out, and are each vying with the others in desperate attempts
to show the medical profession that theirs is the one pure virus, and that all
the others are dangerous and unfit for the use even of a health (?) officer."
Dr. Clarke was an antivaccinationist (the giveaway was that parenthetical
question mark), but he did not exaggerate. As early as 1898, an Alexander
Company advertisement had thrown down the gauntlet: "At the beginning
of this second century [of vaccination] the tendency is to propagate impure
virus, in order to meet the demand for great discounts, thus lowering the

price and making it impossible to propagate in a proper manner." Even assertions of product purity were phrased so as to condemn rivals' wares by implication: "This Vaccine is Entirely Free from Blood Corpuscles," a distributor for the New-England Vaccine Company proudly announced. Parke, Davis did not wait for the Camden crisis to cool down before taking a swipe at Mulford (unnamed) in its advertising. "The most successful vaccination is not the vaccination that inflicts the most suffering upon the patient," said one Parke, Davis ad. "The best virus is our Aseptic Vaccine. It effectually protects against smallpox—it does not infect with disease-breeding organisms." And then came the kicker, underscored and printed in boldface type: "Not a single fatality was ever charged to our Vaccine Virus."[55]

Still, negative advertising was a risky marketing strategy: the American public did not need much encouragement to think that vaccines were vile and dangerous.

The American newspapers followed the Camden vaccine investigation like a criminal trial. The story certainly had the elements of a good police procedural: dead schoolchildren, intimations of a corporate cover-up, and men in laboratory coats keeping a sober vigil over culture dishes and white rats.

To lead its investigation, the Camden Board of Health secured the services of a young Philadelphia physician named Albert C. Barnes. A brilliant and eccentric man who never shrank from a fight, Barnes grew up in the hardscrabble section of South Philadelphia known as "The Neck." Educated at Philadelphia's renowned Central High, he paid his way through the University of Pennsylvania Medical School by boxing and playing semiprofessional baseball. An M.D. at twenty, he studied chemistry at the University of Berlin (and later at Heidelberg). Returning to Philadelphia in 1896, Barnes began working as a consulting chemist for Mulford Company and quickly rose to a full-time position as advertising and sales manager. Placing a Mulford man in charge of an investigation of Mulford products may seem scandalous today. But the move raised few eyebrows at a time when business, medicine, and public health authority often moved in unison. (Not long after the Camden episode, Barnes began amassing his own pharmaceutical fortune by inventing, with a German colleague, the antiseptic Argyrol; he spent that fortune building one of the great private collections of modern French art, the Barnes Foundation in Merion, Pennsylvania.)[56]

Barnes's unique combination of talents made him an able defender of the Camden Board of Health and Mulford. The doctor traveled to New York to keep the city's leading papers and their wire services apprised of the ongoing investigation. Barnes pressed the point that the same virus had been used on a million people living within thirty miles of Philadelphia, "and few, if any, fatal results were reported." The *Tribune* praised the board's man: "Dr. Barnes, the expert employed by the authorities of Camden to look into this trouble, throws a flood of light on its origin." Papers that a few days earlier had impugned Mulford vaccine now lingered over local factors: Camden's dry weather, dusty streets, filthy children, and negligent parents. As Barnes told his audience, the fatal cases had occurred "among the lower class of people, who by their own carelessness poisoned the wounds with tetanus, or lockjaw, bacteria." The vaccine and the physicians who used it were "perfectly blameless." The *Sun*, one of the first newspapers to implicate Mulford, now told its readers that tetanus was simply "in the air," just waiting for "any cut or scratch . . . to give it a lodging place." It was "highly unfortunate," the paper added, "that a period of prevalence of tetanus germs should have coincided with a period of vaccination." The chemist cum adman had sold the press the oldest story in the annals of public health: the poor begot filth, and filth begot disease.[57]

The Camden Board of Health finally released its full report, on November 29, 1901. By then all of the major findings had already been delivered by Barnes to the New York papers. The terse report combined bacteriology and epidemiology with an older emphasis on atmospheric and environmental factors. The board had tracked down samples of the various makes of vaccine used in the city and sent them to the New Jersey state bacteriologist. Laboratory tests failed to detect tetanus in the samples. Meanwhile, physicians at Camden's Cooper Hospital had used vaccine purchased from fifteen separate Camden pharmacies to inoculate white rats, known to be highly susceptible to tetanus. Not one developed the disease. Epidemiological evidence supported the laboratory data. According to standard medical treatises, acute tetanus occurred within five to nine days after the introduction of bacilli in the body. But the Camden children had not fallen ill for about three weeks after vaccination. All of this constituted "indisputable evidence," in the words of the report, "that the tetanus germs were not introduced at the time of vaccination." Following Henry Davis's original suggestion, the report attributed the tetanus outbreak to the peculiar "atmospheric and telluric conditions" (the dry, dusty weather) that had prevailed in Camden that fall. To demonstrate that the germs were present "in the atmosphere," the board cited the case of a boy who got tetanus from a gunshot wound that fall. Other germs had made their way onto the vaccine wounds of a few luckless children who had left their wounds uncovered, wrapped them in filthy rags, or, worse, "scratched the vaccinated area with their dirty fingers and nails and infected the wound." At the conclusion of the report, the board expressed its "unanimous opinion" that compulsory vaccination should resume in Camden.[58]

Medical science and public relations know-how had come to the defense of the vaccine industry at its hour of greatest need. The *American Druggist and Pharmaceutical Record*, an industry trade journal, expressed relief. The *Record* urged "every intelligent person" to "do all that is possible to prevent the spread of unnecessary and ill-founded alarm from the accidental occurrence of tetanus following, but in no wise due to vaccination."[59]

And yet there were doubts. The board's "vigorous ex parte denial," as a *New York Times* editorial skeptically referred to the report, did not silence the public narrative that tied the suffering of little children to tainted commercial vaccine. The Philadelphia *North American* agreed: "The prima facie evidence of connection between vaccination and tetanus is too strong to be refuted by mere assertion of opinion by the vaccinators." Addressing the New York Academy of Medicine, W. R. Inge Dalton, a physician and professor, said he was not persuaded by the report. "In Camden the manufacturer and the medical men have co-operated in exonerating themselves, and have thrown all the blame on the parents of the children," Dalton said. If tetanus bacilli were simply "in the air," it was remarkable that they had a "selective predilection for sores produced by particular kinds of vaccine virus."[60]

In Philadelphia, a scientific debate on the merits of the board's argument had begun even before the report's release. Addressing the Philadelphia Medical Society on November 27, Dr. Robert N. Willson presented a paper about a case he had recently handled. An eleven-month-old child had died of tetanus following vaccination. Willson concluded that the child's father, a coachman, had carried the tetanus from the stable to the nursery. Insisting there had never been any connection between vaccine and tetanus, Willson told his audience that the only cure for "rampant" opposition to vaccination was a "new scrupulousness" toward the vaccination wound. No doubt many of his listeners applauded. But at least one remained unconvinced. Dr. Joseph McFarland, the man who had built Mulford's antitoxin laboratory, took the floor. He had been following the tetanus cases closely, he said, and was conducting his own study of the subject. He had learned enough already to suspect that Willson's "extremely optimistic view . . . concerning the harmlessness of vaccine virus might not be correct." Five months later, the two physicians would meet again in that same room to debate the issue.[61]

Nor had the board's investigation stopped the pain and death in Camden. On the night of November 25, thirteen-year-old Ada Heath died of lockjaw. Her parents had paid a local druggist twenty-five cents to vaccinate her. On November 26 came the death of nine-year-old Georgiana Overby, the first African American child among the afflicted, and the first of the tetanus victims to have received her vaccination in the free dispensary. "[S]he, too, died in agony," the *Tribune* reported. From nearby Jordantown came the news that four-year-old Flora Johnson, also African American, had died, "apparently suffering from tetanus, following vaccination." The final Camden case was reported on December 4. Three days later Bessie Rosevelt, age seven, the daughter of a local horse dealer, died at her home on Ferry Avenue. No two of the new cases had been vaccinated by the same physician. The *Tribune* awkwardly noted that Bessie's was the "fourteenth case since the epidemic [of tetanus] made its appearance, and despite the fact that it has been found that the disease does not come from vaccination lymph, all of the victims have been vaccinated." A headline in the *Omaha World-Herald* suggested that for much of the public, the story was more straightforward: "Poisoned Vaccine Still Proving Fatal at Camden, N.J."[62]

If the mere assertion of expert opinion could not restore public confidence in vaccine, at the height of the most extensive U.S. epidemic of smallpox in recent memory, then what could? The *Times* warned that this was "not a momentary sensation." St. Louis and Camden had done "incalculable injury" to medical progress, while the profession whose "pride and business interest" were most closely tied to that cause stood idly by. In the coming months, the American medical profession would be anything but idle. The New York County Medical Society resolved to investigate the "entire subject" and to determine "the steps that should be taken to guard against the possibility of a repetition of such deplorable disasters." Other societies followed suit, as one local and state organization after another called for investigations of the vaccine industry and debated the need for government control. Physicians stepped away from both the biologics makers and the public health boards, seriously considered their own interests, and worked to restore public confidence in vaccination.[63]

Physicians knew better than anyone that even under the best of circumstances vaccination carried health risks. The same late nineteenth-century developments in bacteriology that had made U.S. military medicine a much safer and more ambitious enterprise had introduced a heightened concern for aseptic practices in routine medical procedures, including vaccination. As Arthur Van Harlingen, a Philadelphia doctor, noted approvingly in 1902, "few men will now come to the delicate infant with the odor of stable and animal on the unwashed hands, or will moisten their instruments with their own saliva." And still physicians knew that introducing animal vaccine into the human system could produce unpredictable results, especially if the patient did not have the constitution for it, or if the vaccine itself was impure.[64]

American doctors had been concerned about vaccine quality since the first wave of the turn-of-the-century smallpox epidemics spread across the southern states in 1898 and 1899. But the doctors had kept their worries mostly to themselves, maintaining a solid (if occasionally splintery) defense of vaccine before the public. Their own medical society minutes and journals told a different story. Physicians and health officials—including a few federal officials such as C. P. Wertenbaker of the U.S. Marine-Hospital Service—complained that contaminated tubes and points were producing sore arms and open rebellions. At a meeting of the North Carolina Medical

Society, local physicians swapped stories about "the violent results" caused by the vaccines they were receiving from northern manufacturers. "The popular prejudice against vaccination is not wholly without justification," one doctor confessed. He recalled many "very sore arms" and lamented the suffering of his "own little daughter [who] was for three days violently ill" after he vaccinated her. As the epidemics spread north, the stories were much the same. From Omaha, Dr. F. T. Campbell wrote of the "vile vaccine" found on the shelves of grocery stores. "[A]nd so the 'sores' ran wild with contiguous and constitutional infection. From such cases came complaints that vaccination was 'worse than smallpox.'" By the time tetanus broke out in Camden, American physicians had good reason to wonder what was really in those skinny tubes and points they carried around in their pockets.[65]

At the Marine-Hospital Service's Hygienic Laboratory in Washington, Milton Joseph Rosenau was wondering the same thing. In the winter of 1901–2, he determined to find out, secretly buying up samples from eight different vaccine makers on the open market and taking them back to his laboratory. The thirty-three-year-old scientist knew Philadelphia and its environs well: a native of the city, like Albert Barnes and Joseph McFarland, he had received his education in its public schools and at the University of Pennsylvania. After completing his medical training in 1889, Rosenau joined the Marine-Hospital Service, serving as a quarantine officer in San Francisco and, at the close of the Spanish-American War, in Santiago. After a decade in the field, he took over the Hygienic Laboratory, which he transformed from a one-man outfit into a leading government scientific institution. A brilliant scientist with the heart of a reformer, Rosenau's scientific interests ranged across bacteriology, chemistry, and pharmacology. As early as April 1900, Wertenbaker had focused Rosenau's attention on the problem of vaccine purity by sending him some points and lymph for testing. A few teeming cultures and one dead mouse later, Rosenau confirmed Wertenbaker's suspicion that the dry points on sale in the South crawled with pathogens. In a private letter, Surgeon General Wyman had cautioned Wertenbaker against reading too much into Rosenau's report. "The work confirms the well known fact that glycerinized lymph is superior to dry points and no other conclusion should be drawn from the report," Wyman advised.[66]

A broader conclusion was inescapable after Rosenau tested the vaccine samples he collected on the open market, at the height of the national vaccine crisis, in the winter of 1901–2. The federal scientist presented his preliminary findings to the New York Academy of Medicine in February 1902. Like Walter Reed before him, Rosenau found a great unevenness in the quality of vaccine on the market. On average, each nonglycerinated dry point Rosenau examined had 4,809 bacterial colonies, while the glycerinated lymph averaged 2,865 colonies per sample. (The journal *Pediatrics* recoiled at this "ridiculous amount of impurity.") The contaminants included staphylococci, pus cocci, and an assortment of molds common to the hay and dust of the stable. What made Rosenau's report news was his argument that vaccine makers placed too much confidence in the germicidal powers of glycerin. The makers had "become careless of contamination, trusting to the glycerin to purify their product." And in their haste to meet the high demand for vaccine during the national wave of smallpox epidemics, makers had not given the glycerin sufficient time to work, flooding the market with "green" virus.[67]

Rosenau did not shy away from the political implications of his data. He told Wyman, "Our results so far have plainly indicated that the manufacture of vaccines is too important a subject to leave to commercial enterprise without restrictions." Many in the medical profession agreed. As the *Medical News* observed, "The enforcement of government inspection with power to prevent the sale of improper material seems to be the desideratum."[68]

Rosenau's paper accomplished what only a federal report could do. Coming so fast on the heels of St. Louis and Camden, it persuaded American doctors and public health officials, working in local communities across the United States, that defective vaccine was a national problem that required a national solution. Many had seen the hideous effects of bad vaccine in their own patients, and their consciences troubled them. "The inoculation of such vaccine is followed by severe reaction, including fever, erysipelatous dermatitis, a deep, sloughing sore, and great swelling of the arm," the *Cleveland Journal of Medicine* reported. And after all of that, some vaccine still produced "no immunity to subsequent smallpox." The *Sanitarian*, a leading voice of the public health profession, lamented "the poisonous character of much of the vaccine that is put upon the market at the present day." Nine tenths of that vaccine might be fine, but there was "no telling how much harm may be done by the remaining one-tenth . . . or how many anti-vaccinationists it may produce." "Something will have to be done," the *Sanitarian* concluded, "to rehabilitate vaccine virus in the estimation of the medical profession as well as of the general public."[69]

The old rhetoric of the vaccination argument had lost its persuasive powers, even for some of the measure's strongest supporters. Cost-benefit arguments were not enough. Vaccination was a political measure, ordered for the most benevolent of purposes. But vaccine was a commercial product, and like all such wares, its success depended upon the confidence of consumers. Public confidence in the market—and thus in the measure— had collapsed. Vaccination itself was, as one New York physician observed, "at a crisis." And that crisis exposed to all the fundamental contradiction characterizing the procedure: the government compelled vaccination, but it would not vouch for vaccine.[70]

Dr. Theobald Smith, a scientist with the Massachusetts Board of Health, was one of the growing number of officials and physicians who demanded reform in 1902. "Without the specific protection given by vaccination, small-pox cannot be efficiently controlled and suppressed," Smith said. "The acceptance of this proposition by the medical profession and the State creates the responsibility of supplying as pure and efficient vaccine virus as can be made under present conditions."[71]

The vaccine crisis seemed to require a new role for the state in controlling production. But what sort of control? Like their European social-democratic counterparts, progressive reformers in the United States insisted that certain areas of life were too precious to leave entirely to the unregulated market. This call for a sort of decommodification—to replace capitalist price with government discipline—was a common thread running through a great many otherwise disparate reform causes, from the movement for public ownership of streetcars to the campaign to ban child labor. The disasters in St. Louis and Camden convinced many physicians and health officials that vaccine production had been left to the free market for too long. "The lesson we have principally to learn from these catastrophes," said Dr. Dalton of New York, "is the necessity of eliminating commercialism from matters pertaining to public health."[72]

The professional debate centered on two options. The first was for states to manufacture their own vaccines, in effect socializing the industry (as Japan had done in 1896). Eugene A. Darling, director of the Cambridge, Massachusetts, Bacteriological Laboratory, noted the ethical clarity in this approach. He said, "The State compels the child to be vaccinated, and should furnish the lymph for the operation, guaranteed to be pure and efficient." The other option was to bring commercial vaccine makers under the discipline of a new regime of licensing and inspection. Since vaccines were an interstate business, most supporters of regulation called for the involvement of the federal government. This, too, was a bold idea: the federal government did not regulate drugs or biologics manufactured in the United States. (Since 1848, federal law had banned the importation of adulterated or spurious drugs, but that law did not touch domestic manufactures.) The entire professional debate took place in the context of rising antivaccination sentiment. In early February, the Massachusetts legislature held hearings on a bill to repeal the state's compulsory vaccination law. The committee heard an emotional appeal from the mother of Annie Caswell, a five-year-old Cambridge girl who had died the previous month from tetanus after vaccination. The bill failed. But that effort and others like it helped keep the vaccine purity question before the press.[73]

The idea of government production, which *American Medicine* dismissed as "almost out of the question," met with powerful opposition from vaccine makers and the druggists who sold their goods. The makers had long enjoyed a cozy relationship with state and local health boards, aggressively seeking their contracts and endorsements. And, of course, every vaccination order created a demand for commercial products. Not surprisingly, the makers did not welcome competition from their longtime sponsors. "A Board has no right to enter into commercial enterprises," the *St. Louis Medical Journal* declared in 1898, a few years after the city health department introduced its ill-fated antitoxin. That same year, the New York County Medical Society sponsored a state bill that would have forbidden the Tammany-controlled New York City Health Department to sell its surplus biologics; the bill failed. In 1900 and 1901, manufacturers and druggists urged Congress to stop the Department of Agriculture from providing ranchers with free vaccine for blackleg, a disease of cattle and sheep. At a time when some of America's more progressive municipal governments were taking steps to provide their citizens with necessary services—including water, electricity, and gas—production of vaccines and antitoxins by local health boards was met with slippery-slope charges of "municipal socialism." (Bona fide socialists bristled at the association. Socialist Labor Party leader Daniel De Leon countered, "The vaccination laws are capitalist laws: they were framed by capitalist legislatures; they have been passed upon by capitalist courts; they are enforced by capitalist officials. From first to last the spirit of capitalism has dominated the whole procedure.")[74]

In the winter of 1901–2, druggists and vaccine manufacturers waged a protracted campaign to beat back government production in the few places it already existed. (The great exceptions were in the new U.S. colonies in Puerto Rico and the Philippines.) On the U.S. mainland, the vaccine interests held up the St. Louis tetanus outbreak as the tragic but inevitable result of placing production in the hands of a political machine. "It is difficult enough to keep politics pure," said the Minneapolis-based *Medical Dial*, "but it is impossible to make pure political antitoxin." Seizing the moment, the makers and druggists pressed Mayor Seth Low of New York to stop the city health department from the "destructively competitive" practice of selling its highly regarded vaccine and antitoxin on the market. Even reformers worried that municipal governments controlled by political machines would produce products more dangerous than those already available on the commercial market. Others insisted there was something un-American about the whole idea. "No government has the right, morally, legally, or commercially to enter into any business for pecuniary profit," declared the *Medical Record*. Neither purity of product nor cheapness to consumers could justify it. "A municipal laboratory is not a shop."[75]

The so-called Continental method of monopolistic government production was not going to happen in the United States. Government regulation was controversial enough. Here, too, there were European models. In Italy, which had the most extensive system of regulation in Europe, would-be makers of any biologics (including antitoxin and vaccine) had to first secure the consent of the interior minister. (Germany, France, and Russia also had national systems of control covering specific biologics). In the United

States, some commentators objected that any such system was impractical and contrary to the American way. "In a country as large as ours, and with our republican form of government," *American Medicine* commented, "it would be very difficult, if not impossible, to carry out the supervision suggested." In the United States a dozen commercial establishments made diphtheria antitoxin. Each had 25 to 250 horses. Was the government really prepared to "test the serums of 100 or more bleedings a day" at sites around the country?[76]

But by the spring of 1902, it increasingly seemed clear to the medical profession that a national licensing and inspection regime was an idea whose time had come. The events in Camden and St. Louis had made such a move seem inevitable to organized physicians and vaccine makers alike. In late March, the *Medical Record* described the emerging professional consensus. "Of late, owing chiefly to the accidents which have occurred recently in this country from the use of diphtheria antitoxin and vaccine virus, there has been a movement in favor of Government control of such products," the journal said. "This proposition is not only highly proper under present circumstances, but absolutely imperative." But regulation was as far as this journal, or the profession, was ready to go. Government competition with free enterprise was unacceptable. Much the same conclusion was reached in an informal discussion at the annual meeting of the American Medical Association that spring. The old arrangement in American public health law—which allowed compulsory vaccination with unregulated products—was no longer tenable. A resolution introduced to the Homeopathic Medical Society of New York caught the spirit of many others: "when the State or local authorities enforce vaccination they are in justice bound to surround it with all the modern safeguards."[77]

There were a few precedents for such state-level regulation. In the most ambitious effort, Pitfield's grand tour of American vaccine farms for the Pennsylvania board in 1896 had demonstrated just how revealing on-site inspections could be. But the power of a state health board only reached so far; it could only use such information to control vaccine sold or produced within the state. The vaccine business was an interstate trade; the larger firms like Parke, Davis even manufactured and marketed their wares beyond the nation's borders. An effective system of government regulation, many reform-minded physicians concluded, would have to be a federal government responsibility. Rosenau's study of the vaccine market had shown the potential of that idea; in fact, Rosenau did not conceal his belief that the Marine-Hospital Service (with his laboratory) was the natural agency for the job.

On April 4, 1902, a bill was introduced simultaneously in the U.S. House and Senate, sponsored by the Medical Society of the District of Columbia, to create a new regime of federal regulation of biologics. The commissioners of the District drafted the bill, which received a strong endorsement from the District's health officer, William C. Woodward. The District was not home to a single biologics manufacturer. But Woodward noted that there was "no legal reason why any person whosoever should not enter into the business at any time." In the nation's capital, as in most American states, no restrictions at all governed the production and traffic in biologics. Woodward explained that the "manner in which these substances are produced and marketed" made it impossible to efficiently control them by inspecting only the finished product. The nature of biologics production justified a more intrusive system of licensing and unannounced inspections of manufacturers.[78]

As if anyone needed reminding, Dr. George M. Kober, chairman of the D.C. Medical Society, advised Congress of the moral urgency of the biologics bill and its connection to the "unfortunate accidents" in St. Louis and Camden that had brought so much discredit upon antitoxin and vaccine. The social value of these lifesaving products—and the considerable risks that attended their manufacture and sale—demanded "that action be taken to preserve the confidence of the medical profession and of the community generally in them." Like Woodward, Kober expressed dismay at the low barriers to entry in this industry of vital national importance: "Any kind of a stable, a little technical skill, and a fair amount of nerve are all that is needed." Individual states were "powerless to protect themselves against impure and impotent materials," especially since most of them consumed biologics made out-of-state. Testing a vial here or a package there was not enough; the whole industry required continuous government surveillance. "For these reasons Federal supervision is necessary," Kober declared. The

House and Senate committees on the District of Columbia went to work on the bill.[79]

M emories of a city and its nine lost schoolchildren lingered in the air of the vaccine debate. The report of the Camden Board of Health had not sat well with everyone. Many Americans refused to accept that the vaccine makers were blameless or that public health officials understood the risks of vaccination better than they. Conscientious physicians entertained doubts about the purity of the vaccine in their hands, and considered the possibility, however remote, that they might infect a patient with tetanus. Even some leading vaccine makers found the circumstantial evidence difficult to dismiss. "I am inclined to believe that the New Jersey cases were due to after infection and that the vaccine was not at fault," confided Ralph Walsh of the National Vaccine Establishment in a private letter, "yet the fact that the cases in Philadelphia, Camden and Atlantic City occurred almost simultaneously and from vaccine propagated by the same party staggers me."[80]

Ultimately, the Mulford Company's complicity in the deaths of the nine Camden children (not to mention scattered other fatalities) was a scientific question. As men of science, Robert Willson and Joseph McFarland determined not to let that question go unanswered. On April 23, 1902, as the two congressional committees considered the biologics bill, the Philadelphia County Medical Society assembled to hear Willson and McFarland present their findings.

Dr. Willson spoke first, taking up the gauntlet Dr. McFarland had thrown at his feet back in November. Since then, Willson had prepared abstracts on fifty-two cases of postvaccinal tetanus, which he had found in the medical literature and through personal correspondence with physicians and health officials. The cases dated as far back as 1839, but the majority of them were in children who had fallen ill between October 1, 1901, and March 30, 1902. Willson had discerned, as well as he was able, the circumstances surrounding the production of the vaccine used in each case, as well as the method of vaccination and the care of the wound. Laboratory tests had never detected evidence of tetanus in vaccine virus. And most physicians now understood the importance of following the best aseptic practices during vaccination. That left the patients. Mulling over his abstracts, Willson observed that in almost every case there had been "some gross breach in the care of the wound." For Willson, the evidence pointing to secondary infections was too strong to dismiss. As he reminded his audience, the streets of American cities were blanketed with tetanus bacilli. The Camden outbreak was unique: there had never been such a cluster of well-marked cases implicating a single maker of vaccine. But Willson concluded this was nothing more than a coincidence. "That vaccine virus may be infected with tetanus no one will deny," he conceded. "But that it has been, and in such cases as here come to view, deserves the full denial that has been given by the clinical symptoms and a careful scientific study."[81]

Joseph McFarland took the floor. Dr. McFarland was anything but a disinterested party. The highly regarded scientist had built the Mulford Company's biologics department back in the 1890s, though his work was primarily in antitoxins, not vaccine. He had left Mulford for a position as professor of pathology and bacteriology at the Medico-Chirurgical College of Philadelphia. McFarland had also been employed, since early 1901, as a consultant for Parke, Davis, Mulford's greatest rival. McFarland's conflict of interest was apparent (Mulford executives certainly thought so). But in the cozy medical world of turn-of-the-century Philadelphia, his position did not discredit his investigation, any more than had the Camden Board of Health's decision to place its investigation in the hands of Mulford's man Albert Barnes. And who in McFarland's audience could resist the chance to hear his paper? It remains to this day a pioneering study in the epidemiology of a pharmaceutical disaster. The quality of the paper is indicated by the fact that it was republished, with only a few significant changes, in *The Lancet*, the preeminent British medical journal of the era and an unwavering advocate of vaccination.[82]

McFarland spoke as a friend of vaccination, not a critic. Since the first reports of postvaccination tetanus from Cleveland and Camden, he had recognized in this complication "a matter of the gravest importance"—not only because tetanus increased the risk of vaccination but because it aroused "the animosity of those who have banded themselves together for organized opposition against this well recognized and only safeguard against smallpox." (In the *Lancet* version, the doctor would insert the words "misguided persons" after "those.") Nor was McFarland above the class prejudices of his peers. Though many Camden parents were still in mourning, he casually observed that the deceased had been "ignorant and filthy children."[83]

Like Willson, McFarland had spent the past few months tracking down American cases of postvaccination tetanus. He had found just fifteen in the medical literature, dating back to the 1850s. All had been attributed to secondary infection of the wound. Through correspondence with physicians and health officials, McFarland had turned up eighty more cases, for a total of ninety-five. (Had McFarland access to modern newspaper search engines, he would have found still more.) The first significant fact about these cases, McFarland said, was that sixty-three of them had occurred in a single year, 1901. Most of those had occurred in a single month, November. "Some exceptional condition," McFarland observed, had "changed an unimportant and infrequent complication into a very important and frequent one."[84]

The scientist proceeded to consider, in turn, each of the conventional explanations for the occurrence of tetanus after vaccination. To the argument (espoused by Willson and the Camden Board of Health) that tetanus was an "accidental secondary infection of the vaccination sore," McFarland conceded that such cases might occasionally occur. But "to content one's self with such a simple explanation may be to fall into egregious error, for if tetanus can thus occur it should do so in all parts of the world, with more or less regularity." According to McFarland's correspondence with the Imperial Health Office in Berlin and the Pasteur Institute at Paris, the complication was unknown in either Germany or France. Evidently the complication was "chiefly American" and had only become important within a single year.[85]

McFarland had still less patience for the argument, made by the board of health, that the Camden epidemic was caused by "atmospheric and telluric conditions." If tetanus were simply "in the air," Camden and the other afflicted areas should have been plagued by more than the usual incidence of ordinary traumatic tetanus. Instead, the board of health reports of both

Camden and Philadelphia showed *fewer* tetanus cases than usual in 1901 (not counting the vaccination-related cases).

To the argument that secondary infections were caused by careless treatment of the vaccination wound, McFarland again raised the question, But why now? Vaccination had been practiced for more than a hundred years, for most of that time "with a total disregard to cleanliness and asepsis." Why was the complication so prevalent now—decades after Koch and Pasteur—when vaccination was practiced with greater aseptic precautions than ever? And why was postvaccination tetanus epidemic only among Americans, rather than, say, among "the densely ignorant and filthy people of the island of Puerto Rico," where the Army had performed 860,000 vaccinations in 1899, with only two or three cases of tetanus reported?[86]

McFarland proceeded to the tougher part of his argument: to show that tetanus must have been present in the vaccine itself. The Camden health board investigators had tested samples of the locally available makes of vaccine and had found no evidence of tetanus in any of them. McFarland, who had made his name in the laboratory, did not present fresh laboratory evidence. What he did offer was evidence, gathered presumably from his correspondents, as to precisely which vaccines had been used in the ill-fated procedures. The rumors had been right. The "great majority of the cases" in 1901—thirty out of the forty cases that he was able to document—had followed the use of a single make of virus. Cleveland, Camden, Atlantic City, Philadelphia—in every locale, the closely clustered cases implicated "chiefly if not exclusively" one vaccine. McFarland named no names (he labeled the offending vaccine "virus E"), but as everyone in that room knew (and as McFarland's personal papers confirm), the maker was his former employer, Mulford. McFarland was ready to stipulate that "no care or expense" had been spared to produce these products. But the evidence, he said, "leads me to conclude that tetanus bacilli may be contained in the virus and distributed with it." In the *Lancet* version, McFarland would strike that "may be" and write "is."[87]

McFarland's most powerful piece of evidence—also epidemiological, rather than bacteriological—came from the Philadelphia Hospital. Smallpox had broken out among the hospital's 4,500 "inmates." Physicians went through the hospital vaccinating everyone, the sick and the well, with the exception of one section, the Men's Insane Department. The inmates of that department "were obliged to wait until a new consignment of the virus arrived." The new consignment was "virus E." All of the men were vaccinated. Now, McFarland had done some digging in the hospital records. Not a single case of spontaneous traumatic tetanus had occurred in the Insane Department for at least twelve years. As vaccination proceeded, though, five men in the department developed tetanus. All of them died. The outbreak caused a great deal of alarm in the hospital, and afterward, the doctors took additional precautions in dealing with suspicious vaccination wounds. Eleven more men fell ill with tetanus; after receiving "enormous doses of antitoxin," all recovered. With one possible exception, every patient who developed tetanus had been vaccinated with "virus E." At this moment, McFarland must have looked out at his audience. "There is something about virus E," he said.[88]

As to how the vaccine of one of the nation's most reputable and scientific makers might have been so terribly corrupted, McFarland invoked the world of the biologics stables that he knew so well: the manure of the calves, the hay, the dusts. . . . Glycerin seemed powerless before tetanus, as the cases implicated all of Mulford's vaccine products: dry points (unglycerinated), glycerinated points, and glycerinated lymph. (Later that year, Milton Rosenau would report that glycerin *preserved* tetanus spores.)[89]

Good scientist that he was, McFarland conceded to his audience that his argument had a "sole weakness." And that was the incubation period. Tetanus usually set in within ten days after an injury. Everyone cited William Osler's standard medical treatise on this point; McFarland had studied under the man at the University of Pennsylvania. In the vaccination cases, though, the average time elapsed between the procedure and the onset of tetanus was twenty-two days. But McFarland had a theory. He suggested that while the tetanus bacilli had been "ingrafted into the skin at the time of vaccination," they did not start to grow until "the development of the vaccine lesion pave[d] the way by the local destruction of tissue." This hypothesis would add about two weeks to the usual incubation period, for a total duration of about three weeks.[90]

We may never know for certain what caused the deadly outbreaks of postvaccination tetanus in Camden and other American communities in the fall of 1901. McFarland put forth compelling evidence to implicate Mulford's vaccine, but the argument's weak point—the incubation period—does leave a remainder of doubt. Still, there is no mistaking the political repercussions of these events. The vaccine crisis that erupted at Camden shocked the nation, roused the medical profession, and, ten weeks after Willson and McFarland presented their findings, ushered in a major change in American political institutions: the creation of the first effective system for regulating the production and sale of biologics.

On July 1, 1902, President Theodore Roosevelt signed the bill now known as the Biologics Control Act. Drafted by the District of Columbia Medical Society, the bill had been introduced by the Republican senator John Coit Spooner of Wisconsin. Although born of a great public controversy, the bill itself seems to have provoked little. Spooner's papers contain little correspondence regarding the legislation, and both houses of Congress enacted it without debate. As *The New York Times* noted, "The bill . . . would involve a dangerous expansion of Federal authority were it not aimed to correct an evil yet more dangerous as directly and immediately affecting the public health." The case for government regulation, the *Times* observed, "has been emphasized by recent experiences with virus and serums charged with tetanus germs and pus organisms."[91]

Although the law originated in the District, its provisions reached the nation. Effective January 1, 1903, the law established a system of licensing and inspection for all biologics sold in interstate commerce or imported from abroad. Practically speaking, this meant that all substantial makers of vaccines, antitoxins, serums, and toxins in the United States would need to seek a federal license to continue to trade in biologics. The act empowered a federal board—composed of the surgeon generals of the Army, Navy, and Marine-Hospital Service—to promulgate regulations to be enforced by the Treasury Department. Unannounced inspections would be carried out at the discretion of the treasury secretary. The act also required manufacturers to plainly label each product with the maker's address and license number and the date "beyond which the contents cannot be expected beyond reasonable doubt to yield their specific results." Penalties included suspension of the license, a maximum fine of $500, and up to one year's imprisonment.[92]

On the same day, Congress passed another law that enlarged the authority of the Marine-Hospital Service and gave it a commensurately bigger name: the U.S. Public Health and Marine-Hospital Service. Service medical officers would serve as the frontline inspectors of the new biologics licensing regime, and Milton Rosenau's Hygienic Laboratory would administer the act. The federal biologics board promulgated its first regulations in February 1903; they became effective that August. To receive a license, makers had to submit to an inspection by a medical officer from the Service. Licenses were good for just one year and could be reissued only after another inspection. If an inspector turned up any problems—bad production standards, impure or impotent products—the government could suspend a maker's license for thirty days; if the maker did not correct the problem, the government could revoke its license. Parke, Davis received license no. 1; H. K. Mulford no. 2; and H. M. Alexander no. 3. By 1904, the government had inspected and licensed thirteen biologics establishments, mostly for the manufacture and sale of diphtheria antitoxin and smallpox vaccine. Forty-one companies would hold licenses by 1921; all told, those companies marketed more than a hundred different biological products.[93]

The new law had an immediate impact on the biologics industry. The government refused to license some shoddy makers and suspended the licenses of others. Some smaller companies simply shut down, knowing they could not afford to meet the new standards. In the first few years of the new regime, Mulford's Pennsylvania rival H. M. Alexander had its license suspended and was twice ordered to remove tainted products from the market. In 1908 and 1909, Mulford and Parke, Davis had their licenses suspended when hoof and mouth disease broke out among their antitoxin horses and vaccine cows. Rosenau's Hygienic Laboratory continued his old practice of secretly buying up biologics on the open market and testing them for potency and purity. Vaccine quality in the United States rose dramatically.

Between 1902 and 1915, laboratory staff routinely tested smallpox vaccine for tetanus bacilli; none were found. The Hygienic Laboratory grew apace with its new responsibilities and powers. From Milton Rosenau's one-man operation in 1902, by 1904, the laboratory had a staff of thirteen, and it would continue to grow. In 1930, the Laboratory would be given a new name: the National Institute (later Institutes) of Health.[94]

The vaccine crisis of 1901–2 also prompted local and state health boards to increase their interventions in the vaccine market. In 1903, the Massachusetts legislature authorized the state board of health to manufacture its own lymph and antitoxin under the supervision of Theobald Smith. "Having provided for compulsory vaccination in this state," *The Boston Globe* commented, "the authorities are at least bound to see to it that the humblest citizen is provided with as perfect vaccine as it is possible to secure." Other state and local boards—including Cleveland's—regularly inspected vaccine lots in their own bacteriological laboratories.[95]

Leading biologics makers, particularly the largest firms, welcomed the new regime. The new system defused the vaccine crisis and gradually strengthened public confidence in vaccine and antitoxin. The new regulatory system, like other progressive business regulations instituted during the early twentieth century, fostered corporate consolidation by driving many small competitors out of the industry altogether (a welcome benefit to the likes of Parke, Davis and Mulford). Government licensing conferred a federal stamp of approval upon commercial vaccines, and the law established the government as a cooperative partner rather than a rival manufacturer (or, worse, a monopolistic one) in the brave new world of biologics. The National Hygienic Laboratory shared its research with private firms, ultimately saving those firms a great deal of money. The revolving door between government, academia, and the pharmaceutical industry continued to spin, as Joseph J. Kinyoun, Rosenau's predecessor at the Hygienic Laboratory, left the government in 1903 for a position as director of the Mulford laboratories in Glenolden. Rosenau himself would leave the laboratory six years later for a position at Harvard.[96]

Over time, all of this government activity increased the quality of American-made vaccines (not to mention other biologics) and assured the physicians and the public that they were not being compelled to undertake unnecessary risks in the name of the public health. The public would accept that assurance only gradually, and never fully. Four years after the passage of the Biologics Control Act, Congress would enact another, much better remembered statute modeled closely after it, the Pure Food and Drug Act. Together, the two laws introduced an unprecedented level of federal regulatory authority over one of the most profitable areas of American commerce and manufacturing, the pharmaceutical industry.[97]

The Biologics Control Act resolved one of the greatest contradictions in the practice of the nation's burgeoning public health systems: compulsory vaccination of the people without any governmental review of product safety. The new inspection regime saved compulsory vaccination at its moment of greatest crisis in the United States. Testifying before a House committee in 1910, Dr. C. T. Sowers of Washington, D.C., recalled the days, before the Biologics Control Act of 1902, when anyone who had a few cows could start up a vaccine farm. "There was no government inspection at that time of these farms, and the consequence was a very impure product," he said. "For us to have enforced vaccination before government inspection I have always regarded as extremely wrong, but now we can do it with the utmost propriety in stopping epidemics of smallpox."[98]

It is possible that Dr. Sowers had always regarded the old arrangements as fundamentally unjust. Or maybe he, like most doctors and public health officials, only came to appreciate that injustice—and its political untenability—after nine children died at Camden and the parents of that city, echoed by the protests of ordinary Americans in communities across the country, demanded a new dispensation of coercion and risk in American law.

For Camden, the new era arrived too late. The tetanus outbreak of November and December 1901 had sharpened public fears of that mysterious product of the stable and the laboratory called vaccine. So many parents revolted against vaccination that school officials delayed reopening the schools after Christmas break. Many residents continued through the winter to tell their doctors that they viewed vaccination as an unacceptable health risk for them and their children. They preferred to take their chances with smallpox, rather than risk exposing their loved ones to tetanus.

No more postvaccination tetanus deaths occurred in Camden after Bessie Rosevelt's death in December. But the toll from smallpox rose. By March 1902, smallpox had struck 165 people in the city, killing 15. Few among the dead in Camden had ever been vaccinated—none of them within the past three years. By the time the epidemic wound down that spring, smallpox had indeed proved more fatal there than vaccination.[99]

SIX

THE POLITICS OF
TIGHT SPACES

In the rear room above Caballo's saloon in East Harlem, behind the door with the big brass padlock, three children lay sleeping one cold February night in 1901. They slept under the bed, on a piece of cloth. Molina Caballo, the eldest, was four. Huddled beside her were her baby sister, Rose, and eighteen-month-old Antoinette Alvena. Some boxes of clothing stood by the bed, like a low wall, blocking the view from the doorway.[1]

Out on the street two hundred and fifty men awaited the order to move. Their breath formed a bank of fog against the winter night. Half of them were doctors—vaccinators and inspectors from the New York City Department of Health. The rest were uniformed patrolmen from the East 104th Street Police Station. It was 9:30, the hour chosen by Dr. Alonzo Blauvelt to ensure that the working people of Italian Harlem would be at home in their beds. The forty-seven-year-old chief inspector of the department's Division of Contagious Diseases had forsaken the warmth of his own bed to lead this raid in person. The vaccination corps aimed to inspect every room, yard, and body between Second Avenue and the East River, moving north from 106th Street to 115th Street. On an ordinary street map, the area didn't look like much: a few blocks on a vast city grid. But to the Department of Health, this stretch of five- and six-story tenements, where as many as five large families crowded onto every floor, marked a trouble spot in the medical geography of Manhattan, one of the island's most thickly populated and disease-ridden Italian "colonies."[2]

Ten weeks had passed since the Thanksgiving smallpox outbreak on All

Nations Block, over on the West Side. In that time, the department had reported nearly two hundred cases—not quite enough to strike terror into a city of three and a half million people, but more than enough to cause the circulation of library books to plummet, the city's regional trade to shrink, affluent families on the Upper West Side to cast out their servants, and the health department to hire seventy-five extra vaccinators. The department's smallpox strategy, as Blauvelt had recently explained it to *The New York Times*, involved isolation of all infected persons, surveillance of their family members and known contacts, and vaccination of "suspicious neighborhoods."[3]

City health officials often reminded the public that the Empire State had no compulsory vaccination law. But their actions said otherwise. The department's strategy for containing smallpox ensured that the full power of public health policing would be felt chiefly in the city's tight spaces—the crowded places where the wage earners lived, worked, prayed, and amused themselves. In those places, made closer still by the sudden entry of a vaccination squad and its armed police entourage, the department's authority proved hard to resist—and yet hard *not* to. What counts as compulsion is a question best answered by the person with her back to the wall. Even Blauvelt had said, after the December raids of the Bowery lodging houses, where his men had vaccinated 4,500 homeless people, that the sight of all those nightsticks "might have been something of a persuader."[4]

The response of American public health departments to epidemic smallpox at the turn of the century revealed progressive social governance at its most powerful and problematic. New York City's methods were exceptional only in their bureaucratic sophistication and scale. The same working principles, tactics, and values drove campaigns against smallpox in urban communities from San Francisco to Boston. The known behavior of smallpox—its tendency to spread like wildfire in crowded places—dictated a spatial response. In fact, smallpox would one day be eradicated across the world using a strategy of isolation, surveillance, and targeted vaccination not so different from that used by New York City to fight this, its last major epidemic of the disease, in 1901 and 1902. But the spatial strategy of disease control generated its own political theater of government coercion and working-class resistance.

Space, a necessary condition for the exercise of human freedom, came at a premium in the modern, urban-industrial society that the United States was so rapidly becoming. No one knew the price of space better than "the masses": the sort who journeyed to America below the water line, in the teeming steerage compartments of steamships, and who sought work in factories and mines, shelter in tenements and lodging houses, leisure in saloons and dance halls, and an education for their children in the public schools. Fighting contagion in the name of the public health meant wielding extraordinary authority in those tight spaces. Public health was, without question, a cutting-edge, progressive enterprise—the marshaling of modern science for the betterment of society. Few stood more to gain than tenement dwellers from successful campaigns against smallpox and other plagues. But as the price for the space they occupied in the nation, such people were expected to bear a level of intrusion and coercion that American governments did not dare ask of their better-off citizens. As a consequence, smallpox control triggered some of the Progressive Era's most dramatic conflicts between working-class people and the government. That is why Blauvelt's medical men traveled with a police escort.

New York's two major Italian "colonies" on the East Side—home to tens of thousands of America's newest immigrants—were closely watched by health officials even when smallpox did not threaten. As workingmen and families from southern Italy poured through New York harbor during the 1880s and 1890s—forming one distinct enclave on the Lower East Side around Mulberry, Elizabeth, and Mott streets, and another up here along the southern edge of East Harlem—their communities had become known to health officers as danger zones. The Italians understood all too well that disease flourished in those crowded, airless, double-decker tenements. Many who had made the move north from Mulberry Bend to East Harlem had done so not just to be closer to the construction and transit companies that were building northern Manhattan but also to live in this relatively cleaner and more open section by the East River. But East Harlem, too, grew thick with people and sickness.[5]

In both settlements, the Italians often welcomed health officials' efforts to improve their environment. In the summer of 1900, Blauvelt met little opposition when he rolled onto Mott Street at the head of a "disinfecting party," equipped with two wagons carrying one hundred gallons of disinfectant. Sanitary inspectors, backed by eighty policemen, moved through hallways, rooms, and cellars, pumping spray into every nook and across every surface they suspected of harboring germs. But when health department tactics collided with cherished cultural practices or the sanctity of the family, the officers encountered strong opposition. No action occasioned greater resistance than when authorities tried to remove an Italian child infected with tuberculosis or smallpox from her mother. Such experiences had convinced charity officials and health officers that Italian tenement mothers—knowing little English and seemingly indifferent to modern hygiene—posed a special threat to their own children and to the public health. "With ignorance of that stamp," said the crusading reformer Jacob Riis, "there is no other argument than force."[6]

With the return of smallpox to New York in late 1900, the eyes of the department were trained once again on the city's "Little Italies." In mid-January 1901, officials discovered a case of smallpox in a Mott Street tenement. In the last few days of the month, a department raiding party removed thirty people with smallpox from Italian Harlem. Inspectors found children tucked away in cupboards. "No one knows the damage that has been done by these Italians," said Dr. Frederick Dillingham, assistant sanitary superintendent for Manhattan. "They have gone from infected homes to work everywhere in this city; they have ridden in street cars, mingled with people, and may have spread broadcast the contagion. The most stringent measures should be taken to stamp out the spread of the disease." Now, on the night of February 1, as Blauvelt's men looked around at all those tenements, they had a good idea what they would find behind their brick and wooden walls.[7]

At Blauvelt's command, the men moved. They followed the same method on each block. With policemen stationed on the roofs, at the front doors, and in the backyards, doctors and police entered the tenements and rapped on doors, rousing men, women, and children. Frightened and furious, the residents moved into the lighted areas, where doctors inspected their faces for pocks and their arms for the mark of vaccination. Some understood the officials' English. They translated for the many who did not. Everyone lacking a good mark had to submit to vaccination. According to the *Times*, which had a reporter on the scene, many residents were "forcibly vaccinated."[8]

While some fought, others fled. Quick-footed men slipped past police at stairwells, doorways, and coal scuttles, bolting into the night. Doctors and police chased a man wearing nightclothes as he leaped over back fences. Catching him, they discovered he had recently been vaccinated—he had the ripe sore on his arm to prove it. He fled because, speaking no English, he did not understand the raid's purpose. He ran as if his life depended on it.[9]

The *Times* reporter recorded the "many dreadful scenes" that marked the progress of the vaccination corps through "the infected district." Italian Harlem was a predominantly male world—a complex and conflicted community forged in the common experiences of separation and alienation. Separation from loved ones back in southern Italy. Alienation from New York's Irish-dominated Catholic Church and Tammany Democratic machine. Only on these blocks did the authority of the Italian workingmen normally prevail. On a typical day, the streets were a male domain of bocce games, card playing, and conversation. Even so, mothers had a special moral authority in the tenements. In rooms where precious space was set aside for shrines to the Madonna, the bond of mother and child received the utmost respect. Now, as doctors and policemen "tore suffering little children from the arms of shrieking mothers," the reporter watched in amazement as "embryo riots" erupted in the rooms, yards, and streets.[10]

Chief Inspector Blauvelt and a group of his men arrived at the three-story wood-framed building on First Avenue that housed Caballo's saloon. They climbed the steps to the second floor. In the rear of the building, they came upon the door with the brass padlock. Tenants insisted those rooms were vacant. But Blauvelt and his men paused at the threshold. According to the *Times* reporter, "after a time they heard someone move within and the faint moan of a child in pain." The men kicked down the door. Inside, they found a second locked door. They forced it open. They came upon the pile of boxes. Pulling them away, they found the children under the bed. All three, the doctors quickly determined, were sick with smallpox "in the most dangerous stage."[11]

The mother of the Caballo children—who must have been in that room all along, the "someone" who moved within—struggled with the men as they carried her children and little Antoinette down the stairs to the street. The doctors tried to calm her, assuring her she could accompany her children to the isolation hospital on North Brother Island. Well-behaved mothers were sometimes allowed that privilege, especially if they were nursing infants. But when she continued her protest on the street, the physicians barred her from the ambulance wagon. Mrs. Caballo, the *Times* reporter wrote, "fought like a tigress on the sidewalk, and her screams aroused the neighborhood for blocks around." At last, she was driven indoors. The ambulance rolled away.[12]

By the end of that long night, Blauvelt's corps had scraped vaccine into the arms of many tenement dwellers, put watches on suspicious people, and removed nine infected children from their homes. Three-year-old Marion Scarroni was already dead when the doctors found her. None of the infected children had ever been vaccinated. In defiance of the law, their families and neighbors had secreted them away for days. Perhaps the parents believed they could best take care of their own children themselves; with smallpox, attentive care could mean the difference between survival and death. Or perhaps the parents feared, as the *Times* reporter supposed they must, that their little ones would "be taken away from them forever."[13]

In the early hours of the morning, the men of the vaccination corps made their way through the still sleeping city to their own homes to get some rest. They would need it. The Department of Health had another raid planned for Italian Harlem the following night.

N*one of the children had ever been vaccinated.* The scarless arms of those nine children of the Italian diaspora tell us something about their political status. Each was, in the words of the Constitution, a "natural born Citizen" of the United States. How could a child's skin say so much? In the final years of the nineteenth century, in the midst of the greatest sustained wave of human migration the world had ever seen, a vaccination scar had become something more than a sign of immunity from smallpox. The scar had become a sort of passport—a stamp-sized tattoo of *political* immunity, required by U.S. law and the quarantine regulations of the nation's major ports for entry into the American body politic. This legal requirement did not apply with equal force to all. The class-based spatial arrangements of the ocean voyage governed migrants' treatment upon arrival; steerage passengers underwent a far more exhaustive medical inspection than did their shipmates traveling in first- and second-class cabins. This much is reasonably certain: at the turn of the century, no child en route from Italy to a place like East Harlem would have made it through the Port of New York without well-defined pockmarks (proving a previous case of smallpox) or a discernible mark of recent vaccination.[14]

Twenty-four million people migrated to the United States between 1880 and 1924, two thirds of them entering the country through the Port of New York. The world over, people were on the move. Within Europe, some two million people picked up and moved each year in the late nineteenth century. Others reached ports like Bremen, Naples, or Liverpool and kept going. The promise of decent jobs and a greater measure of political and religious liberty helped make the United States the foremost destination of the global transoceanic migrations of the era. Until the 1920s, U.S. immigration law—shaped by interests of humanity and political economy—left the borders open to most of the world's peoples. Still, slowly accumulating categories of exclusion tightened the nation's points of entry, revealing the particular contours of the immigrant nation's rising anxiety about newcomers. Congress welcomed all but prostitutes (excluded in 1875); Chinese people, convicts, lunatics, idiots, and paupers (1882); unskilled contract laborers (1885); polygamists and "persons suffering from a loathsome or a dangerous contagious disease" (1891); and epileptics and anarchists (1903).[15]

Immigrants to the United States traveled alone, in families, or even as transplanted communities. Some came only as sojourners, others as the first pioneers in chains of family members intent on permanent settlement. Increasingly, they came from regions of southern and eastern Europe that prior to the 1880s had been insignificant players in the peopling of America. Italy alone contributed tens of thousands of migrants each year during the 1890s, hundreds of thousands annually after 1900. Four fifths of the Italians came from the southern peninsula and Sicily (the *mezzogiorno*). Compared to the familiar English, Scottish, Irish, and Germans, the "new" immigrants from Russia, the Austro-Hungarian Empire, and Italy seemed utterly foreign to many native-born Americans, who associated them with urban squalor, criminality, and, above all, disease. American state and federal governments shared that assessment, and beginning in the 1880s they built an increasingly elaborate system for the control of immigrant ships and the diseases they carried.[16]

Whether they began their journey by foot, wagon, or rail, immigrants from Europe or Asia got their first glimpse of America from a crowded, clamoring steamship. By 1870, steam had replaced wind as the force that powered the Atlantic crossing. During the next three decades, as the immigrant trade exploded, steamships grew larger and faster. Dozens of companies competed for immigrant fares, including Britain's White Star and Cunard lines, France's Companie Générale Transatlantique, Germany's Hamburg-Amerika line, and New York–based Pacific Mail Steamship Company. Steel hulls, better boilers, and stronger engines enabled the construction of great ships weighing five thousand tons or more. Each might carry as many as three hundred passengers in their first- or second-class cabins and a thousand or more belowdecks in the steerage compartments—so named because of their location near the ships' steering machinery.[17]

Companies packed steerage passengers onto tiers of narrow metal bunks that rose from dirty floors to low, sweaty ceilings. Toilet facilities were inadequate, portholes few. The lines running from southern Italy were notorious. One journalist, traveling as an immigrant from Naples in 1906, wondered how a steerage passenger was supposed to "remember that he is a human being when he must first pick the worms from his food . . . and eat in his stuffy, stinking bunk, or in the hot and fetid atmosphere of a compartment where 150 men sleep." The introduction of third-class cabins on some lines around the turn of the century offered passengers a bit more space. But accommodations remained exceedingly tight for the vast majority making the ocean voyage to America.[18]

The discovery of smallpox aboard a crowded ship at sea, a common occurrence in the nineteenth century, was a harrowing event that called forth the full power of the captain. As "master of the vessel," the captain's legal authority over his crew and passengers was, in the words of one law scholar, "necessarily summary and virtually absolute." The captain's men pulled infected passengers from their bunks and isolated them in the ship's infirmary. They fumigated compartments and personal effects. They vaccinated all aboard. Stoner's *Handbook for the Ship's Medicine Chest* instructed that the scabs from the sick passengers had to be carefully gathered up and burned, lest the infectious stuff be "conveyed not only to other parts of the ship, but to any part of the world to which the ship is bound." U.S. quarantine regulations required that the dead be wrapped in a sheet saturated with carbolic acid or bichloride of mercury and then placed in a hermetically sealed coffin or buried at sea. Nineteenth-century practice was to throw the bodies overboard "the instant that life had ceased." When the ship reached its destination, crew and passengers could expect to spend fourteen days in quarantine while medical officers waited to see how widely smallpox had spread among them. Exceptions were often made for travelers in first and second class.[19]

Even without smallpox aboard, travel in steerage was hazardous to the health. Late nineteenth-century American reformers and port officials protested the "heartless treatment" of steerage passengers on journeys that some compared to the "Middle Passage" of the bygone slave trade. Federal law levied a $10 penalty on ship companies for every passenger over eight years of age who died en route to the United States. But as two New York State commissioners of immigration lamented in 1868, the law was little enforced and did nothing for the hundreds of steerage passengers who died each year. The "interest of humanity" and "political economy," these officials declared, required the reform of a system where "emigrants are treated more like beasts of burden than human beings." The New York officers urged Congress to require all immigrant ships bound for America to carry a medical officer.[20]

By the time Congress finally enacted such a law, in 1882, the germ theory was on the rise. "Reasons of hygiene" joined the old "sentiments of charity, morality, and humanity" in congressional deliberations. Consequently, ship surgeons would do much more than care for sick passengers. They would become on-board agents of American quarantine regulations. That same year, 1882, the short-lived National Board of Health called for a new federal law to mandate "the vaccination of all immigrants not previously protected"—a policy that at that time applied only to passengers from foreign ports known to be infected with smallpox. But the board's argument that compulsory vaccination served the national interest—by preventing the constant importation of smallpox and stopping the amassing of "large numbers of susceptibles in circumscribed localities" (cities)—failed to move Congress to adopt a uniform national policy until another decade had passed.[21]

Faster ships, more than sharper laws, made the Atlantic crossing safer. In 1867, the journey took fourteen days or more; by 1900, some steamships could make the trip in under six. But the passenger's relief was the quarantine officer's headache. Speed altered the nature of the threat from smallpox. The average incubation period for the disease was about twelve days; in the age of sail, if anyone on board was infected that fact was likely to become known well before the vessel reached port. With each new increment of speed, the likelihood increased that infected travelers would reach port without presenting symptoms. As Dr. William M. Smith, health officer of the port of New York, reported in 1888, smallpox was the most difficult "latent contagion" to check by maritime quarantines. In that year alone, Dr. Smith's medical officers inspected some 383,000 steerage passengers. Given the rising boat speeds, any number of them might have contracted smallpox in a European village, traveled more than three thousand miles to New York, shown no symptoms at quarantine, boarded a train, and not felt the first fever until reaching the American heartland. Outbreaks in Illinois, Indiana, and Missouri were traced to recently arrived immigrants from Europe. According to Smith, this problem of latent contagion had caused "more anxious reflection" among American port health officers "than any other subject during the past nine years." He called for a strict policy that all passengers not vaccinated within the previous eight years submit to the procedure within two days of boarding a U.S.-bound ship.[22]

Increasingly, immigrant-receiving ports enforced just such a rule. One English opponent of vaccination, arriving in New York aboard a White Star steamship, wrote home that "America was closed against the unvaccinated anti-vaccinator, [who] was fast falling into the condition of the American negro-slave who was hunted down everywhere by everybody." Like New York, the port of Boston required all arriving steerage passengers to present a certificate, signed by the ship's medical officer, stating that they were protected from smallpox due to having survived the disease or by recent vaccination. Anyone failing to meet this requirement would be vaccinated by a port physician on arrival or be detained for fourteen days

on Gallop's Island. Steamship companies posted the port's vaccination re-
quirements, translated in several languages, on their Boston-bound ships.
For many immigrants, seeing this notice was their first encounter with
American law.[23]

For some steerage passengers, vaccination aboard a ship at sea was just
one inconvenience among many. For others, the experience was overwhelming. Steamship companies insisted they were merely providing a
service, one required of them in order to do business in American ports.
Passengers, they said, were at liberty to refuse the service and face the consequences. But the true test of liberty lies in its exercise. Liberal political
theorists since John Locke had suggested that real human freedom and
consent required physical space—"room enough"—for their exercise. Liberty needs an exit.[24]

Mary O'Brien was just seventeen when she boarded the Cunard
Steamship Company's *Catalonia* in Queenstown, Ireland. The *Catalonia* set sail for Boston on the Fourth of July, 1889. Mary had never been
away from home, and her mother had recently died. She made the journey
with her father and brother, traveling in a steerage compartment with three
or four hundred strangers.[25]

When the *Catalonia* was about three days out from Boston, Mary sat
with other female passengers on deck. A ship steward approached and told
them to go below. Not knowing the purpose, Mary descended the staircase
into steerage. At the landing, halfway down, she passed the ship's surgeon,
I. T. M. Griffin, who stood with two stewards. She continued to the bottom
of the stairs. All of the ship's female steerage passengers had been lined up
at the foot of the stairs and were making their way slowly up. The male passengers were nowhere to be seen. (Mary later learned that her father and
brother, along with all the rest, had been taken to another part of the ship.)
As the line moved forward, Griffin inspected each woman's arm and "proceeded to vaccinate those that had no mark." As they passed inspection,
each woman received a card from a steward—a vaccination certificate to be
presented to the port physicians. Mary held back until she was the last
woman on the stairs. She later recalled that she saw "no means of exit except

where the surgeon stood." She told Griffin that she knew from her mother that she had been vaccinated as a baby. He said there was no mark, and she "must be vaccinated."[26]

It seemed to Mary that no time at all had passed between that utterance and the sensation of Griffin's penknife scraping her left arm and the dabbing on of some stuff from a glass tube. By her own admission, she had not spoken out; she had not struggled. But she would later testify before a Boston jury that she had been vaccinated against her will and that the vaccine had made her sick. The judge instructed the jury that there was no evidence to support O'Brien's claim of assault. Hearing the case on appeal in 1891, the Supreme Judicial Court of Massachusetts agreed. To reasonable men of privilege and power—on a bench that included the future Supreme Court justice Oliver Wendell Holmes, Jr.—the young Irishwoman's legal claim may have seemed absurd. But, O'Brien's lawyers argued, "a distinction must be drawn between mere submission and positive consent." In the closed space below the waterline, separated from home and family, the immigrant girl had, by all appearances, passively submitted. Seeing no other exit, she held up her arm to be vaccinated. How many others felt as she did, we will never know.[27]

In 1891, the U.S. government took control of immigration administration. As it did, the poorer immigrants passed through an increasingly elaborate gauntlet of medical inspection at the nation's borders. At many American ports, state quarantine officers continued to inspect immigrants, but they did so in compliance with a burgeoning national regime for the processing of aliens. Mass immigration continued unabated, but immigration policy grew increasingly fraught, a battleground for business interests and organized labor, nativists and humanitarians. Global outbreaks of cholera, smallpox, and other diseases kept hygiene central to the administrative process. In laws of 1891 and 1893, Congress assigned the U.S. Marine-Hospital Service responsibility for keeping migrants with contagious diseases from entering the country. Service officers inspected immigrants at port stations from New York Harbor to San Francisco Bay, as well as at designated crossings along the Canadian and Mexican "frontiers." At a growing number of foreign ports, Service men attached to U.S. consulates inspected immigrant ships *before* departure, advising steamship companies to refuse passage to

those passengers who appeared likely to be turned back for medical rea
sons upon reaching America.[28]

U.S. quarantine regulations in force by 1894 made vaccination a prereq-
uisite to entry. Like the older state rules, the federal requirement treated
steerage passengers as a class: "All passengers occupying apartments other
than first or second cabin shall be vaccinated prior to entry, unless they can
show that they have had smallpox, or have been recently successfully vaccinated." Every steerage passenger bound for America received an inspection card that detailed an elaborate transatlantic process of medical
inspection. Boxes on the front of the card recorded the migrant's passage
through inspection by a U.S. consular agent or Marine-Hospital Service
officer at the port of departure; through quarantine at the port of entry;
and by the U.S. Immigration Bureau. Another box, completed by the ship's
medical officer, called for the passenger's number on the ship's manifest list,
where U.S. inspectors could find the detailed information on each passenger (including a medical history) required by U.S. law. The back of the card
called for an official stamp or signature certifying vaccination. In seven
languages, the card warned its holder, "Keep this card to avoid detention at
quarantine and on railroads in the United States."[29]

A ship entering New York harbor after 1891 first passed quarantine,
which remained the province of New York port authorities. The port health
officer and his assistants boarded, examining the ship's manifest and its bill
of health—a statement from the U.S. consulate detailing the sanitary condition of the ship and the port of embarkation. The inspectors then searched
for passengers infected with any of five quarantinable diseases: smallpox,
cholera, plague, typhus, or yellow fever. Smallpox was a constant concern.
Unlike the mild form of the virus spreading across much of the country
after 1898, the disease making the Atlantic passage was still classic deadly
smallpox.[30]

New York quarantine officials viewed Italian immigrants as a special
threat, despite the fact that Italian state medicine had long been in the vanguard of European smallpox control. The Italians had introduced bovine
vaccine, and Italian law required all children to be vaccinated within six
months of birth and required revaccination for entry into the schools and
factory jobs. But none of the nation's fourteen vaccine-manufacturing es-

tablishments could be found south of Rome. And in southern Italy, where most immigrants to the United States originated, vaccination was far from universal. For Dr. Alvah H. Doty, health officer of the port of New York, smallpox arriving on steamships from Naples was a "constantly recurring" problem. Without the quarantine precautions, "a horde of people would be landed on our shores to scatter smallpox broadcast over our land." It became routine: a huge ship would steam into the harbor, quarantine inspectors would find smallpox aboard, and all of the steerage passengers would be subject to vaccination and detention on Hoffman Island.[31]

If the New York inspectors found no quarantinable diseases aboard, they left the ship. At that point, physicians of the Marine-Hospital Service's Boarding Division took over. They gave passengers in the first- and second-class cabins a perfunctory inspection. Rarely was a first-class passenger singled out for closer inspection; and when this did occur, it usually happened not because the passenger looked especially unhealthy, but because some unspecified social marker made him appear out of place. As one officer of the Service explained, "If a passenger is seen in the first cabin, but his appearance stamps him as belonging in the steerage or second cabin, his examination usually follows."[32]

When the steamship at last arrived at its destination, a wharf or dock in New York City, only passengers traveling in third-class or steerage were ferried to the federal government's immigration depot at Ellis Island to run the gauntlet of medical inspectors known, in Service parlance, as "the line." The inspection at Ellis Island began as soon as the immigrants stepped off the barge. They lined up under the watchful eyes of the medical inspectors, who scanned the crowd for any individual possessing a mental or physical defect. Carrying their baggage, the immigrants climbed the steep stairs to the Registry Room, also known as the Great Hall. Watching from the top of the stairs, Service physicians looked for signs of weakness or heavy breathing that might indicate heart trouble. As the immigrants made their way through the congested gates and cordoned-off areas of the facility, officers examined eyes and scalps, hands and throats, all the while looking for signs that the passenger was unfit to enter the American nation.[33]

The power to exclude migrants from the political space of the nation— ordering their return to their port of origin, at the expense of the steamship

Immigrants from a smallpox-infected ship, detained in 1901 at the quarantine station on Hoffman Island, N.Y. Photo by Elizabeth Allen Austen. COURTESY OF THE LIBRARY OF CONGRESS

company—was the ultimate power entrusted to U.S. officials at points of entry. The exercise of this authority rested upon the medical expertise of the Marine-Hospital Service officers, who by 1903 inspected nearly 900,000 immigrants each year at thirty-two American ports and several overseas. The power to exclude was not exercised often. In an average year, U.S. officials turned back fewer than 1 percent of all arriving immigrants. But medical criteria, rather than political radicalism or poverty, became an increasingly important reason for exclusion, until it was the principal one. No wonder many recalled those hours at Ellis Island as the longest of their entire journey.[34]

Along the borders with Canada and Mexico, U.S. quarantine law called for aliens to enter only through designated points. Such rules proved difficult to enforce, particularly along the Rio Grande. Many Mexicans, accustomed to traveling freely across the border for work or to visit relatives, viewed the tightening system of inspection around the turn of the century as a violation of their rights. In a single week in February 1899, Acting Assistant Surgeon H. J. Hamilton and his staff at Laredo, Texas, inspected more than 2,500 migrants crossing the Rio Grande via the Laredo Foot Bridge, a truss bridge built in the 1880s, or by ferry or train. Most of the people he met at the footbridge insisted upon their "right to pass" without inspection. But that was a privilege the Service extended only to affluent travelers. While the Service routinely inspected all arriving passenger trains from Mexico, checking all second- and third-class passengers for "recent vaccine scars," inspectors allowed travelers in the Pullman cars simply to swear to their immunity. In his time at the post, Hamilton concluded that the poorer class of Mexicans reckoned smallpox a fact of life and feared vaccination far more than the disease.[35]

In the winter of 1899, Surgeon General Wyman received a flurry of dispatches from Laredo, a border city of 15,000 people, the majority of them of Mexican descent. Virulent smallpox had raged there for months, with 376 cases and 83 deaths reported in January and February. (The death rate indicates an epidemic of classic variola major.) Hamilton advised the local authorities "to issue some law compelling vaccination, by force if necessary." In March, Texas health officer W. T. Blunt arrived from Austin. City officials set about fumigating homes, vaccinating, and removing infected residents by force to the pesthouse. The actions targeted the poorer barrios on the east side of town. Meeting strong resistance from the residents, Blunt called in the Texas Rangers. In the ensuing violence, one Mexican American leader was killed, thirteen people were wounded, and twenty-one were arrested. A contingent of the U.S. Tenth Cavalry arrived, and Hamilton took charge of the local vaccination corps. Even with so many soldiers in the area, fifteen residents "had to be reported, arrested, and then vaccinated."[36]

Even beyond the nation's borders, the mark of vaccination became a powerful signifier of American rule. In September 1905, more than 650 black contract laborers from Martinique traveled aboard the French steamship *Versailles* to Colón, a port city located near the Atlantic entrance to the U.S.-controlled Panama Canal Zone. As the crowded ship approached the port, laborers in canoes paddled up to the ship, warning the passengers that poor treatment and harsh conditions awaited them on shore. The messengers said that vaccination, required of all immigrant laborers by the American sanitary regulations of the Isthmian Canal Commission, would produce "an inextinguishable mark" that would make it impossible for them ever to leave the Isthmus. The migrants refused to leave the ship. The next morning, officials persuaded 500 of them to land. But 150 men remained on board and demanded to be returned to Martinique. A force of Panamanian and Canal Zone police forced the migrants from the ship. According to *The Washington Post*, "nearly everyone of them had been clubbed, and several were bleeding from nasty wounds." Many had jumped overboard. Later that same afternoon, all of the laborers were vaccinated, loaded on a train, and shipped out to Corozal, where they were put to work building the canal.[37]

In the hands of a subordinate people, a rumor can be a surprisingly potent political tool—a "weapon of the weak"—even when the rumor is not true. But the canoe riders of Colón did not exaggerate. In the Canal Zone, only the immigrant workers were compelled to be vaccinated. The doctors uniformly scraped their right arms. Foremen and canal officials used the marks—much as the slave catchers of the remembered past had used brands—to identify and apprehend runaway workers in the Panamanian jungle.[38]

Watching with dismay as smallpox spread across the American heartland in 1901, Dr. James Hyde of Chicago's Rush Medical School urged state and local governments to use their full police powers to eradicate this affront to modern civilization. Like many of his professional peers, Hyde found the metaphor of the vaccine scar as passport irresistible. He urged that American governments require this medical mark for entry into the country's civic spaces. "Vaccination should be the seal on the passport of entrance to the public schools, to the voters' booth, to the box of the juryman, and to every position of duty, privilege, profit or honor in the gift of either the State or the Nation," he declared. In one respect, vaccination seemed superior to a printed identity document; this government-certified ticket of immunity was stamped indelibly upon the body. Seasoned health officials did not trust the paper vaccination certificates issued by private physicians; they always asked to see the scar. As one writer noted in *American Medicine*, "This certain, well-defined sign cannot be forged."[39]

That writer was wrong. As health officials and police tightened enforcement of vaccination at public schools, industrial work sites, and railroad depots, Americans started forging scars. Some tried plaster fakes. Others followed recipes printed in unorthodox medical journals and passed along by word of mouth. "Get a little strong nitric acid," advised the Columbus, Ohio–based journal *Medical Talk for the Home*. "Take a match or a toothpick, dip it into the acid, so that a drop of the acid clings to the end of the match. Carefully transfer the drop to the spot on the arm where you wish the sore to appear. Let the drop stand a few minutes on the flesh. Watch it closely." After a few minutes, the skin, stinging, turned red. That meant it was time to blot up the remaining acid. In a week, the nickel-sized spot turned dark. "This sore will gradually heal by producing a scar so nearly resembling vaccination that the average physician cannot tell the difference." Health officials condemned the "vile crime" as the handiwork of a few antivaccination fanatics. But these intimate acts of civil disobedience were part of something larger, a groundswell of popular opposition to "state medicine."[40]

"True compulsory vaccination," as Health Officer Charles V. Chapin of Providence defined it, aimed to secure general immunity from smallpox by requiring every member of the community to be vaccinated and periodically revaccinated. The model was Germany, which boasted the world's most vaccinated population and the one most free from smallpox. German law required that every child be vaccinated in the first year of life, again during school, and yet again (for the men) upon entering military service. The U.S. Constitution, as interpreted at the time, foreclosed any serious talk of achieving such a universal system through federal law. That left the matter to the states. Hard political realities—the diversity of state legal cultures, the uneven development of their public health systems, and the suspicion with which many Americans greeted any government interference with their personal liberties—assured that a German-style system of vaccination, covering the entire U.S. population, never came to pass. Most vaccination laws on the books were the residue of bygone epidemics.

As the emergencies that begot those laws faded from memory, enforcement waned.[41]

For all of these reasons, the epidemics of 1898–1903 found many communities poorly protected by vaccination. New circumstances made health officials' jobs even harder. The advent of a milder type of smallpox and heightened concerns about vaccine safety hindered the efforts of public health officials, who often received little support from lawmakers, government executives, and the public.

Still, when confronted with a costly smallpox epidemic, the same governments that during times of relative health shied away from compulsory measures readily resorted to coercion. The emergency powers they exercised were extraordinary—particularly in thickly populated spaces. In his definitive 1904 treatise *The Police Power*, Professor Ernst Freund of the University of Chicago Law School covered every form of state regulatory action from liquor licensing to the suppression of labor strikes to trust-busting. But he singled out compulsory vaccination to illustrate the outer limits of legitimate state action. "Measures directly affecting the person in his bodily liberty or integrity," he wrote, "represent the most incisive exercise of the police power." During the turn-of-the-century epidemics, millions of ordinary Americans could not enter their work sites, send their children to public school, or travel freely without showing their vaccination scars. To them, the metaphor of the passport seemed real enough.[42]

Besides soldiers, prisoners, and immigrants fresh off the boat, the most vaccinated members of American society were public schoolchildren. School vaccination rules paved the way for a growing array of measures governing the bodies and behavior of children, as more and more states made school attendance mandatory into the teenage years. By 1902, nearly 16 million Americans—72 percent of all children aged five to eighteen—attended public schools; another 1.2 million went to private schools. The great exception was the South, where most state legislatures had yet to compel school attendance or vaccination. In 1901, only five states had laws on the books requiring universal childhood vaccination in the first year or two of life. But most took measures to keep unvaccinated children from the public schools, especially when smallpox threatened. (Some states, including California and Massachusetts, mandated school vaccination by statute;

others, such as New Jersey and Maine, authorized school boards to order vaccination; and in still other states, school boards simply issued orders at their discretion.) Almost everywhere, the requirements applied exclusively to public schools. Parents with the means to send their children to private schools could opt out.[43]

In an era when American governments took ever greater responsibility for children—through child labor laws, school laws, and new child-welfare institutions such as the juvenile court—the vaccination rules served multiple purposes. As some health officers pointed out, it would have been unconscionable for states to require children to spend half their day in crowded classrooms without protecting them against socially transmitted diseases. The measures, coupled with increasingly routine medical inspections in the public schools, also extended state authority from the school into the home, bringing working-class and immigrant parents into line with new progressive norms of hygiene. When unvaccinated children were excluded from school, their parents could face prosecution under education laws. Some officials even imagined that the requirement made a positive impression on the students—"familiarizing the juvenile mind with respect for authority," as one put it, "whatever the merits of the medical expedient may be."[44]

Compulsory vaccination turned American public schools into theaters of conflict. Parents, pupils, teachers, and sometimes even principals challenged the rules with tactics ranging from civil suits to civil disobedience. Parents decried the measures as a violation of their domestic authority and a threat to their children's health. Officials in Chicago and New York uncovered what the *Times* called "an extensive traffic" in phony vaccination certificates. The school strikes that rocked Camden and Rochester after Camden's tetanus outbreak were not isolated incidents. In Gas City, Indiana, two hundred mothers, holding their unvaccinated children by the hand, marched upon the public schools building on a December morning in 1902. Facing down a contingent of policemen at the schoolhouse doors, they demanded that their "scarless" children be admitted.[45]

In nearby Bluffton, Indiana, the school board squared off against the health board, refusing to enforce the latter's vaccination order. In Delaware County, Pennsylvania, a group of female teachers refused to let physicians

New York City schoolboys line up to have their vaccination marks inspected by a public health officer in 1913. COURTESY OF THE NATIONAL LIBRARY OF MEDICINE

examine their arms for scars, protesting a policy that compelled them to undergo a risky medical procedure before entering their workplaces. Students caused trouble, too. Visiting Newburg, Ohio, Cleveland health officer Martin Friedrich came upon some children outside their school. The students called out to each other, "Are you vaccinated? Are you vaccinated?" Friedrich understood: the vaccinators were in the schoolhouse. He slowed his pace and listened. "Pretty soon I knew what they were up to," he recalled. The corner grocery-man had told some of them that they should wash the vaccine from their arms to keep them from getting sore. "They communicated it to each other in a most lively manner, and all hurried as fast as they could to the grocery-store to wash their arms."[46]

Mass vaccinations at American workplaces generated their own dynamics of power and conflict. American workers were vulnerable not only to contagion but to arbitrary dismissal during epidemics. Domestic employers, fearing exposure to infection, shunned servants and laundresses, causing destitution in the tenements. When smallpox broke out, some factory owners abruptly suspended operations, with no thought of compensating their workers for lost wages. In a typical incident in Sayreville, New Jersey, two handkerchief manufacturers, acting upon the advice of physicians, told their employees to stay home until the local epidemic was brought under control. The order affected about three hundred workers, many of them the breadwinners of their families. Workers pleaded with foremen. One factory girl dropped to her knees and prayed. All to no avail. To employers and local health officials, the mere threat of smallpox justified the most overt acts of ethnic scapegoating. When a single Italian worker with smallpox escaped from quarantine in Bethlehem, Pennsylvania, in 1902, Bethlehem Steel Company summarily discharged all of its Italian workers. Italians were forbidden to ride the city streetcars until the outbreak subsided.[47]

Employers normally bristled at workplace health regulations. Key pieces of progressive labor legislation—including factory safety measures and laws to shorten the workday—were justified by reformers as necessary to protect the health of workers and the public. Manufacturers' associations and individual employers challenged such measures in the courts, insisting they violated the "liberty of contract" between worker and employer. But when faced with the potentially expensive emergency of a smallpox epidemic that had a relatively cheap solution (vaccination), many industrial employers readily cooperated with public health officials. They willingly turned their private workplaces into public health stations.[48]

Many employers made vaccine refusal grounds for dismissal. In one 1901 episode, six Brooklyn health department physicians, policemen in tow, appeared at the sugar refineries of Havemeyer & Elder, just in time for payday. As each worker stepped forward to receive his wages, a city doctor vaccinated him. Railroad and streetcar corporations, liable for damages if an employee with smallpox infected a passenger, were particularly vigilant. In the winter of 1903, as smallpox raged in the Pennsylvania coal region, officials of the H. C. Frick Coke Company, a vast industrial enterprise of coal mines and coke works, ordered all of its employees *and* their families to get vaccinated. According to the *Chicago Tribune*, the order affected 300,000 men, women, and children.[49]

When employers joined forces with local health officers and police to enforce vaccination, a crowded factory floor could become as confining as a prison. In April 1901, a female worker at the American Tobacco Company in Passaic, New Jersey, died of smallpox. She had continued to work during

the early contagious stages of her disease. In such an instance, any responsible employer would want to secure the safety of his workplace by assuring
that the workers got vaccinated. But the measures taken at the American
Tobacco Company went well beyond that duty. A squad of government
physicians and police entered the plant, determined to vaccinate all 350
women and girls who worked there. Informed they would have to submit
to vaccination, some workers fainted, "others became hysterical, and there
was a general rebellion," *The New York Times* reported. Two hundred of
the women tried to escape, but they found all of the factory exits locked.
"[A]ll were finally vaccinated."[50]

As C. P. Wertenbaker observed time and again in the South, workers'
natural fears of vaccination were intensified by their need to earn. Many
American industrial workers feared, with good reason, that vaccine would
cause their arms to swell, making it impossible for them to support themselves or their families for a period of days or weeks. And they knew better
than to expect their bosses or the state to support them during that period
of disability. Some washed off vaccine (as Martin Friedrich spied workmen
doing at an Ohio factory). Others walked off job sites rather than be vaccinated. African American workers, in particular, dreaded vaccination.
In June 1900, the New York State Board of Health ordered the vaccination
of five hundred black workers at the Wash & Company brickyard in
Stockport, New York, about thirty miles down the Hudson from Albany.
According to *The New York Times*, when fifty of the laborers "refused to
submit," Governor Theodore Roosevelt sent in the Hudson Company of
the state militia, "ninety men strong," to enforce vaccination against the
"unruly negroes."[51]

Violence was always a possibility when health officials clashed with
American workers. In 1902, smallpox struck the neighboring mining cities
of Lead and Deadwood, in the Black Hills of South Dakota. Both cities
ordered a general vaccination, but the miners balked. The city physician of
Lead—accompanied by four assistants, the sheriff, and five deputies—
conducted a nighttime raid of the city's crowded saloons, gambling dens,
and theaters. At the Gold Mine Saloon, the officers covered both entrances
and proceeded to vaccinate everyone in the place. Several fights broke out,
but eventually the police overwhelmed the miners.[52]

Controlling smallpox on the nation's vast network of railroads was obviously a crucial step to stamping out the American epidemics. But how? In the winter of 1902, Chicago health officials announced a Chicago-sized plan. The Second City stood at the hub of the nation's transportation networks. The same central geographical position that made Chicago such an economic force—bringing grain, lumber, and livestock from the rural hinterland to American markets and sending Montgomery Ward catalogues back in the other direction—made the city vulnerable to smallpox outbreaks all over the Middle West. In January 1902, about 10,000 cases of smallpox—roughly three fourths of all reported cases in the United States—occurred within a few hours' train ride from Chicago. The Chicago Health Department decided to use the Second City's position as the railroad hub of the Middle West to stamp out smallpox in a ten-state region with 25 million inhabitants. City health officials made an agreement with officials of the major companies serving Chicago to spur "wholesale vaccination and revaccination in every infected locality" of the region by enforcing a strict inspection of all travelers from those communities. The railroads also ordered all of their employees serving the Chicago routes to submit to vaccination or lose their jobs. And every car entering the city from any direction had to be fumigated for six hours before new passengers were allowed to enter it.[53]

A cross the American political landscape, public ambivalence about compulsory vaccination during the turn-of-the-century epidemics registered in the statute books. Mississippi, one of the states hardest hit by virulent smallpox in 1900 and 1901, enacted a new law authorizing county boards to order compulsory vaccination (which many refused to do). Rhode Island passed a new law in 1902 that mandated vaccination of all children before their second birthday and empowered the state board of health to order vaccination of all "inmates of hotels, manufacturing establishments, hospitals, asylums, and correctional institutions." That same year, Massachusetts gave local health boards authority to compel vaccination at will.[54]

Other states, though, moved the other way. Wisconsin governor Robert

M. La Follette vetoed a new compulsion statute in 1901, insisting (as the *Journal of the American Medical Association* remarked with disbelief) that "he does not believe an emergency exists which demands a law repugnant to so many good citizens!" In Utah that same year, grassroots opposition to compulsory public school vaccination spurred the legislature to pass a law banning compulsion. The *Wasatch Wave* applauded the statute: "it robs the tyrant of his power to rob the people of their right to 'life, liberty and the pursuit of happiness.'" And two years later, well-organized antivaccination activists in Minnesota persuaded the legislature to forbid compulsion in the absence of an actual smallpox emergency.[55]

New York lawmakers debated a compulsory vaccination bill in 1902. The state had long banned unvaccinated children from the public schools. But beyond that the legislature had not ventured, prompting *The New York Times* to assert, "compulsory vaccination is a thing utterly unknown in this State." In February 1902, State Senator James McCabe, a physician from Brooklyn, introduced a bill that would have been one of America's strongest vaccination laws. It required cities to enforce universal vaccination whenever the health department called for it. Any resident who refused vaccination was subject to a $50 fine and imprisonment for ten days. Companies with more than ten employees were forbidden to hire anyone not vaccinated within the past five years. The New York County Medical Association championed the measure. So did the *Times*. Remarkably, the New York City Board of Health opposed the bill. The city's new health commissioner, Dr. Ernst J. Lederle, explained that the legislation would simply hand the city's antivaccination leagues a tool for recruitment. Compulsion was unnecessary, Lederle insisted. His department had encountered "no serious difficulty . . . in persuading the people to submit to vaccination." The bill died in the New York Assembly.[56]

Residents of New York City—at least those who lived in the tenements or read the daily papers—must have found Ernst Lederle's public position on compulsion baffling. A Ph.D.-bearing chemist, Lederle had taken office in January 1902, appointed by the city's new reform mayor Seth Low to head up both the board of health (which promulgated health regulations for the city) and the department (which carried them out). High on the list of disgraceful conditions that Low's administration promised to eradicate was smallpox, which had continued to spread despite the aggressive tactics of Alonzo Blauvelt's vaccination corps. Nearly 2,000 cases, with 410 deaths, had been reported in the city's five boroughs in 1901, making this New York's worst smallpox epidemic since 1881.[57]

For Lederle, smallpox was the most interesting problem confronting a modern department whose activities covered everything from making vaccine to policing milk dealers to arresting the spitters who spread the city's deadliest endemic disease, tuberculosis. Smallpox concentrated Lederle's mind on the larger purpose of his office: to extend the benefits of modern medicine to the city's "great tenement population—ill-housed, ill-nourished, bred in the foul air of the slums; above all, ignorant of the laws of cleanliness and right living, and willing to go to any lengths to hide the evidence of disease from the municipal physicians." Tellingly, Lederle expressed admiration for the work of the U.S. Army Medical Department in Havana, "a striking example of what can be done in a short time."[58]

Under Lederle, the health department managed compulsion well enough without a law that would have strengthened the political base of antivaccinationists and given Albany a greater hand in the affairs of local health departments. Lederle publicly denied that coercive legal power was necessary, even as his department routinely exercised just such power in the city's tight spaces. Lederle added more than 150 new men to the vaccination corps. By the end of his first year in office the department performed a record-breaking 810,000 vaccinations—more than twice as many as in any previous year. The commissioner sent letters to the owners of all the city's larger factories, offering them the services of a vaccination squad, at any hour of the day or night. His board of health ordered lodging houses to refuse shelter for more than one night to anyone who failed to provide proof of recent vaccination. Discovery of a pimple-faced passenger aboard a trolley in the Bronx in March 1902 was sufficient cause to reroute the train, with all the passengers aboard, to the nearest police station, where a city health officer got busy with lancet and virus. "Those who objected were sternly admonished and the work went on." The following month, James Butler, a hostler, and his wife, Kate, living on the third floor of a Third Avenue tenement in Harlem, were discovered "suffering from smallpox in an advanced stage." A vaccination squad arrived, backed by twenty police officers. Men, women, and children fled down fire escapes or climbed to the roof. "But policemen were at hand at every place of egress, and appeals and entreaties were unheeded," the *Times* reported. By the raid's end, 300 residents had been vaccinated, "the majority of them very much against their will." James Butler was found hiding in a coal bin. After a struggle, he and Kate were taken to North Brother Island.[59]

In November 1902, a health department inspector discovered a person with smallpox in a tenement on West Twenty-sixth Street inhabited by forty African Americans. The inspector summoned the police. They stormed the door. As the *Times* reported, "When the attacking party entered, some of the inmates went to the roof, some climbed out to the fire escape, and others tried to gain the street." City physicians took out their instruments and began vaccinating the residents. Four were vaccinated in the hallway, others "in the corners of rooms where they had huddled together for refuge." Still others received their "treatment" on the roof. One of the lodgers, twenty-four-year-old Eva Gerry, climbed out onto the fire escape, lost her balance, and fell three stories to the sidewalk, breaking both of her arms and several ribs.[60]

The department under Lederle did not do away with compulsion. It expanded the scope and intensity of the same old tactics. In fact, Blauvelt continued to head up the Division of Contagious Diseases. The department's measures undoubtedly did much to bring the New York City smallpox epidemic of 1901–2 to an end. In 1902, the Division of Contagious Diseases reported 1,516 more cases with 309 more fatalities. Most of them occurred in the first six months of the year, after which the epidemic tapered off. In 1903, only 67 cases were reported, with just 4 fatalities; 40 percent of the people with smallpox treated in the municipal hospitals were new arrivals to the city. The department performed an additional 215,000 vaccinations that year, bringing the grand total under Lederle's two-year regime to well over a million, roughly one third of the city's population.[61]

As *Scientific American* noted, in a laudatory article on Lederle's department, the city's "crusade against smallpox" had engendered "bitter opposition." It was strongly "opposed by the ignorant and superstitious, and by a considerable body of the more intelligent who were opposed to vaccination on principle. The inspectors were openly abused and resisted, and it was only through the co-operation of the police that an effective campaign was conducted."[62]

In November 1903, Mayor Seth Low ran for reelection on a campaign that trumpeted his administration's victorious war on smallpox. Campaign posters placed on elevated trains displayed the words of the reformer Jacob Riis, who urged New Yorkers to vote for the man who had driven prostitution from the tenements and "wiped out the smallpox in six months." The voters, though, were not sufficiently impressed. They returned control of City Hall and the health department to the Democrats. Ernst Lederle left the department and founded the profitable Lederle Antitoxin Laboratories, manufacturers of vaccine, sera, and other biological products.[63]

New York was not the only American city to deploy paramilitary vaccination squads. The Chicago Health Department sent teams of physicians and police on nighttime raids to the tenements and into the cheap lodging houses along South Clark Street. In Boston, a notorious "hotbed of antivaccinationism," nineteen citizens were prosecuted for refusing to submit to vaccination as city physicians and police made door-to-door sweeps. One night in November 1901, the health department sent a "virus squad" to the "five and ten cent" lodging houses in the South End. Physicians carrying lancets were accompanied by club-wielding police. The squad busted down doors. Policemen held down struggling men on their cots while doctors performed the operation. According to a *Boston Globe* reporter, the "tramps" fought back. They "kicked and clawed and also fought with teeth and heads against what some of them declared was an assault upon their rights as otherwise free and independent American citizens." The homeless men uttered "every imaginable threat from civil suits to cold-blooded murder."[64]

One American city tried a very different spatial approach to the fight against smallpox. Like most public health authorities of his day, Cleveland health officer Martin Friedrich believed in compulsory vaccination; it was, after all, national policy in his native Germany. With his gold spectacles and close-trimmed beard, the thirty-six-year-old physician might have been mistaken for Sigmund Freud as he entered cheap lodging houses in the middle of the night and urged free vaccination upon the rowdy bachelors he encountered.[65]

In the spring of 1901, mild type smallpox struck the cities along Lake Erie. (More than 1,200 cases would be reported by year's end, but only 20 deaths.) Friedrich launched a wholesale vaccination campaign concentrated in the city's immigrant working-class neighborhoods. But four people died of tetanus following vaccination, and many more took ill. With a candor all too rare for a health official of the day, Friedrich announced that the available vaccines were unreliable at best, toxic at worst. "A man would have to have a heart of stone if he would not melt at the sight of the misery it produces," he said.[66]

Backed by the progressive mayor Tom Johnson, Friedrich ceased vaccination and embarked on a different sort of campaign to fight smallpox. He ordered all smallpox patients isolated from the general population. Then he hired a corps of medical students to go house-to-house with formaldehyde generators and fumigate every home in the city. The disinfection campaign took months to complete, but by the end of 1901 it seemed to bring smallpox under control, making the Cleveland experiment national news and Friedrich a reluctant hero of the antivaccination movement. When a physician named J. H. Belt accused Friedrich of "furnishing aid and comfort to the enemy," the health officer responded that his campaign had won hearts and minds where compulsory vaccination had won only enemies. "A sigh of relief went over the city when I stopped vaccination," he wrote. "The people began to work in harmony with us, opened their houses for us to disinfect them, gave us all the information we wanted, and helped us in every way conceivable."[67]

For the many contemporaries who applauded Dr. Friedrich's Cleveland experiment as a more palatable alternative to coercion, time delivered an unsettling rejoinder. Friedrich's candor about vaccine safety was laudable. His formaldehyde clouds appeared to stamp out the disease, enabling him to duck the most controversial public health issue of his generation—compulsory vaccination. But this dispensation was only temporary. Friedrich's policy left people unprotected.

A homeless man from Hoboken, New Jersey, entered the city in May 1902, carrying in his feverish body smallpox of the severest type. As Friedrich said, it was "the smallpox 'we read about.'" The city launched a sweeping campaign in which more than half the city's residents were vaccinated through an extraordinary public effort involving civic groups, religious leaders, and the local Academy of Medicine. Chastened but still cautious, Friedrich used the city's new bacteriological laboratory to test the vaccines on the market for one that was safe and reliable. The vaccination campaign finally stamped out the epidemic by early 1903. But by that time, 246 people lay dead from smallpox.[68]

On January 25, 1902, the *Philadelphia Medical Journal* published an update on Pennsylvania's smallpox epidemic. The report included the following lines: "At Resetto, an Italian settlement near Bangor, the attempt of the police to bury a woman who died of smallpox, without religious services, resulted in a riot. The Italians seized the coffin, bore it into the church, and then stood guard, chasing the policemen away."[69]

Roseto (as the place was actually called) was a close-knit settlement of fifteen hundred people at the edge of slate quarries in eastern Pennsylvania. The place had recently been named after the hill town in southern Italy from which most of its residents had come. The incident, reported without comment in a leading American medical journal, shows the determination of one immigrant community not to let even the deadly serious matter of smallpox interfere with a proper Catholic burial for one of its members. The people of Roseto rioted. They seized the body from the police. They bore it to a sacred space, their sanctuary. They drove the police from their church and stood guard so that the proper religious rites could be performed. In doing so, they unknowingly contributed a few sentences to a swelling archive of popular opposition to public health authority at the turn of the century—an archive most officials would have agreed showed the ignorance and superstition that hindered their efforts to stamp out smallpox.[70]

The power to remove and isolate an infected body—whether dead or alive—was fundamental to public health. "The power of removal," said Leroy Parker and Robert Worthington in their treatise on American public health law, "is unconditional and unqualified." But as the tenement mothers of Italian Harlem showed Blauvelt's vaccination corps, the power was not uncontested. The most common form of resistance was concealment, hiding sick people, sometimes entire families, from public view. When health officials and police went looking for hidden cases of smallpox—sometimes acting on a tip from suspicious neighbors, school officials, or employers—they often walked into a fight. Experienced health officers expected trouble when they came for children. Fathers and mothers responded with tears, fists, and shotguns.[71]

Charles Chapin of Providence, one of the more self-reflective public health officials of his era, reckoned that people had good reasons for dreading the pesthouse. For their comfort and survival, smallpox patients desperately needed attentive personal nursing in a healthy environment. A few U.S. cities—including Cleveland, Milwaukee, and the District of Columbia—built permanent smallpox isolation hospitals, modern facilities involving large public investments. Chicago spent the unheard-of sum of $83,000 on its isolation hospital, an elaborate campus of buildings on Lawndale Avenue, complete with electricity and ten acres of well-appointed grounds. But the typical American pesthouse was a crude wooden shed, built in haste and on the cheap. Most lacked plumbing, plaster, or decent furniture. They were located far from their patients' friends and families, a hard journey over bad roads or, as in the case of Boston and New York, across water to an island.[72]

American newspapers were filled with pesthouse scandals. A former patient of the New Orleans pesthouse decried the "horrors" of his confinement in a shanty built upon a swamp. Salt Lake City's pesthouse was a public "menace." One survivor of the New York City pesthouse on North Brother Island objected to "the uncleanliness and unsanitary way in which the patients are treated," calling the "mockery for a hospital" a poor example for its inmates. In 1901, James Kerr willingly surrendered his young smallpox-afflicted daughter to city health officials only to have her die—of *tuberculosis*—on North Brother Island. Adding insult to grief, the city returned to Kerr the wrong body. As Chapin recognized, the scandalous conditions of many American pesthouses lay behind much of the resistance to removal of "patients." "It is not to be wondered at that patients and their friends resort to every deception to conceal the disease," he said, "in order that they may not be carried to such a place."[73]

Improvements to the typical pesthouse came only on those rare occasions when a well-to-do smallpox patient was confined in one. The American pesthouse was, without apologies, a class institution—the medical equivalent of steerage. Pesthouses were designed for the isolation and treatment of smallpox patients who lived in tenements and other dwellings too crowded to allow for their isolation at home. By long practice, affluent members of the community who lived in spacious quarters, at some remove from other dwellings, were entitled to convalesce at home. Health officials who failed to heed this commonly recognized American practice risked litigation and political censure. When Mary Kirk of Aiken, South Carolina, returned from missionary work in Brazil with a case of leprosy, the board of health ordered her removed from her house in the heart of the city to the four-room pesthouse by the city dump. Kirk sued. A "woman of culture and refinement" had no business in the pesthouse, a place "coarse and comfortless, used only for the purpose of incarcerating negroes having smallpox and other dangerous and infectious diseases." Awakened to Kirk's plight, the city council promised to build her a "comfortable cottage" on the outskirts of town, "supplied with all modern conveniences." Meanwhile, a circuit judge issued an order, forbidding the board from removing Kirk to the pesthouse. Calling this "an exceptional case," the state supreme court affirmed that action.[74]

The poorest members of an American community were not only the ones most likely to be sent to the pesthouse; they were also the people most likely to have one opened up in their neighborhood. Best public health practices called for locating a pesthouse at a safe remove from the local population. Usually, pesthouses were located on the outskirts of town. In some places, state law forbade public health boards to erect pesthouses too close to other dwellings. There seemed to be sound science behind such rules. While most public health officials believed smallpox contagion could not be carried through the air more than two hundred feet without being destroyed by oxidation or dilution, the *Journal of the American Medical Association* conceded, "This belief is purely empiric; there are no scientific data for its foundation." In one 1903 study, an English health officer suggested that one "smallpox ship," a floating pesthouse moored on the Thames, had caused an epidemic in a village half a mile away. As the London *Times* said, "smallpox hospitals may become sources of serious danger to the un-protected populations in their vicinity."[75]

That sense of danger made a pesthouse, in one medical writer's estima-tion, "the most unpopular neighbor that a man could have." Health officers seeking sites for a new pesthouse were turned back by shotgun-wielding farmers in Durham, North Carolina; writ-bearing "taxpayers" in Omaha, Nebraska; petition-signing citizens in Houston; and blaze-setting residents in Union County, Kentucky. In Bradford, Pennsylvania, three hundred men and women burned down a vacant schoolhouse that local officials had turned into a pesthouse. In Turtle Creek, eight miles outside of Pittsburgh, a "Quaker mob," two thousand in number, rioted to prevent the board of health from trying the same thing. Firemen turned their hoses on the un-ruly Friends.[76]

Whether the agitators were immigrant laborers or white "taxpayers," whether they favored the axe or the writ, collective action to keep out the kept-outs had an inherently conservative aspect. These turf defenders did not necessarily object to the pesthouse as a political response to contagious disease. In most cases, their quarrel would evaporate if the government chose another site—somebody else's backyard. Grievances and interests varied. Property owners feared that a pesthouse in the neighborhood would diminish real estate values. Poor residents protested the endangerment to their health as well as the constant reminder that they lived in their town's dumping ground.

In March 1901, two cases of smallpox were discovered in Orange, New Jersey, a city of 24,000 known for its hat-making industry. The board of health hired a builder to construct a pesthouse at the city dump. But the site was surrounded by tenements filled with Italian workers and their fam-ilies. As the carpenters set to work, a crowd gathered. By evening, 300 angry residents and just two policemen had gathered at the site. The crowd rushed the pesthouse. Someone lit a pile of wood shavings, and within minutes a blaze was making its way toward the structure. Firemen arrived, but a group of the residents stood on their hose, while one tried to cut it with a knife. Clubs flying, the police arrested three men. More police arrived, the crowd was driven back, and the fire was extinguished. The next night, a single pistol shot rang out at the dump. Men carrying axes and crowbars poured out from the surrounding tenements. In a few minutes they reduced the building to splinters. For good measure, a crowd returned later and set fire to the pile of broken wood.[77]

In the wake of the incident, the Orange Common Council refused to authorize construction of another pesthouse. *The New York Times* lamented that the revolt illustrated "the readiness with which well-ordered and generally law-abiding communities revert to barbarism when their fears or evil passions are aroused." But one letter writer from Orange, a self-described "Sympathizer with the People," saw justice in the crowd's actions. "Simply because the residents in the vicinity of the 'dump ground' are working people they are to be made uncomfortable and their health and that of their children endangered because the Board of Health—so-called—chose to put a pesthouse up in the midst of their dwellings," the sympathizer wrote. "Legally, I suppose, the people were in the wrong, but morally they had every right to act as they did."[78]

The altogether ordinary Americans who defied public health measures during the nation's turn-of-the-century war on smallpox left a deep mark upon the historical record. In their actions rather than their words—which, unlike those of the well-organized, predominantly middle-class antivaccinationists, were rarely recorded—they created a public transcript of opposition to the growth of institutional power in everyday life during the Progressive Era.

That record of dissent had political consequences. It forced compulsion to show its true self. It emboldened the antivaccination movement. It raised doubts in the heads of some lawmakers and a governor or two. And it even made an impression upon the institutions most removed from the common people, the courts. "It is a matter of common knowledge that the number of those who seriously object to vaccination is by no means small," observed Justice Orrin Carter of the Illinois Supreme Court, "and they cannot, except when necessary for the public health and in conformity to law, be deprived of their right to protect themselves and those under their

control from an invasion of their liberties by a practically compulsory inoculation of their bodies with a virus of any description, however meritorious it might be."[79]

Compulsion engendered resistance even in those tightest of spaces
whose inhabitants had no legal claim to liberty at all: prisons and jails. Vaccination was a routine part of penal discipline in the United States, as the
young Jack London discovered when he was arrested for vagrancy during
his long tramp across North America in the 1890s. London recounted the
experience in a chapter of his book *War of the Classes* (1905), entitled "How
I Became a Socialist." While traveling near Niagara Falls, he was "nabbed by
a fee-hunting constable, denied the right to plead guilty or not guilty, sen-
tenced out of hand to thirty days' imprisonment for having no fixed abode
and no visible means of support, handcuffed and chained to a bunch of
men similarly circumstanced, carted down country to Buffalo, registered at
the Erie County Penitentiary, had my head clipped and my budding mustache shaved, was dressed in convict stripes, compulsorily vaccinated by a
medical student who practiced on such as we, made to march the lock-step,
and put to work under the eyes of guards armed with Winchester rifles."[80]

For London, living the hobo's life as a member of America's "submerged
tenth," the underclass of his day, compulsory vaccination was but one in a
litany of injustices that prompted his conversion from a working-class individualist into a socialist and a citizen of the world. During the experience,
he said, some of his "plethoric national patriotism simmered down and
leaked out of the bottom of his soul somewhere." In another telling, London recalled with warm solidarity how another inmate, a veteran of the
penal system with whom London had shared some tobacco, advised London to "suck it out"—literally to suck the vaccine from his arm. The writer
was glad that he did. For afterward he saw "men who had not sucked and
who had horrible holes in their arms into which I could have thrust my
fist." London could muster no sympathy for his fellows in prison stripes
who had done nothing to stop the state of New York from making its mark
on their bodies.[81]

"It was their own fault," he said. "They could have sucked."[82]

SEVEN

THE ANTIVACCINATIONISTS

The *Medical News* gave it a billing worthy of P. T. Barnum: "a smallpox case destined to be famous in the history of the progressive victory of therapeutic science over the ranks of ignorance, prejudice, quackery, and sentimentalism." A more neutral observer (if one could be found) might have described the entire affair as a case of medical brinksmanship gone wrong.[1]

It had all started with a dare. On November 25, 1901, Dr. Samuel H. Durgin, lecturer in the Harvard Medical Department and chairman of the Boston Board of Health, made a statement to *The Boston Globe*. "If there are among the adult and leading members of the antivaccinationists," he said, "any who would like an opportunity to show the people their sincerity in what they profess, I will make arrangements by which that belief may be tested and the effect of such exhibition of faith, by exposure to smallpox without vaccination, be made clear." Chairman Durgin said he doubted there was "a man or woman among them"—Boston's small but fervent antivaccination movement—who would accept his challenge.[2]

Boston was battling its most serious smallpox epidemic in a generation. The epidemic of 1872–73, Durgin's first trial as a member of the board, had killed over a thousand people. There was no telling how many would die this time. The first cases, discovered in May 1901 in a Roxbury factory, had killed no one. It seemed that the new "mild type" smallpox, which had been troubling the southern and midwestern states for the past few years, had finally reached Boston. With summer came one small outbreak after another. September brought thirty new cases, October forty-nine, November nearly two hundred. By then, several people had died. With the smallpox hospital on Southampton Street filled to capacity, the board outfitted additional wards at the quarantine hospital on Gallop's Island, in Boston harbor. According to city physicians, nine out of ten patients turning up at the pesthouses had never been vaccinated. The board opened free vaccine stations around the city. Durgin reached out to Archbishop John Joseph Williams, and his appeal for universal vaccination was read aloud at Sunday services across Catholic Boston. And though the board had yet to issue a vaccination order, hoping to preserve the image of voluntarism for as long as possible, the board's "virus squad" began its bruising nighttime raids of the city's lodging houses.[3]

In the midst of this public health emergency, an anonymous circular appeared on the streets of Boston. Addressed to parents, guardians, and the people, it warned that vaccination caused "disease, constitutional debility, death." The circular advised that the state law requiring vaccination for all public school pupils—now being strictly enforced in the city—made an exception for any child who presented a certificate, signed by a physician, stating that the child was an "unfit subject for vaccination." Having won this concession from the legislature in 1894, the antivaccinationists were now making the most of it. "There are hundreds of physicians in Massachusetts who are well aware of the uselessness and evil effects of vaccination," the circular instructed. To them, *no* child was a fit subject for vaccination. "Apply to any one of them for a certificate of exemption for your child." The leaflet provided an address—an office at No. 1 Beacon Street, just steps from the gold-domed State House—to which parents could write for names of such doctors. Asked by the *Globe* for a comment, Durgin issued his challenge.[4]

It must have seemed to Durgin's peers that the stress of the job had finally gotten to him. Had the respected chief of one of the nation's leading public health departments really just dared unvaccinated citizens to expose themselves to smallpox? In all likelihood, Durgin expected no one to take the bait. A man of his experience knew the antivaccinationists were nothing if not sincere. But their beliefs did not constitute a suicide pact. While antivaccinationists considered vaccination a medical fraud and *compulsory* vaccination an "atrocious crime," few imagined themselves invulnerable to smallpox.[5]

One of the few was Dr. Immanuel Pfeiffer of Boston. A Danish immigrant and former dealer in real estate, the sixtyish physician was a handsome man with an erect bearing, a thick head of hair, and a well-groomed beard. He was a public figure of well-known enthusiasms: spiritualism, physical culture, free speech, and, uniting them all, antivaccinationism. An apostle of the idea that the mind possessed almost limitless power over the material world, Pfeiffer offered his own body as the proof of his beliefs, winning a Houdini-like reputation for his vigorous constitution and capacity to withstand physical hardship. In 1900, he garnered national press attention by fasting for twenty-one days. A year later, he fasted for a month. "He has been considered a crank by many people," the *Globe* observed; and yet those who knew the man acknowledged that he had "a brain of unusual power and activity, a fitting concomitant of his stalwart figure and imposing carriage." In his heterodox medical journal, *Our Home Rights*, Pfeiffer taught readers that the best way to ward off disease was through sanitation, proper diet, and impeccable hygiene. He advertised his services as a "renowned natural healer" who "successfully treats all kinds of chronic diseases by the simple laying on of hands, after having been pronounced incurable by regular physicians." *Regular physicians*: to Pfeiffer, that phrase signified unthinking medical orthodoxy and creeping state regulation of the healing arts, a trend he fought as president of the Massachusetts Medical Rights League.[6]

Pfeiffer's views on vaccination were a matter of public record. In December 1901, one month after Durgin issued his challenge, Pfeiffer attended a lecture at a meeting of the Ladies' Psychological Institute of Boston. The speaker was Dr. John H. McCollom of Boston City Hospital, an instructor in contagious diseases at Harvard and a prominent member of the Massachusetts Medical Society—a "regular," through and through. McCollom presented a by-the-book argument for vaccination. As gruesome images of smallpox patients beamed onto a screen from his stereopticon, McCollom narrated humankind's long struggle with smallpox, culminating in the scientific triumph of Jennerian vaccination. He traced the development of vaccine, touting the virtues of modern glycerinated lymph. He marshaled statistics from historical epidemics to demonstrate that well-vaccinated people rarely contracted smallpox and, when they did, suffered far less than their unvaccinated neighbors. The same argument could be found in countless medical journals, government reports, and newspapers. But with smallpox spreading in the city—perhaps in that very room—the audience hung on McCollom's every word. Coming to the end of his lecture, he opened the floor to questions.[7]

Pfeiffer rose. "Is it not true, doctor," he began, "that men of science and immense learning have effectually claimed that persons whose bodies are cleanly, sound and generally healthy are protected from smallpox?"

McCollom responded, "No, it is not true, and I do not recollect of hearing any learned or scientific men making any such claim."

Pfeiffer: "Is it not admitted by eminent physicians and learned men that there are more ills resulting from vaccination than from the disease of smallpox?"

McCollom said he had "never heard a scientific man" say any such thing.

Pfeiffer: "And did not the people of Ohio rise up against vaccination to such an extent that it has been abolished there?" (He was referring to Cleveland health officer Martin Friedrich's recent decision to suspend wholesale vaccination in favor of disinfection.) Before McCollom could answer, Pfeiffer launched into another question. Then another. The cross-examination went on like this for some time, as Pfeiffer exhibited his famous endurance and McCollom—and the audience—approached the limits of theirs.[8]

A month later, on January 18, 1902, Pfeiffer wrote to Durgin, seeking permission to visit the smallpox wards at Gallop's Island "for the purpose of scientifically looking into the disease in all its various forms." The letter indicated that the two men had already spoken; Durgin had asked Pfeiffer to put his request in writing. To this, the chairman readily assented, waiving the hospital's strict requirement that all visitors show evidence of recent vaccination. Pfeiffer had not been vaccinated since infancy. Durgin's dare had a taker after all.[9]

Many would later question the chairman's decision. By January 1, city physicians had already vaccinated 185,000 residents; family doctors and other agencies had vaccinated roughly 300,000, for a total of 485,000 in a city of 586,000. That was an exceptionally high vaccination rate (83 percent) for a U.S. city. But Durgin seemed determined to reach that final 17 percent and to strip Boston of its national reputation as "a hot-bed of the anti-vaccine heresy." That January, under authority of a vaccination order issued by Durgin's board, city doctors and police canvassed East Boston, South Boston, Charlestown, the North End, and the West End. The antivaccinationists stepped up their efforts, petitioning the Massachusetts General Court with bills to abolish compulsion. Nineteen citizens of Boston were prosecuted for resisting vaccination (including one East Boston father, John H. Mugford, who would fight his case all the way to the state's Supreme Judicial Court). Meanwhile, the epidemic continued. By late January, nearly 700 Bostonians had been stricken with smallpox; 108 had died. Durgin held the antivaccinationists responsible, and Pfeiffer was their most visible leader.[10]

On January 23, Pfeiffer toured Gallop's Island in the company of Dr. Paul Carson, the port physician. Carson, a former Dartmouth football star, instructed Pfeiffer in hospital protocol, helping him don the requisite white gown and cap. The two men walked the wards that housed more than one hundred smallpox-stricken patients, stopping at their grim bedsides so Pfeiffer could examine the disease in its various stages. Pfeiffer complimented his host on the cleanliness of the facility. He remarked that the air lacked the infamous smell of smallpox—an odor one country doctor of the era likened to "a hen-house on a warm April morn." Carson suggested that Pfeiffer smell a patient's breath. Pfeiffer leaned in, inhaling deeply. Durgin was not present. But he later told a reporter that he was "glad the suggestion of the breath was made, so that Dr Pfeiffer might be gratified in every conceivable way in his expressed desire." Arriving at the end of the tour, Pfeiffer returned the robe and cap and, on Carson's instructions, washed his hands, face, hair, and beard in disinfectant before boarding the boat back to Boston.[11]

In the days that followed, agents for the board of health kept Pfeiffer under close surveillance. They stood sentry outside his Washington Street office. They shadowed him on his rounds. They trailed him to the State House, where he testified in crowded public hearings on the antivaccination bills. Pfeiffer had drafted one of the bills himself. It called for "obtaining the consent to inject any poisonous substance into the body of any person."[12]

The surveillance went on for a week, eight days, nine, ten. . . . Then, on February 3, the eleventh day after his exposure to smallpox—right about the time when a person infected with the virus would be expected to fall ill and become contagious—Durgin's agents lost Pfeiffer.

I conoclasts! Charlatans!! Cranks!!! Of "the little coterie of obstructionists who call themselves antivaccinationists," the leaders of scientific medical opinion in turn-of-the-century America had little good to say. "To call him an ass," the New York country doctor–cum–memoirist William Macartney said of the antivaccinationist, "is to disparage donkeys in general." With the same stubborn sort in mind, health officials from Kentucky to California called a tough case of smallpox "the fool-killer." Dr. James Hyde, the small-pox expert at Rush Medical School, offered a more searching psychological profile of vaccination's discontents. "A class of men," he imagined them, "whose minds are so curiously constituted that they will select for study the nether side of the social fabric, the weakness of the best of governments, and the minor defects in the character of the world's heroes." For years to come, few medical historians or science writers would feel any professional obligation to soft-pedal their contempt when writing about the "antivac-cine, anti-government, and anti-science crowd."[13]

To be sure, the turn-of-the-century antivaccination movement attracted more than its share of odd characters and showboating extremists. As Boston's Dr. Charles F. Nichols (the author of *Vaccination: A Blunder in Poisons*) observed, "The subject evokes strong language—explosives, not apologetics." The aptly named Dr. Robert A. Gunn told an audience at the Manhattan Liberal Club in 1902 that he would "shoot down as he would a burglar" any health officer who attempted to vaccinate his family, confident "no jury of American freemen" would find him guilty of murder.[14]

With the passage of time, the ideas of the early twentieth-century anti-vaccinationists may seem quaint, or worse. But those ideas, so markedly wrong by modern scientific standards, still offer critical insights into the tumultuous transformation of American society, culture, and government in the Progressive Era. Dr. Hyde's unflattering psychological profile of the antivaccinationists hints at their deeper historical significance. These men and women, for whom opposition to compulsory vaccination had become a political cause, were profoundly disaffected by the growing administrative power and social reach of the American government in their time. For many of them, active opposition to "state medicine"—a term embraced by the state itself—was part of a larger social and cultural struggle against the dramatic extension of governmental power into the realms of education, family life, personal belief, bodily autonomy, and speech.[15]

The antivaccinationists' sense of themselves as members of a political movement distinguished them from the far greater numbers of Americans who resisted compulsory vaccination during the smallpox epidemics of 1898–1903. For the African American coal miners of Birmingham, the tenement mothers of Italian Harlem, or the barrio dwellers of Laredo, resisting compulsory vaccination was indisputably a political act. By rioting, forging vaccination scars, scrubbing vaccine from their children's arms, or driving vaccinators from their neighborhoods, thousands of ordinary Americans rebelled against government authority. Their actions emboldened antivaccinationists, but that did not make every "vaccine refuser" an antivaccinationist. For most refusers, resistance was an act in and of the moment; it lasted only so long as did the threat of compulsion itself. Antivaccinationists were different. They were *activists*—people with a cause. They aimed to win converts, move public opinion, change laws. As John Pitcairn, the wealthy Pittsburgh plate glass manufacturer and president of the Anti-Vaccination League of America, told a committee of the Pennsylvania General Assembly, "There is no money in the cause we represent; it is the cause of truth, the cause of freedom, the cause of humanity." For some, that cause became a lifelong crusade.[16]

Many antivaccinationists had close intellectual and personal ties to a largely forgotten American tradition and subculture of libertarian radicalism. That tradition took on a feverish new life as industrial capitalism, progressive reform, and the professionalization of knowledge fostered the rise of a distinctly modern interventionist state during the Progressive Era. The same men and women who joined antivaccination leagues tended to throw themselves into other maligned causes of their era, including anti-imperialism, women's rights, antivivisection, vegetarianism, Henry George's single tax, the fight against government censorship of "obscene" materials (under the late nineteenth-century "Comstock laws"), and opposition to state eugenics. Seventy-year-old Dr. Montague R. Leverson— an English immigrant, onetime California state assemblyman, and perennial leader of the Brooklyn Anti-Compulsory Vaccination League—was denounced, accurately, by *The New York Times* as "an extreme advocate of personal liberty," an "untiring writer of letters and pamphlets" on "all sorts of impracticable theories" from the injustice of the obscenity laws to the lawlessness of the U.S. war in the Philippines. It was the antivaccinationists' uncompromising defense of personal liberty, as they understood it—and not merely their unorthodox medical beliefs—that placed them, in the eyes of so many of their contemporaries, on the wrong side of history. That same "crankiness" makes their words and works an unusually revealing porthole to their times.[17]

Antivaccinationism was a worldwide phenomenon in the late nineteenth and early twentieth centuries. The American activists were well aware of the vaccination riots that rocked Montreal in 1885 and Rio de Janeiro in 1904. They knew (if only through Kipling's stories) of the grassroots resistance that Britain's vaccination campaigns had aroused across India. But given their common language and the legal and political traditions that they shared, American antivaccinationists always felt an especially close connection to their English counterparts. And together the English and American antivaccinationists proudly claimed the mantle of another unpopular movement: the transatlantic nineteenth-century antislavery movement.[18]

A natural affinity linked abolitionism and antivaccinationism. Both upheld bodily self-possession as the sine qua non of human freedom; both distrusted institutions; and each evoked public scorn in its time as the dangerous cause of a lunatic fringe. Frederick Douglass told an English correspondent in 1882 that compulsory vaccination had long offended his "logical faculty" as a man "opposed to every species of arbitrary power." Some antivaccinationists, including the English leader William Tebb (1830–1917) and the California spiritualist Dr. James Martin Peebles (1822–1922), lived long enough to participate in both movements. For others, antislavery provided a rich source of moral inspiration and political rhetoric. Beginning in 1902, Lora C. Little of Minneapolis edited *The Liberator*, a smartly written antivaccination journal named after William Lloyd Garrison's abolitionist newspaper from antebellum Boston. Little's *Liberator* was well known to Garrison's son, William Lloyd Garrison, Jr. (1838–1909), a businessman reformer whose causes included anti-imperialism, free trade, women's rights, repeal of the Chinese Exclusion Act, and antivaccinationism. During the 1840s the elder Garrison renounced the U.S. Constitution as a pro-slavery compact, a "covenant with death," and "an agreement with hell"; in his son's time, Immanuel Pfeiffer denounced health boards as "covenanters with death and leaguers with hell." Addressing the Western New York Homeopathic Medical Society in 1902, Dr. J. W. Hodge of Niagara Falls thundered, "Compulsory vaccination ranks with human slavery and religious persecution as one of the most flagrant outrages upon the rights of the human race." It may have been the single most quoted line in the American antivaccinationist literature. It is still quoted by antivaccinationists today.[19]

For men and women who espoused a form of radical individualism, critics of vaccination were quick to recognize the power of association. "From all parts of the state, and indeed from all parts of the country," declared the Minneapolis-based *Northwestern Lancet* in February 1901, "come reports of the organization of small anti-vaccination societies, whose first work is to embarrass health and school officials in their efforts to prevent the spread of small-pox." As vaccination enforcement surged, organizations long moribund sprang back to life and new leagues appeared on the scene. The longest-running groups had formed in response to the first major wave of compulsory vaccination laws during the 1870s and 1880s. The granddaddy of them all, the Anti-Vaccination Society of America, was established in New York in 1879, during a visit from England's William Tebb.

Between 1879 and 1900, other organizations formed, including the New England Anti-Compulsory Vaccination League (1882, Hartford), the American Anti-Vaccination Society (1885, New York), the American Anti-Vaccination League (1889, New York, claiming 380 members by 1901), and an Indiana-based organization called the Anti-Vaccination Society of America (1895, claiming 200 members by 1901). Around the turn of the century, state leagues were up and running in California, Colorado, Connecticut, Massachusetts, Minnesota, Missouri, Pennsylvania, Utah, and other states, in addition to the welter of local societies in communities such as Berkeley, Boston, Brooklyn, Cleveland, Milwaukee, and St. Paul. The existence of two distinct organizations, each calling itself "the" Anti-Vaccination Society of America, attests to a lack of coordination in the movement. The antivaccinationists had little of the organizational discipline (or membership base) of a national interest group such as the General Federation of Women's Clubs, whose success in winning protective legislation for female factory workers rested on its ability to mobilize affiliated organizations at every level of the polity. By comparison to the GFWC, the antivaccination movement was an unmade bed.[20]

Still, even their detractors had to admit that the antivaccinationists constituted a genuine movement, complete with its own polemicists, its own journals (notably the Terre Haute–based *Vaccination*, 1898–1906, and *The Liberator*, 1898–1907); its own international literature of pamphlets and books; and its own lawyers (including C. Oscar Beasley of Philadelphia, who specialized in vaccine injury suits, and Harry Weinberger of New York, for whom antivaccination was part of a distinguished career in defense of civil liberties). The societies sent delegates to international congresses in Paris, Cologne, and Berlin. Every well-read American antivaccinationist knew that Leo Tolstoy sympathized with the cause, as he did "with every struggle for liberty in any sphere of life"; that George Bernard Shaw called vaccination "a peculiarly filthy piece of witchcraft"; and that the British naturalist Alfred Russel Wallace had predicted, in 1898, that the practice "will, before many years have passed, be universally held to be one of the foulest blots on the civilization of the nineteenth century." As American antivaccinationists saw the international "Vaccination Question," theirs was the enlightened view of the matter. The apologists for state medicine were the true cranks. The antivaccinationists were determined to wipe the blot of compulsion from the statute books of the United States.[21]

Who were the antivaccinationists?

In England, antivaccinationism fostered a cross-class alliance of factory workers, artisans, clerks, and shopkeepers. English vaccination measures explicitly targeted working-class families, and antivaccinationism gained strongholds in workers' neighborhoods, especially those with robust labor movements. For a half century after the passage of England's first compulsion statute in 1853, hundreds of thousands of parents joined the movement to resist government-mandated vaccination of their children. Many were fined or jailed. Government distraint sales—public auctions of property seized from resisters who failed to pay their fines—spawned riots. An estimated 80,000 to 100,000 people participated in the Leicester Demonstration of 1885, a grand urban spectacle that featured the hanging of Edward Jenner in effigy. Parliament established the Royal Commission on Vaccination in 1889. After studying the subject for seven years, the commission endorsed vaccination as scientifically sound but advised Parliament to create an exemption for "conscientious objectors": people who sincerely believed the procedure threatened their own or their children's health. Parliament introduced that exemption by law in 1898. Within ten years, conscience exemptions reached one quarter of all births in England.[22]

In the United States, organized antivaccinationism never enjoyed such a broad, politicized working-class base. Most activists instead came from the country's broad, educated middle class. A typical league counted among its members businessmen and lawyers, shopkeepers and artisans, schoolteachers and housewives. To an outsider, the most striking fact about antivaccination activists—particularly those who wrote tracts and made public speeches—was how many of them were doctors. Or how many *called themselves doctors*, a regular physician would have said.

The controversy over the vaccination question was closely tied to the contemporary battle over state medical licensing and the increasing dominance of "regular," allopathic medicine. So intertwined were the two issues in some states (including New York and Massachusetts) that at times the political fight over compulsory vaccination could seem little more than a proxy war for the professional struggle over licensure. But it was much more than that.[23]

The ranks of the antivaccination movement teemed with practitioners of the stunningly diverse systems of alternative medicine to be found in turn-of-the-century America. For many so-called irregular practitioners, the rise of state medicine in the late nineteenth century—with its boards of health, medical licensing bodies, and compulsory vaccination orders—was an insidious development. State medicine posed a direct challenge to their livelihoods and to their ways of understanding the body, nature, and the world. For many alternative practitioners, the fights against compulsory vaccination and medical licensure were two fronts in the same war. By discrediting vaccination, the Indiana "Physio-Medical" practitioner Dr. R. Swinburne Clymer declared, "we are striking at the very root and foundation of so-called scientific or 'regular' medicine."[24]

It was a long-running war. In the early republic, state licensing laws had granted a professional monopoly to mainstream physicians of the allopathic school. It had been their idea to call themselves "regular" physicians and their upstart competitors in homeopathy and Thomsonianism "irregulars." During the 1830s and 1840s, those laws were wiped off the books by state lawmakers, part of the broad Jacksonian-era assault on intellectual elitism and government-granted special privileges of all sorts. As the Massachusetts Sanitary Commission lamented in 1850, henceforward "any one, male or female, learned or ignorant, an honest man or a knave, can assume the name of physician, and 'practice' upon any one, to cure or to kill, as either may happen, without accountability. 'It's a free country!'" Free to healers and also free to patients, who could choose among practitioners, all of whom were equally entitled to hold themselves out as "doctor."[25]

By 1900, the United States had an estimated 110,000 orthodox physicians and roughly 20,000 practitioners of alternative medicine. The best-established irregulars were America's 9,000 homeopaths (who treated disease by administering minute doses of remedies known to produce symptoms in a healthy person that were similar to those of the disease) and the eclectics (who favored botanical remedies). Relative newcomers to the medical culture included practitioners of osteopathy, chiropractic, and naturopathy—all forms of drugless healing. Although adherents of each of the unorthodox schools viewed their own system as superior, they shared a general belief in the therapeutic and preventive power of nature—emphasizing the virtues of sound diet, a daily regimen to maintain the integrity of the body, and the administration, in times of illness, of gentle remedies such as herbs. The irregulars rejected the mercurial drugs, bleedings, and other strenuous measures of mainstream practice. They prided themselves on their holistic, empirical, "common sense" approaches to disease. For much of the nineteenth century—the age of heroic surgeries and toxic mercurials—the irregulars' gentler medicine seemed to many patients the safer approach.[26]

For years, the unbridled contempt of the mainstream medical societies had only enlarged the irregulars' self-esteem, and, not incidentally, their market share. From its inception in 1847, the American Medical Association had strived to drive the irregulars (particularly the homeopaths) from the temple of medicine. The association imposed on its members a "consultation clause," which forbade them to consult with doctors who lacked "proper" (regular) medical credentials. Even in the absence of exclusive state licensure laws, this clause effectively barred homeopaths from practicing in many publicly funded hospitals. Regulars who consulted with unorthodox practitioners faced expulsion from their medical societies. The consultation clause was increasingly perceived by the public as petty and dangerous. (The AMA would eventually do away with the mandatory provision in 1903.) And as Dr. Oliver Wendell Holmes acknowledged as early as the mid-nineteenth century, every insulting comment from a regular physician was "a gratuitous advertisement" for his irregular rival. The irregulars, Holmes observed, "understand the hydrostatic paradox of controversy: that it raises the meanest disputant to a seeming level with his antagonist." This was a truism of public debate that the antivaccinationists understood as well.[27]

The final decades of the nineteenth century brought a new campaign for state medical licensing laws, precipitating a struggle between the regulars and irregulars that remained heated well into the early twentieth century. The advent of the germ theory of disease enabled extraordinary advances in medicine, particularly in the field of surgery, an area that alternative practitioners had generally conceded to mainstream physicians. Rising standards of medical education and the general culture of middle-class professionalization in late nineteenth-century America helped win the support of state lawmakers. Nearly every state enacted some form of medical licensing statute. Though homeopaths and eclectics were by that time too well established to legally exclude from the practice of medicine, many still resented the government imprimatur that the new laws conferred upon the regular-dominated state medical societies. In most states newcomers in fields such as chiropractic and naturopathy found themselves subject to prosecution for practicing medicine without a license.[28]

During its long struggle for authority, the regular medical profession established uneasy but increasingly close ties with American state and local governments. As the AMA and the state medical societies pushed for laws to eliminate their irregular competitors, the AMA helped establish the authority of orthodox practitioners through its pursuit of laws criminalizing abortion and the distribution of information about contraception, and by establishing alliances with boards of health in the control of contagious and infectious diseases. The AMA strongly endorsed compulsory vaccination at its annual meeting in 1899, lamenting that "well-meaning but fanatical persons have, for some time past, been endeavoring to excite a prejudice against vaccination."[29]

Those "persons" included a great many irregulars, who perceived that every medical society endorsement of compulsory vaccination carried a rebuke to alternative medicine. Homeopaths (who many regulars grudgingly recognized as well educated and intentioned) were in fact divided on the vaccination question. Some regarded vaccination as clear proof of the homeopathic maxim *simila similibus curentur* ("Let like be cured by like"), while a vocal minority, including J. W. Hodge, regarded "the state-supported vaccination rite" as an exercise in blood poisoning. The 1901 meeting of the New England Eclectic Medical Association adopted a resolution proclaiming "the right to resist the vaccinator in his disseminating of disease." Botanical physicians of the Physio-Medical School contributed several leaders to the cause, such as Dr. Clymer, vice-president of the Terre Haute–based Anti-Vaccination Society of America and author of the intermittently brilliant 1904 tract *Vaccination Brought Home to You*. (Clymer figured out that the best sources of damaging material on vaccination were the regulars' own medical journals, where doctors let down their public guards and shared personal experiences of vaccinations gone wrong.) The vaccination procedure may have garnered the greatest scorn from devotees of the least legitimate (in regulars' eyes) schools of drugless healing—including hydropaths and chiropractors. For Dr. T. V. Gifford of Indiana, a "pioneer in Hygeio-Therapy," antivaccination was simply another part of a sound health regimen, like taking cold baths and avoiding salt, meat, and sex.[30]

Although beset and beleaguered, alternative medicine survived the return of medical licensing laws. Homeopaths and eclectics won their own licensing acts in some states. And even practitioners of the new or more marginal schools held out the hope that their system would eventually triumph over medical orthodoxy. "The day of powder and pill and knife is nearing its end," declared one osteopathic text in 1903.[31]

Another source of support for the antivaccinationists came from the growing communities of faith healers in turn-of-the-century America. The cause had long enjoyed support from spiritualists, a movement of alternative religion that flourished in the nineteenth century. Known for séances and "table-rappings," spiritualists emphasized the fundamental unity of matter and spirit; their anti-institutionalism and strong belief in the sovereignty of the individual tied them to various radical causes, including women's rights, antislavery, and antivaccination. Vaccinators were persona non grata at John Alexander Dowie's Zion City, a settlement established outside Chicago in 1899 that banned alcohol, smoking, dance halls, and medical doctors.[32]

Mary Baker Eddy's Church of Christ, Scientist, established in Boston in 1879 and reaching forty thousand members by 1906, shared the natural healers' concerns about vaccination. Adherents of Christian Science believed in the power of the mind to cure disease through prayer. During the 1890s, Christian Scientists had denounced compulsory vaccination as a violation of the laws of God and their religious freedom. In Beloit, Wisconsin, a Christian Scientist won a major legal victory in 1897, securing the right for his unvaccinated children to attend the public schools. When the city council of Americus, Georgia, where smallpox was epidemic in 1899, passed an ordinance compelling vaccination, local Christian Scientists rebelled, insisting their faith would protect them against the disease. City authorities arrested the resisters, assessing fines from $3 to $30 and imposing jail terms from ten to thirty days. Some Christian Scientists joined antivaccinationist societies, while others, such as Putnam J. Ramsdell of Cambridge, Massachusetts, took an individual stand, refusing to comply with local vaccination orders.[33]

In 1900, with the vaccination controversy heating up across the United States, church leaders adopted a new conciliatory stance toward the government. By that time, the young church had gained extensive experience with the American legal system. Christian Science parents had faced prosecution for failing to provide medical treatment for sick children. In some states, authorities arrested Christian Scientists for practicing medicine without a license. (In their defense, the faith healers argued that they were "practicing religion, not medicine," an argument for religious liberty that American courts increasingly accepted.) In 1900, Eddy issued a terse statement on compulsory vaccination. She advised her followers that "if the law demand an individual to submit to this process, he obey the law; and then appeal to the gospel to save him from any bad results." Two years later, Eddy advised Christian Scientists to cooperate with health boards by reporting contagious diseases, including smallpox. Both actions were taken in a time when the church and its faithful were struggling for recognition and religious liberty in the states. Eddy cited Matthew 22:21: "Render unto Caesar the things that are Caesar's." But reports from local communities showed that some Christian Scientists continued to dodge vaccination and to insist upon healing smallpox-infected family members by prayer alone.[34]

Concerned parents formed the largest recruitment pool for the antivaccination societies. Many American parents, including many who would never formally join a society, viewed school vaccination requirements as an unwarranted usurpation of their domestic authority and an unconstitutional denial of every child's "right" to a public education. More viscerally, many parents feared vaccination would harm their children. Behind almost every antivaccination leader lay a family horror story. J. W. Griggs, president of the Anti-Vaccination Society of St. Paul, recalled how he lost his "faith in the strange practice" of vaccination when his daughter got smallpox, even though she had been vaccinated twice for school. "I began to study the question," he wrote. "As I looked into it, I began to see the dangers of this process of poisoning the fountain of life, and a little at a time to learn of the disasters and deaths resulting from it—some immediately, and others more remotely; and thus I was stimulated actively to oppose the practice and to work for the repeal of the compulsory vaccination law in this State." The Pittsburgh industrialist John Pitcairn, already wary of vaccination as an adherent of homeopathy and the Swedenborgian religion, recalled the suffering of his son Raymond from complications of vaccination. *Liberator* editor Lora Little (of Minneapolis) and Louis H. Piehn (an Iowa banker and first president of the midwestern Anti-Vaccination Society of America) each had a child die from the effects, they believed, of state-mandated school vaccination.[35]

C ritics had trouble making up their minds about the influence of anti-vaccinationist ideas on American public opinion. Reporting on a meeting of the Anti-Compulsory Vaccination League of Brooklyn in 1901, the *Times* sneeringly commented, "Nine men, one boy, and seven reporters were present." Of course, the same words attested to the antivaccinationists' talent for getting their message heard. Health officials dismissed them as inconsequential anonymities, but when their own vaccination campaigns came up short, the same men blamed antivaccinationism. "Although the vaccine house is built upon a rock, and is not likely to fall," declared one Boston health department bulletin in 1902, "the noisy storm has frightened many of our people into a dangerous neglect or opposition to vaccinal protection."[36]

Antivaccinationism was as old as vaccination itself. In the United States, the protest actually preceded the practice. In 1798, two years before Dr. Benjamin Waterhouse of Harvard performed the first American vaccinations, physicians and clergymen in Boston formed the Anti-Vaccination Society, declaring vaccination an act of "defiance to Heaven itself, even to the will of God." American antivaccinationists owed a heavy intellectual debt to their British counterparts, who generated a vast literature on the subject between the rise of compulsory vaccination in the 1850s and the act of 1898. And the Americans, in their continuing search for evidence to support their views, kept tabs on the experience of compulsion and opposition on the Continent (and, to a far lesser degree, in Asia and Latin America). Some contributors to the American literature of antivaccination did little more than compile the arguments and data of others; if the Springfield, Massachusetts, physician C. W. Amerige had an original thought as he wrote *Vaccination a Curse* (1895), he failed to put it on the page. And even the more original and lively writers, such as J. W. Hodge, tended to grow shrill with time, recycling their own arguments at an ever increasing volume. Still, these were not shortcomings unique to antivaccination writing. Their opponents were guilty of the same excesses.[37]

The sharp-penned English polemicist Alfred Milnes observed that the nineteenth-century debate had produced "a double history to vaccination." To mainstream medical leaders, the introduction of vaccination in 1798 was the greatest gift ever bestowed upon civilization by science. To the antivaccinationists, the record of vaccination was a "history of failures."[38]

The historical debate was really a quarrel about the efficacy of vaccination. Did the practice really deserve credit for causing the sharp decline of smallpox in the West during the first thirty years after its introduction? To antivaccinationists, much of that credit belonged not to the adoption of a new medical practice, vaccination, but to the banning of an old one, inoculation. Inoculation (using actual smallpox virus) had once enjoyed the broad support of the medical profession, notwithstanding the serious risk that a person inoculated with smallpox would infect others. With the arrival of vaccination, the profession discredited inoculation. The abrupt cessation of that perverse practice, antivaccinationists argued, was one key factor in the declining incidence of smallpox. The others were stricter isolation of smallpox patients, rising standards of cleanliness, and the large-scale sanitation projects introduced in European and American cities. Antivaccinationists believed smallpox to be preeminently a "filth disease." By diverting public attention and government resources from sanitary measures, they argued, the "vaccine nostrum" had been "instrumental in perpetuating the very disease it is supposed to prevent."[39]

Both sides drew upon the discipline of statistics to make their cases. Defenders of vaccination marshaled hospital data to show that unvaccinated individuals were far more vulnerable to smallpox than the vaccinated. Antivaccinationists in England and America accused their opponents of obtaining their data from biased sources (hospitals) and of missing the data's true significance. "Of course the death-rate is greater among the unvaccinated," said Hodge, building upon an argument made by Wallace. After all, who *were* the unvaccinated? The poor: ill fed, ill housed, ill clothed, and, consequently, just plain ill. The political solution to smallpox was broad-based structural reform to improve the lives of the laboring poor. "It should require no argument to convince a physician that people who live in sanitary dwellings, on clean streets, and who eat wholesome food, drink clean water and breathe pure air are in a better position to resist diseases, smallpox included, than are other people living under opposite conditions."[40]

Statisticians love an army. England's Wallace built much of his case against vaccination in 1898 by citing the incidence of smallpox among the well-vaccinated troops of the British army. American antivaccinationists updated the argument for their own national context, citing the hundreds of smallpox deaths among U.S. soldiers in the Philippines, despite the boast of one Army surgeon that vaccination and revaccination "went on as regularly as the drills at any army post." American antivaccinationists also Americanized the Leicester argument. Wallace (among other English polemicists) had made much of the fact that in the antivaccination stronghold of Leicester, where health officials emphasized sanitation, the citizens suffered far less smallpox per capita than in "well-vaccinated Birmingham." The American Leicester was Cleveland, where Friedrich's wholesale disinfection campaign in 1901 had apparently wiped out a smallpox epidemic. The antivaccinationists tended to leave out the inconvenient fact that smallpox soon returned to Cleveland, killing hundreds of unvaccinated citizens.[41]

Antivaccinationists everywhere had the greatest impact when their arguments resonated with pressing public concerns. In turn-of-the-century America, the "noisy storm" ultimately had less to do with vital statistics than vital issues. The antivaccinationists spoke to three of the Progressive Era's core public concerns: antimonopoly, child protection, and the uncertain meaning of liberty in a modern, urban-industrial society.

The turn of the century was the heyday of federal trust-busting prosecutions and muckraking exposés of the corporate "octopuses" that dominated vital industries such as the railroads, steel, oil, and sugar refining. Antimonopoly and an acute awareness of the role of business interests in corrupting politics at every level were among the most widely resonant reform issues of the era. The antivaccinationists tapped into the pervasive antimonopoly resentments of their day.[42]

Beneath the aura of public service surrounding vaccination policy, charged the antivaccinationists, lay an unholy conspiracy of self-dealing health officials, profit-seeking vaccine makers, and regular physicians bent on monopoly: the "cowpox syndicate." "Vaccination yields fees to lymph-peddlers and baby-slashers," declared the Belgian-born American physician Felix Oswald in his 1901 book, *Vaccination A Crime*. Who could deny the interest of vaccine makers in a policy that generated artificial demand for their product? The interests of private physicians were not much more subtle. During epidemics, many local governments still contracted with private physicians to vaccinate the public. Porter F. Cope of Philadelphia, a banker's son and champion of "medical freedom," estimated the total salaries paid to American public health officials at $14 million. Throw in the $20 million invested in vaccine farms (again, according to antivaccination-ists), and compulsory vaccination constituted a substantial interest. "As long as the golden eggs of that goose can be squeezed out by proper ma-nipulation," wrote Oswald, "Dr. Edward Jenner will continue to be classed with the chief benefactors of the human race."[43]

The profit-seeking of the "vaccine trust," antivaccinationists argued, was a natural result of the regular physicians' *place*-seeking campaign for a "medical monopoly." The prospect of fees was probably far less important to the regulars than the government imprimatur conferred by legislatures and health boards upon vaccination—a measure closely identified with the mainstream physicians' struggle for authority. The return of medical licensing troubled Americans who had nothing personally at stake in the matter. "I don't know that I cared much about these osteopaths," Mark Twain testified before the New York legislature, "until I heard you were going to drive them out of the State; but since I heard this I haven't been able to sleep." For William James, the licensure problem ran deeper still. The power to license doctors was the power to grant a monopoly over belief itself.[44]

The distinguished Harvard psychologist (and older brother of Henry James) testified in March 1898 before a "tremendous throng of men and women" at the Massachusetts State House. The legislature's committee on public health was holding hearings on a bill that would make it a criminal offense to practice medicine without being certified by a state medical board. As everyone understood, the state exam would test for knowl-edge of allopathic medicine. The bill's framers touted it as "a blow at charlatanry—at medical quacks." The crowd of spiritualists, Christian Scientists, mind curers, and antivaccinationists in the room understood that meant them. "Ostensibly an act to protect the community from malpractice," said William Lloyd Garrison, Jr., "this is really meant to secure the monopoly of treating a disease to those who bear the credentials of a recognized school."[45]

James agreed. His quarrel with the bill reflected a set of ideas about the contingency of truth that he would later develop in his famous lectures that became *The Varieties of Religious Experience* (1901–2) and *Pragmatism* (1907). He noted that of the therapeutic methods presently in good repute, many had arisen from outside the regular medical profession. Successful treatments "appealed to experience for their credentials"—not to some state board. In an age of medical hubris, the professor asked for some professional humility. "The whole face of medicine changes unexpectedly from one generation to another in consequence of widening experience; and as we look back with a mixture of amusement and horror at the practice of our grandfathers, so we cannot be sure how large a portion of our present practice will awaken similar feelings in our posterity." To the lawmakers he warned, "You dare not convert the laws of this Commonwealth into obstacles to the acquisition of truth." The committee voted unanimously to reject the bill.[46]

Few antivaccinationists were as open-minded as William James. But like him, the antivaccinationists who railed against medical monopoly saw licensure as a threat to personal beliefs and to scientific progress. Three years later, in April 1901, the Massachusetts General Court debated another medical licensing bill. This time, Immanuel Pfeiffer testified. Though himself a registered physician, Pfeiffer demanded an amendment that would prevent the state from interfering with the practice of "any cosmopath, clairvoyant, hypnotist, magnetic healer, mind curist, masseur, osteopath or Christian Scientist." The lawmakers assented—but only so long as no such healer held himself out as a bona fide "practitioner of medicine."[47]

Antivaccinationism also spoke to the era's heightened social concern for children. Twelve-year-olds tending dangerous machines in textile mills, little boys playing unsupervised in city streets, fourteen-year-old delinquents tried as if they were grown men in municipal police courts: these once familiar sights became unthinkable in a relatively few short years around the century's turn. Infant and child mortality emerged as major social issues, with reformers pushing for better maternal and infant health care. Even as health officials promoted vaccination as a boon to childhood, antivaccinationists reached out to parents with their message that mandatory childhood vaccinations endangered the young, a modern-day reprise of Herod's "Slaughter of the Innocents." "There is a great cry of 'Save the children,'" said Harry Bradford of Kensington, Maryland. "Let us begin by stopping the infliction of compulsory disease on the defenseless."[48]

The vaccine safety issue was always the most politically promising of the antivaccinationists' arguments. Even the staunchest defenders of vaccination had to concede, as did Dr. William Welch of Philadelphia Municipal Hospital, "this measure is not entirely devoid of some danger." The appalling record of American-made vaccines during the 1898–1903 epidemics lent the issue a new urgency. Vaccine safety concerned everyone, especially parents. In most communities, children were the segment of the population most vulnerable to compulsory vaccination and thus to whatever dangers attended the procedure. Many antivaccination texts featured photographs of children—deformed, disabled, or lying dead in their coffins—identified by their captions as "Victims of Vaccination."[49]

The finest American example of the victims-of-vaccination genre was Lora Little's 1906 book, *Crimes of the Cowpox Ring: Some Moving Pictures Thrown on the Dead Wall of Official Silence*. The culmination of Little's work as editor of *The Liberator*, the book delivered on the muckraking promise of its title. Little was the Ida Tarbell of the antivaccination movement, a dogged reporter driven by a powerful vision of the injustices committed by business interests in collusion with corrupt or feckless state governments. Little drew upon the most effective tactics of the contemporary muckraking genre. Hers was a journalism of exposure, built from interviews, affidavits, and the public record, and written in the sensational style that made Lincoln Steffens a household name. And like thousands of muckraking pieces that appeared in American magazines between 1900 and World War I, Little's book narrated a clash of "the people" against organized economic interests through affecting portraits of individuals. With its short profiles of 336 "victims" of vaccination, most of them fatal, *Crimes of the Cowpox Ring* was not just an indictment of vaccination and its per-petrators. The book was a compendium of pain and loss. The most moving story in it was Little's own.[50]

Born in 1856, in a log cabin in the Minnesota Territory, Lora Little had worked as a seamstress, teacher, printer, and homemaker. In *Crimes of the Cowpox Ring*, she described her painful decision to allow her only child, seven-year-old Kenneth, to be vaccinated in 1895 so he could attend public school in Yonkers, New York. "He must go to school, and he could not go to school until he was vaccinated," she recalled. "Here was a risk. Children had died from vaccination. Why subject my only darling to this thing?" But all the other children were getting vaccinated. "He needed the association that school life afforded. If I were to keep him at home and teach him my-self, and he miss the common lot, and be marked as an exception, perhaps as queer, with a freakish mother who would not let him be vaccinated—how would all this affect his life?" It was a dilemma shared by countless mothers and fathers. Little feared not only the loss of the privilege of a public education but social ostracism, for her child and herself. Ultimately, she consented. Kenneth was vaccinated. Soon after, he suffered an attack of "catarrh of severe and stubborn kind," followed by measles, and then diphtheria "without known exposure." It was the diphtheria that killed him. Though she could never prove it, Little was convinced the vaccination was to blame. "My child was as really torn from me by the vaccinator, as tho he had died the day his arm was punctured." Three years later, Little was living with her husband, a civil engineer, in Minneapolis, speaking out against the local school board's vaccination rule and criticizing the Army's system of vaccination.[51]

In *Crimes*, Little argued that vaccination persisted, in the face of great opposition, because it served the economic interests of its "agents and pro-ducers." The "cowpox ring" had always been willing to face down the statis-tical evidence that vaccination was no preventive of smallpox. But they responded with a "conspiracy of silence" to the "other side of the statistical question, the ruin wrought by vaccine virus." This silence was the ring's "last and most impregnable stronghold."[52]

She began collecting cases on January 1, 1902, culling newspapers and conducting interviews with "the afflicted" or a surviving parent or relative.

Even though she was unable to investigate all of the reports and rumors she received, she went to press with the stories of 336 confirmed (to her satisfaction) victims of vaccination from across the United States. She provided names, dates, and locations for each case (including many verifiable in surviving local newspapers). Most of the accidents had happened during the epidemics of 1898–1903. The "victims" suffered postvaccination complications including anemia, blindness, blood poisoning, cancer, diphtheria, erysipelas, impetigo, lockjaw, meningitis, and tuberculosis.[53]

There is no way to confirm that vaccination caused all of this hurt and heartache. It is possible to dismiss Little's project as an exercise in overly simplistic post hoc reasoning: the children died following vaccination, therefore vaccination must have been the cause. Still, many of Little's "victims" had suffered complications acknowledged by medical scientists as possible, if rare, results of vaccination, whether caused by impure vaccine or secondary infection of the vaccine wound.

But Lora Little's book is most powerful at its least rational, as a dutifully compiled archive of belief and grief—not just hers, but of the hundreds of parents who told her their sad stories. "91. *Death*. Henry C., son of H.C. Petterson, St. Paul. Vaccinated Aug. 1901 to go to school. Three vaccinations in succession were necessary to get a take. Child then took sick, and was never able to go to school. Was not confined to bed, but gradually grew weaker til he died, Nov. 2, 1901. He was a fat, healthy little fellow all his life until vaccinated. The sore that formed on his arm never healed. Three doctors tried to save his life." Little patiently recorded hundreds of such stories. Neither doctors nor city health officials nor his boss could persuade railroad conductor Homer E. Sturdevant of Buffalo that his daughter's death from blood poisoning in May 1902 was not caused by the vaccine that had been scraped into her arm thirteen days earlier. Sturdevant paid to have the cause of death, as he saw it, inscribed on Lucille's tombstone in Forest Lawn Cemetery: "Lucille Sturdevant died May 28, 1902, aged 6 years. Vaccination poisoning at School 35."[54]

Like its antimonopoly and child protection arguments, the distinctive libertarian thrust of American antivaccinationism engaged an area of broad public concern. A robust language of personal liberty, anchored in the Anglo-American common law tradition and the state and federal constitutions, lay at the heart of antivaccinationist ideology. "Every man's house is his castle," wrote the San Diego spiritualist James Martin Peebles in 1900, "and upon the constitutional grounds of personal liberty, no vaccination doctor, lancet in one hand and calf-pox poison in the other, has a legal or moral right to enter the sacred precincts of a healthy home and scar a child's body for life." The passage illustrates the rhetorical range of these unlikely radicals: their righteous mixture of religion and constitutionalism, masculine prerogative and republican domesticity, a faith in clean living and a suspicion of state medicine, old-fashioned populism and a new libertarianism that might have startled old John Stuart Mill himself.[55]

The American antivaccinationists were personal liberty fundamentalists. They quoted chapter and verse from Mill's *On Liberty* (1859): "Over himself, over his own body and mind, the individual is sovereign." They reached past Mill to Sir William Blackstone, the eighteenth-century commentator on the common law whose *Commentaries on the Laws of England* (1765–69) formed part of the ideological bedrock of the American Revolution. Blackstone wrote (as Pitcairn reminded his early twentieth-century audiences), "The right of personal security consists in a person's legal and uninterrupted enjoyment of his life, his limbs, his body, his health and his reputation." So precious were the personal rights to life and limb, that the laws of England and America pardoned "even homicide, if committed in defense of them." Compulsory vaccination—the *only* medical procedure required by the state—trampled upon these elemental liberties. The antivaccinationists found support for their beliefs in the fundamental law of their nation. As the New England freethinker George E. Macdonald commented, "The law under which [the vaccinators] operate should carry a clause providing that all sections of the Constitution guaranteeing the security of person or property are hereby repealed."[56]

From alternative medicine, antivaccinationists learned that the key to health was to preserve the body's "integrity"—the soundness of its constitution, the purity of its blood. Vaccinators invaded "the integrity of the healthy body," said Dr. Hodge, penetrating the skin and corrupting the blood. How could introducing pus matter from a diseased cow into a healthy human body possibly protect a person from disease? "The right of every man to his own body, to keep it clean and pure and uncontaminated by poison, the right of every parent to guard the life and health of his children, are among the most sacred of human rights!" declared the New York–based *Anti-Vaccination News and Sanatorian*. Lora Little agreed. "It is because vaccination robs us of our physical integrity, contaminates and destroys our bodies," she wrote, "that we object to it."[57]

The vaccination question always circled back to freedom of belief. Chairman Durgin dared the Boston antivaccinationists to test their "belief" through a public "exhibition of faith, by exposure to smallpox without vaccination." American antivaccinationists proposed their own test of the state's vaccination "rite." "Let those, then, who have faith in the rite get poxed just as often as they choose to, and be satisfied with their own 'protection,'" said J. W. Hodge. "Being themselves 'secure' they can have no valid reason for inflicting the loathsome rite upon the unwilling and unbelieving." Public health officials countered that the purpose of universal vaccination was to render an entire community invulnerable to infection. Still, even some of the most ardent believers in compulsion, such as *The New York Times*, had to concede there was "a shadow of logic" in arguments like Hodge's. The *Times* cited the "natural inclination" of the enlightened public not to see "fellow-mortals cut off untimely by a preventable disease." Beyond altruism, another motive justified compulsion. "[T]he presence of smallpox in any community endangers business as well as life," said the *Times*.[58]

The antivaccinationists' libertarian radicalism seems utterly out of place in the Progressive Era. Their uncompromising defense of personal liberty sounds almost quaint next to the progressive intellectuals' brilliant assault upon laissez-faire and classical liberal individualism. As the forces of industrial capitalism and urbanization fashioned a more connected and self-consciously interdependent society around the turn of the century, leading progressives—including Jane Addams, Louis Brandeis, and John Dewey—called for a new liberalism that would value social interests above individual autonomy. Under modern social conditions, the progressives argued, a new concept of liberty was required. Liberty defined as "freedom from" government interference (the right to be left alone) may have made sense in the agrarian world of Jefferson and Jackson. But in Roosevelt's United States—an industrial nation of cosmopolitan cities, powerful corporations, and stark inequalities between rich and poor—the old liberty fell short. "Real liberty," redefined as the individual citizen's capacity to participate fully in the economy and polity, required purposeful government intervention. In this new self-consciously "social" age in Europe and the United States— with its movements for social Christianity, social democracy, and socialized law—the antivaccinationists carried the torch for individualism.[59]

But their individualism was not simply a quaint artifact of America's agrarian past. No less than the progressives' concept of social interdependence, the antivaccinationists' individualism bore the impress of its historical moment. The antivaccinationists fashioned their defense of a robust conception of personal liberty—bodily integrity, freedom of belief, the right not to participate in a state-sanctioned rite—in response to real changes in American society, culture, and politics. Like Mill, writing in Victorian England, the turn-of-the-century American antivaccinationists wrote at a time when their government was in fact reaching more deeply than ever before into their nation's economy and society. They challenged the expansion of the American state at the very point where state power penetrated the skin.

Was antivaccinationism *antiprogressive*? Most defenders of compulsory vaccination thought so. To them, antivaccinationism was founded in misguided individualism and willful ignorance. Antivaccinationists countered that theirs was the true cause of progress. Vaccination, they pointed out, originated as a folk remedy—"the tradition of the milk-maids"—promoted by Jenner back when physicians still routinely bled their patients. The medical profession's blind adherence to the Jennerian rite had diverted resources from sanitation and hygiene, the real scientific advances of the nineteenth century. The genuine American progressives were men like Tom Johnson and Martin Friedrich of Cleveland, who stood up to the cowpox trust and abandoned the dangerous and unpopular policy of vaccination. Benjamin O. Flower, founder of the reform magazine *Arena*, praised Cleveland's action as an example of "the best progressive thought of the age."[60]

To some antivaccinationists, the progressiveness of their cause lay in their fundamental belief in the right of ordinary citizens in a democracy to participate in scientific deliberation and medical decision making. Antivaccinationists pointed out that the demand for compulsory vaccination laws had not come from the general public but from health officials and medical societies. Which was why compulsory vaccination so often joined the regular physician's lancet to the policeman's nightstick.[61]

Lora Little—the movement's most democratic voice—was a keen student of the burgeoning American archive of popular resistance to compulsory vaccination. Violent imagery pervaded antivaccination texts: the frontispiece of Clymer's book pictured a police officer, armed with a copy of the Vaccination Law, seizing a baby from its mother's lap while the angel of death waited with open arms. Lora Little found material enough in the public record. "It is for this ghoulish work that churches, theaters, business blocks, and whole neighborhoods have been raided," she wrote, "ocean liners' populations cowpoxed; a shipload of negro laborers driven off the vessel with clubs at Panama, and poisoned in spite of resistance; arrests have been made and innocent persons cast into jail and there jabbed with the virus; and most atrocious of all, the annual army of babies graduating from nursery into school are required to bare their little arms and receive this injection of disease." For middle-class antivaccinationists, the plight of working-class vaccine refusers, "pinioned by police officers and vaccinated," revealed the "tyranny" and "despotism" of the entire system of state medicine. "If this can be done and upheld by the legal machinery of this country, what next have we to expect?" asked Clymer. "Why not chase people and circumcise them? It surely would be a good preventative against certain kinds of disease. Why not catch the people and give each a compulsory bath?"[62]

It may sound absurd to contemporary ears, but antivaccinationists were in fact more conscious than were most progressives of the coercive potential of the new interventionist state. In a few short years, American eugenicists would be persuading state legislatures to enact compulsory sterilization laws for the "feeble-minded," epileptics, and other people deemed "unfit" to reproduce. The eugenicists' chief legal precedent for their measures would be compulsory vaccination.[63]

For Lora Little, though, antivaccinationism was ultimately more than a struggle for personal liberty—though it most certainly was that. It was also a progressive movement for the democratization of health. "A first step in health culture," she called it. She envisioned the struggle against compulsory vaccination leading to a broader, popular movement for health, a grassroots culture alternative to, and when necessary in opposition to, the official, top-down health movement of the state.[64]

The most ambitious American antivaccinationists tried to use the political system to abolish compulsory vaccination. The decentralized structure of the American political system made their task fundamentally different from that of their counterparts in England. Although the English Vaccination Acts were administered locally, they were the legislative product of a single national body, Parliament. That focused reform efforts. A half century of protest and lobbying culminated in the hearings before the Royal Commission on Vaccination, which in turn persuaded Parliament to make an exception for conscientious objectors. The U.S. Congress had no such power. When public health officials and medical societies sought authority to enforce vaccination on unwilling members of the public, they necessarily turned to local boards of health and education, city councils, county courts, and, ultimately, to state legislatures. The antivaccinationists had to make their case for abolishing compulsion to the same bodies.

Antivaccinationists used every political weapon available. They flooded legislatures with petitions. They litigated. They turned out the vote. Although the "tyrannical" boards of health were normally appointive bodies, insulated from democratic pressures, local school boards were typically elective. During the epidemics of 1898–1903, a number of communities made their school board elections turn upon the candidates' positions on the vaccination question. The voters of Norwich, Connecticut, turned their board of education into a bulwark against compulsion.[65]

But in the antivaccination fight, the big game was a state law banning compulsory vaccination. From Massachusetts to California, several state legislatures debated such measures around the turn of the century. In the end, the antivaccinationists won their biggest victory in the nation's youngest state.

In 1900, the predominantly Mormon state of Utah was just four years old. With smallpox threatening in the mountain states, Utah became a battleground over compulsory vaccination. That year, three thousand cases of smallpox were reported to the state board of health; twenty-six people had died. The scale of the epidemic alarmed health officials, but its relative mildness (with a case-fatality rate of less than 1 percent) sharpened popular sentiment against compulsion. The new mild type variola virus continued to spread dissension as efficiently as it did disease.[66]

In January, when Salt Lake City boards of health and education moved to compel vaccination of public schoolchildren, a de facto schools strike erupted. Eight thousand of the city's schoolchildren failed to present "the scars of vaccination entitling them to their seats." In April, one Salt Lake father, John E. Cox, won a court order compelling the school board to admit his unvaccinated daughter; on appeal, the Utah Supreme Court upheld the board's action as a "reasonable regulation in the aid of the public health." The Salt Lake Medical Society and the state and local boards of health came to the defense of compulsion. Meanwhile, meetings of the Utah Anti-Compulsory Vaccination League in Salt Lake City attracted crowds of two hundred people or more.[67]

Like many other leagues that first surfaced during the epidemics of 1898–1903, the Utah Anti-Compulsory Vaccination League formed in response to a new effort to enforce vaccination. Unlike the long-standing antivaccination societies (the sort that produced journals and books), these new leagues were not necessarily led by irregular doctors eager to drive back state medicine in general. Instead, these more transient political organizations tended to be single-issue groups with a much broader base of activated people. They borrowed rhetoric and ideas from the antivaccination literature but in the interest of their own immediate fight. These groups could be stunningly effective.

The Utah league left a fuller impression on the historical record than most. The *Salt Lake Herald* covered its meetings and reported the names of the league's leaders, speakers, and members assigned to draft resolutions— a cross-section of nineteen of the most involved members. All of these activists, who came to meetings in the Fourteenth Ward from areas across the city, were white (hardly surprising for Salt Lake City in 1900). And most were male. In economic status, the group ranged more widely. Lucretia Kimball, a banker's wife, served on the resolutions committee with publisher J. H. Parry, bookkeeper D. H. Tatham, wrapper-of-dry-goods H. J. Walk, and hardware salesman James M. Barlow. The first elected officers of the league included President Thomas Hull, an office manager; Vice President Scott Anderson, a bill poster; Secretary C. S. Booth, a bookkeeper; and Treasurer Bernard H. Schettler, a banker. More than half (ten) of the activists had been born outside the United States: a striking number (seven) were natives of Great Britain, two hailed from Sweden, and one from Germany—all countries where compulsory vaccination of infants was national policy. But the nine others were native-born Americans, the majority from Utah. All in all, the group seems to have been a bastion of white, male, taxpaying respectability—neither a working-class "mob" nor a "coterie" of "crank" doctors.[68]

The 1900 Census reveals the most important commonality among these members. All but one was a parent of one or more schoolchildren. (The other, attorney LeGrande Young, had children who were already grown.) Most of the members had large families. H. J. Walk had nine children living at home, including three at school and three school-bound. Of the six children in Bernard Schettler's household, four were still in school. The Utah Anti-Compulsory Vaccination League was an organization of local taxpaying parents with a strong sense of ownership in the city's schools.

Outside critics, including *The Denver Post*, decried the surging antivaccination movement in Utah as a Mormon phenomenon—a charge local newspapers such as the Ogden *Standard-Examiner* roundly denied. Neither census records nor local newspaper accounts identified the religious composition of the league, though its membership certainly matched the profile of a predominantly Mormon organization. Church leaders were in fact divided on the issue. Although Mormon teachings had nothing in particular to say about vaccination, decades of political conflict with the U.S. government prepared Utah Mormons to view with distrust any use of government authority to impose scientific beliefs or behavioral mandates upon the public without democratic deliberation. Distinctly Mormon voices—such as Charles W. Penrose's *Deseret Evening News*, an organ of the Church of Jesus Christ of Latter-day Saints—applauded the public opposition to compulsory vaccination. Still, religious imagery and language is notably absent from the public record of the controversy. The *Deseret Evening News* said the people of Utah were open to persuasion on the vaccination question: "It is the policy of force which arouses the indignity of the great bulk of the citizens." The relative homogeneity of the Utah citizenry may help explain the exceptionally strong support there for antivaccinationism. But there is little evidence to suggest that most Mormons viewed antivaccination as a Mormon cause.[69]

The goals and rhetoric of the Utah Anti-Compulsory Vaccination League reflected its broad social base. Its purpose was not to debate the merits of vaccination, but to prevent the Salt Lake City Board of Health from compelling healthy schoolchildren—*their* healthy schoolchildren—to submit to the procedure. Beyond that, the organization urged the legislature to "keep from the statutes anything that savors of compulsory vaccination." The league made its case in the constitutional keywords of American public life: popular sovereignty, separation of powers, and the rule of law. "The highest medical authority is divided on the question of vaccination," one resolution noted, "many taking the ground that it is always dangerous, and sometimes productive of fatal results." To date, the legislature had faithfully "expressed the sentiment of the people by refusing to pass a compulsory vaccination law." The health board's action—"to compel a medical opera-tion not authorized by law" and not justified by the "condition of the pub-lic health"—threatened to "usurp the authority of the people." The people should resist by "an emphatic protest." And that the people delivered.[70]

The climax of Utah's "vaccination war" came in January 1901, as the legislature debated a bill introduced by Rep. William McMillan, a Mormon bishop from Salt Lake City. The McMillan bill made it unlawful for any public board to compel the vaccination of any "person of any age" or to make vaccination "a condition precedent to the attendance at any public or private school in the state of Utah, either as pupil or as teacher." The bill was the most controversial piece of legislation in the state's short life. While the hearings went on, the Salt Lake Board of Education passed a resolution, on a slim majority of 5 to 4, holding that it was "not the duty" of school officials and teachers to enforce the Utah Board of Health's vaccination order. At the insistence of Dr. T. B. Beatty, secretary of the state board, those five mem-bers of the local school board were arrested. The Utah Anti-Compulsory Vaccination League held a mass meeting, adopting "strong resolutions" in favor of the McMillan bill. Inside the statehouse, the defenders of compul-sion seemed determined to confirm their critics' worst charges about them.

Dr. Beatty testified that the critics of vaccination did not understand science. Dr. Alexander MacLean offered to expose his own vaccinated son to "the most virulent forms of smallpox" in the city pesthouse, if a critic of vaccination agreed to "subject his unvaccinated child to a similar danger."[71]

On January 31, 1901, the Utah legislature passed the McMillan bill by a wide margin: 37 to 6 in the House, 13 to 5 in the Senate. Governor Heber M. Wells vetoed the bill. "To place among our statutes such a bill would be a step backwards, which will be disastrous," he cautioned. Political credibility seemed to loom as large in his mind as public health. He had received dispatches from nearly every American governor, standing "almost as a unit for vaccination." If the law stood, Utah would be one of the few states that forbade local boards of health to order vaccination to stamp out smallpox. Both houses of the legislature voted to override Wells's veto. Newspapers and medical journals across America reported with disbelief the antivaccinationists' triumph. The *Medical Standard* denounced the law as a "pronunciamento"—a Mormon coup d'état. "It is an unpleasant thing to suggest at the present juncture and we hope our friends in Utah may be spared," the journal warned, "but it usually happens that chickens of this kind 'come home to roost.'"[72]

The following year, Immanuel Pfeiffer and the Massachusetts antivaccinationists put several bills before the General Court's joint committee on public health. All of the bills aimed to repeal the state's compulsory vaccination laws. All were killed in committee, an outcome the activists may well have anticipated. Antivaccination bills were a more common event in Massachusetts than in Utah. The packed hearings on Beacon Hill had the aspect of ritualized performances: public bouts between old foes who knew each other's arguments well. But that did not lessen the public drama.

Day after day, committee members and the assembled public heard speeches by health officials (including Chairman Durgin and Dr. McCollom) and doctors from both sides of the vaccination question. Dr. Pfeiffer testified that the board of health's vaccination stations were places unfit to hold cattle. Dr. Caroline E. Hastings of Boston claimed smallpox tended to increase in proportion to the extent of vaccination in a community. Jessica L. Henderson, a mother from suburban Wayland, vowed she would go to jail before allowing her children or herself to be vaccinated. On the other side, Durgin and his peers paid the antivaccinationists the compliment of taking their campaign seriously. The defenders of compulsion assembled a parade of luminaries from the fields of bacteriology, medicine, and public health to testify against the bills—including Harvard professor of pathology William T. Councilman, Massachusetts Medical Society president Francis Draper, MIT professor William T. Sedgwick, and Azel Ames (who told the committee of his recent experience fighting smallpox in Puerto Rico).[73]

The antivaccinationists saved their most powerful witnesses for the final day. The bodies of children—present or remembered—were placed, once again, into evidence. The petitioners presented to the committee one "little child whose head was almost one mass of sores." Mrs. Smith of Winthrop introduced her son Benjamin, who she said had lost the use of his arm following vaccination. Fred W. Hatch of Dorchester said his daughter had suffered a severe case of eczema following vaccination. With the Camden tetanus cases still in the news, Mrs. Caswell of Cambridge told the committee of losing her five-year-old daughter Annie to lockjaw. The death certificate listed tetanus as the cause of death, with vaccination as the contributing cause.[74]

The antivaccinationists failed to move the committee. At the end of February, the committee adversely reported all of the antivaccination bills, effectively killing them. The following month, the committee favorably reported a new vaccination bill, introduced by Chairman Durgin. The Durgin bill, which was soon enacted by the General Court, made the exemption for "unfit" children from the school requirement more stringent. It required that a physician actually examine the child before signing a certificate. The antivaccinationists had tried to squeeze something for their side from the Durgin bill, submitting an amendment that would extend the health exemption to adults as well as children. But lawmakers rejected it.[75]

Despite their string of defeats on Beacon Hill, the antivaccinationists had succeeded in keeping the state lawmakers and the public focused on their cause through much of the winter of 1902. The State House debate provided the high political drama of a larger struggle over vaccination that would continue in the streets, the schools, and, increasingly, the courts.

During the next three years, American antivaccinationists won two more legislative victories. In Minnesota, in 1903, Lora Little and activists from Minneapolis and St. Paul placed an antivaccination bill before the state legislature. The bill made it unlawful for any public board to compel the vaccination of any child or make vaccination "a condition precedent to the school attendance." Dr. Henry M. Bracken, secretary of the state board of health, recalled, "At first this bill hardly seemed worthy of notice on the part of sanitarians." To his dismay, the House passed the bill. When doctors mobilized in opposition, the Senate amended the bill, adding a clause that allowed boards to require vaccination in the event of an actual smallpox epidemic. Little denounced the amended law as "a disgusting piece of legislative folly." But health authorities would later complain that the law was all too effective. In 1906, AMA president William J. Mayo, a Minnesota physician, charged that his state's "inability to enforce vaccination" had unleashed a smallpox epidemic, infecting 28,000 of the state's citizens—"all due to a small but vociferous band of antivaccination agitators."[76]

In California, a crowd of three hundred assembled in Berkeley in 1904 to form an Anti-Compulsory Vaccination Society and protest the "unjust" school vaccination law. The group's leaders included the president of the local board of education and a local minister. The movement gained traction. In the winter of 1905, the state legislature passed a bill banning compulsory vaccination from the schools. Governor George C. Pardee, a physician, vetoed the bill on March 8, 1905. He cited the "vast preponderance of expert medical authority throughout the civilized world" that viewed vaccination as "the prime cause of the practical disappearance of smallpox." Pardee insisted that the number of vaccination accidents was "infinitesimal" compared to the "millions of times that this beneficent procedure is practiced." The legislature let Pardee's veto stand. In the wake of this political defeat, antivaccinationists in Berkeley announced plans to open a private school, a separatist institution where students and teachers would not be required to show proof of vaccination in order to receive an education.[77]

From Boston to Berkeley, the vaccination issue revealed tensions at the heart of American public life in the Progressive Era. The conflict pitted scientific authority against democracy, rising government social intervention against an uncompromising individualism, an increasing paternalism in public policy against the rights of parents themselves. Striking communities across the United States with a disease often perplexingly mild, the epidemics brought old debates to a head and provided both sides with new fuel for argument.

For the antivaccinationists, the epidemics provided a welter of fresh evidence. They cited the deaths from smallpox of hundreds of previously vaccinated U.S. soldiers in the Philippines. Martin Friedrich's Cleveland experiment replaced the antivaccination stronghold of Leicester, England, as the American antivaccinationists' favorite exhibit in their case for a sanitary approach to smallpox. To the Rivalta, Italy, syphilis outbreak and other Old World examples of vaccination gone awry, 1901 brought Camden—an appalling new American monument to the "victims of vaccination." The violent clashes between virus squads and working-class populations in innumerable local places provided a powerful public record of the czarist "tyranny" inflicted by public health boards upon the public they were meant to serve.

Lora Little was one of the few American antivaccinationist writers whose vision of the question extended to racial politics. Seemingly alone among her peers, she saw the connection between the bludgeoning of Martinican laborers in the Panama Canal Zone and physical force vaccination in American tenement districts. It was Little, the careful student of newspapers and medical journals, who protested the "brutal invasion" of an African American faith-healing church in Philadelphia by a vaccinating force. "It is time we had a Reconstructed North," she declared. To Little, writing from her desk in Minneapolis, the routine violence that attended public health enforcement in so many African American neighborhoods showed how far the nation had fallen from "the true idea of freedom and equality before the law which has been the professed ideal of our government." For Little, at least, the constitutional problem of compulsory vaccination was not just the harm it did to liberty; in practice, the measures also trampled the promise of equal protection of the laws.[78]

For health officials, too, the epidemics provided a fund of new data and experience. Some were moved to question the practicality of compulsion, convinced by the experience of those years that persuasion might be the better way to achieve their goal of a well-vaccinated community. But others were strengthened in their belief that ignorance was best met with force. From health departments and hospitals across the United States came the evidence: the unvaccinated suffered far worse than the well vaccinated. Before the Boston epidemic ended, in May 1903, 1,596 cases of smallpox were reported, with 270 deaths. A majority of the sufferers showed no evidence of previous vaccination. They died at twice the rate of vaccinated patients.[79]

And so, to their nemeses the antivaccinationists, leading American public health officers and physicians threw down the gauntlet. The dares issued by men like Boston's Samuel Durgin and Salt Lake City's Alexander Mac-Lean were born of medical certitude and frustration. To such men, the smallpox epidemics provided many stories of the proverbial chicken "coming home to roost," as the trusted "fool-killer" smallpox stole the health and lives of a number of committed opponents of compulsory vaccination. In July 1902, *The New York Times* reported that the well-known Christian Scientist Putnam J. Ramsdell of Cambridge, Massachusetts, had "die[d] of the disease he defied." In Charlotte, North Carolina, five vaccine refusers died of the disease later that year. In June 1903, on the very same day that the Minnesota legislature enacted the anticompulsion law he had championed, the Minneapolis antivaccinationist Charles Stevens died of smallpox at his home. "Providence seems to have been somewhat against the antivaccinationists," smirked Secretary Bracken of the Minnesota Board of Health. The *Times* could barely contain itself when fifteen Dowieites fell ill at Zion City in August 1904. "Now that smallpox has broken out in 'Zion,'" the paper declared, "there is likely to be an excellent, though rather dangerous, opportunity to see what can be done with a disease of that sort by the exercise of 'faith.'"[80]

But for America's anti-antivaccinationists, no case of smallpox was sweeter than the one that nearly killed Immanuel Pfeiffer.

The manhunt lasted five days. Only later would the public learn the details of those tense hours. The interrogation of Pfeiffer's clerk, who insisted the doctor was away in Philadelphia. The interview with the janitor of a Charlestown apartment house, who had seen the doctor, looking weak and accompanied by an unnamed woman, exit by the back door and enter a hack. The search for the hack and its driver, who had taken Pfeiffer and his "companion" (presumed, it appears from newspaper accounts, to be his mistress) to the offices of a certain Boston doctor. The doctor's denial that he had seen Pfeiffer. The discovery that Pfeiffer and "the woman in question" had engaged another carriage bound for Bedford, the town twenty miles northwest of Boston where Pfeiffer's wife, Olive, and their children lived on a dairy farm he rarely visited. The health officers' race to Bedford. The rounding up of the local selectmen. The drive to the farmhouse, where a doctor examined Pfeiffer and declared him "in a very serious condition from a thoroughly developed case of smallpox." The announcement, by the Boston Board of Health, that Dr. Pfeiffer "probably will not recover."[81]

How many had been exposed to smallpox in the days between Pfeiffer's disappearance and the arrival of the health officials at his Bedford bedside? No one knew. Bedford officials placed the Pfeiffer farm under quarantine, ordering all on the premises vaccinated. Learning that Pfeiffer's two daughters had been to school since his arrival, officials ordered all the town's pupils to get vaccinated or stay home. Boston authorities tracked down the two carriages in which Pfeiffer had traveled and disinfected them. All of the residents of the Charlestown apartment house were vaccinated.

To everyone's surprise (except perhaps his own), Immanuel Pfeiffer's famous constitution pulled him back from the brink of death, and he began his long recovery. The race for the moral high ground began even before his survival was assured. Durgin announced that several other physicians had visited Gallop's Island that season, and, having previously been vaccinated, none had come down with smallpox. *The Boston Globe* dubbed Pfeiffer "a victim of his own zeal and bravado." The Pfeiffers' Bedford neighbors took no pity on the man one called an "old chump." Medical authorities across the nation reminded their publics that the moment was larger than the man. They praised Durgin for his "wisdom and his scientific foresight" in orchestrating this "object lesson" for the American people. Meanwhile, the intended recipients of that lesson—the antivaccinationists—condemned Pfeiffer, too. Boston antivaccinationist B. F. Nichols could find no sympathy for any man "who recklessly exposed himself to contagion."[82]

As the days passed, the realization dawned (at least to some observers) that Pfeiffer and Durgin were a dangerous match. The episode showed how far a committed antivaccinationist and an equally determined vaccination advocate would go to make a point. The citizens of Bedford, stuck with a bill of $1,000 for containing the resulting emergency, recognized this better than anyone. Some called for lawsuits against *both* parties—Pfeiffer, for failing to notify the local authorities of his disease, and the City of Boston for the "inexcusable negligence" of its health authorities.[83]

In the end, the people of Bedford dropped the matter and moved on. But they'd had a point. Both Durgin and Pfeiffer were true believers who had played Russian roulette with the public health. A jury of their peers, though, might have discerned a difference of culpability between the two men. Pfeiffer believed that vaccination was a sham and that a man of his constitution, psychic power, and cleanly habits was impervious to smallpox; he had, as *The New York Times* conceded, shown the "courage of his convictions," however wrongheaded those convictions might have been. Durgin, a sworn government officer of the public health, had staged a public event whereby an unvaccinated man was exposed to smallpox; he had done so with full knowledge of the risks to that man and the general public. Pfeiffer may have been misguided. But Durgin was reckless.

EIGHT

SPEAKING LAW TO POWER

It is one of the more ennobling characteristics of the American system of government that the greatest of constitutional questions may arise in the most humble of places. A coach on a Louisiana train. An elementary school in Topeka, Kansas. A pool hall in Panama City, Florida. The seminal case in modern American public health law began at the threshold of a tenement house apartment in a neighborhood filled with wage earners and immigrants.[1]

On March 15, 1902, Dr. E. Edwin Spencer, chairman of the Cambridge, Massachusetts, Board of Health, called upon Pastor Henning Jacobson in his apartment at 95 Pine Street, in the neighborhood of Cambridgeport, about a mile east of Harvard Yard. A man little known beyond his Swedish congregation at the nearby Augustana Lutheran Church, Jacobson lived with his wife, Hattie, and their sons Fritz, David, and Jacob. Spencer had practiced medicine in Cambridge for thirty years and headed the board of health for almost ten of them. Spencer informed Jacobson of the board's "vote" declaring smallpox prevalent in the city and ordering all inhabitants who had not been vaccinated within the past five years to submit to the procedure at once or incur a $5 fine, as provided for by the Massachusetts compulsory vaccination law. The penalty was not trivial: the average weekly wage of an American factory worker was about $13, and it is unlikely that an immigrant minister earned much more than that. Jacobson, forty-five, had not been vaccinated since childhood. Spencer offered to vaccinate him "then and there," free of charge. But Jacobson "absolutely refused." He was later summoned to court, tried, and found guilty of "the crime of refusing vaccination." Rather than pay his fine, Jacobson appealed.[2]

During the next three years, Pastor Jacobson would pursue his cause all the way to the U.S. Supreme Court, prompting the Court's first ruling on the subject of compulsory vaccination. In the words of Justice John Marshall Harlan, who wrote the opinion for the majority in *Jacobson v. Massachusetts*, the minister claimed that "a compulsory vaccination law is unreasonable, arbitrary, and oppressive, and, therefore, hostile to the inherent right of every freeman to care for his own body and health in such way as to him seems best." More than a century on, it is difficult to appreciate just how radical that claim must have sounded when first uttered. Henning Jacobson was asking the nation's highest court to contemplate the true extent of constitutional liberty in the United States.[3]

The *Jacobson* case marked the end of the great wave of smallpox epidemics that had swept across the United States at the turn of the century. It also signaled the beginning of the long struggle to reconcile twentieth-century Americans' ever-increasing expectations of personal liberty with the far-reaching administrative power needed to govern a modern, urban-industrial society.

A man in his prime, with deep-set eyes and a touch of gray in his beard, Henning Jacobson was an unlikely troublemaker. He was an institution builder, the spiritual leader of the Swedish American community of eastern Massachusetts.

Born in rural Yllestad, Sweden, in 1856, he had immigrated to America with his family in 1869. The Jacobsons' adopted country was in the throes of its post–Civil War Reconstruction and just entering the explosive period of growth that would make it the world's most productive industrial economy by 1900. As a young man, Jacobson took out naturalization papers and became a U.S. citizen. He studied at Augustana College in Rock Island, Illinois, an institution founded by Swedish Lutheran immigrants in 1860 to prepare young men for the ministry. Jacobson founded the college orchestra. He played the contrabass, anchoring the music with deep-pitched authority.[4]

Swedish Lutheranism was not a radical religious sect. It was the official state church of Sweden, the faith of the overwhelming majority of Jacobson's countrymen who migrated to the United States during the peak decades of Swedish immigration after the Civil War. Jacobson received his ordination in Kansas, in the rural heartland of Swedish America. But his future lay in an eastern industrial city. The Church of Sweden Mission Board called him in 1892 to build the Augustana Lutheran Church in Cambridge. He conducted services in his native tongue and became a regular at the Boston docks, meeting newly arrived Swedes and taking them back to Cambridge, where he helped them find jobs and homes. He would remain pastor of the Cambridge church until his death in 1930.

Nothing in the conservative biblical doctrine of Swedish Lutheranism dictated defiance to vaccination, but Jacobson practiced a form of pietism that filled the daily details of life with religious significance. His brief to the Massachusetts Supreme Judicial Court—written by his lawyers but submitted under his name—decried compulsory vaccination as an unconscionable state sacrament. "We have on our statute book," it said, "a law that compels such a man to offer up his body to pollution and filth and disease; that compels him to submit to a barbarous ceremonial of blood-poisoning."[5]

That reference to blood-poisoning held a literal meaning for Jacobson. Though antivaccinationism ran rife in the Swedish countryside, he had undergone vaccination as a child, in accordance with national law. Early childhood vaccination spread quickly in Sweden after 1800 and became compulsory in 1816—nearly forty years before Massachusetts enacted America's first vaccination law. Sweden was an international public health success story, championed in the American medical literature. Smallpox killed 300,000 people in the country between 1750 and 1800, most of them children. Mortality levels fell sharply after the introduction of vaccination, and by 1900 the disease had virtually disappeared. But young Henning's vaccination had gone badly. He experienced "great and extreme suffering" that instilled in him a lifelong horror of the practice. Henning and Hattie Jacobson knew all too well the perils of a nineteenth-century childhood. Married for eighteen years by the time a U.S. Census-taker knocked on their door in 1900, they had created five children together, but only three survived. One of Jacobson's boys (he did not say which) suffered adverse effects from a childhood vaccination, convincing the minister that some

Pastor Henning Jacobson, circa 1902. Courtesy of the Evangelical Lutheran Church in America

hereditary condition in his family made vaccine a particular hazard for them. Jacobson's belief that smallpox vaccine threatened his family's existence seemed as deeply ingrained as his religious faith.[6]

If Jacobson made an unlikely rabble-rouser, neither did the man who stood across his threshold that March day fit the part of the heartless bureaucrat. E. Edwin Spencer had a starkly different medical background and leadership style from his counterpart across the Charles River, Chairman Samuel Durgin of the Boston Board of Health. Unlike the Harvard-educated Durgin, Spencer had studied a form of alternative medicine. Born to a Rhode Island farming family in 1833, he graduated from the Eclectic Medical College in Cincinnati, a young institution that considered itself a citadel of freedom in medical education. The eclectics favored botanical remedies, eschewing "heroic" interventions and mercurial medicines. Spencer moved to Massachusetts and received another degree from the short-lived Worcester Medical College, an eclectic school that received its charter from the state in 1849 over strenuous professional opposition. He settled in Cambridge, where he practiced medicine, held the office of city physician, and earned an appointment to the board of health.[7]

Working in a field dominated by allopathic physicians, Spencer never severed his ties to "irregular" medicine. A onetime president of the Massachusetts Eclectic Medical Society, he remained an officer of that organization until his death in 1903. Unlike many eclectics, Spencer believed in the theory of vaccination. But he showed a marked reluctance to impose the beliefs of the mainstream medical profession upon unwilling members of the public. It is hard to imagine Spencer relishing a public confrontation with Immanuel Pfeiffer. In his interactions with Jacobson, Spencer proceeded with caution and deliberation, as he had ever since smallpox first broke out in Cambridge several months earlier.

Smallpox had already been spreading for months in Boston and other cities of eastern Massachusetts by the time Cambridge reported its first case on October 25, 1901. The outbreak, in a tenement by the Charles River, still caught the city unprepared. Despite the entreaties of the board of health— a three-member board consisting of Dr. Spencer and two laymen, lawyer William Peabody and engineer Charles Harris—the city government had balked at spending taxpayer money on precautionary measures. Cambridge had no pesthouse, and in recent years vaccination had fallen off. Harvard required all of its students and employees, from the professors to the African American waiters at Memorial Hall, to get vaccinated; during the months to come the university reported not a single case of smallpox. But Harvard and the elite bastions of Brattle Street and Avon Hill stood as islands of privileged homogeneity in a diverse city of 95,000 people that teemed with brickworks, factories, and thickly settled neighborhoods. By the end of December, the city suffered fifteen smallpox cases, three of them fatal.[8]

Spencer's response was decisive but temperate. The board established a pesthouse on New Street, near the Fresh Pond marshes, and opened public vaccination stations, where thousands of citizens lined up for free vaccine. The voluntary vaccination effort hit a setback on January 4, when the *Cambridge Chronicle* reported that Annie Caswell, just five years old, had "died of tetanus, or lockjaw, following vaccination." The news came less than one month after the last Camden, New Jersey, child had died from postvaccination tetanus. According to the report, the doctors who had tried to save Annie believed "the vaccine used might have been impure or that some foreign substance may have gotten into the sore." Dr. Edwin Farnham, the chief inspector for the Cambridge Board of Health, swiftly declared his belief that vaccination could not have caused Annie's death. There would be no investigation.[9]

As the outbreak of smallpox continued, with twenty-six cases and three more deaths reported during January and February 1902, the board declined to use its full powers. Spencer publicly defended his cautious quarantine policy, saying the city had "no right" to placard the home of a resident merely because she may have been exposed to smallpox. The board must be "absolutely certain" the resident had been infected. And the board held on to compulsory vaccination as a last resort.[10]

Spencer seemed determined to avoid the sort of public standoffs with antivaccinationists that the more aggressive actions of Durgin's Boston board had sparked in the streets, the criminal courts, and the State House. That January, as the Boston virus squad stepped up enforcement in working-class neighborhoods, the doctors and police had run up against many determined refusers, including nineteen residents willing to face prosecution rather than submit.[11]

Charles E. Cate, a South End laborer, refused vaccination even as his wife lay sick in the Southampton Street pesthouse; he served fifteen days in Charlestown Jail rather than pay his $5 fine. As a force of 125 city-employed physicians moved from house to house in East Boston, vaccinating five thousand residents in a single day, a Canadian-born grocer named John H. Mugford refused to allow Dr. John Ames to vaccinate him or his daughter, Eva. Dr. Ames assured Mugford that the vaccine points he carried, on small quills, were perfectly safe. But Mugford did not relent. "I told him I studied the question too long to allow any poison to be put into my system," the grocer testified at his trial. The court found Mugford guilty on both charges of refusing vaccination. He appealed his case to the Supreme Judicial Court.[12]

Even when Spencer's Cambridge board finally took steps to enforce vaccination, it moved with an exceptional degree of caution. The board ordered vaccination on February 27, 1902. Spencer waited two more weeks before dividing the city into districts and sending seventeen physicians from house to house to vaccinate "all the inhabitants they could find."

Thousands were vaccinated in this way, while better-heeled citizens paid their family doctors to perform the procedure. For the city vaccinators, finding the inhabitants was not always easy. Some bolted. Others shooed the doctors from their doorsteps. The board compiled a catalogue, containing a card for every house in a large swath of the city. Each card listed the names of the inhabitants and the date each had last been vaccinated. Vaccine refusers were noted. Among them were Albert M. Pear, a prominent city official, and Pastor Henning Jacobson, whom Spencer visited himself. The board prosecuted no one.[13]

For a time, it seemed that compulsion in name only was all Cambridge would require. By the time some local residents got around to forming an antivaccination society in April, the epidemic seemed to have subsided. Vaccination slowed to a halt. With the arrival of spring, normalcy returned to Cambridge. It did not last.[14]

A t midnight on June 5, the phone rang at Spencer's home. The caller reported a dead body at 77 Norfolk Street. When Spencer arrived at the tenement, he was shocked at the appearance of the body—"one of the worst cases of smallpox I had ever seen." The deceased, an African American boarder, had suffered for weeks with no medical care. Spencer examined the family that lived in the house. Three of the children had smallpox. Spencer had to assume that many in the densely populated neighborhood had been exposed. He called the undertaker, who buried the body that same night.[15]

Waiting out the incubation period of smallpox could be an unnerving experience. For a week, the board of health heard of no new cases. Then came the deluge: a full-blown outbreak on the blocks around 77 Norfolk Street, a section of Cambridgeport that lay just north of Massachusetts Avenue, the main road running from Central Square into Boston. Between June 14 and 28, ambulances carted nearly fifty infected adults and children to the New Street hospital. Seven from the neighborhood died. The board disinfected homes; closed schools and churches; and renewed its call for universal vaccination. In a single week, 4,000 people flocked to the free station in Central Square, just a few blocks from the infected district. Vaccinators canvassed the neighborhood, one of them vaccinating 260 people in just two days. But conflict impeded the corps' progress. "Many refuse to be vaccinated," the *Chronicle* reported, "while others evade the doctors when they call at the house."[16]

The board issued another vote: all vaccine refusers would now be prosecuted. Now accompanied by police, city vaccinators were under strict orders to "see the vaccination mark instead of merely taking a person's word." At the end of June, the board reported that "almost all persons" in the infected district had been vaccinated.[17]

One of the holdouts was Pastor Jacobson, who lived just two blocks from 77 Norfolk Street. None of these details would make it into the legal record of his case, leaving later generations of readers of *Jacobson v. Massachusetts* with no real context for Justice Harlan's statement that the Cambridge Board of Health had battled "the evils of a smallpox epidemic that imperiled an entire population." Jacobson really did take his stand against compulsory vaccination at the epicenter of a smallpox emergency. His own neighbors were falling sick and dying. More than three months had passed since Dr. Spencer first visited his apartment. The stakes had risen dramatically. But the pastor hadn't budged.[18]

Meanwhile, at the height of the Cambridgeport outbreak, which would be remembered as the most serious phase of the city's 1901–2 epidemic, Spencer still refrained from prosecuting anyone. Although his vaccination campaign helped keep the epidemic from reeling out of control, outbreaks continued to strike across the city in July, reaching North Cambridge and the brickyards, where several French Canadian laborers would die of the disease. One of the Cambridge residents afflicted that month was Putnam J. Ramsdell, a Christian Scientist who publicly denounced vaccination. The smallpox killed him.[19]

On July 17, 1902, Edwin Spencer finally swore out a criminal complaint against Henning Jacobson. Like hundreds of other Americans at the turn of the century, the minister found himself summoned before a local judge, charged with the crime of refusing vaccination.[20]

Jacobson appeared for trial on July 23 in the Third District Court of Eastern Middlesex County, before Associate Justice Samuel W. McDaniel. Local "inferior courts" like McDaniel's were the workhorses of the American legal system. Sometimes called "poor man's courts," they handled the great mass of everyday civil suits—landlords and tenants suing each other, laborers fighting bosses for unpaid wages, collection agencies demanding payment from debtors—as well as criminal cases below the grade of felony. McDaniel was exceptionally well qualified for the position. A graduate of Harvard Law School, he had served on the school board and the city council.[21]

Entering the courtroom, Jacobson noticed that he was not alone. Vaccination cases were typically recorded, in the custom of America's adversarial legal culture, as a conflict involving only two parties: the state versus the lone defendant. But many of these legal conflicts arose from collective, or nearly simultaneous, acts of resistance. Three other men, presumably strangers to one another, waited to be tried alongside Jacobson for the same offense. They were Albert Pear; Frank W. Cone, an inspector with the city water department; and Ephraim Gould, a Canadian-born carpenter. Two other vaccine refusers had been summoned to court that day. Gould's wife, Maggie, defaulted. Paul Morse, a French Canadian brick burner, had relented and submitted to vaccination. Judge McDaniel dismissed the case against him.[22]

Of the four remaining defendants, the press showed an interest only in Albert Pear. Dashing and "widely respected," the thirty-one-year-old Pear was a public figure. The son of a local Republican Party leader, he had served Cambridge for eight years as assistant city clerk, and he had acquired a reputation as "one of the most strenuous antivaccinationists in the city." As he told a *Boston Globe* reporter at the courthouse, "I do not propose that the board of health shall dictate to me what medicine I shall put into my system." Troubled by muscular rheumatism, Pear said his doctor had advised him against vaccination and had given him some "powders" to ward off smallpox.[23]

Judge McDaniel tried the four defendants together, without a jury. City Solicitor Gilbert A. A. Pevey stated the case against them: the state law authorized local health boards to order vaccination during smallpox epidemics; the Cambridge board had done so; the defendants knew their legal duty but had refused to be vaccinated. Simple as that. Pevey might as well have been prosecuting the men for public drunkenness.[24]

The first sign of anything unusual in the proceedings was the appearance of a defense attorney—a rarity in an inferior court. James Winthrop Pickering introduced himself as the attorney for Frank Cone, though he appeared to be sizing up all four defendants. A Harvard-trained Boston lawyer, Pickering represented the Massachusetts Anti-Compulsory Vaccination Society. Though no lawyer made a specialty of vaccination cases—there weren't enough to pay the bills—the cases tended to attract attorneys of a particular bent: self-styled civil libertarians who were unafraid to lose. Like Harry Weinberger of New York—who cut his teeth on vaccination cases before representing Emma Goldman and other radicals in a string of celebrated World War I–era free speech cases—Pickering viewed compulsory vaccination as a particularly insidious example of the creeping, state-imposed regimentation of American life.[25]

Seven years earlier, Pickering had argued a sensational free speech case alongside his attorney father, James F. Pickering, before the Massachusetts Supreme Judicial Court. Their client, Reverend William F. Davis, was an open-air evangelist who had been arrested repeatedly for delivering sermons without a permit on the Boston Common. Davis's crowds numbered in the thousands. His case became a cause célèbre among evangelical Christians and free speech advocates. The elder Pickering argued that the Boston ordinance violated Davis's fundamental right to preach the Gospel. But the argument failed to persuade Justice Oliver Wendell Holmes, Jr. Although Holmes would later become one of America's greatest defenders of free speech, at the time he showed little regard for individual rights as such, especially when they conflicted with the will of the majority as expressed in law. For the government to forbid public speaking in a public park, Holmes declared, was "no more an infringement of the rights of a member of the public than for the owner of a private house to forbid it in his house." Individual rights were not absolute, natural entities that existed in opposition to the state; a right existed when the public force could be counted on to protect it. If Holmes's opinion chastened the younger Pickering, the effect did not last.[26]

Representing Frank Cone in Judge McDaniel's court, Pickering made a forceful plea against the Massachusetts vaccination law. He said it violated his client's rights as a citizen of Massachusetts and the United States. Pickering explained that his client was merely acting in accordance with the "common knowledge" that vaccination was dangerous and "no sure preventative of smallpox." Sensing where Pickering was headed, McDaniel said that he "doubted his power," as an inferior court judge, to review the constitutionality of a state law.[27]

Jacobson's attempt to defend himself was a comedy of errors. But his sole court appearance without a lawyer did offer the purest statement of his grievance. Uncertain how to proceed, Jacobson asked to make a statement to the court. Solicitor Pevey asked him if it would be in the form of an argument or testimony. Jacobson did not know how to answer that. The minister was "finally induced to appear on the witness stand," where he started to explain his belief that his physical condition and experience "did not warrant him in being vaccinated." Pevey objected, and McDaniel sustained. The state vaccination law, the judge explained, did not allow any exceptions for adults to a health board's order—even if an individual's medical history made the procedure dangerous for him. (The state code did make such an exception for children, if they could provide a doctor's certificate to that effect.) After Pear indicated that he, too, planned to argue that he was an unfit subject for vaccination, Judge McDaniel told him to sit down.[28]

McDaniel found all four men guilty and fined each $5. Ephraim Gould had had enough. He would pay the fine. The other three defendants—Pear, Cone, and Jacobson—appealed their cases to the Middlesex County Superior Court, the next rung up the judicial ladder. Each would receive a new trial, this time before a jury.[29]

Then and there a constitutional test case was born. And its name (at least for the time being) was *Commonwealth v. Pear*. The Massachusetts Anti-Compulsory Vaccination Society decided that Albert Pear was their man to test the state law. He must have seemed the obvious choice. Several of the Boston and Cambridge defendants seemed motivated to go the distance. But Cate, the South End laborer, had already served his jail time. Jacobson and Mugford, the East Boston grocer, were both immigrants, which may have made them less than ideal plaintiffs. Moreover, Mugford's litigation was complicated, legally and morally: he had been convicted of refusing vaccination for himself and *neglecting* to have his child vaccinated. (Cone did not pursue his case beyond the superior court level.)

Commonwealth v. Pear, by contrast, distilled the vaccination question to its most controversial form. Here stood an adult, male, natural-born citizen, taxpayer, and public servant—an American in the prime of manhood—being told by the state how to take care of his own body. If that failed to move the brethren of the Supreme Judicial Court, nothing would. Besides, Pear was one of the antivaccinationists' own. Pastor Jacobson had attended a meeting or two, but he was not a man of the movement. There is no evidence to suggest that he ever used the power of his pulpit to urge his flock to refuse vaccination.[30]

When Pear appeared before the Middlesex Superior Court for his second trial, on November 13, 1902, all knew that the proceedings were merely "the second necessary step" to getting his case before the Supreme Judicial Court. Now represented by Pickering, Pear offered no evidence. Pickering asked Judge William Cushing Wait to instruct the jury that the state law was void because it violated "the rights secured to the defendant by the preamble of the Constitution of the United States." He asked Judge Wait for further instructions to the effect that the law violated the Constitution's Fifth Amendment, the Fourteenth Amendment, and several provisions of the Massachusetts constitution, including its famous "free and equal" clause, which the Supreme Judicial Court had used in 1783 to effectively abolish slavery in the state.[31]

Pickering's plea for instructions revealed his ambitions for the case. He was already preparing the ground for an appeal to the U.S. Supreme Court. The federal constitutional claims he was making were unorthodox. The status of the Preamble—which declared it among the Constitution's purposes to "secure the blessings of liberty" to the American people—was uncertain at best. And by invoking the Fifth Amendment, Pickering seemed ready to make an argument that the Fourteenth Amendment applied the Bill of Rights to the states, an argument the Supreme Court had rejected three decades earlier in the famous *Slaughter-House Cases*. Lawyers making personal liberties arguments at the turn of the century had to be creative.[32]

Rejecting Pickering's proposed instructions, Judge Wait advised the jurors that if they believed the evidence showed that Pear had violated the law (which no one disputed it did), they would be warranted in finding him guilty. The jurors never left their seats. They found Pear guilty. The court accepted Pickering's motion to present a bill of exceptions, so the case could go before the Supreme Judicial Court.[33]

The Massachusetts Anti-Compulsory Vaccination Society met in Tremont Temple Baptist Church on December 1 and voted to continue to support Pear in his "contest with the board of health." Tensions continued to mount in the Boston area. Forty-one residents of Somerville had refused vaccination. Officials there had decided to await the outcome in the Pear case before prosecuting anyone. In Cambridge, at least three more residents had been summoned to court since July for refusing vaccination. All three submitted to the procedure rather than face prosecution and the inevitable fine.[34]

Henning Jacobson, meanwhile, continued to pursue his case. His Superior Court trial had been postponed until February 1903. Although *The Boston Globe* indicated the antivaccination society was backing Pear as its test case, Pickering was now representing Jacobson, too, presumably on the society's dime. Jacobson even attended one of the society's monthly meetings. According to the *Globe*, the minister told the audience of "the terrible experiences of himself and children from vaccination, and of his own knowledge of the uselessness of the practice."[35]

With Pickering at his side, Jacobson stood trial in Middlesex Superior Court, before a jury of his peers, on February 27, 1903. The trial covered the same ground as Pear's, with one major difference: Jacobson had a case he wanted to make to the jury. From those first awkward moments in Judge McDaniel's courtroom—and, one imagines, earlier, when Spencer first appeared at his door—the minister had shown an overwhelming desire to explain himself. He wanted to show that his refusal to obey the law was, as he now proposed to prove to this jury, "prompted by his knowledge of the danger and his dread of the terrible consequences of vaccination."[36]

Jacobson offered to prove fourteen points "by competent evidence." Many of the points had the flavor of an antivaccinationist pamphlet: vaccination caused injury, disease, and death; "as a rule," it rendered a person temporarily incapable of "performing his usual duties and labors"; vaccine manufactured in America was often "impure"; its "evil and dangerous effects" included tetanus and syphilis; sanitation and isolation were the only reliable safeguards against smallpox. Jacobson may have believed all of these points, but their inclusion in his case was clearly the price for the support of the antivaccination society. He saved his two most personal points for last. In childhood he had experienced "great and extreme suffering, for a long period, by a disease produced by his vaccination." And he had "witnessed a similar result of vaccination in the case of his own son, and had personally known a great number of other instances of the same kind." Jacobson's will to fight against compulsion arose from those experiences rather than from antivaccination ideology.[37]

Judge Wait ruled that all of those assertions were "immaterial." He excluded them all. And so in Pickering's request for instructions to the jury, the attorney added another item to those he had asked for in Pear's case. He asked the judge to tell the jury that the board of health order was unreasonable because it made no exceptions for individuals to whom vaccine posed a special risk. Judge Wait refused. The jury had little choice but to find Jacobson guilty. A few days later, Pickering filed his exceptions for appeal to the Supreme Judicial Court. The state's high court could consider Jacobson's and Pear's cases together; their causes were once again joined, now as "plaintiffs-in-error."[38]

Constitutional controversies often outlive the events that gave rise to them. The Cambridge smallpox epidemic had run its course by the winter of 1903, when Assistant District Attorney Hugh Bancroft, representing the Commonwealth, and J. W. Pickering and his new cocounsel, Henry Ballard of Vermont, representing Pear and Jacobson, prepared their briefs for the Supreme Judicial Court. All told, 187 patients had been taken to the New Street hospital. Thirty-five Cambridge residents had died. The board of health had vaccinated 30,000 people, private physicians 26,000. And the citizens now held the bill: the highest tax rate in the city's history. The epidemic looked to many like yet another verdict for vaccination. Of the cases isolated at New Street, none had been vaccinated within the past five years. On January 19, 1903, a few months after smallpox loosened its grip on the city, E. Edwin Spencer died at his Cambridge home, just two weeks shy of his seventieth birthday.[39]

The three lawyers had a different historical subject in mind as they compiled their briefs in the cases of *Commonwealth v. Pear* and *Commonwealth v. Jacobson*. The cases compelled them to come to terms with the most contentious issue in American constitutional law since the Civil War: the explosive growth of the police power and the great wave of constitutional struggles that had grown up with it.

Bancroft, a novice who graduated from Harvard Law School in 1901, knew enough to understand that he had the easy side of the case. His briefs in the two cases were nearly identical. "The legislature has an extensive undefined power," he said in both of them, "usually called the police power, to pass laws for the common good." The legislature's "wide discretion cannot be controlled by the courts unless its action is clearly evasive." Whether the theory of vaccination was sound or not was a question for lawmakers, not judges. But if the Supreme Judicial Court should choose to consider that question, it would surely take notice of the fact that vaccination is "the most effective known preventive of one of the most dangerous diseases to which the human race is subject."[40]

The briefs for the "plaintiffs in error" contained a few lunatic flourishes. (Again, the bodies of the two briefs were virtually identical; but Ballard contributed an addendum to Jacobson's brief in order to address the issue of the excluded evidence.) Did Pickering and Ballard really expect the members of the Supreme Judicial Court to swallow their argument that compulsory vaccination was "a greater outrage than the scalping of a living victim by an Indian savage"? Or that this state-imposed "rite" was a "form of worship of the Sacred Cow?" Like the antivaccinationist literature on which they drew, the briefs decried vaccination as a barbaric practice unworthy of a civilized people.[41]

But the lawyers' argument for Albert Pear and Henning Jacobson cut much deeper. Their briefs raised *the* central question of American constitutional law at the turn of the century: Where should the courts draw the line between police power and individual liberty? Was there a line at all?

The Massachusetts Supreme Judicial Court enjoys pride of place as "the oldest court in continuous existence in the Western Hemisphere." Known in colonial times as the Superior Court of Judicature, the institution opened in 1692 and was immediately busy with the trials of accused witches from Salem. The court acquired its modern name in 1780, when the new Commonwealth of Massachusetts ratified its state constitution, drafted by John Adams (and now the world's oldest written constitution). In the nineteenth century, the Supreme Judicial Court established itself as a leader in the development of an American common law. Massachusetts industrialized early, and its high court handed down influential decisions in property, torts, and master-servant law, helping to lay the legal foundation for American capitalism. The office of chief justice had been occupied by such legal luminaries as Adams, Theophilus Parsons, and Lemuel Shaw. Marcus Perrin Knowlton, who took it upon himself to write the court's opinion in the vaccination case, had assumed that position only in December 1902, when President Theodore Roosevelt appointed his predecessor, Oliver Wendell Holmes, Jr., to the U.S. Supreme Court. Holmes stepped into the vacancy left by another former chief justice of the Massachusetts court, Horace Gray.[42]

In its storied history, the Supreme Judicial Court had more than once had occasion to consider the scope of the police power. Chief Justice Shaw's 1851 decision in *Commonwealth v. Alger* remained, more than half a century later, the definitive American statement on the subject. Assistant D.A. Bancroft cited it prominently in his briefs for the vaccination case. *Alger* involved a classic police power controversy, pitting one citizen's property rights against the right of the legislature to defend the people's welfare. The state legislature had established a wharf line in Boston Harbor, beyond which no private structure could be built. The law aimed to preserve the free use of the harbor as "a common and public right." A Boston jury found Cyrus Alger guilty of breaking the law by building a pier, on his own property, that extended beyond the line. On appeal, the Supreme Judicial Court upheld the law in a resounding defense of the police power. Shaw wrote:

> We think it is a settled principle, growing out of the nature of a well-ordered society, that every holder of property, however absolute and unqualified may be his title, holds it under the implied liability that his use of it may be so regulated, that it shall not be injurious to the equal enjoyment of others having an equal right to the enjoyment of their property, nor injurious to the rights of the community. . . .

Rights of property, like all other social and conventional rights, are subject to such reasonable limitations in their enjoyment, as shall prevent them from being injurious, and to such reasonable restraints and regulations established by law[.] The power we allude to is . . . the police power; the power vested in the legislature by the constitution to make, ordain, and establish all manner of wholesome and reasonable laws, statutes, and ordinances, either with penalties or without, not repugnant to the constitution, as they shall judge to be for the good and welfare of the Commonwealth. . . . It is much easier to perceive and realize the existence and sources of this power than to mark its boundaries, or prescribe limits to its exercise.[43]

The police power enjoyed the sanction of the state and federal constitutions, but it did not originate there; it flowed from the wellspring of sovereignty itself. The concept of "police" had deep roots in English and European traditions of governance. Its scope far exceeded the law enforcement function of municipal police forces, which first appeared on the streets of New York, Philadelphia, and Boston during the 1840s and '50s. When considering the almost indeterminate scope of the police power, nineteenth-century American jurists referred to two great common law maxims: *sic utere tuo ut alienum non laedas* (use your own so as not to injure another) and *salus populi suprema lex est* (the welfare of the people is the supreme law). In "well-ordered societies," state governments and municipalities served the people's welfare in ways too numerous to list: they upheld public morals by policing saloons and brothels, ensured public safety through fire and crime prevention, governed the marketplace through price regulations and licensing, and protected the public health by policing noxious trades and enforcing quarantines to check contagious diseases.[44]

As significant as Shaw's expansive meditation on legislative power was his parsimonious discussion of individual rights. Later generations of Americans would imagine the nineteenth century as the epoch of rugged individualism and laissez-faire. But the century's preeminent state judge recognized a very different reality. Individual rights—even rights as elementary to American law and politics as property—were "social" and "conventional," not natural entities inherent in human beings. As citizens like

Cyrus Alger learned time and again, in the name of the common good state and local governments trod heavily on property rights and personal liberties, with no obligation to compensate private parties for their losses. Like other American judges, Shaw recognized certain constitutional restraints on police power, but they were few. Laws must apply equally to all under like circumstances, to avoid creating an undue advantage for particular individuals. (Sadly, Shaw found room enough in this "equality" principle to permit the Boston schools committee to require African American children to attend separate schools.) In addition, "ex post facto laws" were forbidden. Finally, government interferences with individual rights must be "reasonable"—they must have a clear relation to some legitimate legislative purpose. Beyond those outer limits, until the late nineteenth century most courts stayed out of the way of police power.[45]

That included federal courts. Prior to the Civil War, state and local police measures were virtually unreviewable by the federal courts, unless a measure invaded an area of exclusive congressional control (such as the power to regulate interstate commerce) or violated some specific state-restraining provision of the U.S. Constitution, like the Contract Clause. Even those limitations were controversial. And as Chief Justice John Marshall himself had reminded the American people in *Barron v. Baltimore* (1833), the U.S. Constitution's Bill of Rights restrained only the federal government. If a state subjected prisoners to cruel and unusual punishments, forbade newspapers to speak ill of the legislature, or seized private property for public use without compensation, the citizens had no remedy in federal court. They had to seek relief in their state courts under their state constitutions.[46]

And then the war came. The Civil War transformed the nation, remade the Constitution, and attached individual rights more closely than ever before to the federal government. Still, the sweeping nation-building events of the Reconstruction period—including the adoption of the Thirteenth, Fourteenth, and Fifteenth Amendments—had remarkably little immediate impact on the theory and practice of the police power. The U.S. Supreme Court ensured that this was so.

The Court's first opportunity to consider the Fourteenth Amendment involved a public health law. In 1873, delivering the majority opinion in the *Slaughter-House Cases*, Justice Samuel F. Miller announced that the police

power had survived the war intact. The decision affirmed a Louisiana statute that had incorporated a massive slaughterhouse, located downriver
from New Orleans, and forbade the slaughtering of animals elsewhere in
the city. The law aimed to protect the public health by containing a noxious trade. But the law's monopoly provision proved controversial. The
plaintiffs, a group of white butchers, charged that the law violated their new
rights under the first two Reconstruction amendments. Justice Miller made
quick work of the butchers' Thirteenth Amendment claim; the law, he said,
did not create a system of involuntary servitude.[47]

The Fourteenth Amendment claims could not be so easily dismissed.
The butchers grounded their claims in the amendment's crucial first section, which had established a framework of new constitutional restraints
on state power. The passage forbade any state to "abridge the privileges or
immunities of citizens of the United States"; to "deprive any person of life,
liberty, or property, without due process of law"; or to deny to any person
the "equal protection of the laws."[48]

But Justice Miller cautioned the American people that the Fourteenth
Amendment had not turned the Court into "a perpetual censor" upon the
states. The equal protection clause targeted only state action that discrimi-
nated against African Americans; Miller said the Court "doubt[ed] very
much" whether any action not directed against "Negroes as a class . . . would
ever be held to come within the purview of this provision." The due process
clause gave the federal government power to prevent the states from violating the procedural rights already protected from federal intrusion by the
Fifth Amendment. Miller's opinion read the "privileges or immunities"
clause narrowly. That phrase, he said, referred to a limited array of long-
standing rights, already protected by federal law, such as the right of all
citizens to come to the seat of the national government; it did not apply the
Bill of Rights to the states. To uphold the butchers' claims, Miller concluded, would effect a great "departure from the structure and spirit of
our institutions." It would "fetter and degrade the State governments" by
subjecting them to federal oversight "in the exercise of powers heretofore
universally conceded to them of the most ordinary and fundamental
character."[49]

If the majority's astonishingly narrow reading of the Fourteenth

Amendment defended the pre–Civil War status quo, the dissenting opinions written by Justice Stephen Field and Justice Joseph Bradley mapped out a new direction in American constitutional jurisprudence. Field and Bradley took aim at the state-created monopoly as a violation of fundamental economic rights. As Field put it, under the "pretense" of a sanitary regulation, the legislature had unjustly invaded the butchers' "right to pursue a lawful and necessary calling"—a liberty and property right protected from state interference by the due process clause. During the next thirty years, the Field and Bradley dissents—and particularly their close identification of "due process" with economic liberty—would become key weapons in the constitutional attack on state social legislation.[50]

Industrialization had a greater immediate impact upon the police power and its constitutional status than did the Civil War. The police power exploded in the postwar decades, as organized labor and social reformers pushed state legislatures to regulate some of the worst human consequences of America's dramatic and often violent transformation into an urban-industrial society. "The law of the police power is practically a growth of the last thirty or forty years," the progressive University of Chicago legal scholar Ernst Freund observed in his authoritative 1904 treatise *The Police Power*, "and much of it remains unsettled." Freund's tome covered everything from the control of monopolies to the suppression of labor strikes. The field of public health and safety alone comprised an extraordinary range of government activities, many of them new: medical inspection of immigrants at the nation's ports, factory regulations in the industrial heartland, tenement laws and pure milk standards in the cities. Much of the social legislation supported by labor-friendly progressive reformers was justified by state lawmakers on the grounds that it promoted the public health—a claim that made many such laws vulnerable to constitutional challenge when the connection between the state action and the health of the public was at all controversial or indirect.[51]

As the reach of the police power grew, so did the number of constitutional challenges to it. During the 1880s and '90s, plaintiffs, lawyers, treatise writers, and, increasingly, state supreme court judges emphasized the supposedly timeless "constitutional limitations" on the police power. Traces of these arguments could be seen in the prewar period (almost invariably on the losing side of cases), but they were largely a product of the late nineteenth-century struggle over the political economy of industrialism. Building upon the foundation laid by Justices Field and Bradley in their *Slaughter-House* dissents, critics of regulation breathed a new meaning into the due process clauses of the state and federal constitutions. Those clauses—forbidding government to deprive a person of life, liberty, or property *without* due process of law—had their origin in the ancient English Magna Carta, and they had long been understood by American courts as guaranteeing good common law procedure. The passage of reasonable legislation, its enforcement by duly constituted public officers, the right of a defendant to a fair trial—that was the essence of due process. The police power was not at odds with due process, as pre–Civil War judges like Lemuel Shaw understood it. In a fundamental respect, the police power *was* due process. In late nineteenth-century America, the due process clauses were taking on a broader meaning—as critics of government regulation used them to define the substance of the life, liberty, and property rights that could not be invaded, under almost any circumstances, by the state.[52]

Judges did not simply upend a century of jurisprudence to clear the way for a business-friendly laissez-faire constitutionalism. But dozens of hard-fought labor laws, whether a New York ban on tenement sweatshops or an Illinois eight-hour law for female factory workers, met an untimely death in a state supreme court for interfering with property rights or a newly minted "liberty of contract." By the turn of the century, conservative treatise writers such as Christopher G. Tiedeman had helped convince many judges that the police power was an almost unnatural force, best kept under close judicial control. "The unwritten law of the country is in the main against the exercise of police power," Tiedeman claimed.[53]

By the late 1890s, having largely repudiated the civil rights of African Americans, the U.S. Supreme Court was reading broad economic liberties into the Constitution via the Fourteenth Amendment's due process clause. Several key opinions were written by a newcomer to the Court, Justice Rufus Peckham. In *Allgeyer v. Louisiana* (1897), the Court invalidated a Louisiana statute regulating out-of-state insurance companies that did business in the state. In his opinion for the Court, Peckham imported the controversial new doctrine of "liberty of contract" into the Constitution:

The liberty mentioned in [the Fourteenth Amendment] means not only the right of the citizen to be free from the mere physical restraint of his person, as by incarceration, but the term is deemed to embrace the right of the citizen to be free in the enjoyment of his faculties; to be free to use them in lawful ways; to live and work where he will; to earn his livelihood by any lawful calling; to pursue any livelihood or avocation, and for that purpose to enter into all contracts which may be proper, necessary and essential to his carrying out to a successful conclusion the purposes above mentioned.

By itself, *Allgeyer* did not spark a revolution in jurisprudence. During the next several years, the Court upheld a good deal of social legislation, including a Colorado law (upheld over the dissents of Justice Peckham and Justice David Brewer) that forbade the employment of workers in mines for more than eight hours per day. But Peckham's expansive vision of economic liberty foretold the Court's increasing willingness to assume the very role that Justice Miller had warned against in *Slaughter-House*: a "perpetual censor" on state legislation that interfered with individual liberty.[54]

At the turn of the century, the rising generation of progressive intellectuals and activists regarded such talk of a constitutionally protected sphere of individual liberty with great skepticism. The United States had become a "modern," urban-industrial society, they observed. The emergence of a national economy—bound by railroads, built by corporate might and wage labor, and giving rise to a new density of urban life—fostered a new era of human association and social responsibility. Leading progressives from Jane Addams of Chicago to Louis Brandeis of Boston valued social interdependence over personal autonomy. The legal scholar Roscoe Pound and the philosopher John Dewey argued that individual rights existed not for themselves but because they served important social interests. Under the press of urban-industrial social conditions, the progressives argued, "real liberty" meant more than freedom from government.[55]

Outlook magazine, a leading organ of progressive opinion, expressed the position well. "In our time the man of progressive temperament is an advocate of organization, the man of conservative temper is an individualist," the magazine said. "Real liberty for the laborer requires labor organization; real liberty of travel requires government control of the instruments of travel; real liberty in food, clothing, and home requires law to guard against disease and death, threatened by conditions of modern society; real liberty to speak and teach effectively requires organization, educational and religious." In a time when the crowded conditions of everyday urban life evoked the inescapable social connectedness of an epidemic, progressives took up the germ theory as a powerful political metaphor. From the cities to the statehouses to Washington, the reformers decried prostitution, sweatshops, and poverty as "social ills." A stronger state, they said, held the "cure."[56]

With good reason, progressives condemned the judicial language of individual liberty as old-fashioned, formalistic, and fake—thin cover for the presumed laissez-faire prejudices of the judges themselves. The progressives' charges of judicial "usurpation" centered on the courts' invalidation of labor legislation and other forms of economic regulation. But there was another front in the era's great struggle over the police power.[57]

At the turn of the century, ordinary Americans were just beginning to turn to the law to challenge the increasing reach of administrative power into areas of life to which we now attach the most fundamental of civil liberties: freedom of speech and belief, parental rights, and the right to bodily integrity. No public policy crystallized those inchoate concerns more powerfully than did compulsory vaccination. In the name of public health and safety, Freund acknowledged, the modern state had been "readily conceded more incisive powers than despotic governments would have dared to claim in former times."[58]

Critics of the burgeoning interventionist state agreed. St. Louis's *Central Law Journal*, a leading voice of conservative legal opinion, condemned compulsory vaccination as "one of the most serious and unwarrantable encroachments upon the personal liberty of the citizen that has been committed in recent years under the guise of the police power."[59]

A s Bancroft, Pickering, and Ballard researched the state of the art of police power jurisprudence for their briefs, they naturally paid particular attention to the recent proliferation of state court cases challenging compulsory vaccination. Remarkably, the legal issues involved were still novel. Vaccination laws had been on the books in Massachusetts and other states for decades. But the first legal challenge had not reached a state supreme court until 1890—at the very moment police power cases began to stream into the courts. Vaccination litigation escalated dramatically as smallpox spread at the turn of the century. The law remained unsettled. The Supreme Judicial Court had the opportunity to bring some much-needed clarity to the subject.

So far, the American vaccination cases had taken several distinct forms. In the most common type, parents asked courts to order local school boards or principals to admit their "scarless" children. Unsurprisingly, in a legal culture that privileged men, most of the parents named in these cases were fathers. Some, like George R. Mathews of Kalamazoo, Michigan, were Christian Scientists, who opposed compulsory vaccination as an infringement of their "religious belief and scruples"; others, such as stenographer Frank D. Blue of Terre Haute, Indiana, were members of antivaccination societies; and others followed Michael Breen, a farmer from Lawrence County, Illinois, who demanded his rights as "a resident and taxpayer." In another type of case, public schoolteachers, including women like Mary Helen Lyndall of the Philadelphia Girls' High School, sued for the right to enter their workplaces unvaccinated. A third class of litigants—including the North Carolina merchant W. E. Hay and a Georgia factory worker named Morris—challenged their treatment under general vaccination orders, arguing that compulsory vaccination was a form of bodily assault.[60]

Given the long tradition of judicial deference to the police power, especially in the area of public health, it is remarkable that so many Americans could imagine that compulsory vaccination violated their rights. This unshakable belief arose from their sense that compulsory vaccination was unprecedented—a radical and especially dangerous form of governmental power, different in kind from all previous public health measures.

Prior to the Civil War, the paradigmatic compulsory health measure had been quarantine, a form of physical restraint that raised conventional due process questions: was the detention carried out in a lawful manner, following good common law procedures? Compulsory vaccination involved an invasive medical technology. It raised questions about the *substance* of personal liberty: could the state *ever* penetrate a citizen's body and insert a mysterious biological substance into a healthy human system? Until the 1890s, no state appellate court had ever upheld such a right of government.[61]

Some legal experts argued that compulsory vaccination was far less intrusive than quarantine. Under quarantine, a smallpox "suspect" could be detained by the government for two full weeks. The vaccination operation lasted but a few minutes. "If the protection of public health allows quarantine," Freund mused, "it is difficult to see why it should not justify compulsory vaccination."[62]

All of this made perfect sense from a conventional due process perspective, which saw seizure of a man's body or property, in the absence of public necessity and proper common law procedure, as an act of the purest tyranny. But for critics of compulsory vaccination (in Europe as well as the United States), any similarity to quarantine ended the moment lancet touched skin. One involved temporary detention of someone officials believed to have been exposed to contagion; the other entailed insertion of an animal virus into a presumably healthy human system. "There is a better way," Ballard wrote in Jacobson's brief. "In case of a quarantine of the unvaccinated, no risk or danger would ever be run to anybody's health or life—and nobody's feelings would ever be shocked or outraged by it." What Freund and others saw as the lesser of two necessary evils, vaccination litigants and their lawyers regarded as the far greater invasion of personal liberty.[63]

The personal liberty claims made in the vaccination cases bore the impress of a changing legal culture, as Americans and their lawyers reached for—and expanded upon—the newly minted language of substantive due process. Lawyers representing vaccination litigants (if not always the litigants themselves) showed that they were well versed in the economic due process arguments that had made headway in recent years in the courts. They marshaled substantive due process onto a new terrain—from the field of contract and property to the domain of personal liberties and the body.

The doctrine of substantive due process became increasingly important in the vaccination cases. In the first case to reach a state supreme court, *Abeel v. Clark* (1890), Santa Cruz parents challenged California's 1889 school vaccination law on the narrowest of technical grounds. The statute, they said, violated the state constitution because the law's subject was not clearly expressed in its title and it was "not general in its scope" (it reached only public schoolchildren, not the general public). The court upheld the law as a reasonable exercise of police power.[64]

Four years later, Andrew Jackson Duffield's suit against the Williamsport, Pennsylvania, School District made a far more expansive due process argument, signaling a new direction in the litigation. With smallpox "epidemic in many near by cities and towns," the local school board ordered all pupils to show proof of vaccination. Duffield, a real estate dealer and local constable, went to the Lycoming County Common Pleas Court seeking a writ of mandamus—an order that would compel the school board to admit his unvaccinated son. The court refused. In a time of "imminent danger," the court declared, school directors had the "right as well as the duty" to do "everything in their power" to prevent the spread of disease. The constable appealed.[65]

Duffield's attorney got to work. William H. Spencer was a local lawyer who had gone to work in anthracite coal mines at the age of twelve. His brief to the Pennsylvania Supreme Court defined the police power in the narrow terms advocated by the conservative legal scholars Thomas Cooley and Christopher Tiedeman (whose treatises he cited). "The police power is grounded upon inevitable necessity—the necessity that all men are under of so exercising their own rights so as not to infringe upon the equal rights of others." This was, of course, the common law *sic utere tuo* principle. But Cooley and Tiedeman had recast that venerable maxim in the modern libertarian mold of John Stuart Mill. Like those writers, Spencer said little about the other great maxim of the police power, *salus populi*, which put the people's welfare above all else. Citing the due process clauses of the Fourteenth Amendment and the Pennsylvania Constitution, he called compulsory vaccination an assault by the state "against the body of a healthy child."[66]

Duffield lost his case. The Pennsylvania Supreme Court affirmed the broad power of the school board to adopt "reasonable health regulations for the benefit of their pupils and the general public." The court insisted that no one had compelled Andrew Duffield to vaccinate his son; the board claimed only the right to exclude unvaccinated children. Conceding that "medical men differ" about the effectiveness of vaccination, the court concluded that the board's action reflected "the present state of medical knowledge." The board had acted "in the utmost good faith," at a time when smallpox actually threatened Williamsport.[67]

That same winter, the U.S. Supreme Court upheld the right of New York to enact legislation protecting its fisheries. In the decision, the Court added, for the first time, a new example to the long list of government actions that state appellate courts had found permissible under the police power: "the compulsory vaccination of children." The language was what lawyers call "dicta"; it did not amount to a constitutional holding affirming compulsory vaccination of schoolchildren or anyone else. But the casual addition of compulsory vaccination to a litany that included "the regulation of railways" and "the restraint of vagrants" suggested the Court saw no problem with it.[68]

In the absence of an actual Supreme Court ruling, however, the outcomes of the school vaccination cases varied from state to state, fostering a degree of uncertainty that encouraged more litigation. As Pickering and Ballard could plainly see from the state court reports in their libraries, the general trend in the case law since *Duffield* was to uphold the power of legislatures, health boards, and school boards to require vaccination for admission to the public schools. Parents argued that vaccination was a positive right that the states could not deny (especially to the children of taxpayers). But the courts responded with a very parental-sounding lesson: a public education was a privilege, not a right, and when the state granted a privilege, it had the authority to dictate the conditions under which that privilege might be enjoyed. As Hugh Bancroft argued in his briefs for the Commonwealth of Massachusetts in the Pear and Jacobson cases, the schools cases represented a solid line of precedents supporting compulsory vaccination. But the briefs contained a few surprises. Vaccination plaintiffs had won some major concessions from the courts.[69]

Wisconsin led the way with an 1897 ruling. The state board of health had ordered that no child be admitted to any school in the state without a certificate of vaccination, signed by a "reputable physician." In covering private, parochial, and public schools, the measure was exceptionally broad. The board of education of Beloit ordered principals and teachers to enforce the provision. At the time, only a few cases of smallpox existed in the entire state, and Beloit had none. A city resident named E. J. Adams, a

Christian Scientist, refused to allow his three schoolchildren to be vaccinated, stating his belief that "the laws of God permit no such operation."
The children were expelled. Adams went to the Rock County Circuit Court
and secured a peremptory writ ordering the school board to reinstate his
children. The era's record of vaccination litigation was filled with such local
victories, but they often fell on appeal. But Adams won again at the state
level, sparking a minor sensation in the press.[70]

Clearly, for Adams, his case raised a question of religious liberty. But his
legal team, led by a prominent Wisconsin Republican named Ogden H.
Fethers, assaulted the board of health's vaccination order on different
grounds. The legislature, Fethers argued, could create a board of health, but
it could not delegate to that agency its power to make laws. And the board's
rule, an absolute mandate that required children to get vaccinated even in
the absence of an epidemic, would have been void even if enacted by the
legislature itself, because such a requirement was "unreasonable and not
enacted by necessity."[71]

Fethers's argument raised a question of high importance in the Progressive Era: what were the limits of administrative power—especially when
important liberties were at stake? The modern administrative-welfare state
was still in its infancy. But municipalities, states, and even the federal government were rolling out new administrative agencies—from railroad com-
missions to parole boards—to govern new fields of social and economic
regulation. The new administrative bodies made their own rules, adjudi-
cated cases, and exercised extraordinary discretionary powers. Critics protested that the rule of law was withering away in America. State boards of
health, which first appeared in some places as early as the mid-nineteenth
century, were among the oldest administrative agencies. And Fethers was
asking the Wisconsin Supreme Court to rein in their rule-making powers.

Remarkably, the court did just that. The opinion in *Adams v. Burdge* was
written, with passion, by sixty-year-old Justice Silas U. Pinney, a former
mayor of Madison and a veteran on the court. Pinney noted that the board
of health was "purely an administrative body" and one "not directly responsible to the people." (The Wisconsin Supreme Court, unlike the health
board, was an elective body.) The board had "no legislative power, properly
so called, and none could be delegated to it." Pinney conceded that in order

to fulfill its statutory purpose, the board must have authority to make reasonable regulations. But in the absence of a public emergency, the board's sweeping vaccination order was not reasonable. "[T]here was no epidemic of smallpox in or near the city of Beloit," Pinney wrote, "and yet, by an arbitrary rule, as by a single stroke of the pen, every child of school age, throughout the entire state, that had not been vaccinated, was excluded from the common schools." The rule would not stand.[72]

Adams v. Burdge was roundly praised and condemned as a victory for religious freedom. *The New York Times* lamented that once a state court yielded to the conscience claims of Christian Scientists and antivaccinationists, legalized polygamy was around the corner. But Justice Pinney had in fact said little about religion. He did say that since the police power pressed upon "the natural and private rights of individuals," it must be founded upon "the law."[73]

The Adams case set an important precedent for holding modern administrative power accountable to law. Its logic was widely adopted. In three more cases from 1897 to 1902, state supreme courts imposed clear limitations on the power of administrative boards to order pupils to get vaccinated. In the absence of a state law mandating vaccination as a condition for admission, no board could impose such an order unless confronted with the "pressing necessity" of a smallpox epidemic. Ernst Freund described the rule as a "present danger" standard. Some fifteen years before Justice Oliver Wendell Holmes, Jr., immortalized this phrase in the American law of free speech, state courts had articulated this civil liberties concept in order to protect citizens against unwarranted government health orders.[74]

Other parents pressed state courts for relief from the double bind that compulsory education and compulsory vaccination measures imposed upon them. A public education might be a privilege, but in a growing number of states compulsory education laws now made that privilege a legal obligation for parents who could not afford to send their children to a private school. By a bare 3 to 2 majority, in 1901 the Michigan Supreme Court ordered the Kalamazoo school board to admit the healthy but unvaccinated children of George R. Mathews, a Christian Scientist. The smallpox epidemics hadn't reached Kalamazoo. The dissenters in the case made the old

argument that denying admission to unvaccinated children did not constitute compulsory vaccination. But the court's majority would not have it.
Under the state's education law, a parent was liable to a fine or imprisonment for failing to send a child to school. "The practical result, if this rule
can be sustained, is to give the board of education the power to compel vaccination," the court declared. Since the legislature had never directly given
the board that authority, "the school board exceeded its power."[75]

And so by the time the Massachusetts Supreme Judicial Court heard the
Jacobson and Pear cases, the school vaccination cases had established a
complex line of precedents. No court had invalidated a statewide school
vaccination law, but at least five courts had imposed some form of "present
danger" standard as a limitation on the rule-making powers of boards of
health and education. As the *Central Law Journal* proclaimed after the
Mathews victory, "Compulsory vaccination is evidently a gross interference
of individual liberty and can be justified on only one ground—an 'overwhelming necessity,' which is the only real justification of what is known
as the police power." Overruling necessity—the community's right of
self-defense—was a very old rationale for police power. But it had never
been the only one. The vaccination litigants were pressing the courts toward
a subtle shift in their understanding of that doctrine. Once a phrase that
could justify all manner of state action, "overruling necessity" was taking on
a double life as a legal standard for limiting official action—particularly of
administrative bodies—whenever personal liberties were at stake.[76]

Of course, Albert Pear and Henning Jacobson were not schoolchildren.
In the thirty years since *Slaughter-House*, laws that interfered with the economic rights of men—whether for their own good or for the good of the
community—had become vulnerable to substantive due process arguments. In 1886, the Pennsylvania Supreme Court invalidated a state law
that forbade iron mills to pay their workers in company scrip, rather than
real currency. The court declared the provision "utterly unconstitutional
and void" because it prevented two competent individuals—employer and
employee—from freely contracting with each other. Never mind that the
companies always had the upper hand. The court called the scrip ban "an
insulting attempt to put the laborer under a legislative tutelage, which is not
only degrading to his manhood, but subversive of his rights as a citizen of

the United States." Since 1886 state courts had repeatedly used similar reasoning to invalidate state laws that set maximum hours or minimum wages for American workingmen. If the government couldn't tell a grown man to call it a day after eight or ten hours on a sweltering factory floor, could it tell him to bare his arm and take his medicine?[77]

During smallpox epidemics, local councils and boards of health issued general vaccination orders, sometimes under the express authority of a state law (as the Cambridge Board of Health had done) but more often not. These orders were not directed at children seeking access to a public institution; they applied, at least officially, to everybody. Whether carried out in big cities by virus squads or in small towns by sheriffs or physicians, these orders were wildly unpopular, especially among the workers, African Americans, and immigrants who bore the brunt of them.

Reports of excessive force enraged some judges. In 1895, Judge William Gaynor of the Kings County Supreme Court (a trial-level court) lashed out against Brooklyn's overzealous health commissioner. Z. Taylor Emery had ordered vaccination raids without authority of a state law. In habeas corpus proceedings, Judge Gaynor (the future mayor of New York) ordered the release of two Brooklyn expressmen, William H. Smith and Thomas Cummings, who had been quarantined in their own Franklin Street stable after they refused to be vaccinated. "The discretion you claim is limitless," Gaynor thundered at Emery. "I am of the opinion that you have no such power." The New York Court of Appeals later upheld Gaynor's ruling: Commissioner Emery had interfered not only with the men's personal liberty but with their "pursuit of a lawful avocation" without proving that their isolation was warranted by "an extraordinary and dangerous emergency." When vaccination orders reached adult men, personal liberties concerns often evoked the contemporary struggle over economic rights—a fact that plaintiffs' lawyers, including Pickering and Ballard, sought to use to their clients' advantage.[78]

Pickering and Ballard could find only three state supreme court cases that considered the constitutionality of a general vaccination measure like the one their clients had violated. Two were decided in North Carolina, the other in Georgia—southern states hard hit by "mild type" smallpox. As C. P. Wertenbaker had so often observed during his smallpox work, southern communities were riven with conflict over vaccination, due in large part to the harsh effects of the bacteria-laden dry points in wide use there. Assistant D.A. Bancroft urged that the three cases had raised the "precise question" of the Pear and Jacobson litigation, and in all three cases, "statutes substantially the same as the one before us have been upheld."[79]

In *Morris v. Columbus* (1898), the Georgia Supreme Court upheld an 1890 state law that gave municipalities the right to compel vaccination in order to prevent smallpox. The litigation arose from the prosecution of three men in Columbus, where local officials believed an epidemic was "imminent." One of the men was a factory worker who had refused to be vaccinated at his workplace. "In no proper sense can the act of the General Assembly attacked in this case be said to deprive the plaintiffs in error of any right without due process of law, or to deny them the equal protection of the laws," the state court declared. "We do not propose to enter into a discussion as to whether or not [vaccination] is a preventive of smallpox." Five months later, the same court held that municipalities were not liable for injuries caused by impure vaccine used by their health officers. If the Supreme Judicial Court wanted a model of unquestioning judicial deference to public health power, Georgia was it.[80]

The North Carolina Supreme Court had also defended the right of municipalities to issue general vaccination orders when authorized by a state law. In 1900, the court reviewed the case of the Burlington merchant W. E. Hay, who had been prosecuted for violating a local vaccination ordinance. Hay told the local trial court that he had been advised that the operation would be dangerous for him due to his physical condition. To test the validity of the ordinance, the local court issued a special verdict for the defendant, enabling the city solicitor to appeal. The supreme court approved compulsory vaccination with the resounding declaration that "Salus populi supreme lex, 'the public welfare is the highest law,' is the foundation principle of all civil government." The court even marshaled government statistics to show that the legislature had good reason to believe vaccination protected communities against smallpox. Writing for the majority, Justice Walter McKenzie Clark, a Confederate Army veteran, compared the community's right to vaccinate to its right to repel an invasion. He added that modern social conditions—the incessant movement of people, goods, and viruses from place to place—made this method of checking smallpox ever more necessary.[81]

The next year, the North Carolina court heard the case of Koen Levin. An itinerant Jewish peddler, Levin sued the Piedmont town of Burlington for "wrongful arrest, detention, and ill treatment." Levin's case presented public health at its most extreme. In February 1899, the peddler stayed overnight at Mary Ingle's boardinghouse. The next morning, he drove his wagon nine miles to the Altamaha factory, where he planned to sell his wares. A Burlington police officer caught up with him there, arrested him, and carried him back to the town. Evidently, another boarder at Ingle's house had come down with smallpox. The officer took Levin back to the boardinghouse, where he was kept in quarantine for twenty-one days, forcibly vaccinated twice, and even made to pay for the vaccine. He was also ordered to wait on the patient. (It is hard to imagine that Levin's status as a Jew had nothing to do with his treatment.)[82]

The peddler sought $5,000 in damages for the "great indignity" of this experience, which had caused him "great agony of mind" and the loss of several months' business, as the people of the area, knowing he had been exposed to smallpox, wanted nothing to do with him. Town officials did not dispute Levin's version of events. As Chief Justice David Furches put it, no one denied Levin had "received heroic treatment and was damaged." But he added, "it is not every damage that creates a cause of action." Citing the principle of sovereign immunity, Furches said, "a municipal corporation can not be held liable in damages for the enforcement of a public law for the public good."[83]

Levin was an unblinking affirmation of the police power, and Pickering and Ballard knew Bancroft would cite it. But as the attorneys noted in their own briefs for Pear and Jacobson, the decision was controversial. (The *Central Law Journal* had issued "a trumpet blast of indignation.") Unlike Bancroft, they recounted the ugly facts of the case for the Massachusetts justices to mull over. No other state court decision had even indirectly approved of physical-force vaccination.[84]

And even the North Carolina court, in *State v. Hay*, had said some things that Pickering and Ballard recognized ought to strengthen Jacobson's case. Perhaps owing to W. E. Hay's status as a leading local merchant (rather than an itinerant peddler), the court had disliked the idea of a man being compelled to undergo vaccination against his doctor's advice. The state court upheld the vaccination order, but as Pickering and Ballard noted, there was more to the case than a simple affirmation of the law. The court conceded that for some individuals, personal health conditions might make vaccination unsafe, providing "a sufficient excuse for noncompliance." Even though the Burlington ordinance (like the Massachusetts vaccination law, at least as far as adults were concerned) provided no health exemptions, the court ruled that Hay ought to have the right to make his case for a health exception directly to a jury.[85]

Pickering and Ballard highlighted the concurring opinion in the same case. The opinion eloquently expressed the unease that many judges felt toward the extraordinary administrative power of public health officials. It happened to be written by Justice Robert M. Douglas, the son of the legendary Illinois senator Stephen A. Douglas. Justice Douglas went even further than the majority opinion in reading a health excuse into the law. "[T]here may be cases where vaccination, owing to certain exceptional conditions of health, may be dangerous or even fatal," Douglas said. "We cannot suppose that the Legislature intended to enforce the rule under such cases." If the letter of the law did not provide such an excuse, the courts would. After all, it was in the courts, Justice Douglas admonished, "where all of the rights of the citizen are determined and administered." A court should not grant a public health officer "any presumption of professional infallibility. He must take his chances before the jury, like any other witness."[86]

The North Carolina Supreme Court had articulated a novel principle of public health law that is now called "harm avoidance." Ballard applauded Justice Douglas's opinion. He wrote, "No better brief can be written, or better argument made" in support of Jacobson's contention that the Massachusetts statute was unreasonable because it lacked a health exemption for adults. And the North Carolina court had also provided a precedent for the admissibility of precisely the sort of medical evidence that Jacobson had tried twice to put before the trial courts. As Douglas had said in *Hay*, "the defendant has a right to be heard."[87]

And so, Pickering and Ballard built their case for Pear and Jacobson on the shoulders of the many vaccination litigants who had come before them.

Although the case law since 1890 had generally affirmed the right of the state to compel vaccination under its police powers, during the past few years state judges had imposed some meaningful conditions on that right. The "present danger" standard limited the rule-making discretion of administrative bodies. The harm avoidance principle presumed that personal health conditions could be a defense against prosecution in vaccination cases. Of course, the Supreme Judicial Court of Massachusetts had the right to make up its own mind. Pickering and Ballard urged the justices of the renowned court to abolish compulsory vaccination just as their predecessors had abolished slavery in the state 120 years earlier.

Curiously, Pickering and Ballard overlooked one particularly relevant federal case. Unlike most of the era's important public health cases, *Wong Wai v. Williamson* (1900) had nothing to do with smallpox. The case arose from the turn-of-the-century bubonic plague epidemic in San Francisco. A federal circuit court issued an injunction to prevent health officials from carrying out a plan that forbade Chinese residents to leave the city without submitting to vaccination. The plague vaccine, Haffkine's prophylactic vaccine, had been invented just three years earlier. It was highly toxic and had serious side effects, as Chinese residents of the city had learned when a few voluntarily submitted to inoculation. Chinese residents put up a good fight against compulsory inoculation—in the streets and in the courts. Wong Wai, a merchant, sued, insisting the inoculation plan violated the Equal Protection Clause of the Fourteenth Amendment. Judge William Morrow agreed. The plan, he said, was "boldly directed against the Asiatic or Mongolian race as a class, without regard to the previous condition, habits, exposure to disease, or residence of the individual." The defendants had provided "no evidence" to show that the Chinese were more susceptible to the plague than other races. Morrow cautioned the San Francisco Board of Health that the police power, "however broad and extensive, is not above the constitution." *Wong Wai* established equal protection as an important standard for reviewing compulsory health measures.[88]

In their final briefs Pickering and Ballard presented the Supreme Judicial Court with a libertarian indictment of the growth of police power since the Civil War. The lawyers charged that the government "has surrounded the citizen with a multitude of restrictions as to his right of choice and individual action, and has imposed almost countless conditions upon his exercise of his legal rights, in respect to his use of his own skill and labor, in earning a livelihood, his employment of others, his use of his own property, and his dealings with his fellow citizens." Compulsory vaccination revealed the extreme tendencies of the police power. It stole from the individual "the most sacred right that man has ever claimed and defended as his own—the right to the inviolability and integrity of his person." Every citizen had the "privilege" to decide to what "medical cult, if any, he will entrust his protection against the contagion of small-pox." Given the risks of vaccine—the lawyers cited Joseph McFarland's recent report on the Camden tetanus deaths— every citizen had the right to "take his chance of small-pox." The briefs culminated with the obligatory dance on the slippery slope. If compulsory vaccination was constitutional, then so must be "compulsory hypodermic injections of the public with all the known anti-toxins," the attorneys declared. "Operative surgery, also, must have its turn, and we shall have compulsory removal of appendices, of warts and wens, and compulsory reformations of human architecture generally, and so have a compulsorily reformed and rehabilitated society."[89]

It was an absurd argument, intended to jolt the justices from familiar ways of thinking. Pickering and Ballard could not have known that four years later Indiana would enact America's first eugenical sterilization law.

On April 2, 1903, the Supreme Judicial Court handed down its unanimous decision in *Commonwealth v. Pear; Same v. Jacobson*. The opinion was written by Chief Justice Marcus P. Knowlton. A Massachusetts native and Yale graduate, Knowlton had a long career in public life, including service in both branches of the state legislature and sixteen years as a superior court justice before he was appointed to the Supreme Judicial Court in 1887.[90]

Knowlton's opinion closely followed the path laid out for him in Bancroft's brief. "The rights of individuals must yield, if necessary, when the welfare of the whole community is at stake," Knowlton declared. "This is true of the right to personal liberty as well as the right to property." If quarantine and conscription were reasonable exercises of governmental power, then so was compulsory vaccination. "It is a fact of common knowledge that smallpox is a terrible disease whose ravages have sometimes swept away thousands of human beings in a few weeks," Knowlton wrote. "It is equally well known that a large majority of the medical profession and of people generally consider vaccination, repeated at intervals of a few years, a preventive of the disease." He cited the line of state cases upholding compulsory vaccination, noting that even cases such as *Adams v. Burdge*, which struck down measures issued by health boards, assumed that a legislature may interfere with individual rights of the unvaccinated "when smallpox is prevalent."[91]

Knowlton also ruled that the trial court had properly excluded Jacobson's offers of evidence. Jacobson's propositions regarding the danger vaccination posed to him were matters of his personal belief, which could neither "affect the validity of the statute, nor entitle him to be excepted from its provisions." The "theoretical possibility" that enforcement might result in an individual injury was insufficient to show that the statute itself was unreasonable. "The application of a good law to an exceptional case may work hardship." Knowlton mused that the law still gave the "exceptional" individual an out: "the worst that could happen to him under the statute would be the payment of a penalty of $5." (In fact, there was nothing to stop the government from prosecuting a single vaccine refuser again and again for repeatedly committing the same offense.)[92]

The Supreme Judicial Court handed the antivaccination movement a major defeat, affirming one of America's strongest vaccination laws. But Knowlton added a note of caution, sending an unmistakable signal to local boards of health. In certain instances, he said, "the time and manner of enforcement" might call for stricter judicial scrutiny. "If a person should deem it important that vaccination should not be performed in his case, and the authorities should think otherwise, *it is not in their power to vaccinate him by force*."[93]

This was no casual aside. As anyone who read the Boston newspapers knew, physical force vaccination was hardly uncommon in turn-of-the-century America. Not everyone received a polite visit from the chairman of the board of health. From the African American shacks of Middlesboro, Kentucky, to the tenements of Italian Harlem to the huts of the Philippine city of Iloilo, American health officials, police, and soldiers had on numerous occasions enforced vaccination at the point of a gun or the end of a billy club. Like the "tramps" who had uttered "every imaginable threat from civil suits to cold-blooded murder" when the Boston virus squad burst into their South Boston lodging house in the middle of the night, Knowlton recognized that forcible vaccination was beyond the pale. Getting this no-force principle stated for the public record by one of the nation's most venerable state courts was a major achievement.[94]

The court handed down its decision that same day in the Commonwealth's cases against John H. Mugford. The court stated its ruling in a single sentence: "These cases are governed by *Commonwealth v. Jacobson*." The verdicts against Mugford would stand.[95]

For Albert Pear, too, the Supreme Judicial Court was the end of the fight. He made no further appeal. But Jacobson had not finished litigating. It seems likely that the Massachusetts Anti-Compulsory Vaccination Society played a role in Pear's decision to step aside and let Jacobson appeal his case alone to the nation's highest court. Although Pear had a higher local profile, Jacobson's case presented a richer set of legal issues.

When Reverend Jacobson appeared for sentencing in the Middlesex County Superior Court on June 15, 1903, he had a new lawyer with him, George Fred Williams. The court fined Jacobson $5; Williams immediately filed a petition for a writ of error to the U.S. Supreme Court. The defendant asked for reversal on the grounds that the Massachusetts law violated the U.S. Constitution—specifically the Preamble, the Fifth Amendment, the Fourteenth Amendment, and the "spirit of the Constitution." The superior court had also erred, Williams charged, in excluding Jacobson's offer of evidence.[96]

In 1904, the Supreme Court had no choice but to hear the case. Congress did not give the Court power to pick and choose its own constitutional cases until 1925. Appeals went out in alternative medical journals across the nation for donations to help the Massachusetts Anti-Compulsory Vaccination Society pay Henning Jacobson's legal costs. The minister's case had become a national cause célèbre for the movement, the first vaccination case to reach the Supreme Court.[97]

. . .

George Fred Williams was fifty years old when he took on Jacobson's case: a famous lawyer, political insurgent, and former U.S. congressman. Born to a patrician family in Dedham, Massachusetts, he attended Dartmouth College and the universities of Heidelberg and Berlin. As a young Boston lawyer in the 1880s, Williams emerged as an impassioned leader—along with the future mayor Josiah Quincy and the lawyer Moorfield Storey—of the Massachusetts Mugwumps, reform-minded men of privilege who bolted the Republican Party to support Grover Cleveland's 1884 presidential campaign. Once in the Democratic Party, Williams never left. He showed a greater interest than most Mugwumps ever had in the problems and politics of "the slums."[98]

Williams was no stranger to long-shot political causes. As William Jennings Bryan's top political lieutenant in New England, he spoke out against the Spanish-American War and for Philippine independence, advocated tariff reduction and public ownership of utilities, called for an eight-hour workday and a progressive system of taxation that would "require full contribution from wealth and bear as lightly as possible on labor and the poor," and stood for "liberty and self-government everywhere under the stars and stripes." He ran as the Democratic nominee for Massachusetts governor three times in the 1890s, and lost every time. But he remained a force, bearing the Bryan standard at state and national conventions. By 1904, "this David of Massachusetts," as the Boston *Arena* styled him, had largely retired from politics. But he still loved a good fight. As recently as 1903 Williams had argued, and lost, a bankruptcy case before the Supreme Court.[99]

On December 6, 1904, a large audience, including several members of the Massachusetts Anti-Compulsory Vaccination Society, filled the Old Senate Chamber in the U.S. Capitol to watch the Supreme Court hear oral argument in *Jacobson v. Massachusetts*. With Williams leading Jacobson's legal team, the pastor's constitutional case assumed a different tone. The well-reasoned brief that Williams and his partner, James A. Halloran, submitted to the Supreme Court contained few of the libertarian fireworks of the Pickering and Ballard briefs. Williams scotched the Fifth Amendment argument—a claim that was both futile (because the Supreme Court had long maintained that the Bill of Rights did not reach the states) and unnecessary (because the Fourteenth Amendment *did*). The new brief gave the police power its due, even acknowledging the right of states to regulate the practice of medicine. If Jacobson had actually been infected with smallpox, Williams conceded, the state would have had every right to defend the community against him. The brief disclaimed any objection to *voluntary* vaccination and conceded the right of any state to exclude unvaccinated children from its schools. But by entrusting local boards with arbitrary powers to inoculate a healthy individual with disease—without making any exception for adults with special health conditions—the Massachusetts legislature had deprived Jacobson of his liberty without due process of law. And by making health exceptions only for children, the law violated the Fourteenth Amendment's equal protection clause. "In the history of our Republic, and indeed of England," Williams declared, "there is no parallel to such legislation."[100]

In the brief and in oral argument before the Court, Williams offered his own version of the recent history of smallpox in the United States. He recalled the collapse of public confidence in American vaccine, and Cleveland's decision to fight smallpox with sanitation rather than vaccination. "Smallpox has ceased to be the scourge it once was," Williams said, in a clear reference to variola minor, "and there is a growing tendency to resort to sanitation and isolation rather than vaccination." Painting Massachusetts as an outlier state, the brief said only eleven of the nation's forty-four states had compulsory vaccination laws, while only thirteen excluded unvaccinated children from the public schools. While technically correct, this claim glossed over the important fact that during the epidemics many American communities had ordered vaccination at will, under their local police powers. Williams noted the passage of noncompulsion laws in Utah, West Virginia, and Minnesota, and cited Governor La Follette's veto of a compulsion bill in Wisconsin, quoting his statement that in other states such laws "have resulted in riots and strife which have outlived the epidemic." And in his discussion of the state vaccination cases, Williams called special attention to *State v. Hay*. Placing America's vaccination controversy in a global context, the brief applauded Parliament's 1898 conscientious objector clause and reminded the justices that antivaccination riots had rocked Brazil as recently as November 1904.[101]

The final words of Jacobson's brief to the Supreme Court paid tribute to the post–Civil War constitutional amendments, particularly the Fourteenth, adopted the year before young Henning sailed to America with his family. Like the Thirteenth and Fifteenth Amendments, the Fourteenth— with its promises of equal protection and due process of law to all within the nation's domain—guaranteed "the freedom of the African race and the security and perpetuation of that freedom." In the decades since Reconstruction, the juggernaut of industrial capitalism and the rise of the social question in the United States had prompted the courts to read expansive new freedoms into those clauses. And so Jacobson's cause posed the question: did not the liberty protected by the Fourteenth Amendment embrace the right of a free man to control his own body and health? "As the Fourteenth Amendment has so often been appealed to for the protection of property," Williams concluded, "this plaintiff appeals to it with confidence for the protection of his freedom."[102]

The Supreme Court handed down its decision in *Jacobson v. Massachusetts* on February 20, 1905. Associate Justice John Marshall Harlan, the Court's longest-serving justice, delivered the opinion for the 7 to 2 majority. Harlan was an interesting choice for the assignment. One of the Court's more contrarian members, he was perhaps best known for his dissents. He also hailed from Kentucky—one of the states hardest hit by the smallpox epidemics.

At seventy-one, Justice Harlan still cut an imposing figure. A former slaveholder, he had served as a colonel with the Kentucky Volunteers, on the Union side, during the Civil War. Justice Holmes, who didn't like Harlan much, called him "the last of the tobacco-spitting judges." Justice Brewer said of Harlan, "He goes to bed every night with one hand on the Constitution and the other on the Bible, and so sleeps the sweet sleep of justice and righteousness."[103]

During an era when justices still read their opinions from the bench, Harlan preferred to deliver his opinions extemporaneously, like a good sermon. In his long judicial career, he had unexpectedly emerged as the Court's conscience on civil rights. When the Court announced the doctrine of "separate but equal" in *Plessy v. Ferguson* (1896), giving constitutional sanction to Jim Crow apartheid in the South, the man who had once opposed the Thirteenth Amendment because it invaded states' rights issued a thundering dissent: "The Constitution is colorblind, and neither knows nor tolerates classes among citizens." One of the Court's more progressive members, he championed the right of the federal government to break up business trusts, and he often bristled at laissez-faire arguments dressed up in the language of substantive due process. Recently, Justice Harlan had faced down the army of lawyers representing a group of railroad barons and financiers that included James J. Hill and J. Pierpont Morgan, as he delivered the Court's decision to allow the Roosevelt administration to dissolve their trust, the Northern Securities Company. "Liberty of contract," Harlan proclaimed, "does not imply liberty in a corporation or individuals to defy the national will, when legally expressed."[104]

So Jacobson and Williams had no reason to expect good news from Justice Harlan. Harlan wasted few words dismissing all of the plaintiff's claims that depended on the Preamble (it "has never been regarded as the source of any substantive power," he said) or the "spirit of the constitution" (the "plain" words of the Constitution "must control our decision"). The trial court's rejection of Jacobson's offers of proof, he added, "does not strictly present a Federal question." And he rejected Jacobson's equal protection argument, stating that there were "obviously" reasons why a regulation appropriate for adults might "not be safely applied to persons of tender years." Setting all of those issues aside, Harlan arrived at the heart of the matter: "Is the statute . . . inconsistent with the liberty which the Constitution of the United States secures to every person against deprivation by the State?"[105]

The short answer was no. Harlan did not give a short answer. In a richly textured if at times convoluted opinion, the justice tacked back and forth between power and liberty.

Harlan's rendering of the status of American constitutional liberty in 1905 bore the unmistakable impress of its times. Jacobson insisted the state had invaded his liberty—"the inherent right of every freeman to care for his own body and health in such way as to him seems best." The Court disagreed. Even in America, liberty was necessarily conditional.

> [T]he liberty secured by the Constitution of the United States to every person within its jurisdiction does not import an absolute right in each person to be, at all times and in all circumstances, wholly freed from restraint. There are manifold restraints to which every person is necessarily subject for the common good. On any other basis organized society could not exist with safety to its members. Society based on the rule that each one is a law unto himself would soon be confronted with disorder and anarchy. Real liberty for all could not exist under the operation of a principle which recognizes the right of each individual to use his own, whether in respect of his person or his property, regardless of the injury that may be done to others.

There were principles here that dated back a century or more, but Harlan tellingly expressed them in the political key words of progressivism. The interests of a modern "organized society"—with its teeming urban centers, powerful business corporations, and national labor unions—called for new and powerful forms of social and economic governance. The allusion to "anarchy" required no explanation in a nation that just three and a half years earlier had lost its president to an anarchist's bullets. Most broadly, Harlan invoked the progressive concept of "real liberty." It was the tenet around which the entire ideology of American progressivism revolved: amid the overwhelming social and economic forces of modern urban-industrial life, to secure to each individual the actual capacity to make the most of her opportunities called for a new understanding of liberty itself. In such a world, the old freedom to be left alone was no freedom at all. Real liberty required a new social conscience and a powerful interventionist state.[106]

Harlan posed the vaccination question in the starkest terms: as a conflict that pitted the most basic duty of the state—protecting the population from peril—against the personal liberty of individuals who feared vaccination even more than they feared smallpox. Speaking for a Court whose members included three Civil War veterans—the former colonel likened the community's right to fight smallpox to its right and duty to defend itself from a military invasion. "Upon the principle of self-defense, of paramount necessity, a community has the right to protect itself against an epidemic of disease which threatens the safety of its members." He recalled that smallpox was epidemic in the city of Cambridge when the board of health issued its order. "[U]nder the pressure of great dangers," he said, an individual's freedom must yield to public necessity. During an epidemic—no less than in a time of war—no man had the right to refuse the call of his country. "[H]e may be compelled, by force if need be, against his will and without regard to his personal wishes or his pecuniary interests, or even his religious or political convictions, to take his place in the ranks of the army of his country and risk the chance of being shot down in its defense."[107]

To Harlan and the Court's majority, the Massachusetts compulsory vaccination law was unquestionably constitutional. But the decision was not, as some would later imagine it, a blank check. In fact, the opinion articulated new limitations on police power that would have stunned a nineteenth-century jurist like Lemuel Shaw. Since 1897, the vaccination cases had nudged state courts toward a more cautious balancing of state power and individual rights appropriate to an era of rapid technological and institutional change. Echoing the "present danger" standard established in the schools cases, Harlan emphasized that public health power was itself contingent. The right of a community to compel vaccination existed because of the "necessities of the case," the dangerous presence of smallpox. And even during a life-threatening epidemic, said Harlan, the authorities might go too far. "[I]t might be that an acknowledged power of a local community to protect itself against an epidemic threatening the safety of all, might be exercised in particular circumstances and in reference to particular persons in such an arbitrary, unreasonable manner, or might go so far beyond what was reasonably required for the safety of the public, as to authorize or compel the courts to interfere for the protection of such persons." Harlan left the details open. But in just the past few years, several courts had done just that. In *Wong Wai*, a federal circuit court had established equal protection as an inviolable constitutional standard in vaccination cases. In its Pear and Jacobson decision, the Massachusetts Supreme

Judicial Court had declared that government officials had no right to enforce vaccination by physical force.[108]

At the end of his opinion, Justice Harlan delivered a surprise. With language that evoked the Eighth Amendment of the Bill of Rights, Harlan carved into the Massachusetts law a medical exemption for adults. It was "easy," Harlan said, "to suppose the case of an adult who is embraced by the mere words of the act, but yet to subject whom to vaccination in a particular condition of his health or body, would be cruel and inhuman in the last degree. We are not to be understood as holding that the statute was intended to be applied to such a case, or, if it was so intended, that the judiciary would not be competent to interfere and protect the health and life of the individual concerned." The Massachusetts court had explicitly rejected this reading of its own state's law. It seems that Williams's emphasis on *State v. Hay* in his brief attracted Harlan's notice. The justice defended his rendering of the harm avoidance principle with a noteworthy rule of statutory construction: "General terms should be so limited in their application as not to lead to injustice, oppression, or absurd consequence."[109]

Of course, Henning Jacobson had been making precisely that argument since he first set foot in Judge McDaniel's Cambridge courtroom more than two and a half years earlier. Unschooled in American legal traditions, he had tried to explain to the court his sincere belief, founded in his own family's experience with vaccination and the stories he had heard from others, that the operation threatened his health. Justice Harlan, however, was unwilling to concede that Jacobson might himself fall under the novel standard of protection he had just outlined. "No such case is here presented," Harlan declared, without foundation. "It is the case of an adult, who for aught that appears, was himself in perfect health and a fit subject of vaccination, and yet, while remaining in the community, refused to obey the statute" at a time when the people of Cambridge were "confessedly endangered by the presence of a dangerous disease."[110]

Justice David J. Brewer and Justice Rufus Peckham, the Court's two most conservative members, dissented from the decision without comment.

Pastor Henning Jacobson had reached the end of his legal odyssey. He would return one last time to the Middlesex County Superior Court and pay his $5 fine, perhaps only dimly aware that his case would become the most important legacy of the turn-of-the-century smallpox epidemics. Even in defeat, the minister had won some valuable constitutional safeguards for individual liberty and due process—if not for him, then for the rest of us.

The *Jacobson* ruling drew loud applause from the medical profession. The *Wisconsin Medical Journal* called it "a decision of very far-reaching significance." Public health officers welcomed this vindication from the nation's highest court. As one New York official said of the decision, "it has elevated our profession." The Cambridge and Boston newspapers hailed the decision for resolving a question that had caused so much controversy in their cities. As the *Boston Journal* commented, "Thus falls the theory of the few who wilfully blind themselves to the enormous good accomplished by vaccination, that personal liberty is violated by the enforcing of a salutary and reasonable health regulation." *The New York Times* relished the moment. "This will not end the discussion of vaccination as a measure against the one disease which it perfectly controls," the *Times* declared, "but it should end the useful life of the societies of cranks formed to resist the operation of laws relative to vaccination. Their occupation is gone." Once again, the *Times* underestimated the antivaccinationists.[111]

The antivaccinationists' reactions to the decision were appropriately ambivalent. To be sure, some decried it as an unmitigated disgrace. The Providence, Rhode Island, bookseller Sidney S. Rider compared the decision to *Dred Scott*. "This Court once decided that a negro had no rights which a white man was bound to respect," Rider seethed. "Is it going now to decide that a white man who abhors vaccination as a deadly poison has no rights which a doctor is bound to respect?" But many critics of compulsory vaccination recognized that the *Jacobson* litigation had in fact secured important gains for personal liberties—including the Massachusetts Supreme Judicial Court's public condemnation of forcible vaccination and the important safeguards Harlan had worked into his Supreme Court opinion. The *Medical Advance*, a homeopathic journal, highlighted Harlan's admonition to health boards that their measures could be so "arbitrary and oppressive as to justify the interference of the courts." "This warning deserves attention," the journal noted, "and may afford persons suffering from constitutional dyscrasia legal ground for protest." In fact, for the antivaccination movement, the next twenty years would bring a burst of new organizing and initiatives to topple school-based smallpox vaccination mandates at the local and state levels.[112]

Many observers instantly recognized that the *Jacobson* decision had important ramifications beyond the vaccination question. Much of the progressive reform agenda—including the great welter of labor legislation enacted in the states in recent years—had been justified on the grounds that it promoted the public health. If the Supreme Court had ruled that the states had no right to compel vaccination during a smallpox epidemic, how would other measures, less directly related to the public health, have survived constitutional challenge? The *New York Tribune* observed that the *Jacobson* ruling had "a special interest for New-York," because of its implications for an ongoing suit to strike down the state's tenement house law. "It is reassuring to find the Supreme Court taking a view of the scope of the State's police power in which the community's right to protection against sanitary abuses cannot be jeopardized by individual obstinacy or individual greed."[113]

But the Supreme Court itself muddied the constitutional waters just a few months after *Jacobson* with its instantly notorious decision in *Lochner v. New York*. In a 5 to 4 decision (written by Justice Peckham) the Court struck down the state's ten-hour law for bakers as an unconstitutional violation of the right of bakers and their employers to contract freely with one another. It was the first time the Court had brandished the controversial concept of liberty of contract, in a case not involving interstate commerce, to override the ruling of a state court and restrain the legislative exercise of the police power. Peckham distinguished the case from *Jacobson*, claiming there were no legitimate public health purposes at stake in the bakers law.[114]

In dissent, Justice Harlan made a mockery of that claim. He cited medical studies that documented the many ailments suffered by bakers due to the long days spent working on their feet, inhaling flour dust in the extreme heat of a bakery. Harlan found much evidence to support the legislature's belief that more than ten hours of work each day in a bakery "may endanger the health, and shorten the lives of the workmen, thereby diminishing their physical and mental capacity to serve the State, and to provide for those dependent upon them."[115]

Justice Holmes wrote a separate dissent. Objecting that the majority seemed to have forgotten the Court's decision, just "[t]he other day" in *Jacobson*, Holmes said Peckham's opinion relied on a "perverted," laissez-faire reading of the word "liberty" in the Fourteenth Amendment. "A reasonable man," said Holmes of the bakers law, "might think it a proper measure on the score of health." Without a shred of justification or precedent, the majority had usurped "the right of a majority to embody their opinions in law."[116]

For more than a century afterward, constitutional scholars and historians would remember the first decades of the twentieth century as the "Lochner era," a dark period in the history of American law, when the U.S. Supreme Court used a business-friendly rhetoric of individual liberty to strike down urgently needed social legislation. *Lochner* was an important decision. But it was less important for its holding than for its cultural reverberations. The decision outraged and focused the intellectual energies of an entire generation of progressive legal thinkers and activists, who would over the next quarter century lay the conceptual groundwork for the New Deal. But even the progressives did not make the mistake of seeing *Lochner* as the emblematic court decision of their era. The decision was outrageous because it was so out of line with the general tendency of American courts to approve greater and greater exercises of state police power—a tendency the progressives viewed as necessary and thus almost inevitable.[117]

Instead, many contemporaries continued to look to *Jacobson* as the better reference point for understanding the real extent of government power in America's modern, urban-industrial epoch. *Lochner* notwithstanding, American judges and legal scholars immediately began citing *Jacobson* as the authoritative statement of the almost unlimited extent of the police power in the United States.

In the decades after *Jacobson*, even as antivaccination societies continued to form and fight school vaccination mandates in the state legislatures and courts, the vaccination question became a touchstone in the American legal imagination. In his 1914 book on antitrust law, for example, former president William Howard Taft cited compulsory vaccination as a synecdoche for the entire rising regulatory edifice of modern American government. "Changing conditions prevailing in society," necessarily led the government to impose a host of new restraints on personal freedom. "Take, for instance, the compulsory vaccination laws sustained by the Supreme Court," Taft wrote, recalling his years in the Philippines. "I have had an opportunity to witness the effect of such laws in the Philippines upon a people that had not had popular government and had been steeled to arbitrary rule, and yet they resented the health laws as savoring of intolerable cruelty." That almost primal resistance to compulsory vaccination, he suggested, was all the more strongly resented by a liberty-loving people accustomed to democracy and the rule of law. But a maturing urban-industrial society had to put away such childish liberties. Taft's very next paragraph traced the connection between modern health laws and the array of other regulations that had necessarily been imposed on industrial society, including tenement house laws, child labor laws, and maximum hours laws. In Taft's view, *Lochner* was an aberration. *Jacobson* better reflected the real state of American constitutional law.[118]

Despite the careful safeguards Harlan laid out in his *Jacobson* opinion, the decision initially had a negative impact for civil liberties. With the coming of World War I, the federal and state governments crushed dissenting political speech with an extraordinary wave of repressive measures. Among the thousands of Americans placed under surveillance by J. Edgar Hoover's new Bureau of Investigation for alleged seditious activities in 1918 were several activists involved in what one special agent called "the anti-vaccination crusade." They included the chiropractor William Heupel of Iowa, the activist Jessica Henderson of Massachusetts, and the former *Liberator* editor Lora C. Little, who now lived in Portland, Oregon. The federal agents viewed these antivaccinationists as subversive and un-American—and not only because their propaganda threatened to undermine the Army's vaccination program.[119]

The war years opened up a new front of civil liberties controversies— this time over the question of the proper bounds of political speech. Significantly, the landmark constitutional cases that emerged from the wartime civil liberties battles bore distinct echoes of the earlier fights over vaccination, as the phrases "conscientious objector" and "present danger" took on new, now familiar meanings. As Justice Holmes, who had signed Harlan's

Jacobson decision, suggested in a personal letter to Judge Learned Hand in 1918, all of these liberty questions were connected. It was in this wartime context that Holmes told Hand, "free speech stands no differently than freedom from vaccination."[120]

Holmes still regarded compulsory vaccination as a reference point for how far the democratic majority might rightfully override the liberty interests of minorities. When Holmes first articulated his famous "clear and present danger" standard in 1919, he altered the meaning of a phrase that had arisen in the vaccination cases as a limitation on administrative discretion. In Holmes's initial formulation, in *Schenck v. United States*, the "clear and present danger" standard gave Congress sweeping power to restrain speech. Later that same year, however, Holmes restated his own standard in language more receptive to speech rights—and more consistent with the present danger standard that state judges had established in the vaccination cases. "It is *only* the present danger of immediate evil or an intent to bring it about that warrants Congress in setting a limit to the expression of opinion where private rights are not concerned," Holmes declared.[121]

Even after Holmes established himself as one of the nation's greatest champions of First Amendment rights, compulsory vaccination remained for him a powerful metaphor for the reasonable sacrifices that the state could demand of its citizens. In 1927, the justice cited *Jacobson v. Massachusetts*, and nothing else, as he upheld the right of the state of Virginia to sterilize an allegedly "feeble-minded" woman named Carrie Buck against her will. "The principle that sustains compulsory vaccination is broad enough to cover cutting the Fallopian tubes," Holmes wrote in some of the most chilling words ever delivered from the Supreme Court. "Three generations of imbeciles are enough."[122]

Holmes, though, did not have the last word. Over time, *Jacobson v. Massachusetts* would attain a more complex place in American law—leaving a legacy more in keeping with the double-sided quality of Justice Harlan's original opinion. For Harlan had attempted to resolve the Progressive Era struggle between individual liberty and government power with a ruling that bolstered both.

In its first century of life, *Jacobson* has been cited as precedent numerous times in Supreme Court cases to defend extraordinary exercises of governmental power. It has been used to uphold eugenical sterilization laws, to support the claim that a warrantless entry by law enforcement officials may be legal when there is a compelling need and little time, and, in a recent dissent, to defend the federal government's right during the twenty-first-century war against terror to detain a U.S. citizen as an "enemy combatant" without due process.[123]

But on the other side of the balance, Jacobson provided a crucial source of constitutional authority for the post–World War II "rights revolution." Constitutional scholars have often noted that in the great reproductive rights decisions of the late twentieth century, civil liberties attorneys and the U.S. Supreme Court revived the old discredited language of substantive due process and changed its basic purpose from the protection of economic rights to the creation of private rights of bodily autonomy and integrity. But the antivaccinationists had made such arguments well over a half century earlier in the long line of cases that culminated in Jacobson. As civil liberties attorneys, women's rights advocates, and liberal judges fought to extend constitutional due process to encompass reproductive rights during the 1960s and 1970s, they brandished Harlan's language from Jacobson. Supreme Court Justice William O. Douglas cited Harlan's words in Doe v. Bolton, a 1973 decision that overturned Georgia's abortion law, to support the proposition that "the freedom to care for one's health and person" was "fundamental" and only a "compelling state interest" could justify interference with that liberty. In other major reproductive rights cases, the Court cited Jacobson to defend the existence of a constitutional right to sexual privacy and to support the claim that "a State's interest in the protection of life falls short of justifying any plenary override of individual liberty claims."[124]

The Jacobson decision has assumed a significance that neither Pastor Henning Jacobson nor Justice John Marshall Harlan could have anticipated in 1905. But the long afterlife of that case underscores an important fact about the contentious history of civil liberties in modern America: free speech wasn't the half of it. Beginning with the vaccination struggles of the turn of the century, in an era of fast-growing institutional power, ordinary Americans again and again challenged the courts to create new protections for personal liberties—including rights to individual autonomy, medical privacy, and bodily integrity. Harlan's opinion had treated those claims with a measure of respect. At the very least, he recognized that they were worth fighting for. He said, "There is, of course, a sphere within which the individual may assert the supremacy of his own will and rightfully dispute the authority of any human government, especially of any free government existing under a written constitution, to interfere with the exercise of that will."[125]

But Harlan recognized that under the necessitous conditions of modern life, human freedom sometimes meant little without purposeful governmental action. And so, in *Jacobson v. Massachusetts*, the U.S. Supreme Court gave its blessing to an unpopular but effective public health technology that would one day be used to eradicate the most deadly disease the world has ever known.

EPILOGUE

Gone are the days of the pesthouse and the detention camp—the tent city thrown up at the edge of town, its gas-fired torches standing sentry through the night. Gone, too, the days when we looked into the pockmarked face of a stranger on a crowded streetcar, or a loved one across the table. We have lost the habit of rolling up our sleeves to display our vaccination scars to the medical inspector at the border, the nurse at the schoolhouse door, or the conductor on the departing train. With each passing year, more of us have no scar to show. All of these things are gone, because smallpox is gone.

America's turn-of-the-century war on smallpox did not kill humankind's ancient foe. But it did mark the beginning of the end for the disease in the United States. The deadly New York smallpox epidemic that started in All Nations Block on Thanksgiving Day 1900, setting Alonzo Blauvelt's vaccination corps into motion in the tenements and factories, was to be the city's last. Boston, too, had seen its final smallpox epidemic during the deadly 1901–3 visitation that sealed the city's reputation as a "hotbed of the anti-vaccine heresy." Over the next twenty-nine years, the city reported a hundred-odd cases, just four of them fatal, and then the pox vanished for good. The story was much the same in Philadelphia, Cleveland, Seattle, and other places where smallpox had raged during the first years of the century.[1]

By World War I, a rough pattern had taken hold. Outbreaks of malignant variola major became rare events, aggressively stamped out by America's increasingly well-organized health departments through a combination of mass vaccination and swift isolation of patients. Having learned something on the vaccination battlegrounds of the turn of the century, public health professionals self-consciously eschewed compulsion and force for public education and the promotion of the idea that every citizen had a positive right to good health. As C.-E. A. Winslow of the Yale School of Medicine observed, "Public health conceived in these terms will be something vastly different from the exercise of the purely police power which has been its principal manifestation in the past." Of course, every profession seeks to elevate itself by disclaiming the backwardness of its predecessors. And the new public health, far from a retreat, implied a much more ambitious program for governing everyday life in America. But over time, ordinary Americans did more fully accommodate themselves to the call for mass vaccination when the deadlier form of smallpox invaded their communities. When variola major reappeared in Detroit in 1924, causing 163 deaths, a half-million residents submitted to vaccination in a single month.[2]

But the new mild type of the disease remained far more difficult to control. Variola minor became the dominant form of smallpox in the United States. Between 1921 and 1930, the United States reported nearly 400,000 cases of smallpox, with a case-fatality rate of less than 1 percent. During the next decade, 108,000 cases were reported, with a case-fatality rate of just .38 percent. As smallpox continued to lose its lethal force, Americans remained ambivalent—or apathetic—about smallpox vaccination. Health departments relied on school mandates and voluntary action to maintain vaccination levels. But by the 1930s, only nine states had compulsory vaccination laws on the books, and four states had laws banning compulsion. During the 1930s, public health experts voiced the old refrain that "the United States lags behind other civilized countries in vaccination protection." And they were right. With 5,000 to 50,000 cases still occurring each year, health officials estimated that only one in two Americans had ever been vaccinated.[3]

The antivaccination movement had continued to challenge the authority of American public health officials. As the Birmingham, Alabama–based *Southern Medical Journal* lamented in 1921, "All the fools are not dead yet." Since the Supreme Court's ruling in *Jacobson v. Massachusetts*, antivaccinationists had relentlessly railed against school vaccination requirements. They would continue to do so even after the Court, in a 1922 opinion written by Justice Louis D. Brandeis, dismissed a constitutional challenge to a local school vaccination mandate, stating that the *Jacobson* ruling had effectively decided the question.[4]

Time and again, however, when malignant variola major reared its head, the American people bared their arms. As Assistant Surgeon General R. C. Williams of the U.S. Public Health Service commented in 1946, "When you get a scare, everyone within 100 miles gets vaccinated."[5]

In 1947, when a traveler on a bus from Mexico City carried smallpox to Manhattan, more than six million New Yorkers lined up in a single month to get vaccinated. In dramatic contrast to the 1901–2 epidemics in the city, the New York City Health Department did not resort to compulsion and force, instead reaching out to the public through the radio and newspapers, while using the full agencies of the local government to trace cases and contacts. In the end, the city suffered only twelve cases and just two deaths.[6]

By the time of the New York outbreak, smallpox had grown scarce in the United States. America's last confirmed outbreak struck Hidalgo County, in the lower Rio Grande Valley of Texas, in 1949.[7]

At the time, few American states mandated smallpox vaccination. Beginning in the late 1930s, nine states and the Territory of Alaska enacted the first laws mandating immunization for another deadly childhood disease—diphtheria. The discovery of the polio vaccine and the ensuing national vaccination campaign during the 1950s changed everything, turning compulsory immunization from a political liability into a popular cause. Between 1958 and 1965, all fifty states enacted new legislation requiring schoolchildren to undergo vaccination for smallpox and other diseases. By 1969, twelve states had mandated a full slate of childhood immunization shots that included smallpox, measles, polio, diphtheria, pertussis, and tetanus. And more states were jumping on board each year. A new era of compulsory immunization had begun.[8]

With no reported cases of smallpox in the United States in more than twenty years, the annual tally of six to eight deaths from complications of vaccination became increasingly unacceptable. In 1971, the United States Public Health Service, the agency that seventy years earlier had sent C. P. Wertenbaker across the South to help communities fight smallpox, recommended that routine childhood vaccinations against smallpox be discontinued. Within three years, every American state had repealed its smallpox vaccination mandate for schoolchildren.[9]

As of 1967, smallpox still killed 2 million people every year across the globe. The World Health Organization—leading an unprecedented international campaign—launched an offensive to wipe smallpox from the planet. In an exceptional example of Cold War–era cooperation, the eradication campaign was heavily funded by the United States with the Soviet Union providing enormous quantities of vaccine. The geographical canvas for this massive effort spanned dozens of developing countries in Asia, Africa, and Latin America. Two inventions proved crucial: the introduction of freeze-dried vaccine (which retained its efficacy for months at high heat) and the manufacture of the bifurcated needle, a cheap forked tool that enabled health workers to get four times as many vaccinations from a single unit of vaccine.[10]

The eradicators developed a strategy, known as "ring vaccination" or "surveillance-containment," that resembled a modern, high-tech version of the methods employed by Manhattan's turn-of-the-century vaccination corps. As each new outbreak of smallpox was reported, a vaccination team descended on the scene, vaccinating everyone they could find in the immediate vicinity and placing the area under close surveillance until the outbreak had subsided. Taking the fight to smallpox, rather than striving for universal vaccination, the surveillance-containment strategy enabled the eradicators to cut short the transmission of smallpox, even in countries that had poorly vaccinated populations. The eradicators had to work around civil wars and surmount cultural barriers; in rural Afghanistan, for example, vaccinators ran up against purdah traditions that limited their access to women and children.[11]

When containment teams met outright resistance, they responded with verbal pressure, legal coercion, and, in extreme cases, forcible vaccination. One senior WHO epidemiologist, a physician from the American Centers for Disease Control and Prevention (CDC) named Dr. Stanley Music, recalled how his team's initial efforts to carry out the containment policy in rural Bangladesh "resembled an almost military style attack on infected villages. . . . In the hit-and-run excitement of such a campaign, women and children were often pulled out from under beds, from behind doors, from within latrines, etc. People were chased and, when caught, vaccinated." Dr. Music explained the thinking of the vaccinators. "We considered the villagers to have an understandable though irrational fear of vaccination," he said. "We just couldn't let people get smallpox and die needlessly. We went from door to door and vaccinated. When they ran, we chased. When they locked their doors, we broke down their doors and vaccinated them." The strategy proved highly effective at containing smallpox. But it came at a high price. As one historian of the South Asia eradication program delicately observed, "coercion can leave behind a residue of resentment that sours public attitudes toward the next vaccination campaign."[12]

As reported smallpox cases dwindled, teams conducted "scar surveys" of high-risk areas, inspecting people for vaccination scars or facial pockmarks, just as U.S. military surgeons had done when the Army moved across Luzon during the Philippine-American War. The last naturally occurring case of variola major occurred in a young girl in Bangladesh in late 1975. The final case of variola minor was reported in a hospital cook in Merca, a port town in southern Somalia, on October 31, 1977. On May 8, 1980, the World Health Assembly declared, "[T]he world and all its peoples have won freedom from smallpox, which was a most devastating disease sweeping in epidemic form through many countries since earliest time, leaving death, blindness and disfigurement in its wake." The Assembly recommended that countries across the world discontinue smallpox vaccination.[13]

The smallpox eradication program severed smallpox from its human host—a monumental achievement. Alas, the campaign did not annihilate the variola virus. As immunization levels around the world fell after 1980, the virus took on a new and ominous existence in the laboratory.

The WHO had authorized two laboratories to keep frozen stocks of variola—the CDC in Atlanta and the Research Institute for Viral Protections in Moscow. By the time the Soviet Union collapsed in 1990, British and American intelligence agencies had believed for some time that the USSR had been developing weapons-grade variola. Those fears were confirmed in the mid-1990s. Civil defense agencies prepared for the worst. Long-standing concerns about the proliferation of weaponized smallpox virus intensified after the terrorist attacks of September 11, 2001, soon followed by the anthrax murders.[14]

On December 13, 2002, President George W. Bush announced his administration's plan to protect the nation from a smallpox attack. The plan, which many in the scientific community had opposed, involved compulsory vaccination of a half-million U.S. military personnel, followed by a voluntary campaign of a roughly equal number of frontline hospital workers and members of public health departments—the most likely health workers to come into contact with the virus during an outbreak. After that, the plan called for the voluntary vaccination of some 10 million firefighters, police, and other "first responders." The military vaccination campaign went smoothly enough. But the civilian campaign quickly collapsed. Only 38,000 health workers agreed to be vaccinated, and many American hospitals refused to participate at all.[15]

The complex concerns elicited by the civilian program would have been familiar to the many Americans who refused vaccination at the turn of the twentieth century. Many of the health workers believed they had a specific medical condition that made smallpox vaccination particularly hazardous for them. (In fact, experts believe as many as one in five Americans today may have contraindications to smallpox vaccination, including immune systems weakened by HIV.) Others worried about the common side effects of smallpox vaccine—still known as "the most dangerous vaccine." Many felt the risk of a bioterrorist attack was too low to make getting vaccinated a good bet. (The invasion of Iraq had revealed that Saddam Hussein held no secret stockpile of variola.) Another key factor was the lack of a federal program, in the first stages of the vaccination campaign, to compensate people for death, injury, or lost work due to the vaccination. In the end, the failed civilian program reported nearly nine hundred adverse reactions to vaccine, including one death. The military program reported seventy-five cases of heart inflammation and one death.[16]

It was a revealing episode. In the absence of a palpable threat of an outbreak, few twenty-first-century Americans would step forward and get vaccinated against smallpox. Clearly, ignorance had little to do with it. Presumably, the 400,000 health workers who declined to roll up their sleeves were exceptionally well-informed about the risks. Even the relatively small risks of the vaccine were deemed unacceptable as long as the threat of a smallpox attack seemed remote.

Even as smallpox itself disappeared from America and the world in the final decades of the twentieth century, vaccines themselves proliferated. Thanks in large part to the polio success story, so did vaccine laws. By the century's end, all fifty states mandated that children receive immunization shots to protect them against seven different diseases. The number continues to grow. State-mandated vaccination is far more extensive than it was a century ago. But most states now provide precisely the sort of exemptions that the turn-of-the-century antivaccinationists in Europe and the United States had demanded. The people may now ask to be exempted for medical and religious reasons, or even, in some states, for conscientious objections to vaccination.[17]

For all of this, public distrust of vaccines is on the rise, caused in part by the unprecedented complexity of the childhood immunization landscape and fueled by the explosive communicative power of the Internet. No longer do rumors of sore arms and lost limbs circulate via word of mouth across communities of workers; a bottomless archive of information and misinformation about vaccines is just a few keystrokes away. According to the CDC's National Immunization Survey, in 2008 nearly 40 percent of American parents of young children refused or delayed giving them at least one routine shot—up from 22 percent in 2003. One quarter of American parents believe vaccines cause autism, though there is no scientific evidence to support that belief and at least a dozen major scientific studies have concluded there is no connection. In March 2010, the federal "vaccine court" ruled that the theory that a mercury-containing preservative long used in vaccines caused autism was "scientifically unsupportable." But no one now expects a single court ruling to silence the vaccination controversy.[18]

The vaccination question a century ago was in important respects markedly different from the current debate. Then the controversy centered on a single vaccine used to fight one horrific infectious disease. Today, healthy children under six routinely receive nearly a dozen separate vaccines, some mandated by state law, all recommended by the CDC, that offer protection against viruses ranging from varicella (chicken pox) to the human papillomavirus. Each of these vaccines raises its own particular issues of safety, parental authority, or even, in the case of the HPV vaccine, sexual mores. Trying to check actual epidemics of smallpox, turn-of-the-century health officials likened their power to the military defense of the nation. Today's vaccination skirmishes are by comparison a peacetime struggle, mostly fought out in the absence of visible diseases—an absence made possible, in large part, by vaccines. The vaccine politics of the present moment reflect twenty-first-century Americans' still evolving conceptions of the family, their affective ties to particular local and virtual communities, and their complex views of a modern administrative and welfare state that was still in its infancy a century ago. Antivaccination arguments today often convey an attenuated sense of social responsibility that is all too pervasive in contemporary American culture. Our politics of health must be understood in its own historical context.[19]

Even so, the long-gone epidemics that swept across the United States over a century ago hold important lessons for us. In our post-9/11 moment, civil libertarians have dusted off the *Jacobson* decision, finding in that complex opinion a set of useful standards for balancing governmental power and individual rights during a health emergency. The experience of those historical epidemics also underscores the abiding importance of public education and political candor in matters affecting personal health. People care deeply about their bodies. To ask them to accept the risk of bodily harm for the sake of others is at times essential. But the decision to make that request of the people has the greatest prospect of success when it is made with the care and public deliberation worthy of a democratic society.

In a broader sense, the history of America's turn-of-the-century fight against smallpox cautions us against making reflexive judgments about the innumerable people, the world over, who greet scientific innovation and expert authority with skepticism, resentment, or steadfast resistance. To dismiss so many people as merely ignorant and irrational is worse than intolerant. At a time when the ability of democratic nations to promote the security and health of their citizens depends ever more on science, it is the purest folly. It tells us little about the root causes of ambivalence toward medical science or how to bridge the gap between popular beliefs and the imperatives of preventive medicine. Scientific innovations that in hindsight seem manifestly rational, benign, and inevitable often appear far more problematic to people on the ground. Unthinking scientific triumphalism is no sounder an approach than antiscientific denialism to the social conflict and political contention that are likely to continue to haunt the human quest to make ours a healthier world.

Acknowledgments

Generous fellowships and grants underwrote this project. The Radcliffe Institute for Advanced Study at Harvard gave me a full year to do the initial research and furnished a marvelous setting in which to do it. I am immensely grateful to Radcliffe, to the brilliantly diverting Fellows Class of 2004–5, and especially to Drew Faust and Judy Vichniac for the gift of that year. I am also deeply grateful to the American Council of Learned Societies for the Charles E. Ryskamp Fellowship (named for a warm and generous scholar no longer with us), which bought me a full year of writing time and other support. Brandeis University provided a semester of leave time on each end of this project, as well as smaller grants to cover costs, for all of which I give thanks.

I owe a special debt to four exemplary historians who wrote in support of my fellowship applications: my mentor Kathy Conzen, Tom Haskell, Jackie Jones, and Laura Kalman. I hope this book repays your confidence in some small way.

Along the way, I presented pieces from the project to workshops and audiences at the American Society for Legal History, Boston College, Boston University, Brandeis University, Canisius College, Cleveland State University, Harvard University, Johns Hopkins University, New York University, Stanford University, the University of Minnesota, the University of Nevada, Las Vegas, the University of Pennsylvania, the University of Wisconsin–Milwaukee, the University of Virginia, and Yale University. I want to thank my many hosts for their hospitality and the members of those audiences for their challenging comments. Ironically, a bout with the H1N1 flu virus (before I had a chance to get vaccinated) forced me to cancel a presentation at the University of Michigan, but I am grateful to Tom Green, Bill Novak, and their legal history students for sending me such crisp comments on my paper. A line here and there in this book first appeared in my article "'The Least Vaccinated of Any Civilized Country': Personal Liberty and Public Health in the Progressive Era," *Journal of Policy History*, 20 (2008): 76–93; I wish to thank the journal for permission to use that material here.

I also want to thank Ann Mary Olson, who provided excellent research assistance during my year at Radcliffe; and Fred Turner, who did some helpful digging for me in the Spooner Papers.

A great many friends and colleagues read pieces of this project along the way or heard me out as I worked through my ideas in conversation. For their insights, research leads, and camaraderie, I particularly want to thank Brian Balogh, Norma Basch, Mary Bilder, Henry Bolter, Chris Capozolla, Andrew Cohen, Tino Cuellar, Jane Dailey, Matt Daniels, Michele Dauber, Peter Garlock, Patsy Gerstner, Julian Go, Bob Gordon, Sally Gordon, Hank Greely, Rob Heinrich, Daniel Hulsebosch, Robert Johnston, Michael Katz, David Kennedy, Daniel Kosoy, Dan Kryder, Gerry Leonard, Jill Lepore, Kenneth Levin, Charlie Lord, Rob McGreevey, Harry Marks, Bill Novak, Robert Orsi, David Rabban, Heather Richardson, Elizabeth Sanders, Dennis Scannell, Mark Schmeller, Bruce Schulman, Daniel Sherman, Lindsay Silver Cohen, Ross Silverman, Jonathan Stapley, Tom Sugrue, David Tanenhaus, Geoff Tegnell, Chris Tomlins, Barbara Welke, John Witt, Rich Young, and Julian Zelizer.

I am proud to be a founding member of a Boston area writing group that over the past six or seven years has included the likes of Steve Biehl, Jona Hansen, Jane Kamensky, Stephen Mihm, Mark Peterson, John Plotz, Seth Rockman, Jennifer Roberts, Dan Scharfstein, and Conevery Valencius. Many thanks to you all for your sharp comments, good company, and the example of your fine prose.

Brandeis University has been my institutional home throughout this project. It is in many ways a remarkable place, and I feel blessed to have such outstanding students and engaging colleagues. In particular, I want to thank Dean Adam Jaffe and Provost Marty Krauss for their continuing support and all of my colleagues in the History Department for their warm collegiality and intellectual engagement. I have learned a good deal from Rudy Binion, Greg Freeze, Paul Jankowski, Bill Kapelle, Alice Kelikian, Govind Sreenivasan, and Ibrahim Sundiata. I especially want to thank a small group of colleagues with whom I have worked especially closely over the past decade in the American History Graduate Program: Silvia Arrom, Brian Donahue, David Engerman, David Hackett Fischer, Mark Hulliung, Jane Kamensky, and my much missed colleague, Jackie Jones. I owe a special thanks to Jane Kamensky, who has been a constant source of ideas, moral support, and excellent humor.

I am especially grateful to a few individuals who read a draft of the manuscript late in the game and who provided thoughtful, expert comments: Art Bookstein (my father-in-law and a voracious reader of nonfiction), Jon Cohen (a close friend from our *City Paper* days and a first-rate science writer), David Igler (one of my oldest friends and a stellar historian), Charles E. Rosenberg (the dean of medical historians), and Conevery Valencius (who possesses an unusually deep knowledge of the medical beliefs of rural nineteenth-century Americans). D. A. Henderson, a man whom I have never met (but about whom I have read a great deal due to his leadership of the World Health Organization's smallpox eradication program), generously read the manuscript and provided expert comments. Like most people today, I have never seen a case of smallpox, and it was both intimidating and rewarding to be able to share this project with a scientist who knows the disease and its ways so well.

Laura Stickney at the Penguin Press has been an ideal editor for this book. As fluent as she is smart, she has edited with a sharp eye and a light hand. I am also grateful to my outstanding agent, Geri Thoma, for her unflagging support and for helping me find my way in the world of trade publishing.

I owe everything to my family.

Art and Lynne Bookstein have given me steady, unconditional support since I married their beautiful daughter fifteen years ago. Many thanks to Dari Pillsbury, who is a great friend and our in-house photographer extraordinaire.

Through their steadfast love, encouragement, and the example of their own lives and work, my parents, Mason Willrich and the late Patricia Rowe Willrich, nurtured my passions for reading, writing, and teaching, and I thank them both for everything. I also wish to thank Wendy Webster Willrich for her support. I am deeply grateful to my siblings and their wonderful partners—Chris and Susan, Stephen and Kelly, and Kate and Erik—for challenging me and supporting me through the years. You're an amazing family, and I am lucky to have you. I'll see you soon on Stinson Beach.

I have saved my greatest debts for last, knowing words will never be enough. Max and Emily, I am so proud of you both. Thank you for your constant reminders of the things that really matter. I love you. And Wendy Jayne Willrich, you *know* I couldn't have done it without you. You know the tune: "I'm giving you a longing look. . . ." With respect, gratitude, and the deepest love, I dedicate this book to you.

Wellesley, Massachusetts

Notes

Archival Collections

AGOMHP	Old Army Records, Record Group 94: Records of the Adjutant General's Office, Entry 547: Medical History of Posts, National Archives (Washington)
CHM	Center for the History of Medicine, Countway Library of Medicine, Harvard University
CPWL	Charles P. Wertenbaker Letterbooks, 1889–1913, Library of the University of Virginia, Special Collections
GFP	Garrison Family Papers, 1694–2005, Sophia Smith Collection, Smith College
HWP	Harry Weinberger Papers, 1915–1944, Yale University Library, Manuscripts and Archives
JCSP	John Coit Spooner Papers, Manuscript Division, Library of Congress
PCPW	Papers of Charles Poindexter Wertenbaker, 1878–1916, Library of the University of Virginia, Special Collections
SLL	Social Law Library, Boston
WFP	Wertenbaker Family Papers, Library of the University of Virginia, Special Collections
WTC	William T. Corlett photography collection, Dittrick Medical History Center Archives, Case Western Reserve University, Cleveland

Published Government Documents

ABOH 1883–84	*Report of the Board of Health of the State of Alabama, for the Years 1883 and 1884* (Montgomery, 1885)

BOSHD 1901   *Thirtieth Annual Report of the Health Department of the City of Boston for the Year 1901* (Boston, 1902)

BOSHD 1902   *Thirty-first Annual Report of the Health Department of the City of Boston for the Year 1902* (Boston, 1903)

CALBOH 1890–92   *Twelfth Biennial Report of the State Board of Health of California for the Fiscal Years from June 30, 1890, to June 30, 1892* (Sacramento, 1892)

CAMBOH 1901   City of Cambridge, *Annual Report of the Board of Health for the Year Ending November 30, 1901* (Cambridge, Mass., 1902)

CAMBOH 1902   City of Cambridge, *Annual Report of the Board of Health for the Year Ending December 31, 1902* (Cambridge, Mass., 1903)

DODGECOM   56th Congress, 1st Session, Senate Doc. No. 221, *Report of the Commission Appointed by the President to Investigate the Conduct of the War Department in the War with Spain* (Washington, 1900)

FBOH 1904   *Sixteenth Annual Report of the State Board of Health of Florida* (Jacksonville, 1905)

IBOH 1897   *Ninth Biennial Report of the Board of Health of the State of Iowa for the Fiscal Period Ending June 30, 1897* (Des Moines, 1897)

KBOH 1896–97   *Biennial Report of the State Board of Health of Kentucky, 1896–7* (Louisville, 1897)

KBOH 1898–99   *Biennial Report of the State Board of Health of Kentucky, 1898–9* (Louisville, 1899)

KBOH 1900–01   *Biennial Report of the State Board of Health of Kentucky, 1900–1901* (Louisville, 1901)

KBOH 1902–03   *Biennial Report of the State Board of Health of Kentucky, 1902–1903* (Louisville, 1904)

LBOH 1898–99   *Biennial Report of the Louisiana State Board of Health, 1898–1899* (Baton Rouge, 1900)

MBOH 1899–1901   *Biennial Report of the Board of Health of the State of Mississippi, from September 30th, 1899, to September 30th, 1901* (Jackson, 1901)

NCBOH 1897–98   *Seventh Annual Report of the North Carolina Board of Health, 1897–1898* (Raleigh, 1899)

NCBOH 1899–1900   *Eighth Biennial Report of the North Carolina Board of Health, 1899–1900* (Raleigh, 1900)

NCBOH 1903–04   *Tenth Biennial Report of the North Carolina Board of Health, 1903–1904* (Raleigh, 1905)

NJBOH 1901   *Twenty-fifth Annual Report of the Board of Health of the State of New Jersey and Report of the Bureau of Vital Statistics, 1901* (Trenton, 1902)

NJBOH 1902   *Twenty-sixth Annual Report of the Board of Health of the State of New Jersey, 1902* (Trenton, 1903)

NOBOH 1900–01   *Biennial Report of the Louisiana State Board of Health, 1900–1901. Part II: Report of the Board of Health of the City of New Orleans* (Baton Rouge, 1902)

NYCBOH 1901   *Annual Report of the Board of Health of the Department of Health of the City of New York for the Year Ending December 31, 1901* (New York, 1902)

NYCBOH 1902   *Annual Report of the Board of Health of the Department of Health of the City of New York for the Year Ending December 31, 1902* (New York, 1903)

NYCBOH 1903   *Annual Report of the Board of Health of the Department of Health of the City of New York for the Year Ending December 31, 1903* (New York, 1905)

PABOH 1900   *Sixteenth Annual Report of the State Board of Health and Vital Statistics of the Commonwealth of Pennsylvania* (1900) (State Printer, 1901)

PABOH 1903   *Nineteenth Annual Report of the State Board of Health and Vital Statistics of the Commonwealth of Pennsylvania* (1903) (State Printer, 1904)

PBOH 1901   *Third Annual Message of Samuel H. Ashbridge, Mayor of the City of Philadelphia, with Annual Reports of the Director of the Department of Public Safety and Bureau of Health, for the Year Ending December 31, 1901* (Philadelphia, 1902)

PBOH 1902   *Fourth Annual Message of Samuel H. Ashbridge, Mayor of the City of Philadelphia, with Annual Reports of the Director of the Department of Public Safety and the Bureau of Health, for the Year Ending December 31, 1902* (Philadelphia, 1903)

PHR   *Public Health Reports* (official journal of the U.S. Marine-Hospital Service, the federal agency which in 1902 became the U.S. Public Health and Marine-Hospital Service)

USCB 1900   United States Census Bureau, *Twelfth Census of the United States* (1900)

USMCSW   Walter Reed, Victor C. Vaughan, and Edward O. Shakespeare, *Abstract of Report on the Origin and Spread of Typhoid Fever in the U.S. Military Camps During the Spanish War of 1898* (Washington, 1900)

USPCRP 1900   U.S. Philippine Commission, *Report of the Philippine Commission to the President* (Washington, 1900)

USPCRP 1901   56th U.S. Congress, Senate Doc. No. 138, *Report of the Philippine Commission to the President* (Washington, 1901)

USPC 1904   U.S. War Department, Bureau of Insular Affairs, *Fifth Annual Report of the Philip-pine Commission, 1904* (Washington, 1905)

USPC 1905   59th U.S. Congress, 1st Session, H.R. Doc. No. 2, *Annual Reports of the War De-partment for the Fiscal Year Ended June 3, 1905, Vol. 11: Report of the Philippine Commission*, Part 2 (Washington, 1905)

USPC 1907   59th U.S. Congress, H.R. Doc. No. 2, *Annual Reports of the War Department for the Fiscal Year Ended June 30, 1906, Vol. 8: Report of the Philippine Commission*, Part 2 (Washington, 1907)

USPC 1908   War Department, *Annual Reports, 1908*, Vol. 8: *The Philippine Commission, Part II* (Washington, 1909)

USSGPHMHS 1894   *Annual Report of the Supervising Surgeon-General of the Marine-Hospital Service of the United States for the Fiscal Year 1894* (Washington, 1895)

USSGPHMHS 1898   *Annual Report of the Surgeon-General of the Marine-Hospital Service of the United States for the Fiscal Year 1898* (Washington, 1899)

USSGPHMHS 1899   *Annual Report of the Surgeon-General of the Marine-Hospital Service of the United States for the Fiscal Year 1899* (Washington, 1900)

USSGPHMHS 1900   *Annual Report of the Surgeon-General of the Marine-Hospital Service of the United States for the Fiscal Year 1900* (Washington, 1901)

USSGPHMHS 1901   *Annual Report of the Surgeon-General of the Marine-Hospital Service of the United States for the Fiscal Year 1901* (Washington, 1902)

USSGPHMHS 1902   *Annual Report of the Surgeon-General of the Public Health and Marine-Hospital Service of the United States for the Fiscal Year 1902* (Washington, 1903)

USSGPHMHS 1903   *Annual Report of the Surgeon-General of the Public Health and Marine-Hospital Service of the United States for the Fiscal Year 1903* (Washington, 1904)

USSGPHMHS 1904   *Annual Report of the Surgeon-General of the Public Health and Marine-Hospital Service of the United States for the Fiscal Year 1904* (Washington, 1905)

USSGPHMHS 1905   *Annual Report of the Surgeon-General of the Public Health and Marine-Hospital Service of the United States for the Fiscal Year 1905* (Washington, 1906)

USSGPHMHS 1907   *Annual Report of the Surgeon General of the Public Health and Marine-Hospital Service of the United States for the Fiscal Year 1907* (Washington, 1908)

USSGPHMHS 1908   *Annual Report of the Surgeon General of the Public Health and Marine-Hospital Service of the United States for the Fiscal Year 1908* (Washington, 1909)

USSGPHMHS 1909   *Annual Report of the Surgeon General of the Public Health and Marine-Hospital Service of the United States for the Fiscal Year 1909* (Washington, 1910)

USSGPHMHS 1910   Annual Report of the Surgeon General of the Public Health and Marine-Hospital
Service of the United States for the Fiscal Year 1910 (Washington, 1911)

USSGPHMHS 1911   Annual Report of the Surgeon General of the Public Health and Marine-Hospital
Service of the United States for the Fiscal Year 1911 (Washington, 1912)

USPRMG 1900   56th U.S. Congress, 2d Session, H.R. Doc. No. 2, *Annual Reports of the War Department for the Fiscal Year Ended June 30, 1900,* Part 3: *Report of the Military
Governor of Porto Rico on Civil Affairs* (Washington, 1902)

USROSENAU   Public Health and Marine-Hospital Service of the United States, Hygienic Laboratory Bulletin No. 12, Milton J. Rosenau, *The Bacteriological Impurities of Vaccine
Virus, An Experimental Study, March 1903* (Washington, 1903)

USSCOP   57th U.S. Congress, 1st Session, Senate Doc. No. 331, *Affairs in the Philippine Islands. Hearings Before the Committee on the Philippines of the United States Senate*
(Washington, 1902)

USWDAR 1898   55th U.S. Congress, 3d Session, H.R. Doc. No. 2, *Annual Reports of the War Department for the Fiscal Year Ended June 30, 1898: Report of the Secretary of War.
Miscellaneous Reports* (Washington, 1898)

USWDAR 1899   56th U.S. Congress, 1st Session, H.R. Doc. No. 2, *Annual Reports of the War Department for the Fiscal Year Ended June 30, 1899* (Washington, 1899)

Frequently Cited Journals

ADPR   American Druggist and Pharmaceutical Record

AJPH   American Journal of Public Health

AIM   Annals of Internal Medicine

BHM   Bulletin of the History of Medicine

BMJ   Buffalo Medical Journal

BMSJ   Boston Medical and Surgical Journal

BRMJ   British Medical Journal

CLJ   Central Law Journal

CMJ   Cleveland Medical Journal

ILLMJ   Illinois Medical Journal

JAMA   Journal of the American Medical Association

JHMAS   Journal of the History of Medicine and Allied Sciences

MC	*Medical Communications* (Massachusetts Medical Society)
MN	*Medical News*
MR	*Medical Record*
NEJM	*New England Journal of Medicine*
NYMJ	*New York Medical Journal*
PHPR	*Public Health Papers and Reports*
PMJ	*Philadelphia Medical Journal*
PSM	*Popular Science Monthly*
SCI	*Science*
YMJ	*Yale Medical Journal*

Frequently Cited Newspapers

AC	*Atlanta Constitution*
BG	*Boston Globe*
BS	*Baltimore Sun*
CC	*Cambridge Chronicle*
CO	*Charlotte Daily Observer* (North Carolina)
CT	*Chicago Tribune*
DMN	*Dallas Morning News*
LAT	*Los Angeles Times*
LMH	*Lexington Morning Herald*
MWH	*Middlesboro Weekly Herald* (Kentucky)
MWR	*Middlesboro Weekly Record* (Kentucky)
NYEW	*New York Evening World*
NOP	*New Orleans Picayune*
NYS	*New York Sun*

NYT   *New York Times*

NYTRIB   *New York Tribune*

NYW   *New York World*

OSE   Ogden *Standard-Examiner* (Utah)

PI   *Philadelphia Inquirer*

PNA   *Philadelphia North American*

RNO   *Raleigh News and Observer* (North Carolina)

SFC   *San Francisco Call*

SLH   *Salt Lake Herald*

WM   *Wilmington Messenger* (North Carolina)

WP   *Washington Post*

PROLOGUE

1. U.S. Census Bureau, *Twelfth Census of the United States* (1900), Schedule 1—Population, Manhattan, New York, New York, District 461. Note: all enumeration district-level census data cited in the notes to follow was retrieved using the U.S. Federal Census Collection in the online database Ancestry Library Edition, ancestry.com (Provo, UT). "Smallpox on West Side," *NYT*, Nov. 30, 1900, 2. Robert W. DeForest and Lawrence Veiller, eds., *The Tenement House Problem: Including the Report of the New York State Tenement House Commission of 1900* (New York: MacMillan, 1903), 53.
2. "Jumped Through a Window," *NYT*, Nov. 29, 1900, 4. "West Side Robberies," *NYT*, Nov. 29, 1900, 5. "Chinaman Whips a Gang," *NYT*, Dec. 6, 1900, 2.
3. "Smallpox in Manhattan," *NYT*, Nov. 28, 1900, 3. "Chemists Report on Water," *NYT*, Nov. 29, 1900, 5. For a concise contemporary description of the pathology of smallpox, see U.S. Treasury Department, Public Health and Marine-Hospital Service, *Handbook for the Ship's Medicine Chest*, by George W. Stoner, M.D., 2d ed. (Washington: Government Printing Office, 1904), 21–24.
4. "Smallpox in Manhattan."
5. Ibid. On the New York City Health Department, see John Duffy, *A History of Public Health in New York City, 1866–1966* (New York: Russell Sage Foundation, 1974); Evelynn Maxine Hammonds, *Childhood's Deadly Scourge: The Campaign to Control Diphtheria in New York City, 1880–1930* (Baltimore: The Johns Hopkins University Press, 1999).
6. "Smallpox on West Side." "Columbia Beat Indians," *NYT*, Nov. 30, 1900, 8. "Thanksgiving Day Cheer," *NYT*, Nov. 30, 1900, 3.
7. D. H. Bergey, *The Principles of Hygiene: A Practical Manual for Students, Physicians, and Health-Officers* (Philadelphia: W. B Saunders, 1904), 374. George Henry Fox, *A Practical Treatise on Smallpox* (Philadelphia: J. B. Lippincott Company, 1902), 26–31. Dr. Fox was the consulting dermatologist to the New York City Health Department.
8. "Smallpox on West Side." "Fighting the Smallpox," *NYT*, Dec. 1, 1900, 16.

9. William Welch and Jay F. Schamberg, *Acute Contagious Diseases* (Philadelphia: Lea Brothers & Co., 1905), 160. For the state-of-the-art scientific knowledge about smallpox, as it existed in the United States circa 1900, see Surgeon General Walter Wyman's "Précis Upon the Diagnosis and Treatment of Smallpox," *PHR*, 14 (Jan. 6, 1899), 37–49. The authoritative modern treatise on the subject is F. Fenner et al., *Smallpox and Its Eradication* (Geneva: World Health Organization, 1988). See also Ian Glynn and Jenifer Glynn, *The Life and Death of Smallpox* (New York: Cambridge University Press, 2004); D. A. Henderson, *Smallpox: The Death of a Disease* (Amherst, NY: Prometheus Books, 2009), esp. 34.

10. "Fighting the Smallpox."

11. On the germ theory and its reception in the United States, see Nancy Tomes, *The Gospel of Germs: Men, Women, and the Microbe in American Life* (Cambridge, MA: Harvard University Press, 1998).

12. "The Spread of Small-pox by Tramps," *Lancet*, Feb. 13, 1904, 446–47. See also "Smallpox and Tramps," *JAMA*, 22 (1894): 635.

13. "Smallpox on West Side." "Fighting the Smallpox." "Smallpox up the State," *NYT*, Jan. 4, 1901, 3. "New York," *PHR*, 16 (Feb. 8, 1901): 238–39. See W. Michael Byrd and Linda A. Cayton, *An American Health Dilemma: A Medical History of African Americans and the Problem of Race*, 2 vols. (New York: Routledge, 2000, 2002).

14. "Fighting the Smallpox." "Race Riot on West Side," *NYT*, Aug. 16, 1900, 1.

15. "Forty Smallpox Cases," *NYT*, Dec. 5, 1900, 5; "Smallpox Case in Hoboken," *NYT*, Dec. 3, 1900, 5. "The Smallpox Epidemic," *NYT*, Dec. 4, 1900, 8.

16. "Fighting the Smallpox." "Two New Smallpox Cases," *NYT*, Dec. 7, 1900, 2. "Smallpox Still Spreading," *NYT*, Dec. 15, 1900, 6.

17. "Smallpox Epidemic."

18. "Smallpox Epidemic." "Topics of the Times," *NYT*, Dec. 12, 1900, 8. See Michael Willrich, *City of Courts: Socializing Justice in Progressive Era Chicago* (New York: Cambridge University Press, 2003).

19. *NOBOH 1900–01*, 23. *PBOH 1902*, 38. Michael R. Albert et al., "The Last Smallpox Epidemic in Boston and the Vaccination Controversy, 1901–1903," *NEJM*, 344 (1901), 375. *NYCBOH 1901*, 7–9, 56. *NYCBOH 1902*, 8–9. *NYCBOH 1903*, 8, 238. See James Nevins Hyde, "The Late Epidemic of Smallpox in the United States," *PSM*, 59 (Oct. 1901): 557–67; and Charles Fletcher Scott, "The Fight Against Smallpox," *Ainslee's Magazine,* July 1902, 540–45.

20. *USSGPHMHS 1898*, 598. *USSGPHMHS 1901*, 15. *USSGPHMHS 1903, 72. USSGPHMHS 1904*, 19. The Service fiscal year ran from July 1 to June 30. On underreporting, see *USSGPHMHS 1899*, 755–56; *USSGPHMHS 1910*, 189. "Echoes and News," *MN*, Sept. 21, 1901, 470. "The number of cases notified each year represents at most 20% of those that actually occurred; many patients did not see a physician and many others who did were not reported as having smallpox." Fenner et al., *Smallpox and Its Eradication*, 329. From my own research, I judge Fenner's 20 percent figure to be very conservative.

21. *USSGPHMHS 1903*, 72. *USCB 1900*, Vol. 4—*Vital Statistics Part II, Statistics of Death*, 228.

22. Welch and Schamberg, *Acute Contagious Diseases*, 207–8. Charles V. Chapin, "Variation in Type of Infectious Disease as Shown by the History of Smallpox in the United States, 1895–1912," *Journal of Infectious Diseases*, 13 (1913), 194.

23. Pamela Sankar et al., "Public Mistrust: The Unrecognized Risk of the CDC Smallpox Vaccination Program," *American Journal of Bioethics*, 3 (2003), esp. W22. Edward A. Belongia and Allison Naleway, "Smallpox Vaccine: The Good, the Bad, and the Ugly," *Clinical Medicine and Research*, 1 (2003): 87–92. Vincent A. Fulginiti et al., "Smallpox Vaccination: A Review, Part II. Adverse

Effects," *Clinical Infectious Diseases*, 37 (2003): 251–71. Welch and Schamberg, *Acute Contagious Diseases*, 58–83.

24. The literature on American antivaccinationism is growing, and it is no longer easy to dismiss the movement, as John Duffy once did, as "filled with cranks, extremists, and charlatans." *History of Public Health in New York City,* 152. See, esp., James Colgrove, "'Science in a Democracy': The Contested Status of Vaccination in the Progressive Era and the 1920s," *Isis*, 96 (2005): 167–91; idem, *State of Immunity: The Politics of Vaccination in Twentieth-Century America* (Berkeley: University of California Press, 2006); Nadav Davidovitch, "Negotiating Dissent: Homeopathy and Antivaccinationism at the Turn of the Twentieth Century," in *The Politics of Healing: Histories of Alternative Medicine in Twentieth-Century North America,* ed. Robert D. Johnston (New York: Routledge, 2004), 11–28; Robert D. Johnston, *The Radical Middle Class: Populist Democracy and the Question of Capitalism in Progressive Era Portland, Oregon* (Princeton: Princeton University Press, 2003), 177–220; idem, "Contemporary Anti-Vaccination Movements in Historical Perspective," in Johnston, ed., *Politics of Healing*, 259–86. Martin Kaufman, "The American Anti-Vaccinationists and Their Arguments," *BHM*, 50 (1976): 553–68; Judith Walzer Leavitt, *The Healthiest City: Milwaukee and the Politics of Health Reform* (Princeton: Princeton University Press, 1982), 76–121. On England, see Nadja Durbach, *Bodily Matters: The Anti-Vaccination Movement in England, 1853–1907* (Durham: Duke University Press Books, 2005). For an overview, see Arthur Allen, *Vaccine: The Controversial Story of Medicine's Greatest Lifesaver* (New York: W. W. Norton, 2007).

25. Chapin, "Variation in Type," 194.

26. "The Vaccination Question and the Purity of Vaccine," *Therapeutic Gazette*, 26 (1902): 98–99.

27. For an excellent revision of the conventional periodization of free speech, see David M. Rabban, *Free Speech in Its Forgotten Years* (New York: Cambridge University Press, 1997). Holmes to Hand, June 24, 1918, in Gerald Gunther, "Learned Hand and the Origins of Modern First Amendment Doctrine: Some Fragments of History," *Stanford Law Review*, 27 (1975), Appendix, 757.

28. Michael Willrich, "'The Least Vaccinated of Any Civilized Country': Personal Liberty and Public Health in the Progressive Era," *Journal of Policy History*, 20 (2008): 76–93.

ONE: BEGINNINGS

1. Henry F. Long, "Smallpox in Iredell County," *NCBOH 1897–98*, 208.

2. U.S. Census Bureau, *Twelfth Census of the United States* (1900): Schedule No. 1—Population, Iredell County, North Carolina. "Dr. John F. Long Dead," *CO*, Apr. 29, 1899, 4. Federal Writers' Project, *North Carolina: A Guide to the Old North State* (Chapel Hill: University of North Carolina Press, 1939), 71–78, 401–7. Hugh Talmage Lefler and Albert Ray Newsome, *North Carolina: The History of a Southern State* (Chapel Hill: University of North Carolina Press, 1954), 481–83.

3. Long, "Smallpox in Iredell County," 214. My account of Harvey Perkins's case also draws upon "From Bulletin, February 1898," in *NCBOH 1897–98*, 82–85; C. P. Wertenbaker, "Smallpox at Statesville, N.C.," *PHR*, 13 (Jun. 24, 1898), 634–35; and "Harvey Perkins Dead," *CO*, Feb. 22, 1898, 6.

4. Long, "Smallpox in Iredell County," 208.

5. *USSGPHMHS 1898*, 627, 598–99. "Warning Against Smallpox," Mar. 25, 1898, in *KBOH 1898–99*, 23. C. P. Wertenbaker, "Investigation of Smallpox at Columbia and Sumter, S.C.," *PHR*, 13 (May 13, 1898), 470. See "From Bulletin, February 1898," in *NCBOH 1897–98*, 82; "Smallpox in the United States as Reported to the Supervising Surgeon-General United States Marine-Hospital Service, December 29, 1896, to December 31, 1897," *PHR*, 12 (Dec. 31, 1897), 1421–22; C. P. Wertenbaker, "Smallpox at Middleborough, Ky.," *PHR*, 13 (Mar. 25, 1898), 273–74. See also W. Michael Byrd and

Linda A. Clayton, *An American Health Dilemma, Vol. 1: A Medical History of African Americans and the Problem of Race: Beginnings to 1900* (New York: Routledge, 2000), 322–414.

6. "From Bulletin, January 1898," *NCBOH 1897–98*, 80. "From Bulletin, February 1898," ibid., 84. C. P. Wertenbaker, "One Case of Smallpox in Wilmington, N.C.," *PHR*, 13 (Jan. 14, 1898), 25. C. P. Wertenbaker, "Investigation of Smallpox at Charlotte, N.C.," *PHR*, 13 (Feb. 18, 1898), 140–41.

7. C. P. Wertenbaker's transmission to Mayor E. B. Springs is published in "From Bulletin, February 1898," 84.

8. Ibid., 84. "Harvey Perkins Dead."

9. "From Bulletin, February 1898," 85.

10. Long, "Smallpox in Iredell County," 210. Lewis, "Annual Report of the Secretary," 28. C. P. Wertenbaker, "Smallpox at Statesville, N.C.," 634–35.

11. Long, "Smallpox in Iredell County," 216.

12. Dr. H. Y. Webb, "Smallpox in Greene County," *ABOH 1883–84*, 129.

13. At the turn of the century, public health reports in many places had yet to adopt a standardized, bureaucratic format. The biennial reports issued by the Kentucky and North Carolina boards of health, for example, as well as the weekly *Public Health Reports* published by the U.S. Marine-Hospital Service, consisted chiefly of letters and telegraphic transmissions from local health authorities, who leavened their smallpox dispatches with a wealth of local social and political detail. On the dramaturgic character of epidemics as social events, see Charles E. Rosenberg, "What Is an Epidemic? AIDS in Historical Perspective," in *Explaining Epidemics and Other Studies in the History of Medicine* (New York: Cambridge University Press, 1992), 278–92.

14. *KBOH 1898–99*, 61, 81, 133, 92. *PHR*, 14 (Mar. 3, 1899), 278. *PHR*, 13 (Jul. 29, 1898), 781. "Vigorous Measures Have Been Adopted," *The State* (Columbia, SC), Apr. 5, 1898, 2.

15. James Nevins Hyde, "The Late Epidemic of Smallpox in the United States," *PSM*, 59 (Oct. 1901), 557–67, esp. 557.

16. H. F. Long, "Report of the State Small-Pox Inspector," *NCBOH 1899–1900*, 29.

17. "Thou shalt not be afraid for the terror by night; nor for the arrow that flieth by day; Nor for the pestilence that walketh in darkness; nor for the destruction that wasteth at noonday." —King James Bible, Psalm 91:5–6.
    This psalm was quoted, albeit inaccurately, in the most important vaccination decision handed down by the North Carolina Supreme Court. In the majority opinion, Justice Clark insisted upon the right of the community to protect itself against "the deadly pestilence that walketh by noonday." *State v. W. E. Hay*, 126 N.C. 999, 1001 (1900).

18. *KBOH 1896–97*, 46–47. *KBOH 1898–99*, 30.

19. Col. A. W. Shaffer, "Small-pox and Vaccination for Plain People. By One of Them," *NCBOH 1897–98*, 173.

20. F. Fenner et al., *Smallpox and Its Eradication*, (Geneva, 1988), 217–44, esp. 210, 217. Sergei N. Shchelkunov, "How Long Ago Did Smallpox Virus Emerge?" *Archives of Virology*, 154 (2009): 1865–71. See also Ian Glynn and Jenifer Glynn, *The Life and Death of Smallpox*, 6–54, esp. 4; and Donald R. Hopkins, *Princes and Peasants: Smallpox in History* (Chicago: University of Chicago Press, 1983).

21. By "natural" host range, I mean outside the laboratory. See S. S. Kalter et al., "Experimental Smallpox in Chimpanzees," *Bulletin of the World Health Organization*, 57 (1979): 637–41. For a useful overview of the virology of variola and the other orthopoxviruses, see Fenner et al., *Smallpox and Its Eradication*, 69–119.

22. See C.-E. A. Winslow, "Communicable Diseases, Control Of," in *Encyclopaedia of the Social Sciences*, ed. Edwin R. Seligman (New York: MacMillan, 1937), vol. 3: 66–78. The death toll figure is from Richard Preston, "The Demon in the Freezer," *New Yorker*, July 12, 1999, 47. See also Preston's

Foreword to D. A. Henderson, *Smallpox: The Death of a Disease* (Amherst, NY: Prometheus Books, 2009), 12.

23. U.S. Treasury Department, Public Health and Marine-Hospital Service, *Handbook for the Ship's Medicine Chest*, by George W. Stoner, M.D., 2d ed., 21. See also Fenner et al., *Smallpox and Its Eradication*, 117.

24. Macaulay quoted in Hopkins, *Princes and Peasants*, 38. Glynn and Glynn, *Life and Death of Smallpox*, 1, 4. Fenner et al., *Smallpox and Its Eradication*, 169–208.

25. Jennifer Lee Carrell, *The Speckled Monster: A Historical Tale of Battling Smallpox* (New York: Dutton, 2003). Fenner et al., *Smallpox and Its Eradication*, 224, 229. Henderson, *Smallpox*, 40–43. Mary Beth Norton et al., *A People and a Nation: A History of the United States*, 6th ed. (Boston: Houghton Mifflin, 2001), 26. See Alfred W. Crosby, *The Columbian Exchange: Biological and Cultural Consequences of 1492* (Westport, CT: Greenwood, 1972). For a compelling reconsideration of the "virgin soil" theory, see David S. Jones, "Virgin Soils Revisited," *William and Mary Quarterly*, 60 (2003): 703–42.

26. Fenner et al., *Smallpox and Its Eradication*, 224.

27. "Précis upon the Diagnosis and Treatment of Smallpox," *PHR*, 14 (Jan. 6, 1899), 37–49. Hopkins, *Princes and Peasants*, 13. Preston, "Demon in the Freezer," 48.

28. Fenner et al., *Smallpox and Its Eradication*, 71.

29. "Smallpox in the United States as Reported to the Supervising Surgeon-General United States Marine-Hospital Service, January 1 to December 30, 1898," *PHR* (Dec. 30, 1898), 1559–62.

30. "Précis." The following description of the clinical course of smallpox relies heavily on the exhaustive research compiled by a team of World Health Organization scientists in Fenner et al., *Smallpox and Its Eradication*, esp. chs. 1 and 3. Running more than 1,400 pages, the tome is often referred to as "The Big Red Book of Smallpox." It is by far the single most comprehensive source on the science of smallpox and vaccination.

  For a more concise medical discussion of the pathology of smallpox, see Hopkins, *Princes and Peasants*, 3–9. Like Frank Fenner and his coauthors, Dr. Hopkins, a physician and epidemiologist, worked in the WHO smallpox eradication program.

31. "Précis," 38.

32. "Smallpox Rumor," *CO*, Feb. 26, 1898, 6. Fenner et al., *Smallpox and Its Eradication*, 266, 45. Hopkins, *Princes and Peasants*, 3.

33. "Précis," 38. Fenner et al., *Smallpox and Its Eradication*, 5, 44, 167. See also Michael R. Albert et al., "Smallpox Manifestations and Survival during the Boston Epidemic of 1901 to 1903," *AIM*, 137 (Dec. 17, 2002): 993–1000, esp. 993.

34. "Précis," 38. See also Fenner et al., *Smallpox and Its Eradication*, 6; Michael Kelly, "Small-Pox: Its Medical Treatment," *MC*, Jan. 1, 1902, 171.

35. Long, "Smallpox in Iredell County," 214. Hopkins, *Princes and Peasants*, 277–81, esp. 277.

36. J. C. Wilson, *Fever-Nursing*, 2d ed. (Philadelphia: J. B. Lippincott Company, 1895), 165. Fenner et al., *Smallpox and Its Eradication*, 19, 189.

37. On the names of smallpox, see Fenner et al., *Smallpox and Its Eradication*, 229; Preston, "Demon in the Freezer," 44.

38. "Précis," 38–39. Preston, "Demon in the Freezer," 47. Fenner et al., *Smallpox and Its Eradication*, 19, 21, 56, 130. See also Stoner, *Handbook for the Ship's Medicine Chest*, 21.

39. "Précis," 37, 38.

40. Long, "Smallpox in Iredell County," 216.

41. Stoner, *Handbook for the Ship's Medicine Chest*, 21, 22. "Précis," 39. Long, "Smallpox in Iredell County," 215–16. Fenner et al., *Smallpox and Its Eradication*, 19, 22.

42. Long, "Smallpox in Iredell County," 217. "Report of Dr. Llewellyn Eliot, M.D.," July 1, 1895, in *Annual Report of the Commissioners of the District of Columbia For the Year Ended June 30, 1895,*

Serial Set Vol. No. 3391, Session Vol. No. 24, 54th U.S. Congress, H.R. Doc. 7, p. 1296. Fenner et al., *Smallpox and Its Eradication*, 68.

43. Fenner et al., *Smallpox and Its Eradication*, 50–54.

44. "Supply of Coffins Is Short," *AC*, Mar. 8, 1900, 8. See "Guarding Public Health," ibid., Mar. 23, 1901, 3; "Will Not Ask for Increase," ibid., Dec. 11, 1901, 4.

45. "Précis," 39. Fenner et al., *Smallpox and Its Eradication*, 22, 139, 167.

46. "Précis," 38–39. Fenner et al., *Smallpox and Its Eradication*, 32, 4, 167. Preston, "Demon in the Freezer," 50. See also Stoner, *Handbook for the Ship's Medicine Chest*, 22.

47. WTC. The image of the scarred man is #1500, titled "Small Pox (after recovery)."

48. See, for example, the display advertisement for the John H. Woodbury Dermatological Institute in New York City, *NYT*, Jan. 26, 1908, 6; and "Woman Choked to Death," ibid., Jul. 15, 1910, 7. See also "Sheriff's Department," *Houston Post*, Feb. 15, 1897, 6; "Priest's Murder Was Incited by a Rare Jewel," *NYEW*, May 27, 1907, 2.

49. See generally John Duffy, *The Sanitarians: A History of American Public Health* (Urbana and Chicago: University of Illinois Press, 1990); idem, *From Humors to Medical Science: A History of American Medicine*, 2d ed. (Urbana and Chicago: University of Illinois Press, 1993); Gerald Grob, *The Deadly Truth: A History of Disease in America* (Cambridge, MA: Harvard University Press, 2002). Nancy Tomes, *The Gospel of Germs: Men, Women, and the Microbe in American Life* (Cambridge, MA: Harvard University Press, 1998). For a concise overview, see C.-E. A. Winslow, "Public Health," in *Encyclopaedia of the Social Sciences*, ed. Edwin R. A. Seligman, vol. 11, 646–57. The best introduction to the legal aspects of public health administration in the early twentieth century is James A. Tobey, *Public Health Law: A Manual of Law for Sanitarians* (Baltimore: The Williams & Wilkins Co., 1926).

50. Fenner et al., *Smallpox and Its Eradication*, 146.

51. Elizabeth A. Fenn, *Pox Americana: The Great Smallpox Epidemic of 1775–82* (New York: Hill and Wang, 2001). Fenner et al., *Smallpox and Its Eradication*, 217, 245–58. Hopkins, *Princes and Peasants*, 249–53.

52. Fenner et al., *Smallpox and Its Eradication*, 258–73.

53. James Gillray, "The Cow Pock—or—the Wonderful Effects of the New Inoculation!" The cartoon appeared in *Vide—The Publications of the Anti-Vaccine Society*, June 12, 1802. It is now held in the National Library of Medicine Collection, and may be viewed in vivid color at http://www.nlm.nih.gov/hmd/frankenstein/frank_promise.html, accessed November 9, 2006. For a fascinating discussion of the cultural context, see Tim Fulford and Debbie Lee, "The Jenneration of Disease: Vaccination, Romanticism, and Revolution," *Studies in Romanticism*, 39 (2000): 139–64.

54. "Précis," 42.

55. "Précis," 39–40, esp. 40. Fenner et al., *Smallpox and Its Eradication*, 27, 65.

56. Peter Baldwin, *Contagion and the State in Europe, 1830–1930* (Cambridge: Cambridge University Press, 1999), 244–354. See also Fenner et al., *Smallpox and Its Eradication*, 258–76.

57. See generally Tobey, *Public Health Law*.

58. According to the "Précis," "The French army numbered 23,000 deaths by it [smallpox], while the German army had only 278." "Précis," 43. I am using the numbers here from Fenner et al., *Smallpox and Its Eradication*, 232, assuming them to be more accurate.

59. "Précis," 43. *USSGPHMHS 1898*, 630.

60. For phony certificates, see "Vaccination Certificate Frauds," *NYT*, May 9, 1904, 8. For evidence of families taking care of their own (and then being discovered by the authorities), see "Smallpox Nest in Brooklyn," ibid., Mar. 20, 1901, 2; "Defies the Health Board" (Harrison, NJ), ibid., Jul. 27, 1901, 2; "Fight for a Sick Child" (Newark, NJ), ibid., Nov. 12, 1901, 3. For escapes from quarantines or pesthouses, see "'Mother' Jones Arrested" (in a Utah mining camp), ibid., Apr. 27, 1904, 3. For resistance to vaccination in other U.S. settings, see "Miners Resist Vaccination" (Lead, SD), ibid.,

Apr. 25, 1902, 1; "Object to Vaccination" (African American railway workers on the Western Maryland Improvement), *WP*, May 3, 1901, 9. For Filipino resistance to U.S. compulsory vaccination in the Philippines, see "Manila Is Healthful," *NYT*, Aug. 19, 1903, 8. Note these are just a few examples, and they are taken only from the first few years of the twentieth century. I also have collected many examples from the 1890s and further into the decades of the 1900s and 1910s.

61. "Smallpox and Vaccination," *BMJ*, 40 (Feb. 1901), 525.
62. See for example C. P. Wertenbaker, "Investigation of Smallpox at Columbia and Sumter, S.C.," *PHR*, 13 (May 13, 1898), 468–70.

TWO: THE MILD TYPE

1. G. M. Magruder, "Passed Assistant Surgeon Magruder's Report on Smallpox at Little Rock, Ark.," *PHR*, 13 (May 6, 1898), 437. See Louis Leroy, *Smallpox: Its Diagnosis, Treatment, Restriction and Prevention, with a Few Remarks upon the Present Epidemic*, issued by the Tennessee State Board of Health (Nashville: Tennessee State Board of Health, 1900).
2. See Charles V. Chapin, "Variation in Type of Infectious Disease as Shown by the History of Smallpox in the United States 1895–1912," *Journal of Infectious Diseases*, 13 (1913), 171–96, esp. 173; Charles V. Chapin and Joseph Smith, "Permanency of the Mild Type of Smallpox," *Journal of Preventive Medicine*, 6 (1932): 273–320.
3. C. P. Wertenbaker, "Plan of Organization for the Suppression of Smallpox," p. 62, typescript in CPWL, vol. 6.
4. On public health administration in the southern United States, see Francis R. Allen, "Development of the Public Health Movement in the Southeast," *Social Forces*, 22 (1943): 67–75. On the lack of administrative systems for tracking disease and vital statistics in the states, especially in the South, see *USSGPHMHS 1910*, 189; *USSGPHMHS 1911*, 241; U.S. Census Bureau, *A Discussion of the Vital Statistics of the Twelfth Census*, by Dr. John Shaw Billings (Washington, 1904), esp. 7–8; and Chapin, "Variation in Type," 171–72.
5. "Warning Against Small-Pox," Feb. 15, 1898, *KBOH 1898–99*, 22. See Chapin, "Variation in Type," 173, 174; G. M. Magruder, "Work of the Service in Suppressing Smallpox in Alabama," *PHR*, 13 (Mar. 18, 1898), 246–51; *KBOH 1900–01*, 17; *NCBOH 1903–04*, 13; *USSGPHMHS 1898*, 598–99.
6. Richard H. Lewis, "Annual Report of the Secretary of the North Carolina Board of Health, 1898–99," in *NCBOH 1899–1900*, 23. See, e.g., C. P. Wertenbaker, "The Smallpox Outbreak in Bristol, Va.-Tenn.," *PHR*, 14 (Nov. 3, 1899), 1890; "Value of Vaccination," *PHR*, 14 (Feb. 10, 1899), 180.
7. *LBOH 1898–99*, 55, 129. *NOBOH 1900–01*, 23–24. "Guarding Public Health," *AC*, Mar. 23, 1901, 3. As late as 1909, Surgeon General Wyman said no one could predict "whether" the mild type of smallpox would "change to the more usual fatal form." *USSGPHMHS 1909*, 201.
8. Chapin, "Variation in Type," 196. In 1932, Chapin and his coauthor Joseph Smith published another major scientific article on the subject; Chapin and Smith, "Permanency of the Mild Type," esp. 319, emphasis added. The authors observed: "The statement should rather be, that it [mild type smallpox] has *for the most part* bred true, for it is not intended to prejudge the question whether it *ever* reverts to the classical type. That it does not revert is the belief of practically all American epidemiologists who have had experience with this disease." Ibid., 276. See Fenner et al., *Smallpox and Its Eradication*, 96.
9. Fenner et al., *Smallpox and Its Eradication*, 3, 96–103, 329–32. K. R. Dumbell and Farida Huq, "The Virology of Variola Minor Correlation of Laboratory Tests with the Geographic Distribution and Human Virulence of Variola Isolates," *American Journal of Epidemiology*, 123 (1986): 403–15.
10. Fenner et al., *Smallpox and Its Eradication*, 3.
11. Chapin, "Variation in Type." 171–96. Charles and Smith, "Permanency of the Mild Type." Fenner

et al., *Smallpox and Its Eradication*, 3, 96–103, 329–32. J. Pickford Marsden, "Variola Minor: A Personal Analysis of 13,686 Cases," *Bulletin of Hygiene*, 23 (1948): 735–46.

12. The phrase "creative destruction" comes, of course, from Joseph A. Schumpeter, *Capitalism, Socialism and Democracy* (New York: Harper and Brothers, 1942).

13. On the fascinating history of Middlesboro, see Harry M. Caudill, *Theirs Be the Power: The Moguls of Eastern Kentucky* (Urbana: University of Illinois Press, 1983), 16–35; John Gaventa, *Power and Powerlessness: Quiescence and Rebellion in an Appalachian Valley* (Urbana: University of Illinois Press, 1980); Kenneth W. Kuehn et al., eds. *Geologic Impacts on the History and Development of Middlesboro, Kentucky* (Lexington: Kentucky Society of Professional Geologists, 2003); Ann Dudley Matheny, *The Magic City: Footnotes to the History of Middlesborough, Kentucky, and the Yellow Creek Valley* (Middlesboro, KY: Bell County Historical Society, 2003).

14. Quoted in Gaventa, *Power and Powerlessness*, 47. See ibid., 47–83. On British investment in the United States, see Eric Rauchway, *Blessed Among Nations: How the World Made America* (New York: Hill and Wang, 2006), 42–52, esp. 48.

15. Katie Algeo, "Historical Overview: Settlement History of the Cumberland Gap Region," in Kuehn et al., eds., *Geologic Impacts*, 3–8.

16. 55th U.S. Congress, 2d Session, H.R. Doc. 10, *Annual Report of the Comptroller of the Currency* (Washington, 1897), vol. I: 496–97. "Encouraging. Middlesborough Town and Lands Company Has a Meeting in London," *MWH*, Dec. 3, 1897, 4. See Algeo, "Historical Overview," 7–8; Gaventa, *Power and Powerlessness*, 76–78; Matheny, *Magic City*, xxii–xxiv, 102–21.

17. "Mingo," *MWH*, Nov. 26, 1897, 1. "Furnaces," ibid., 4. Untitled editorial, *MWR*, Feb. 24, 1898, 4. See also "Encouraging," *MWH*, Dec. 3, 1897, 4. On school enrollments, see "Report of Public School for November," ibid., Dec. 3, 1897, 1. *USCB 1900*, Vol. I—Population, Part I (Washington, 1901), 618. U.S. Census Bureau, *Twelfth Census of the United States* (1900): Schedule No. 1—Population: Bell County, Kentucky, Middlesboro, Enumeration Districts 18 and 19. For a warmer portrait of race relations in Middlesboro, see Matheny, *Magic City*, 127–32.

18. U.S. Census Bureau, *Negroes in the United States* (Washington, 1904), 11, 13, 60. Herbert R. Northrup, "The Coal Mines," in *Blacks in Appalachia*, ed. William H. Turner and Edward J. Cabbell (Lexington: The University Press of Kentucky, 1985), 159–71. On rural industry in the South, see Jacqueline Jones, *The Dispossessed: America's Underclasses from the Civil War to the Present* (New York: Basic Books, 1992), 127–66. On post–Civil War railroad development in Appalachia, see Robert L. Frey, "Railroads," in *Encyclopedia of Appalachia*, ed. Rudy Abramson and Jean Haskell (Knoxville: University of Tennessee Press, 2006), 715–17.

19. G. M. Magruder, "Work of the Service in Suppressing Smallpox in Alabama," *PHR*, 13 (Mar. 18, 1898), 246. "A Big Scare," *MWR*, Nov. 18, 1897, 1. "Unwarranted," *MWH*, Nov. 19, 1897, 4.

20. "A Big Scare," *MWR*, Nov. 18, 1897, 1.

21. L. L. Robertson, "Bell County Board of Health," in *KBOH 1900–01*, 24–25. "Laws, Rules and Regulations," in *KBOH 1898–99*, 177–78. "A Big Scare," *MWR*, Nov. 18, 1897, 1. "Unwarranted," *MWH*, Nov. 19, 1897, 4.

22. "Laws, Rules and Regulations," in *KBOH 1898–99*, 173–80, 186. *Nelson County Court v. Town of Bardstown*, Superior Court of Kentucky (1885) in ibid., 173–76, esp. 176.

23. On the state board's vaccination estimates, see "The State Board of Health Urges All Kentucky Cities and Towns to Take Prompt Action," *LMH*, Feb. 8, 1899, 4. For the Middlesboro estimate, see Matheny, *Magic City*, 226.

24. "Unwarranted," *MWH*, Nov. 19, 1897, 4. Untitled editorial, *MWR*, Nov. 18, 1897, 4. See also "Smallpox," *LMH*, Nov. 17, 1897, 1.

25. "Quarantine Raised," *MWH*, Dec. 10, 1897, 4.

26. See "Quarantine Jottings," *MWR*, Feb. 17, 1898, 2.

27. "Aunt Mariah _____," *MWR*, Feb. 24, 1898, 2. Due to the poor quality of the microfilm, the last part of the headline is illegible.

28. "Chicken-Pox," *MWR*, Nov. 26, 1897, 5. "Quarantine Raised," ibid., Dec. 10, 1897, 4. "Smallpox," ibid., Feb. 3, 1898, 3. *KBOH 1898–99*, 21.

29. *Tazewell Progress* quoted in untitled editorial, *MWR*, Feb. 10, 1898, 4. "Smallpox," ibid., Feb. 3, 1898, 3. See Matheny, *Magic City*, 228.

30. See "Laws, Rules and Regulations," in *KBOH 1898–99*, 171–86.

31. Judge Charles Kerr, ed., *History of Kentucky* (New York: American Historical Society, 1922), vol. 4: 450. John E. Kleber, ed., *The Kentucky Encyclopedia* (Lexington: The University Press of Kentucky, 1992), 592. The best sources on J. N. McCormack's ideas and work are the reports of the state board.

32. *KBOH 1898–99*, 28.

33. J. N. McCormack viewed the quarantine power as "an indispensable weapon" against "counties and towns whose authorities failed or refused to adopt proper precautions against the disease." *KBOH 1900–01*, 11. For an example of such a quarantine order (issued against Greenup County in December 1900), see ibid., 12. See also "Small-Pox Up-to-Date," *MWR*, Feb. 17, 1898, 2.

34. "Small-Pox Victim Dies," *LMH*, Feb. 13, 1898, 8. "Small-Pox Up-to-Date," *MWR*, Feb. 17, 1898, 2. "Spreading," *LMH*, Feb. 15, 1898, 8. On the Ball brothers, see Matheny, *Magic City*, 141–54.

35. "Smallpox in Middlesboro," *WP*, Feb. 16, 1898, 9. "Small-Pox Up-to-Date," *MWR*, Feb. 17, 1898, 2. "Uncle Sam Fumigating," ibid., Feb. 24, 1898, 1. The advertisements appeared in ibid., Feb. 17, 1898, 1.

36. "Small-Pox: Situation More Grave," *MWR*, Mar. 3, 1898, 6. "Laws, Rules and Regulations," 177.

37. A. T. McCormack's brief report on the smallpox epidemic at Middlesboro appears in *KBOH 1898–99*, 47–48.

38. A. T. McCormack's report.

39. Short, untitled reports of postvaccination illnesses appear in the *MWR*, Dec. 9, 1897, 3; Feb. 24, 1898, 1; Mar. 10, 1898, 1–2.

40. Untitled editorial, *MWR*, Mar. 3, 1898, 4. *Plessy v. Ferguson*, 163 U.S. 537 (1896).

41. A. T. McCormack's report, 47. "Small-Pox: Situation More Grave," *MWR*, Mar. 3, 1898, 6.

42. A. T. McCormack's report, 47–48. C. P. Wertenbaker, "Smallpox at Middlesborough, Ky.," *PHR*, 13 (Mar. 25, 1898), 273–74.

43. *KBOH 1898–99*, 48. Untitled Editorial, *MWR*, Mar. 10, 1898, 4.

44. Much of the correspondence arising from this episode is reprinted in *KBOH 1898–99*, 47–61. Fifty-fifth U.S. Congress, *Congressional Directory* (Washington, 1897), 52. For an excellent history of federal disaster relief, see Michele Landis Dauber, "The Sympathetic State," *Law and History Review*, 23 (2005): 387–442.

45. *KBOH 1898–99*, 48–49. The emphasis in Colson's quotation is mine.

46. Walter Wyman to C. P. Wertenbaker, Mar 10, 1898, CPWL, vol. 1.

47. I have formed my impressions of Wertenbaker by reading his personal papers and letter books (collected at the Library of the University of Virginia) and his published dispatches and reports. For an overview of his career, see "Death, Here, of Noted Surgeon," *Daily Progress* (Charlottesville, VA), July 13, 1916, 1.

48. Wertenbaker, "Smallpox at Middlesborough," 273.

49. Ibid., 274. "Death of Dr. A. T. McCormack" (U.S. Children's Bureau), *The Child*, 8 (1943), 47.

50. Wertenbaker, "Smallpox at Middlesborough," 273–74. "Investigating," *LMH*, Mar. 15, 1898, 3. "Spreading," ibid., Mar. 15, 1898, 8. "The Smallpox Situation at Middlesboro," *Grand Forks Herald*

(North Dakota), Mar. 15, 1898, 8. See also C. P. Wertenbaker, "One Case of Smallpox in Wilming-ton, N.C.," *PHR*, 13 (Jan. 14, 1898), 25; C. P. Wertenbaker, "Investigation of Smallpox at Charlotte, N.C.," *PHR*, 13 (Feb. 18, 1898), 140–41.

51. Untitled editorial, *MWR*, Mar. 10, 1898, 4. "Smallpox Situation at Middlesboro." "Starving in a Pesthouse," *NYT*, Mar. 15, 1898, 3. "Seventy Cases of Smallpox," *AC*, Mar. 16, 1898, 5. Werten-baker, "Smallpox at Middlesborough," 274.

52. "Uncle Sam to the Rescue," *MWR*, Mar. 17, 1898, 3. *KBOH, 1898–9*, 49.

53. A. T. McCormack's report, 47.

54. Ibid., 49–50.

55. Ibid., 50.

56. Ibid.

57. Ibid.

58. Ibid., 51.

59. Ibid.

60. "Uncle Sam in Charge of the Small-Pox Cases at Middlesboro," *LMH*, Mar. 20, 1898, 5.

61. For a useful short history of public health in Jefferson County, see "History," Jefferson County Department of Health Web site, http://www.jcdh.org/default.asp?ID=10, accessed January 25, 2007. In one of his several irate letters to Walter Wyman regarding the Service takeover at Mid-dlesboro, Secretary J. N. McCormack of the Kentucky Board of Health said, "*We hesitated to give you absolute control because of the ineffectual methods adopted by your Service in Alabama*, which had permitted the present epidemic in Tennessee and Kentucky." If this complaint was genuine, McCormack was acting on erroneous information. The arrival of the miner Scott in Middlesboro preceded the Service's takeover at Birmingham by at least two months. Secretary McCormack to WW, Apr. 9, 1898, published in *KBOH 1898–99*, 59.

62. "Three New Cases of Smallpox," *AC*, Jul. 29, 1897, 3. G. M. Magruder, "Smallpox in Birmingham, Ala.," *PHR*, 13 (Jan. 14, 1898), 22–25.

63. G. M. Magruder, "Work of the Service in Suppressing Smallpox in Alabama," *PHR*, 13 (Mar. 18, 1898), 246–51. See also "Three New Cases of Smallpox," *AC*, Jul. 29, 1897, 3; "Smallpox Scare in Birmingham," ibid., Aug. 7, 1897, 2; "Prevent Smallpox Spread," ibid., Aug. 8, 1897, 2; "Why Smallpox Is Not Checked," ibid., Aug. 9, 1897, 2; "Wyman Sends Surgeons South," ibid., Jan. 7, 1898, 1; "Pest Prevails in Alabama," ibid., Jan. 14, 1898, 2.

64. Magruder, "Work of the Service," esp. 246–47, 250.

65. Ibid., 247–48.

66. Ibid.

67. Ibid., 248–50.

68. Ibid., 250. The white cases equaled 57.5 percent of the total reported cases. The U.S. Census of 1900 found that 45.2 percent of the population of Alabama was black. *Negroes in the United States*, 20.

69. C. P. Wertenbaker, "Smallpox at Middlesborough, Ky.,—(Continued.)," *PHR*, 13 (Apr. 1, 1898), 300–303. "Locals," *MWR*, Mar. 24, 1898, 1.

70. Wertenbaker, "Smallpox at Middlesborough, Ky.,—(Continued.)," 301. "A Decided Improve-ment," *MWR*, Mar. 24, 1898, 4.

71. Hill Hastings, "Smallpox at Middlesborough, Ky.—(Concluded.)," *PHR*, 13 (Apr. 22, 1898), 379–81, esp. 379. Wertenbaker, "Smallpox at Middlesborough, Ky.,—(Continued.)," 300. "Decided Improvement."

72. Wertenbaker, "Smallpox at Middlesborough, Ky.,—(Continued.)," 301–2. Hastings, "Smallpox at Middlesborough," 380.

73. Hastings, "Smallpox at Middlesborough, Ky.—(Concluded.)," 379–81.

74. *KBOH 1898–99*, 23–24.

75. Ibid., 23–24, 34–35.

76. *Bell County v. Blair*, filed May 11, 1899, in *KBOH 1898–99*, 179–80.

77. Matheny, *Magic City*, 229. *KBOH 1900–01*, 18.

78. Surgeon General Walter Wyman, "Principles Governing the Extension of Aid to Local Authorities in the Matter of Smallpox," in *USSGPHMHS 1898*, 630. The cash figure is from an untitled item in the *MWR*, Apr. 14, 1898, 6.

79. Wyman, "Principles," 630.

THREE: WHEREVER WERTENBAKER WENT

1. Photographs of Wertenbaker in the uniforms of the Warrenton Rifles and the Marine-Hospital Service, as well as various medals for his service in the Virginia Volunteers (state militia), survive in PCPW. C. P. Wertenbaker note, "In the event of my death . . . ," Dec. 27, 1915, ibid. See U.S. Marine-Hospital Service, *Regulations Concerning Uniforms* (Washington, 1891).

2. Wertenbaker describes his smallpox inspection suit in "Plan of Organization for the Suppression of Smallpox," draft, CPWL, vol. 6.

3. On the geographical mobility of southern laborers, particularly in the rural nonagricultural sector, see Jacqueline Jones, *The Dispossessed: America's Underclasses from the Civil War to the Present* (New York, 1992), 127–66.

4. James A. Tobey, *Public Health Law*, 1. On the Service, see Laurence F. Schmeckebier, *The Public Health Service: Its History, Activities, and Organization* (Baltimore: Johns Hopkins Press, 1923); Robert Straus, *Medical Care for Seamen: The Origin of Public Medical Services in the United States* (New Haven: Yale University Press, 1950). Ralph Chester Williams, *The United States Public Health Service, 1798–1950* (Washington: Whittet E. Shepperson, 1951). See also John Duffy, *The Sanitarians*, 157–74, 239–55; Alan M. Kraut, *Silent Travelers: Germs, Genes, and the "Immigrant Menace"* (Baltimore: The Johns Hopkins University Press, 1994).

5. In addition to running its 22 hospitals and 107 relief stations for the nation's merchant marine, manning immigrant inspection stations, and advising southern communities as they fought smallpox, the Service was occupied with an outbreak of bubonic plague in San Francisco. [Walter Wyman], "Resume of the Operations of the U.S. Marine-Hospital Service," *PHR*, 14 (Dec. 22, 1899), 2275–83.

6. "Death, Here, of Noted Surgeon." "Genealogical Material Re the Wertenbaker and Related Families," PCPW. Historical Data Systems, comp., *American Civil War Soldiers* (Provo, UT: Generations Network, 1999).

7. U.S. Census Bureau, *Ninth Census of the United States* (1870): Schedule 1—Population: Fredericksville Parish, Albemarle County, Virginia. U.S. Census Bureau, *Tenth Census of the United States* (1880): Schedule 1—Population: Charlottesville, Albemarle County, Virginia, Enumeration District 14. "Family Record of Charles Poindexter Wertenbaker," PCPW. See Gerald N. Grob, *The Deadly Truth*, 116–19, 142, 192–94.

8. "Death, Here, of Noted Surgeon."

9. Williams, *United States Public Health Service*, 508–9. C. P. Wertenbaker, "University of Virginia Alumni in the U.S. Public Health Service and Marine-Hospital Service," *University of Virginia Alumni Bulletin*, [no date], 197, CPWL, vol. 2. Among those alums Wertenbaker mentioned by name was George M. Magruder, who headed the smallpox control effort at Birmingham.

10. See generally Williams, *United States Public Health Service*.

11. Margaret Humphreys, *Yellow Fever and the South* (New Brunswick, NJ: Rutgers University Press, 1992).

12. *USSGPHMHS 1902*, 30. Wertenbaker, "University of Virginia Alumni," 196–97. Williams, *United States Public Health Service*, 492.

13. Williams, *United States Public Health Service*, 500.

14. "John William Branham," eulogy pamphlet dated Aug. 23, 1893; CPWL, vol. 1. See also "John

Frederick Groenvelt," eulogy pamphlet dated Jul. 7, 1891, in ibid., vol. 1. "Dead in the Line of Duty," *WP*, Aug. 21, 1893, 1. See also "Death of Acting Asst. Surg. Stuart Eldridge": "He was a man of fine personal appearance, a cultured physician, and genial gentleman, and the U.S. Marine-Hospital Service has lost an able officer from an important post"; *PHR*, 16 (Nov. 22, 1901), 2709.

15. C. P. Wertenbaker to J. D. Church, New York Life Insurance Co., Aug. 3, 1898, in CPWL, vol. 6.

16. *Slaughterhouse Cases*, 16 Wall. 36 (1873). Tobey, *Public Health Law*. See Akhil Reed Amar, *The Bill of Rights: Creation and Reconstruction* (New Haven: Yale University Press, 1998); William J. Novak, *The People's Welfare: Law and Regulation in Nineteenth-Century America* (Chapel Hill: University of North Carolina Press, 1996), 191–248.

17. Florence Kelley, *Notes of Sixty Years: The Autobiography of Florence Kelley*, ed. Kathryn Kish Sklar (Chicago: Charles H. Kerr, 1986), 88. See Chicago Department of Health, *General and Chronological Summary of Vital Statistics* (Chicago, 1919), 1446; "Dr. Burson's Resignation Accepted," *CT*, Mar. 1, 1894, 8; R. M. Woodward, "The Cholera Quarantine Conducted by the U.S. Marine-Hospital Service in 1893," paper read before the Cleveland Medical Society, Nov. 23, 1894, reprint from *Western Reserve Medical Journal*, January 1895. See also Kathryn Kish Sklar, *Florence Kelley and the Nation's Work: The Rise of Women's Political Culture, 1830–1900* (New Haven: Yale University Press, 1995), 265–68.

18. C. P. Wertenbaker, "Arrival of Steamship Earnwell at Delaware Breakwater Quarantine with Three Cases of Smallpox," *PHR*, 9 (Sept. 4, 1896), 826. See Sir Graham S. Wilson, *The Hazards of Immunization* (London: Athlone Press, 1967).

19. U.S. Census Bureau, *Negroes in the United States* (Washington, 1904), 276. Works Progress Administration, Federal Writers' Project, *North Carolina: A Guide to the Old North State*, 249. See also, Glenda Elizabeth Gilmore, *Gender and Jim Crow: Women and the Politics of White Supremacy in North Carolina, 1896–1920* (Chapel Hill: University of North Carolina Press, 1996), 105–14; Hugh Talmage Lefler and Albert Ray Newsome, *North Carolina: The History of a Southern State*, 520–22.

20. "The Marine Hospital," *Wilmington Messenger*, Jan. 30, 1898, 9. Photos of the Wilmington home and one photo of Alice and Alicia Wertenbaker out for a ride in the station wagon survive in WFP. See "Girardeau—Wertenbaker," *Boston Daily Advertiser*, May 2, 1895, 8; "Wertenbaker Rites Slated for Today," *WP*, Jan. 24, 1955, 20; Society Section, ibid., Sept. 9, 1917, E9.

21. C. P. Wertenbaker to Frank Gilmer, May 22, 1899, CPWL, vol. 6. C. P. Wertenbaker, "Plan of Organization for Suppression of Smallpox in Communities Not Provided with an Organized Board of Health," *PHR*, 14 (Oct. 22, 1899): 1765–80.

22. C. P. Wertenbaker, "One Case of Smallpox in Wilmington, N.C.," *PHR*, 13 (Jan. 14, 1898), 25. "Smallpox in Wilmington," *Fayetteville Observer*, Jan. 13, 1898, no page.

23. "Smallpox in the City," *WM*, Jan. 13, 1898, 1. "A Riot Threatened," ibid., Jan. 14, 1898, 4. "Map: Residential Patterns by Race, 1897," in 1898 Wilmington Race Riot Commission, *Final Report*, May 31, 2006, http://www.history.ncdcr.gov/1898-wrrc/report/maps/residential-patterns-by-race_1897.pdf, accessed October 5, 2009.

24. "A Riot Threatened," *WM*, Jan. 14, 1898, 4. "The Smallpox Scare," ibid., Jan. 15, 1898, 4.

25. "Smallpox in Wilmington." "Burned the House Down," *CO*, Jan. 15, 1898, 1. "Another Case of Smallpox in Wilmington," *BS*, Jan. 17, 1898, 7. "Wilmington and the Smallpox," *Fayetteville Observer*, Jan. 17, 1898, no page. "Compulsory Vaccination," *RNO*, Jan. 18, 1898, no page. "General News of Interest," *Fayetteville Observer*, Feb. 8, 1898, no page.

26. "Smallpox in the City." "Compulsory Vaccination," *WM*, Jan. 25, 1898, 1. "Smallpox Petered Out," ibid., Feb. 1, 1898, 1. "Do You Want to Be Vaccinated?" ibid., Feb. 1, 1898.

27. "Afraid of Vaccination," *WM*, Jan. 27, 4.

28. "Compulsory Vaccination," *WM*, Jan. 27, 1901, 1. "The Vaccinators Still at Work," ibid., Jan. 29, 1898, 4.

29. *NCBOH 1897–98*, 28. "Items of State News," *CO*, Jan. 28, 1898, 4.

30. J. W. Babcock to Senator B. R. Tillman, Apr. 20, 1898, in CPWL, vol. 1. C. P. Wertenbaker, "Investigation of Smallpox at Charlotte, N.C.," *PHR*, 13 (Feb. 18, 1898), 140–41.

31. Wertenbaker, "Plan of Organization," 1779.

32. *Gibbons v. Ogden*, 9 Wheat. 1 (U.S., 1824). *State v. W. E. Hay*, 126 N.C. 999, 1001. Tobey, *Public Health Law*. See Michael Les Benedict, "Contagion and the Constitution: Quarantine Agitation from 1859–1866," *JHMAS*, 25 (1970), 177–93; and Novak, *People's Welfare*, 191–233. *KBOH 1898–99*, 82–84.

33. C. P. Wertenbaker, "The Smallpox Outbreak in Bristol, Va.-Tenn.," *PHR*, 14 (Nov. 3, 1899), 1890. See, e.g., C. P. Wertenbaker, "Report on a Case of Smallpox at Reidsville, N.C.," *PHR*, 13 (Jul. 15, 1898), 714–15; C. P. Wertenbaker, "Smallpox in Georgia," *PHR*, 14 (Nov. 3, 1899), 1891–92.

34. *KBOH 1898–99*, 43. *NCBOH 1903–04*, 15. See, e.g., "Case of Smallpox at Camak," *AC*, Mar. 26, 1901, 2; "Wright Crazed by Smallpox," ibid., Apr. 4, 1901, 2.

35. *NCBOH 1897–98*, 31, 32. "Will Consider Smallpox," *AC*, Mar. 15, 1900, 4; "Lawmakers Show an Ugly Temper," ibid., May 15, 1901, 3. J. F. Hunter, "Law for Compulsory Vaccination in Mississippi," *PHR*, 15 (Mar. 2, 1900), 467. See John G. Richardson, "Variation in Date of Enactment of Compulsory School Attendance Laws: An Empirical Inquiry," *Sociology of Education*, 53 (1980), 157.

36. *NCBOH 1899–1900*, 173. "Smallpox in *Nashville, Tenn.*—Vaccination Compulsory," *PHR*, 15 (Feb. 16, 1900), 325. Wertenbaker, "Plan of Organization," 1769. On Savannah, see "Kick Against Vaccination," *AC*, Mar. 29, 1900, 3.

37. C. P. Wertenbaker, "Report on Inspection of Smallpox at *Winston, High Point, and Greensboro*, N.C.," *PHR*, 15 (Feb. 16, 1900), 324. "Doctors Roughly Treated," *AC*, Feb. 15, 1901, 7. W. P. McIntosh, "Smallpox in *Girard and Phoenix, Ala., and Columbus, Ga.*," *PHR*, 16 (Jan. 11, 1901), 47.

38. W. C. Hobdy, "Smallpox in Georgia," *Public Health Reports*, 16 (June 7, 1901), 1253.

39. *KBOH 1898–99*, 130. *NCBOH 1899–1900*, 21. "Vaccination in Raleigh," *CO*, Apr. 19, 1899, 8.

40. See, e.g., Michael Dougherty, "Diary of Michael Dougherty, December 1863," *Prison Diary, of Michael Dougherty, Late Co. B., 13th Pa., Cavalry: While Confined in Pemberton, Barrett's, Libby, Andersonville and Other Southern Prisons* (Bristol, PA: C. A. Dougherty, 1908), 16–17; Oliver Otis Howard to Joseph Hooker, Apr. 19, 1863, in *Chronicles from the Nineteenth Century: Family Letters of Blanche Butler and Adelbert Ames . . .* , vol. 1, comp. by Blanche Butler Ames (Clinton, MA, privately issued, 1957); Mason Whiting Tyler, "Memoir of Mason Whiting Tyler," in *Recollections of the Civil War: With Many Original Diary Entries and Letters Written from the Seat of War* (New York: G. P. Putnam's Sons, 1912), 47. Donald R. Hopkins, *Princes and Peasants*, 273–82. Jonathan B. Tucker, *Scourge: The Once and Future Threat of Smallpox* (New York: Atlantic Monthly Press, 2001), 32.

41. Col. A. W. Shaffer, "Small-pox and Vaccination for Plain People. By One of Them," *NCBOH 1897–98*, 176.

42. *KBOH 1900–01*, 79. *NCBOH 1899–1900*, 13, 21. "The Old, Old Enemy," *DMN*, Mar. 9, 1900, 6.

43. C. P. Wertenbaker, "Investigation of Smallpox at Columbia and Sumter, S.C.," *PHR*, 13 (May 13, 1898), 470. *KBOH 1896–97*, 80.

44. *KBOH 1902–03*, 172. "Precautions Against Smallpox," *Columbus Daily Enquirer* (Georgia), Mar. 10, 1899. "Vaccination: Ugly Accidents Arising from the Smallpox Preventive," *DMN*, May 14, 1899, 3.

45. Kinyoun in *NCBOH 1897–98*, 114. *NCBOH 1899–1900*, 49. Smock in *KBOH 1898–99*, 149. W. P. McIntosh, Surgeon, MHS, "Smallpox in Houston County, Ga.," *PHR*, 15 (Dec. 14, 1900), 3029. *KBOH 1900–01*, 18.

46. Washington quoted in *Finding a Way Out: An Autobiography*, by Robert Russa Moton (Garden City, NY: Doubleday, Page & Co., 1921), 182.

47. C. P. Wertenbaker, "Smallpox in Georgia," *PHR*, 14 (Nov. 3, 1899), 1891.

48. G. M. Magruder, "Passed Assistant Surgeon Magruder's Report on Smallpox at Little Rock, Ark.," *PHR*, 13 (May 6, 1898), 437. D. S. Humphreys, "Smallpox in Greenwood, Miss.," *PHR*, 15 (Mar. 9, 1900), 516. According to the 1900 Census, African Americans constituted one third of the population of North Carolina, and less than one quarter of the population of Tennessee. Census Bureau, *Negroes in the United States*, 109. See, e.g., "Brunswick and the Smallpox," *AC*, Jan. 7, 1900, 4.

49. C. P. Wertenbaker, "Report on the Smallpox Situation in Danville, Va.," *PHR*, 14 (Jul. 27, 1899), 1038. *KBOH 1898–99*, 135, 79. *KBOH 1902–03*, see photo between 36 and 37.

50. W. F. Brunner, "Report of Smallpox in Montgomery County," *PHR*, 14 (Jul. 21, 1899), 1124.

51. C. P. Wertenbaker to Dr. H. L. Sutherland, Chief Health Officer, Bolivar Co., Mississippi, July 30, 1910, CPWL, vol. 5.

52. S. B. Jones, "Fifty Years of Negro Public Health," *Annals of the American Academy of Political and Social Science*, 49 (Sept., 1913): 138–46. See Edward H. Beardsley, *A History of Neglect: Health Care for Blacks and Mill Workers in the Twentieth-Century South* (Knoxville: University of Tennessee Press, 1987), esp. 11–36; W. Michael Byrd and Linda A. Clayton, *An American Health Dilemma: Volume 1*, idem, *An American Health Dilemma: Volume 2: Race, Medicine, and Health Care in the United States 1900–2000* (New York: Routledge, 2000), esp. 80; James H. Jones, *Bad Blood: The Tuskegee Syphilis Experiment*, expanded ed. (New York: Free Press, 1993), esp. 16–21; Todd L. Savitt, "Black Health on the Plantation: Masters, Slaves, and Physicians," in *Sickness and Health in America: Readings in the History of Medicine and Public Health*, ed. Judith Walzer Leavitt and Ronald L. Numbers (Madison: University of Wisconsin Press, 1997), 351–68; Steven M. Stowe, *Doctoring the South: Southern Physicians and Everyday Medicine in the Mid-Nineteenth Century* (Chapel Hill: University of North Carolina Press, 2004); Werner Troesken, *Water, Race, and Disease* (Cambridge, MA: MIT Press, 2004).

53. W. E. B. Du Bois, *The Philadelphia Negro: A Social Study* (1899; reprint ed., New York: Schocken Books, 1967), 147–63, esp. 163. U.S. Census Bureau, *A Discussion of the Vital Statistics of the Twelfth Census*, by John Shaw Billings (Washington, 1904), 10–11. Byrd and Clayton, *American Health Dilemma*, Vol. 2, esp. 80.

54. Du Bois, *Philadelphia Negro*, 162. See Beardsley, *History of Neglect*, 11–36; Byrd and Clayton, *American Health Dilemma*, Vol. 1, 355.

55. Jones, "Fifty Years of Negro Public Health," 142. Beardsley, *History of Neglect*, 35. See Todd L. Savitt, *Race and Medicine in Nineteenth- and Early-Twentieth-Century America* (Kent, OH: Kent State University Press, 2007).

56. *NCBOH 1897–98*, 79, 88. *KBOH 1898–99*, 79, 139. J. C. Ballard, "Smallpox in Concordia Parish, Louisiana," *PHR*, 14 (Nov. 3, 1899), 1893.

57. "Why Smallpox Is Not Checked," *AC*, Aug. 9, 1897, 2. C. P. Wertenbaker, "Report on the Investigation of Smallpox in North Carolina and Georgia," *PHR*, 15 (Feb. 2, 1900), 216. C. P. Wertenbaker, "Review of Operations in Advisory Capacity in Suppressing Smallpox in Georgia," *PHR*, 14 (Nov. 3, 1899), 1844.

58. *KBOH 1898–99, 74*.

59. Ibid., 139, 140. See Steven Hahn, *A Nation Under Our Feet: Black Political Struggles in the Rural South from Slavery to the Great Migration* (Cambridge, MA: Belknap Press, 2003), 412–64.

60. "General Vaccination Ordered," *WP*, Dec. 20, 1900, 1.

61. *KBOH 1898–99*, 96.

62. Ibid., 81, 80, 98, 145. *NCBOH 1897–98*, 35.

63. "Itching Skin Diseases," *WM*, advertisement, Jan. 26, 1898, 2. John D. Long, "Report on the

Inspection of a Gang of Workmen En Route from Clarksburg, W. Va., through Washington to the South," *PHR*, 61 (Jan. 4, 1901), 1–2. See Wertenbaker, "Investigation of Smallpox at Columbia and Sumter," 468–70.

64. *NCBOH 1899–1900*, 172.

65. *KBOH 1898–99*, 29. *KBOH 1896–97*, 72.

66. C. P. Wertenbaker, "Investigation of Smallpox at Charlotte," 140–41. Wertenbaker, "Smallpox Situation in Danville, Va.," 1038. On rumor, see Hahn, *Nation Under Our Feet*.

67. W. G. Dailey to State Board of Health, Aug. 11, 1898, *KBOH 1898–99*, 63–64. B. W. Smock in ibid., 104. *KBOH 1900–01*, 107. *NCBOH 1899–1900*, 158.

68. *USSGPHMHS 1898*, 598–99. See, e.g., "Bullitt County," in *KBOH 1898–99*, 64–65.

69. Wertenbaker, "Review of Operations . . . Georgia," 1884.

70. Shirley Everton Johnson, "Conquering a Small-Pox Epidemic in Kentucky," in *KBOH 1898–99*, 107–14, esp. 108.

71. Wertenbaker, "Review of Operations . . . Georgia," 1884.

72. Wertenbaker, "Report on Inspection of Smallpox at Winston, High Point, and Greensboro," 324.

73. Wertenbaker, "Plan of Organization," 1779.

74. See, for example, Wertenbaker, "Report on Inspection of Smallpox at Winston, High Point, and Greensboro," 323–24; Wertenbaker, "Smallpox Situation in Danville, Va.," 1038. Wertenbaker may have picked up this technique from North Carolina health officials, who in the fall of 1898 had staged a sort of whistle-stop campaign around the state to "preach the propaganda of vaccination." *NCBOH 1899–1900*, 13–16.

75. Wertenbaker, "Investigation of Smallpox at Charlotte," 140–41; Wertenbaker, "Investigation of Smallpox at Columbia and Sumter," 468–70; Wertenbaker, "Measures to Prevent the Spread of Smallpox in Georgia," *PHR*, 14 (Mar. 3, 1899), 273–78. See "Vaccination: Ugly Accidents," *DMN*, May 14, 1899, 3. See also W. C. Hobdy, "Report on Smallpox in Wilson, N.C.," *PHR*, 17 (Jan. 24, 1902), 164–65.

76. *NCBOH 1897–98*, 35.

77. Ibid., 39, 37, 113.

78. *NCBOH 1899–1900*, 156. *NCBOH 1897–98*, 91.

79. Wertenbaker, "Plan of Organization," 1779.

80. M. J. Rosenau, "Report on the examination of dried lymph and glycerinized vaccine lymph," Apr. 2, 1900, CPWL, vol. 1.

81. Wertenbaker, "Smallpox Outbreak in Bristol," 1891. Henry F. Long, "Smallpox in Iredell County," in *NCBOH 1897–98*, 210.

82. Wertenbaker, "Plan of Organization," 1766, 1770, 1780.

83. Ibid., 1779.

84. C. P. Wertenbaker to Walter Wyman, Feb. 11, 1900, CPWL, vol. 6.

85. C. P. Wertenbaker, *Colored Antituberculosis League: Proposed Plan of Organization* (Washington: Government Printing Office, 1909). "Death, Here, of Noted Surgeon." "Oral History Interview with Alicia Wertenbaker Flynn," July 14, 1976, Library of the University of Virginia, Special Collections.

86. On the history of this beautiful cemetery, see David Mauer, "Set in Stone: The Serenity of U.Va.'s Cemetery Belies a Colorful Past," *University of Virginia Magazine*, Spring 2008, 40–44.

FOUR: WAR IS HEALTH

1. Margherita Arlina Hamm, *Manila and the Philippines* (London: F. Tennyson Neely, 1898), 89–95. *The Official Records of the Oregon Volunteers in the Spanish American War and Philippine Insurrection*, comp. by Brigadier General C. U. Gantenbein, 2d ed. (Salem, OR: W. H. Leeds 1906), 449–52.

2. J. N. Taylor, "On Pacific Swells," *BG*, Oct. 18, 1899, 7. Taylor, "Ready to Sail," *BG*, Sept. 21, 1899, 7; "Like Two Worlds," ibid., Oct. 22, 1899, 9; "Voyage of 26th," ibid., Nov. 29, 1899, 7. See also "Small-pox Among Troops," ibid., Sept. 21, 1899, 7; "John N. Taylor, Long Globe Employee, Dead," ibid., Sept. 9, 1918, 3.

3. J. N. Taylor, "Cleaning Cities," *BG*, Mar. 16, 1900, 3. Jose P. Bantug, *A Short History of Medicine in the Philippines During the Spanish Regime, 1565–1898* (Manila: Colegio Medico Farmaceutico De Filipinas, 1953), 103.

4. Taylor, "Cleaning Cities."

5. Ibid.

6. Ibid.

7. Vincent J. Cirillo, *Bullets and Bacilli: The Spanish-American War and Military Medicine* (New Brunswick, NJ: Rutgers University Press, 2004), esp. 1.

8. Pirogoff quoted in Victor Robinson, *Victory over Pain: A History of Anesthesia* (New York: Henry Schuman, 1946), 167. See Ken De Bevoise, *Agents of Apocalypse: Epidemic Disease in the Colonial Philippines* (Princeton, NJ: Princeton University Press, 1995), esp. ix; M. R. Smallman-Raynor and A. D. Cliff, *War Epidemics: An Historical Geography of Infectious Diseases in Military Conflict and Civil Strife, 1850–2000* (New York: Oxford University Press, 2004).

9. Rudyard Kipling, "The White Man's Burden," *McClure's Magazine*, February 1899, 290–91. Arthur J. Stringer, "Kipling: His Interpretation of the Female Character," *NYT*, Dec. 10, 1898, BR 835. Roosevelt quoted in Patrick Brantlinger, "Kipling's 'The White Man's Burden' and Its Afterlives," *English Literature in Translation, 1880–1920*, 50 (2007), 172.

10. Kipling, "White Man's Burden." There is a large literature on colonial health in India. See especially David Arnold, *Colonizing the Body: State Medicine and Epidemic Disease in Nineteenth-Century India* (Berkeley: University of California Press, 1993), esp. 116–58; Arnold, "Smallpox and Colonial Medicine in Nineteenth-Century India," in *Imperial Medicine and Indigenous Societies*, ed. David Arnold (Manchester, UK: Manchester University Press, 1988), 45–65; Sanjoy Bhattacharya, Mark Harrison, and Michael Warboys, *Fractured States: Smallpox, Public Health, and Vaccination Policy in British India, 1800–1947* (New Delhi: Orient Longman, 2005).

11. Hall quoted in "News and Other Gleanings," *Friends' Intelligencer*, Mar. 4, 1899, 180.

12. Rudyard Kipling, "The Tomb of His Ancestors," in *The Writings in Prose and Verse of Rudyard Kipling* (New York: Charles Scribner's Sons, 1899), vol. 13: *The Day's Work*, 128, 170. "Vaccination in India," *BRMJ*, Jun. 3, 1899, 1341. Kipling, "White Man's Burden." On the idealism and violence of colonial public health, see Dipesh Chakrabarty, "Postcoloniality and the Artifice of History: Who Speaks for 'Indian' Pasts?" in *Contemporary Postcolonial Theory: A Reader*, ed. Padmini Mongia (Delhi: Edward Arnold, 1997), 242–43.

13. "Taft Declares Americans Lead in Disease Fight," *PI*, May 5, 1911, 1. For a lucid conceptual discussion of U.S. colonialism in the Philippines, see Julian Go, "Introduction: Global Perspectives on the U.S. Colonial State in the Philippines," in *The American Colonial State in the Philippines: Global Perspectives*, ed. Julian Go and Anne L. Foster (Durham, NC: Duke University Press Books, 2003), 1–42.

14. "Taft Declares Americans Lead." John E. Snodgrass, "Sanitary Achievements in the Philippine Islands, 1898–1915," Part 1 in *Sanitary Achievements in the Philippines, 1898–1915; Smallpox Vaccination in the Philippine Islands, 1898–1914; Leprosy in the Philippine Islands* (Manila: Bureau of Printing, 1915). See Christopher Capozzola, "Empire as a Way of Life: Gender, Culture, and Power in New Histories of U.S. Imperialism," *Journal of the Gilded Age and Progressive Era*, 1 (2002): 364–74; Ann Laura Stoler, "Tense and Tender Ties: The Politics of Comparison in North American History and (Post) Colonial Studies," *Journal of American History*, 88 (2001): 829–65; and Robert J. McMahon, "Cultures of Empire," ibid.: 888–92.

15. "Origin and Spread of Typhoid Fever in the United States Army during the Spanish War," *MR*, 59 (Jan. 19, 1901), 98.

16. "School of Tropical Medicine," *DMN*, Feb. 5, 1899, 8. Reprinted from *BS*. See Roy Porter, *The Greatest Benefit to Mankind: A Medical History of Humanity* (New York: W. W. Norton & Company, 1997), 462–92. For a marvelous analysis of the anxieties involved in U.S. colonial medicine in the Philippines, see Warwick Anderson, "The Trespass Speaks: White Masculinity and Colonial Breakdown," *American Historical Review*, 102 (1997): 1343–70.

17. Azel Ames, M.D., "Compulsory Vaccination Essential. The Example of Porto Rico," *MN*, Apr. 19, 1902, 722. James C. Scott has argued that a central challenge of modern states is "to make a society legible, to arrange the population in ways that simplified the classic state functions of taxation, conscription, and prevention of rebellion." This process was particularly important in colonial spaces, such as the U.S.-controlled Philippines, where the terrain and its people were at first so little known to the colonizers. James C. Scott, *Seeing Like a State: How Certain Schemes to Improve the Human Condition Have Failed* (New Haven: Yale University Press, 1998), 2.

18. On public health and police power, see esp. William J. Novak, *The People's Welfare: Law and Regulation in Nineteenth-Century America* (Chapel Hill: University of North Carolina Press, 1996), 191–233. See also Lawrence O. Gostin, *Public Health Law: Power, Duty, Restraint* (Berkeley: University of California Press, 2000); James A. Tobey, *Public Health Law*.

19. When the global eradication campaign came in the 1960s and 1970s, it was to be an enormous international effort, overseen by the World Health Organization, with the United States playing one of several leading roles. See Ian Glynn and Jenifer Glynn, *The Life and Death of Smallpox*; D. A. Henderson, *Smallpox*.

20. Whitman quoted in Ira M. Rutkow, *Bleeding Blue and Gray: Civil War Surgery and the Evolution of American Medicine* (New York: Random House, 2005), 232; see ibid., 217–18. George M. Sternberg, "Medical Department," in *DODGECOM*, vol. 1, 179. Cirillo, *Bullets and Bacilli*, 20–30, esp. 30.

21. Dr. Carroll Dunham, "Medical and Sanitary Aspects of the War," *American Monthly Review of Reviews*, 18 (October 1898), 417. *DODGECOM*, vol. 1, 265. Cirillo, *Bullets and Bacilli*, 32–33.

22. Roosevelt in "Military Surgeons Meet," *NYT*, June 6, 1902, 6. *The Military Laws of the United States*, 4th ed. (Washington, 1901), 350–65. See Edgar Erskine Hume, "The United States Army Medical Department and Its Relation to Public Health," *SCI*, new ser., 74 (1931): 465–76; and Mary C. Gillett, *The Army Medical Department, 1865–1917* (Washington: U.S. Army, 1995); Champe C. McCulloch, Jr., "The Scientific and Administrative Achievement of the Medical Corps of the United States Army," *Scientific Monthly*, 4 (1917), 410–27.

23. George M. Sternberg, *A Text-Book of Bacteriology*, 2d ed. (1896; New York: William Wood and Company, 1901). Martha L. Sternberg, *George Miller Sternberg: A Biography* (Chicago: American Medical Association 1920). See Cirillo, *Bullets and Bacilli*, 20–30.

24. "Officers of the Medical Department of the Army shall not be entitled, by virtue of their rank, to command in the line or in other staff corps." *Military Laws*, 353. Line officer quoted in Cirillo, *Bullets and Bacilli*, 4. Whitman quoted in M. Jimmie Killingsworth, *The Cambridge Introduction to Walt Whitman* (New York: Cambridge University Press, 2007), 9.

25. *USMCSW*. For a very thoughtful treatment of this issue, see Warwick Anderson, *Colonial Pathologies: American Tropical Medicine, Race, and Hygiene in the Philippines* (Durham, NC: Duke University Press Books, 2006), 22–30.

26. *DODGECOM*, vol. 1, 113, 169.

27. Hoff quoted in Anderson, *Colonial Pathologies*, 30. See Sternberg, "Medical Department," 169–70, esp. 170; Sternberg in *DODGECOM*, vol. 1, 113.

28. Hoyt quoted in Anderson, *Colonial Pathologies*, 31. "Dr. Azel Ames Dead," *BG*, Nov. 13, 1908, 8. "Groff, George G.," *The National Cyclopaedia of American Biography* (New York: J. T. White,

1904), vol. XII: 301. Henry F. Hoyt, M.D., "Sanitation in St. Paul," in *PHPR*, 14 (1888): 33–39. "Brevet Rank for Gallant Conduct," *MR*, 61 (Mar. 29, 1902), 500.

29. C. P. Wertenbaker, "Investigation of Smallpox at Columbia and Sumter, S.C.," *PHR*, 13 (May 2, 1898), 468–70. *USWDAR 1898*, 622.

30. Sternberg, "Medical Department," 176. *DODGECOM*, vol. 5, 1684. John Van Rensselaer Hoff, "Experience of the Army with Vaccination as a Prophylactic Against Smallpox," *Military Surgeon*, 28 (1911), 498, 502.

31. *USMCSW*, 167–93, esp. 178. "Origin and Spread of Typhoid Fever in the United States Army during the Spanish War," *MR*, 59 (Jan. 19, 1901), 98.

32. "Horrors of Chickamauga," *NYT*, Aug. 27, 1898, 3. "Camp Alger a Pest Hole," ibid., Aug. 6, 1898, 2. *USMCSW*, 167–93, esp. 190. Cirillo, *Bullets and Bacilli*, 57–90.

33. "Shafter's Men to Flee from Fever," *NYT*, Aug. 5, 1898, 7. See also, Nicholas Senn, "The Invasion of Porto Rico from a Medical Standpoint," *MN*, 73 (Sept. 17, 1898), 369.

34. McKinley, in *DODGECOM*, vol. 1, 237.

35. Reed quoted in Gaines M. Foster, "The Demands of Humanity: Army Medical Disaster Relief" (Washington, U.S. Army, 1983), ch. 3, p. 2, http://history.amedd.army.mil/booksdocs/misc/disaster/default.htm, accessed June 23, 2008. McCulloch, "Scientific and Administrative Achievement," 414, 419. Cirillo, *Bullets and Bacilli*, 111–35. Smallman-Raynor and Cliff, *War Epidemics*, 370–96.

36. J. N. Taylor, "Cleansing Cities," *BG*, Mar. 16, 1900, 3. Captain L. P. Davison, "Sanitary Work in Porto Rico," *Independent*, Aug. 10, 1899, 2128, 2131. Foster, "Demands of Humanity," ch. 3,p. 4. See Martin V. Melosi, *The Sanitary City: Urban Infrastructure in America from Colonial Times to the Present* (Baltimore: The Johns Hopkins University Press, 1999).

37. *USPC 1905*, Appendix A: "Report of the Commissioner of Public Health, Sept. 1, 1904, to August 31, 1905," 72. Davison, "Sanitary Work," 2131. See *USPC 1905*, 10.

38. Taylor, "Cleansing Cities."

39. Smallman-Raynor and Cliff, *War Epidemics*, 625–39, 685. Matthew Smallman-Raynor and Andrew D. Cliff, "War and Disease: Some Perspectives on the Spatial and Temporal Occurrence of Tuberculosis in Wartime," in *Return of the White Plague: Global Poverty and the "New" Tuberculosis*, ed. Matthew Grandy and Alimuddin Zumla (London: Verso, 2003), esp. 70–76.

40. Clara Barton, *The Red Cross: A History of This Remarkable International Movement in the Interest of Humanity* (Washington: American National Red Cross, 1898), 520. "Havana Now a Pest Hole," *NYT*, May 29, 1898, 12. "Topics of the Times," ibid., Mar. 18, 1897, 6. "Smallpox Ravaging Cuba," ibid., Mar. 31, 1897, 2. "Big Conspiracy in Cuba," ibid., Jan. 1, 1898, 3.

41. Senn, "Invasion of Porto Rico," 369, 370, 372.

42. De Bevoise, *Agents of Apocalypse*, ix, 8–44, esp. 18; Smallman-Raynor and Cliff, *War Epidemics*, 311.

43. De Bevoise, *Agents of Apocalypse*, 41.

44. Hoyt quoted in Anderson, *Colonial Pathologies*, 38–39; ibid., 31. See Senn, "Invasion of Puerto Rico," 369.

45. John Van Rensselaer Hoff, "The Share of the 'White Man's Burden' That Has Fallen to the Medical Departments of the Public Services in Puerto Rico," *PMJ*, 5 (Apr. 7, 1900), 797. De Bevoise, *Agents of Apocalypse*, 43. Arnold, "Smallpox and Colonial Medicine," 48.

46. McCulloch, "Scientific and Administrative Achievement," 422. Mary C. Gillett, "U.S. Army Medical Officers and Public Health in the Philippines in the Wake of the Spanish-American War, 1898–1905," *BHM*, 64 (1990), 567–81, esp. 581. Foster, "Demands of Humanity," ch. 3, 4–5. See Davison, "Sanitary Work."

47. John Van R. Hoff, "Report of the Superior Board of Health of Porto Rico," June 30, 1900, in *USPRMG 1900*, 479.

48. Davison, "Sanitary Work," 2130. George M. Sternberg, "Report of the Surgeon General," in *USWDAR 1899, Reports of the Chiefs of Bureaus*, vol. 1, part 2: 597–98. P. Villoldo, "Smallpox and Vaccination in Cuba," 1914 article reprinted in "Public Health Reports 2006 Supplement 1," *PHR*, 121 (2006): 47–49. See also Foster, "Demands of Humanity," ch. 3, 7–8; and Mariola Espinosa, *Epidemic Invasions: Yellow Fever and the Limits of Cuban Independence, 1878–1930* (Chicago: University of Chicago Press, 2009).

49. Hoff, "Share of the 'White Man's Burden,'" 797, 796.

50. James Robb Church, "John Van R. Hoff," *Military Surgeon* (1920), 204–7. "Approves Hoff Memorial," *NYT*, Jan. 26, 1931, 14. Gillett, *Army Medical Department*, 84–87, 197 note 15. See Jacob A. Riis, *Theodore Roosevelt, the Citizen* (New York: The Outlook Co., 1904).

51. Church, "John Van R. Hoff," esp. 205. John Van Rensselaer Hoff, "Experience of the Army with Vaccination as a Prophylactic Against Smallpox," *Military Surgeon* (1911), 492.

52. Gillett, *Army Medical Department*, 258. Hoff, "Experience of the Army with Vaccination," 493. C. H. Alden, "Puerto Rico; Its Climate and Its Diseases," *NYMJ*, 74 (1901), 21.

53. Alden, "Puerto Rico," esp. 19. For a useful contemporary overview of the island, from the Army's perspective, see *USPRMG 1900*.

54. *USPRMG 1900*, 26, 152. Alden, "Puerto Rico," 19–22, esp. 19. *Report of Brig. Gen. Geo. W. Davis, U.S.V. on Civil Affairs of Puerto Rico 1899* (Washington, 1900), 18.

55. Major Azel Ames, "Vaccination of Porto Rico—A Lesson to the World," *Pacific Medical Journal*, 45 (1902), 518. Alden, "Puerto Rico," 19. *USPRMG 1900*, 94.

56. *USPRMG 1900*, 19–20, 23, 26. *Downes v. Bidwell*, 182 U.S 244 (1901). See Robert McGreevey, "Borderline Citizens: Puerto Ricans and the Politics of Migration, Race, and Empire, 1898–1948," PhD diss., Brandeis University, 2008.

57. George M. Sternberg, "Smallpox," in *USWDAR 1899, Reports of the Chiefs of Bureaus*, 596–602, esp. 598. Ames, "Compulsory Vaccination Essential," 722. George G. Groff, "Vaccinating a Nation," *MN*, Nov. 25, 1899, 679. Alden, "Puerto Rico," 21.

58. Hoff, "Experience of the Army with Vaccination," 492. "Small-Pox Scare," *PI*, Oct. 9, 1898. "Deaths in Porto Rico," *DMN*, Dec. 24, 1898, 3. Dr. S. H. Wadhams, "Smallpox in Puerto Rico," *YMJ*, 6 (1899–1900), 279.

59. George Foy, "The Introduction of Vaccination to the Southern Continent of America and to the Philippene [sic] Islands," *Janus*, 2 (1897–98): 216–20. See José G. Rigau-Perez, "The Introduction of Smallpox Vaccine in 1803 and the Adoption of Immunization as a Government Function in Puerto Rico," *Hispanic American Historical Review*, 69 (1989): 393–423; Catherine Mark and José G. Rigau-Perez, "The World's First Immunization Campaign: The Spanish Smallpox Vaccine Expedition, 1803–1813," *BHM*, 83 (Spring 2009), 63–94.

60. Rigau-Perez, "Introduction of Smallpox Vaccine."

61. Hoff, "Experience of the Army with Vaccination," 492. *USPRMG 1900*, 150. Alden, "Puerto Rico," 21. Groff, "Vaccinating a Nation," 679–80. José G. Rigau-Perez, "Strategies That Led to the Eradication of Smallpox in Puerto Rico, 1882–1921," *BHM*, 59 (1985), 75–88, esp. 79.

62. *USPRMG 1900*, 153.

63. "General Orders, No. 7," Jan. 27, 1899, in *USWDAR 1899*, 572–73. C. H. Lavinder, "The Marine-Hospital Service," in *USPRMG 1900*, 277–81.

64. Ames, "Compulsory Vaccination Essential," 723.

65. Azel Ames published two detailed accounts of the vaccination campaign. Ames, "Compulsory

Vaccination Essential" and "Vaccination of Porto Rico." See Bhattacharya, *Fractured States*, 52–69; De Bevoise, *Agents of Apocalypse*, 105.

66. Ames, "Vaccination of Porto Rico," 513. As a special commissioner with the Massachusetts Department of Labor in the 1870s, Ames published a pioneering study of women in industry. Ames, *Sex in Industry: A Plea for the Working Girl* (Boston: James R. Osgood and Company, 1875). Azel Ames appeared frequently in the newspapers. See "Suspension of a Boston Doctor from the Pension Bureau," *BG*, Nov. 15, 1883, 6; "Indicted for Pension Frauds," *NYT*, Mar. 26, 1884, 2; "Not Agreed as to His Guilt," ibid., Jun. 25, 1885, 3; "Dr. Azel Ames Dead," *BG*, Nov. 13, 1908, 8. He fell on hard times after returning from Puerto Rico, filing for bankruptcy in 1902. He died in the Danvers State Hospital for the Insane in 1908.

67. Ames, "Vaccination of Porto Rico," 524, 523.

68. Ibid., 527, 525–26. Sternberg, "Report of the Surgeon General," 598. Wadhams, "Smallpox in Puerto Rico," 282.

69. Groff, "Vaccinating a Nation," 680.

70. Sternberg, "Report of the Surgeon General," 598. Groff, "Vaccinating a Nation," 680, 681. Wadhams, "Smallpox in Puerto Rico," 283. "Alumni and School Notes," *YMJ*, 7 (1901), 333.

71. "Circular No. 3," March 18, 1899, in "Report of Brig. Gen. Geo. W. Davis on Civil Affairs in Puerto Rico," *USWDAR 1899*, 630. Groff, "Vaccinating a Nation," 682.

72. Ames, "Vaccination of Porto Rico," 529.

73. "General Order No. 80," June 17, 1899, in "Report of Brig. Gen. Geo. W. Davis on Civil Affairs in Puerto Rico," 588.

74. Groff, "Vaccinating a Nation," 681. Hoff, "Share of the 'White Man's Burden,'" 798.

75. Ames, "Compulsory Vaccination Essential," 728. Hoff, "Share of the 'White Man's Burden,'" 799.

76. Ames, "Vaccination of Porto Rico," 515, 517. Many positive stories on the Puerto Rican campaign appeared in American newspapers, usually as a new piece of evidence in the argument against the antivaccinationists. See, for example, "Latest Vaccination Argument," *Omaha World Herald*, Aug. 24, 1902. "Vaccination in Porto Rico," *Duluth News-Tribune*, Dec. 20, 1902, 6.

77. *KBOH 1898–99*, 115.

78. Secretary of State John Hay quoted in *Liberty, Equality, Power: A History of the American People*, ed. John M. Murrin and James M. McPherson (New York: Harcourt Brace, 1999), 739. Hoff, "Experience of the Army with Vaccination," 493. Brian McAllister Linn, "The Long Twilight of the Frontier Army," *Western Historical Quarterly*, 27 (1996), 142.

79. Charles R. Greenleaf, "A Brief Statement of the Sanitary Work So Far Accomplished in the Philippine Islands, and of the Present Shape of Their Sanitary Administration," *PHPR*, 27 (1901), 164. Charles Burke Elliott, *The Philippines, to the End of the Commission Government: A Study in Tropical Democracy* (Indianapolis: Bobbs-Merrill, 1917), 186. See Paul A. Kramer, *The Blood of Government: Race, Empire, the United States, and the Philippines* (Chapel Hill: The University of North Carolina Press, 2006).

80. Greenleaf, "Brief Statement," 163. The forty thousand figure, which appears to have originated with the U.S. colonial health official Victor Heiser, was widely quoted in official reports and press accounts and has since been accepted as at least plausible by leading historians of disease in the Philippines. Snodgrass, *Sanitary Achievements in the Philippine Islands*, 15. See also Elliott, *Philippines*, 187; Warwick Anderson, "Immunization and Hygiene in the Philippines," *JHMAS*, 62 (2006), 8; De Bevoise, *Agents of Apocalypse*, 104, 117. "Filipino Minister Surrenders; Aguinaldo's Infant Son Dies at Manila from Smallpox," *NYT*, Mar. 16, 1900, 7. *USSCOP*, Part 3: 2033.

81. De Bevoise, *Agents of Apocalypse*, esp. 94–95.

82. Ibid., 105–10, esp. 108. *USPCRP 1901*, vol. 14, 32. Anderson, "Immunization and Hygiene in the Philippines," 5–6.

83. De Bevoise, *Agents of Apocalypse*, 41–42.

84. Greenleaf, "Brief Statement," 157. "Testimony of Dr. Frank S. Bourns," July 29, 1899, in *USPCRP 1900*, Vol. 2: *Testimony and Exhibits* (Washington, 1900), 347–68, esp. 348–49. (Hereafter Bourns, "Testimony.") See Frank S. Bourns and Dean C. Worcester, *Preliminary Notes on the Birds and Mammals Collected by the Menage Scientific Expedition to the Philippine Islands* (Minneapolis: Harrison & Smith, 1894); and Kramer, *Blood of Government*, 180.

85. Frank S. Bourns, Report to Provost-Marshal-General, Jun. 30, 1899, in *USWDAR 1899: Annual Report of the Major-General Commanding the Army*, Part 2: 260–61. (Hereafter Bourns, "Report.")

86. Bourns, "Testimony," 350, 351. Bourns, "Report," 260–61. Greenleaf, "Brief Statement," 157–58. Foster, "Demands of Humanity," ch. 3, p. 6. On the fascinating career of T. H. Pardo de Tavero, see Kramer, *Blood of Government*, 181–82.

87. Sternberg, "Smallpox," 601, 596. Soldier quoted in De Bevoise, *Agents of Apocalypse*, 115. The Army also tightened the medical inspection and vaccination of troops before they disembarked at San Francisco and paid closer attention to the geographic and racial profile of the American recruits. Sternberg, "Smallpox," 596–97.

88. 55th Cong., 3d Session, Senate Doc. No. 99, *Health of Troops in the Philippines* [containing dispatch from Major-General Otis to Secretary Alger, dated Feb. 3, 1899], first page. Bourns, "Report," 260.

89. Sternberg, "Smallpox," 596, 600. "Smallpox Epidemic Among Troops at Manila," *Rocky Mountain News* (Denver), Nov. 3, 1898, 5. "To Prevent Smallpox," *Grand Forks Herald*, Mar. 25, 1899, 4.

90. Snodgrass, "Smallpox and Vaccination in the Philippine Islands," 15.

91. Anderson, *Colonial Pathologies*, 38. See "Pesky Rebels," *LAT*, Feb. 12, 1900; "Week of War," *BG*, Apr. 23, 1900, 1.

92. Greenleaf, "Brief Statement," 158. Le Roy, "Philippines Health Problem," 778. Smallman-Raynor and Cliff, *War Epidemics*, 311.

93. Maus quoted in De Bevoise, *Agents of Apocalypse*, 116. Gillett, *Army Medical Department*, 178.

94. *USSGPHMHS 1904*, 168. Taylor, "Cleaning Cities," *BG*, Mar. 16, 1900, 3. Snodgrass, "Smallpox and Vaccination in the Philippines," 15.

95. LeRoy, "Philippines Health Problem," 778. Greenleaf, "Brief Statement," 165, 159.

96. "Philippine Tariff Bill Passed by House," *NYT*, Dec. 19, 1901, 1. On conditions in Batangas, see Florencio R. Caedo, provincial secretary, to William Howard Taft, Civil Governor of the Philippines, Dec. 18, 1901, in *USSCOP*, Part 2: 887. "Telegraphic Orders Issued by Brig. Gen. J. F. Bell to Station Commanders in the Provinces of Tayabas, Batangas, and Laguna," in ibid., Part 2: 1606–31.

97. For concise accounts of the Batangas campaign, see Amy Blitz, *The Contested State: American Foreign Policy and Regime Change in the Philippines* (New York: Rowman & Littlefield Publishers, 2000), 42–43; Kramer, *Blood of Government*, 152–54; and Brian McAllister Linn, *The Philippine War, 1899–1902* (Lawrence: University Press of Kansas, 2000), 219–24, 300–305. For a fuller history, see Glenn Anthony May, *Battle for Batangas: A Philippine Province at War* (New Haven: Yale University Press, 1991).

98. Blitz, *Contested State*, 42–43.

99. Bell, "Telegraphic Circular No. 22," Dec. 24, 1901, in *USSCOP*, Part II: 1628. Bell, "Telegraphic Circular No. 17," Dec. 23, 1901, in ibid., Part II: 1621; "Telegraphic Circular No. 19," Dec. 24, 1901, in ibid., Part II: 1621; "Telegraphic Circular No. 20," in ibid., Part II: 1626.

100. On reconcentration, see Kramer, *Blood of Government*, 152–53.

101. Smallman-Raynor and Cliff, *War Epidemics*, 614–24. De Bevoise, *Agents of Apocalypse*.

102. *USSCOP*, Part 3: 2878.

103. "Directions for Vaccination of Natives. Copy of Telegram. Batangas, January 16, 10:40 a.m.," in *AGOMHP*, Vol. 528: San Pablo, Laguna Province, P.I. [first entry], Dec. 31, 1901, 4. Accompanying telegram from General J. F. Bell in ibid., 4–5. See De Bevoise, *Agents of Apocalypse*, 117.

104. Blitz, *Contested State*, 43. Linn, *Philippine War*, 219. Smallman-Raynor and Cliff, *War Epidemics*,

307–48. On Filipinos' memories of the epidemics and the war, see De Bevoise, *Agents of Apocalypse*, ix.

105. Edward Thomas Curran, "Treatment of Filipinos," *NYT*, May 3, 1903, 23.

106. "Stamping Out Disease in the Philippines," *NYT*, June 23, 1902, 1.

107. "Topics of the Times," *NYT*, Aug. 18, 1902, 6. See, for example, "Havana's Health Is Good: Wonderful Changes Wrought by the Army of Occupation," *WP*, Mar. 23, 1902, 6; LeRoy, "Philippines Health Problem"; "Manila Is Healthful," *NYT*, Aug. 19, 1903, 8; "Life in the Philippines," *Omaha World Herald*, May 25, 1905, 4. See also Carl Crow, *America and the Philippines* (Garden City and New York: Doubleday, Page & Co., 1914), 107; Robley D. Evans, *An Admiral's Log: Being Continued Reflections of Naval Life* (New York: D. Appleton and Company, 1910), esp. 222–23; and the quotations presented in Kristine A. Campbell, "Knots in the Fabric: Richard Pearson Strong and the Bilibid Prison Vaccine Trials, 1905–1906," *BHM*, 68 (1994), esp. 606–12.

108. *USPC 1905*, 72, 11. *USSGPHMHS 1907*, 81.

109. *USPC 1907*, 73, 76. Snodgrass, "Smallpox and Vaccination in the Philippines," 15. In the finest study of the Philippine health crisis of the war years, Ken De Bevoise suggests that the claims of American officials in this regard should be taken seriously. Writing of the 1902–3 period, De Bevoise says, "The successful immunizations . . . may have provided a radical discontinuity with past experience sufficient to impel changed beliefs and behaviors. As popular resistance to vaccination began to break down, the cultural groundwork for future control efforts was laid." De Bevoise, *Agents of Apocalypse*, 117.

110. *USPC 1904*, 105. De Bevoise, *Agents of Apocalypse*, 188. Warwick Anderson has suggested that "Probably not more than half the vaccinations were successful." Anderson, "Immunization and Hygiene," 9. Glynn and Glynn, *Life and Death of Smallpox*, 193. On eradication, see Ken De Bevoise, "Until God Knows When: Smallpox in Late-Colonial Philippines," *Pacific Historical Review*, 59 (1990), 185; and De Bevoise, *Agents of Apocalypse*, 188. De Bevoise notes that "a case imported into Mindoro allowed the disease to take one last bow in 1948–1949." Idem, "Until God Knows When," 185.

111. Ames, "Vaccination of Porto Rico," 513. *USSGPHMHS 1907*, 81. Snodgrass, "Smallpox and Vaccination in the Philippines," 18.

FIVE: THE STABLE AND THE LABORATORY

1. "New Jersey Notes," *PI*, June 3, 1902, 3. On the development of product liability law during the early twentieth century, see *MacPherson v. Buick*, 217 NY 382 (1916); and H. Gerald Chapin, *Handbook of the Law of Torts* (St. Paul: West Publishing Co. 1917), 517–20. See also Barbara Young Welke, *Recasting American Liberty: Gender, Race, Law, and the Railroad Revolution, 1865–1920* (New York: Cambridge University Press, 2001), esp. 14–20; John Fabian Witt, *The Accidental Republic: Crippled Workingmen, Destitute Widows, and the Remaking of American Law* (Cambridge, MA: Harvard University Press, 2004), esp. 2–3, 75–76.

2. Franklin Delano Roosevelt, Annual Message of the President to Congress, Jan. 6, 1941 (excerpt), http://avalon.law.yale.edu/20th_century/decade01.asp, accessed March 3, 2009. Old-age pensions, unemployment insurance, compulsory health insurance, and labor regulations for men (outside of extremely dangerous industries such as mining) were dead on arrival in the United States. *Escola v. Coca Cola Bottling Co.*, 24 Cal. 2d 453 (1944). See David A. Moss, *Socializing Security: Progressive-Era Economists and the Origins of American Social Policy* (Cambridge, MA: Harvard University Press, 1995); Theda Skocpol, *Protecting Soldiers and Mothers: The Political Origins of Social Policy in the United States* (Cambridge, MA: Harvard University Press, 1992).

3. In a useful short account, Jonathan Liebenau has examined the vaccine controversy as an important moment in the consolidation of the pharmaceutical industry in the United States; *Medical Science and Medical Industry* (Baltimore: The Johns Hopkins University Press, 1987), 79–88.

Arthur Allen provides a brisk narrative of the episode in *Vaccine*, 79–82, 92–96. A thinner account, with errors, is David E. Lilienfeld, "The First Pharmacoepidemiologic Investigations: National Drug Safety Policy in the United States, 1901–1902," *Perspectives in Biology and Medicine*, 51 (Spring 2008): 188–98.

4. "No Vaccination in Camden's Boundaries," *NYT*, Nov. 19, 1901, 7. "Vaccine and Antitoxin," ibid., Dec. 8, 1901, 6. "Vaccination and Lockjaw," *NYS*, Nov. 21, 1901, 6. F. M. Wood, "The Various Methods of Vaccination and Their Results," *PMJ*, 9 (Mar. 22, 1902), 541–42. "The Cleveland Experiment," *Cincinnati Lancet-Clinic*, May 31, 1902, 580–82.

5. "Rubbed Off Vaccine Virus," *NYT*, Dec. 7, 1901, 2. See, for example, "Death Follows Vaccination," *NOP*, Dec. 15, 1893, 4; "Death Caused by Vaccination," *Interocean* (Chicago), Feb. 15, 1894, 3; "Parents Fear Vaccination," *Milwaukee Sentinel*, Feb. 16, 1894, 8; "Caused by Vaccination: A School Girl's Awful Suffering," *Bismarck Daily Tribune*, Aug. 10, 1895; "Danger in Vaccination," *Macon Telegraph* (Georgia), Dec. 24, 1897; "Died of Virus Poisoning," *PNA*, Nov. 17, 1899, 7; "Death Probably Due to Vaccination," *WP*, Mar. 21, 1901, 3. See, generally, Sir Graham S. Wilson, *The Hazards of Immunization*.

6. On the implications of progressive thinking about social interdependence, see Thomas L. Haskell, *The Emergence of Professional Social Science* (Urbana: University of Illinois Press, 1977). Michael Willrich, *City of Courts*.

7. *Wyatt v. Rome*, 105 Ga. 312 (1898). Even after the enactment of the federal Biologics Control Act of 1902, state and local governments remained insulated from liability for unsafe vaccines. "The State is not a guarantor of the purity of such biological products and is not liable for injury caused by impure ones." James A. Tobey, *Public Health Law*, 58. See ibid., 175–76. On the regulatory environment as it existed in 1901, see Charles V. Chapin, *Municipal Sanitation in the United States* (Providence: The Providence Press, 1901), 573–98, esp. 580–84. On the growth of social intervention in American law during this period, see Willrich, *City of Courts*.

8. Walter Wyman, "Précis upon the Diagnosis and Treatment of Smallpox," *PHR*, 14, Jan. 6, 1899, 37. "Vaccination and Revaccination," *CMJ*, 1 (July 1902), 381. On more recent developments in U.S. vaccine regulation, see Thomas F. Burke, *Lawyers, Lawsuits, and Legal Rights: The Battle over Litigation in American Society* (Berkeley: University of California Press, 2002), 142–70; Vincent A. Fulginiti et al., "Smallpox Vaccination: A Review, Part II. Adverse Effects," *Clinical Infectious Diseases*, 37 (2003), 251–71; and Julie B. Milstein, "Regulation of Vaccines: Strengthening the Science Base," *Journal of Public Health Policy*, 25 (2004): 173–89.

9. "Commercial Virus and Antitoxin," *NYT*, Nov. 18, 1901, 6.

10. A burgeoning field of social science research has shed new light on the mental strategies—or "heuristics"—that ordinary people use to understand the risks of their world. For an introduction, see Paul Slovic, "Perception of Risk," *SCI*, new ser. 236 (1987): 280–85. For an interesting critique of Slovic's ideas, see Cass R. Sunstein, "The Laws of Fear," review of Paul Slovic, *The Perception of Risk* (2000), *Harvard Law Review*, 115 (2002): 1119–68.

11. "Vaccinia is a specific disease, the cause of which has not been determined. We are, therefore, working somewhat in the dark." Milton J. Rosenau of the federal Hygienic Laboratory, in *USROSENAU*, 6.

12. *USCB 1900*, Vol. I: *Population*: Part I: *Population of States and Territories*, 1900, 430, 513, 549. Ibid., Vol. 8: *Manufactures: States and Territories*, 556. *NJBOH 1901*, 152.

13. "Camden's Lockjaw Panic," *NYS*, Nov. 16, 1901, 4. The *Sun* mistakenly reported the family surname as Ludwig. See U.S. Census Bureau, *Twelfth Census of the United States* (1900): Schedule No. 1—Population: Camden, New Jersey, Supervisor's District No. 6, Enumeration District No. 63.

14. *NJBOH 1901*, 371. *NJBOH 1902*, 39–42. *PBOH 1901*, 14–18, 37–48. "Smallpox Situation in Philadelphia and Camden," *MN*, Nov. 30, 1901, 867–68.

15. "Camden's Lockjaw Panic." "Smallpox," *MN*, Oct. 26, 1901, 667. On sore arms during this epidemic, see F. M. Wood, M.D. [city physician of Camden], "The Various Methods of Vaccination and Their Results," *PMJ*, 9 (Mar. 22, 1902), 541–42; Alexander McAllister, M.D. [of Camden], "The Cause of Sore Arms in Vaccination," *Transactions of the Medical Society of New Jersey, 1902* (Newark, 1902), 153–57.

16. *NJBOH 1901*, 371–72.

17. "Vaccinated Boy, Tetanus Stricken, May Recover," *PNA*, Nov. 11, 1901, 1. "Five Victims of Lockjaw," *NYT*, Nov. 17, 1901, 3. W. J. Lampton, "Tetanus Epidemics" (letter to the editor), *NYS*, Nov. 21, 1901, 6. George Miller Sternberg, *Infection and Immunity: With Special Reference to the Prevention of Infectious Diseases* (New York: G. P. Putnam's Sons, 1903), 272–78, esp. 277. William Brown, "Tetanus in Toy-Pistol Wounds," *BRMJ*, 1 (1934): 1116–17. See also Frederic S. Dennis, ed., *System of Surgery* (Philadelphia: Lea Brothers & Co., 1895), vol. 1, 426–27; William Hallock Park and Anna Wessels Williams, *Pathogenic Micro-organisms: Including Bacteria and Protozoa; a Practical Manual for Students, Physicians and Health Officers* (Philadelphia: Lea Brothers & Co., 1905), 222. The contemporaneous accounts of the unfolding Camden tetanus outbreak that were published in newspapers, medical journals, and the Camden Board of Health's official report, contain a number of discrepancies (including some conflicting dates, different spellings of the victims' names, and differing ages for the children). I have been able to locate most of these children in the 1900 census. In my own account, I have wherever possible used information that I have been able to confirm in at least two sources. For the Camden Board of Health report, which appears to contain a few factual errors about the cases, see "Official Report of the Camden Board of Health Concerning the Cases of Tetanus Which Occurred in Patients Who Had Been Vaccinated," Nov. 29, 1901, reprinted in *Bulletin of the North Carolina Board of Health*, 16 (Dec. 1901): 112–18. (Hereafter: "Camden Board of Health Report.")

18. Mrs. Brower and Dr. Kensinger quoted in "Vaccinated Boy, Tetanus Stricken, May Recover." Dr. Kensinger's name is mispelled as "Kinsinger" in this newspaper story. On the Brower family, see *Twelfth Census of the United States* (1900): Schedule No. 1: Population, Camden, NJ, Supervisor's District No. 6, Enumeration District No. 77.

19. "Camden's Lockjaw Panic." *Twelfth Census of the United States* (1900): Schedule No. 1—Population: Camden, NJ, Supervisor's District No. 6, Enumeration District No. 77. "Camden Board of Health Report," 114.

20. "Another Death from Lockjaw," *NYTRIB*, Nov. 14, 1901, 6. "Camden's Lockjaw Panic." "Vaccination and Lockjaw," *NYT*, Nov. 14, 1901, 2. "Vaccination Leads to a Boy's Death," *PNA*, Nov. 14, 1901, 3. *Twelfth Census of the United States* (1900): Schedule No. 1—Population: Camden, NJ, Supervisor's District No. 6, Enumeration District No. 73. "Camden Board of Health Report," 114.

21. "Camden's Lockjaw Panic," *NYS*, Nov. 16, 1901, 4. "Vaccination Claims Another," *NYTRIB*, Nov. 15, 1901. *Twelfth Census of the United States* (1900): Schedule No. 1—Population: Camden, NJ, Supervisor's District No. 6, Enumeration District No. 59. "Camden Board of Health Report," 114.

22. Davis quoted in "Vaccination Claims Another." Dowling quoted in "Epidemic of Lockjaw Arouses a Whole City," *NYW*, Nov. 20, 1901, 6.

23. "Vaccination Claims Another." "Camden's Lockjaw Panic." See *Twelfth Census of the United States* (1900): Schedule No. 1—Population: Camden, NJ, Supervisor's District No. 6, Enumeration District No. 73 (Warrington); ibid., Enumeration District No. 49 (Cavallo). "Camden Board of Health Report," 114. The unnamed victim appears to have been William J. Bauer, aged seven, who according to Camden officials was the tetanus outbreak's first fatality: vaccinated October 12, he showed tetanus symptoms on November 1 and died two days later. Ibid., 113. On the Bauer family, see *Twelfth Census of the United States* (1900): Schedule No. 1—Population: Camden, NJ, Supervisor's District No. 6, Enumeration District No. 85.

24. "Lockjaw Deaths Continue," *NYT*, Nov. 17, 1901, 6. "Five Victims of Lockjaw," *NYT*, Nov. 17, 1901, 3. "Camden Board of Health Report," 114.

25. "Five Victims of Lockjaw." "Camden's Lockjaw Panic."

26. "Ibid. Other newspaper accounts and medical journal articles intimated that a single maker had been involved in the tetanus cases in Camden, but refrained from revealing the maker's identity. On Mulford see Liebenau, *Medical Science and Medical Industry*, esp. 57–78, 80–81.

27. "Camden's Lockjaw Panic." Cochran did not have many dollars to spare. The fifty-one-year-old teamster lived in a rented house on Mechanic Street, about a mile from the Delaware River, with his wife Sarah and their children. In their twenty-six years of marriage, Sarah had given birth to six children. Annie was their second to die. James was going to know who was responsible for this loss. *Twelfth Census of the United States* (1900): Schedule No. 1—Population: Camden, NJ, Supervisor's District No. 6, Enumeration District No. 59. "Epidemic of Lockjaw Arouses a Whole City," *NYW*, Nov. 20, 1901, 6.

28. "Camden's Lockjaw Panic." "No Vaccination in Camden's Boundaries." *Cooper v. Shore Elec. Co.*, 63 N.J.: 558 (1899). See John Fabian Witt, "From Loss of Services to Loss of Support: The Wrongful Death Statutes, the Origins of Modern Tort Law, and the Making of the Nineteenth-Century Family," *Law and Social Inquiry*, 25 (2000), 717–55; Vivian A. Zelizer, *Pricing the Priceless Child: The Changing Social Value of Children* (New York: Basic Books, 1985), ch. 5.

29. "Camden's Lockjaw Panic." "No Vaccination in Camden's Boundaries." "Epidemic of Lockjaw Arouses a Whole City." "Tetanus Following Vaccination," *MN*, Nov. 23, 1901, 829.

30. "Tetanus in Philadelphia," *NYT*, Nov. 19, 1901. "Commercial Virus and Antitoxin," ibid., Nov. 18, 1901, 6. On Atlantic City (Bessie Kessler, age nine), see "Death in Atlantic City," *NYT*, Nov. 19, 1901. "Vaccination Proves Fatal," *SFC*, Nov. 19, 1901, 4. On Bristol (Joseph Goldie), see "Tetanus Follows Vaccination," *CO*, Nov. 19, 1901, 4. See also "St. Louis; Camden, N.J.; Bristol, Pa.," *Duluth News Tribune* (Minnesota), Nov. 15, 1901, 4; "Compulsory Vaccination Exciting Camden, N. J.," *Wilkes-Barre Times*, Nov. 20, 1901, 1. On Cleveland, see Martin Friedrich, "How We Rid Cleveland of Smallpox," *CMJ*, 1 (Feb. 1902), 77–83, esp. 79. Joseph McFarland, "Tetanus and Vaccination: An Analytical Study of 95 Cases of the Complication," *Lancet*, Sept. 13, 1902, 730–35, esp. 731.

31. "A Health Board Arraigned," *NYT*, Nov. 19, 1901. "The St. Louis Tragedy," *Medical Dial* (Minneapolis), 3 (December 1901), 301–2. "St. Louis; Camden, N.J.; Bristol, Pa.," *Duluth News-Tribune*, Nov. 15, 1901, 4. A separate committee, appointed by the St. Louis Board of Health, later confirmed the coroner's judgment and recommended that the Health Department stop making antitoxin. The department complied. Ramunas A. Kondratas, "The Biologics Control Act of 1902," in *The Early Years of Federal Food and Drug Control*, ed. James Harvey Young (Madison, WI: American Institute of the History of Pharmacy, 1982), 15.

32. "A Tempest in Rochester: Frightened Parents Refuse to Allow School Children to Be Vaccinated," *NYTRIB*, Nov. 20, 1901, 6.

33. "No Vaccination in Camden's Boundaries." "Resolutions of the Camden Board of Health," *MN*, Nov. 23, 1901, 828. "Lockjaw Checks All Vaccination," *PNA*, Nov. 19, 1901, 3.

34. See Louis Galambos with Jane Eliot Sewell, *Networks of Innovation: Vaccine Development at Merck, Sharp & Dohme, and Mulford, 1895–1995* (New York: Cambridge University Press, 1995); Liebenau, *Medical Science and Medical Industry*; John P. Swann, *Academic Scientists and the Pharmaceutical Industry: Cooperative Research in Twentieth-Century America* (Baltimore: The Johns Hopkins University Press, 1988).

35. For a lucid short discussion, see Ian Glynn and Jenifer Glynn, *The Life and Death of Smallpox*, 177–89.

36. *NCBOH 1897–98*, 35. Chapin, *Municipal Sanitation*, 580. Donald R. Hopkins, *Princes and Peasants*, 77–81. Fenner et al., *Smallpox and Its Eradication*, 263.

37. George Henry Fox, *A Practical Treatise on Smallpox*, 26. Herbert Spencer, *Facts and Comments*

(New York: D. Appleton and Co., 1902), 271, 107. *USROSENAU*, 6. Hopkins, *Princes and Peasants*, 85. The persistent association of vaccination with syphilis persisted long after the curtailment of the arm-to-arm method ended the problem. See, e.g., Sylvanus Stall, *What a Young Man Ought to Know*, rev. ed. (Philadelphia: Vir Publishing Company, 1904), 142.

38. Francis G. Martin, "The Propagation, Preservation, and Use of Vaccine Virus," address to the American Medical Association, May 7, 1896, in *IBOH 1897*, 169.

39. Samuel W. Abbott, "Vaccination," in *A Reference Handbook of the Medical Sciences*, rev. ed. by Albert H. Buck, vol. 8 (New York: William Wood and Company, 1904), 111–53, esp. 133–34.

40. Abbott, "Vaccination," 133–34.

41. Martin ad in *BMSJ*, unpaginated advertising sheet, Aug. 29, 1872. "A Vaccination Farm," *Arkansas Gazette*, Sept. 25, 1877. "Animal Vaccination: Dr. Martin's Vaccine Farm at Brookline, Mass.," *Frank Leslie's Illustrated Newspaper* (New York), Aug. 6, 1881, 382.

42. "Virus: The Difference Between Humanized and Animal Matter—Rearing Calves for Purposes of Vaccination," *St. Louis Globe-Democrat* [orig. from *Brooklyn Eagle*], Jan. 6, 1876, 3. John Duffy, *A History of Public Health in New York City, 1866–1966*, 151. Massachusetts enacted the nation's first compulsory education law in 1852 and its first compulsory vaccination law in 1855. By 1918, every state had compulsory education. Compulsory vaccination spread far less uniformly, with many state legislatures leaving the matter to local communities and their boards of health.

43. J. W. Compton & Son advertisement, *Transactions of the Indiana State Medical Society*, 1882 (Indianapolis, 1882), 331. Wyeth advertisement, *Drugs and Medicines of North America* (Cincinnati, 1884–1885), Vol. 1: 21. "A Vaccination Farm," *Arkansas Gazette*, Sept. 25, 1877. "Animal Vaccination," 382. Oscar C. DeWolf, "Remarks on Sources and Varieties of Vaccine Virus," *Chicago Medical Journal and Examiner*, 42 (1881): 481–86. J. W. Hodge, "What Is the Stuff Variously Termed 'Vaccine Virus,' 'Bovine Virus,' 'Animal Lymph,' 'Calf Lymph,' 'Pure Calf-Lymph,' Etc.," *Medical Advance*, March 1908, 160–71, esp. 168.

44. More recently DNA analysis has confirmed that vaccinia, cowpox, and smallpox are distinct. See Glynn and Glynn, *The Life and Death of Smallpox*, 177–89.

45. Walter Reed, "What Credence Should Be Given to the Statements of Those Who Claim to Furnish Vaccine Lymph Free of Bacteria," *Journal of Practical Medicine*, 5 (July 1895), 532–34. W. F. Elgin, "The Propagation of Vaccine and Glycerinated Lymph," *Proceedings of the Fifteenth Annual Meeting of the Conference of State and Provincial Boards of Health of North America*, Atlantic City, June 1–2, 1900 (Providence, 1900), 51.

46. R. L. Pitfield, "Report on the Vaccine Farms and Antitoxin Propagating Establishments of the United States, and Their Products, and on Certain Imported Antitoxins," *Twelfth Annual Report of the State Board of Health and Vital Statistics of the Commonwealth of Pennsylvania* (1896) vol. 1 (State Printer, 1897), 186, 193, 196, 154.

47. Abbott, "Vaccination," 142. *USROSENAU*, 6. Glynn and Glynn, *Life and Death of Smallpox*, 172–73. J. J. Kinyoun, "The Action of Glycerin on Bacteria in the Presence of Cell Exudates," *Journal of Experimental Medicine*, 7 (1905): 725–32.

48. Mulford Company display advertisements, *Medical World*, 19 (December 1901), 17. On the connection between cities and hinterlands in the late nineteenth century, see William Cronon, *Nature's Metropolis: Chicago and the Great West* (New York: W. W. Norton & Company, 1991).

49. Richard Hofstadter wrote, "The United States was born in the country and has moved to the city." *The Age of Reform: From Bryan to F. D. R.* (New York: Random House, 1955), 23. Liebenau, *Medical Science and Medical Industry*, 57–78; Galambos with Sewell, *Networks of Innovation*, 9–32. Curiously, the latter work does not mention the Camden episode.

50. Mulford display advertisement, *Medical Dial*, 2 (Apr. 1900), xii. Galambos with Sewell, *Networks of Innovation*, 9–32.

51. Mulford display advertisement, *Medical Dial*, 2 (Apr. 1900), xii.

52. Elgin, "Propagation of Vaccine," 46–55. See also, "How Mulford's Vaccine Is Made," display advertisement, *ILLMJ*, 51 (May 1902), pages not numbered. To compare Mulford's production practices with those of other makers, see esp. Abbott, "Vaccination," 138–44; Chapin, *Municipal Sanitation*, 584; Francis C. Martin, "The Propagation, Preservation, and Use of Vaccine Virus," *MR*, 49 (May 30, 1896), 757–59; "The Public Health Laboratories of New York City and Their Products," *New York State Journal of Medicine*, 2 (Feb. 1902): 37; Theobald Smith, "The Preparation of Animal Vaccine," *MC*, Jan. 1, 1902, 101–16; "Virus and Antitoxin of the Health Board," *NYT*, Nov. 24, 1901, 5. On Canadian practices, see Pierrick Malissard, "'Pharming' à l'ancienne: les Fermes Vaccinales Canadiennes," *Canadian Historical Review*, 85 (2004): 35–62. See "Vaccine Calves on Market," *CT*, Mar. 3, 1901, 14.

53. Chapin, *Municipal Sanitation*, 580–84. Abbott, "Vaccination," 138, 147–49.

54. John Duffy, *A History of Public Health in New York City 1866–1966*, 242.

55. W. B. Clarke, "The Pot Calls the Kettle Black," *American Homeopathist*, 26 (May 1900), 159, 160. Otis Clapp & Son display advertisement, *New England Medical Gazette*, Dec. 1897, unnumbered page in advertising section. Parke, Davis & Company display advertisement, *ILLMJ*, 51 (Feb. 1902), unpaginated advertising page.

56. John Anderson, *Art Held Hostage: The Battle over the Barnes Collection* (New York: W. W. Norton & Company, 2003), 7–30. Richard J. Wattenmaker, "Dr. Albert C. Barnes and the Barnes Foundation," in *Great French Paintings from the Barnes Foundation: Impressionist, Post-impressionist, and Early Modern* (New York: Alfred A. Knopf, 1993), 3–27.

57. "Lockjaw in Camden," *NYTRIB*, Nov. 21, 1901, 8. "Virus Did Not Cause Lockjaw," ibid., Nov. 20, 1901, 6. "Smallpox Virus Was Pure," *NYS*, Nov. 20, 1901, 5. "Vaccination and Lockjaw," ibid., Nov. 21, 1901, 6. See also, Albert C. Barnes, "Facts About the Camden Cases of Tetanus," letter to the editor, *NYT*, Nov. 21, 1901.

58. "Camden Board of Health Report," 112–18, esp. 113. "No Lockjaw Germs in Virus," *WP*, Dec. 1, 1901, 24.

59. "The Tetanus Cases in Camden and St. Louis," *ADPR*, Nov. 25, 1901, 310.

60. "Vaccine and Antitoxin," *NYT*, Dec. 8, 1901, 6. "The Tetanus Problem," *PNA*, Nov. 30, 1901, 8. "Smallpox: Vaccination and Tetanus," *Current Literature*, 32 (April 1902), 486. W. R. Inge Dalton, "Responsibility for the Recent Deaths from the Use of Impure Antitoxins and Vaccine Virus," *Canadian Journal of Medicine and Surgery*, 11 (Jan. 1902), 35.

61. Robert N. Willson, "Tetanus Appearing in the Course of Vaccinia; Report of a Case," *Proceedings of the Philadelphia County Medical Society*, 22 (Nov. 1901), 353–66, esp. 364. "Discussion," ibid., 367–69, esp. 367.

62. "Three Children Expire from the Disease After Vaccination," *NYTRIB*, Nov. 27, 1901, 14; "Another Case of Tetanus," ibid., Dec. 5, 1901, 6. "More Deaths from Tetanus: Poisoned Vaccine Still Proving Fatal at Camden, N.J.," *Omaha World-Herald*, Nov. 27, 1901, 1. "More Deaths from Lockjaw," *Medical News*, Dec. 7, 1901, 909. "Another Tetanus Victim Succumbs," *Philadelphia Inquirer*, Dec. 8, 1901, 7. *Twelfth Census of the United States* (1900): Schedule No. 1—Population: Camden, NJ, Supervisor's District No. 6, Enumeration District No. 67 (Overby); ibid., Enumeration District No. 73 (Rosevelt). Neither Heath nor Johnson was recorded in the 1900 census in Camden County. "Camden Board of Health Report," 115.

63. "Vaccine and Antitoxin," *NYT*, Dec. 8, 1901, 4. "A Medical Inquiry as to Vaccine and Antitoxin," ibid., Dec. 28, 1901, 6.

64. Arthur Van Harlingen, "Remarks on Vaccination in Relation to Skin Diseases and Eruptions Following Vaccination," *PMJ*, 9 (Jan. 25, 1902), 184–86, esp. 186. John H. McCollom, "Vaccination: Accidents and Untoward Effects," *MC*, Jan. 1, 1902, 125–38.

65. *NCBOH 1897–98*, 37-38. F. T. Campbell, "Vaccination," *PMJ*, 9 (Apr. 12, 1902): 668. See also *CAMBOH 1902*, 8.

66. M. J. Rosenau, "Report on the examination of dried lymph and glycerinized vaccine lymph," enclosed with Walter Wyman to C. P. Wertenbaker, Apr. 6, 1900, CPWL, vol. 1. "Dr. Rosenau Dies," *NYT*, Apr. 10, 1946, 25. "Milton J. Rosenau, M. D.," *MMWR Weekly*, Oct. 15, 1999, 907.

67. Milton J. Rosenau, "Dry Points Versus Glycerinated Virus, From a Bacteriologic Standpoint," *USSGPHMHS 1902*, 446–49, esp. 449. "New York Academy of Medicine," *Pediatrics*, 13 (May 1, 1902): 344–49.

68. Rosenau, "Dry Points Versus Glycerinated Virus," 446. "Society Proceedings: New York Academy of Medicine," *MN*, 80 (Mar. 22, 1902), 562ff. Rosenau published his full report in March 1903, *USROSENAU*. "Conference of State and Provincial Boards of Health of North America," *MR*, Nov. 15, 1902, 789.

69. *Cleveland Medical Journal* quoted in "Vaccine Lymph," *Sanitarian*, March 1902. Ibid., 240, 239. "This state of affairs is causing profound disquietude among conscientious medical practitioners." "Commercial Virus and Antitoxin," *NYT*, Nov. 18, 1901, 6.

70. John W. LeSeur, "Vaccination, A Privilege or a Duty?" in *Transactions of the Homeopathic Medical Society of the State of New York for the Year 1902*, vol. 37 (Rochester, 1902), 52.

71. Theobald Smith, "The Preparation of Animal Vaccine," in *MC*, Jan. 1, 1902, 114–15.

72. Dalton, "Responsibility for the Recent Deaths," 35. On decommodification, see Daniel T. Rodgers, *Atlantic Crossings: Social Politics in a Progressive Age* (Cambridge, MA: Belknap Press, 1998); Amy Dru Stanley, *From Bondage to Contract: Wage Labor, Marriage, and the Market in the Age of Slave Emancipation* (New York: Cambridge University Press, 1998), 267–68.

73. Eugene A. Darling, "Vaccination: The Technique," *MC*, Jan. 1, 1902, 118. Ann Bowman Jannetta, "Public Health and the Diffusion of Vaccination in Japan," in *Asian Population History*, ed. Ts'ui-jung Liu, et al. (New York, 2001), 292–305. "Hearing Over," *BG*, Feb. 5, 1902, 4. "Death from Lockjaw," *CC*, Jan. 4, 1902, 5. R. E. Doolittle, "Inspection of Imported Food and Drug Products," *Yearbook of the United States Department of Agriculture, 1910* (Washington, 1911), 201.

74. "Regulation of Serum" [from *American Medicine*], *WP*, Dec. 25, 1901, 11. "Should Cities Go into the Drug Business?" *St. Louis Medical and Surgical Reporter*, 74 (March 1898), 152. "Vaccine Makers Protest," *WP*, Mar. 16, 1900, 5. "On Government Competition," *ADPR*, Oct. 14, 1901, 218. W. R. Inge Dalton, "Municipal Socialism of a Dangerous Kind," letter to the editor, *NYT*, Nov. 18, 1901, 5. Daniel DeLeon, "Hiding Their Own Crimes," *Daily People*, Nov. 19, 1901, http://www.slp .org/pdf/de_leon/eds1901/nov19_1901.pdf, accessed Feb. 23, 2009.
Practical considerations also worked against manufacture by state and local health boards. In many states, the limited demand for the product during long periods when smallpox was not prevalent could not justify the cost of maintaining a state farm. The southern states had virtually no vaccine production facilities, either state or commercial; even in states with relatively strong health boards, such as Kentucky and North Carolina, officials were content to recommend vaccines manufactured in the Northeast or Middle West. See Gardner T. Swarts, "Is It Advisable for a State to Provide Vaccine Virus," in *PABOH 1900*, 467–68.

75. Editorial favorably quoting an unnamed writer, in "The St. Louis Tragedy," *Medical Dial*, 3 (Dec. 1901), 302. "Vaccine and Antitoxin," *NYT*, Dec. 8, 1901, 6. "Government Control of Therapeutic Serums, Vaccine, Etc.," *MR*, Mar. 29, 1902, 495. See "Topics of the Times," *NYT*, Mar. 20, 1902, 8. "Vaccine Virus and Antitoxin," *Sanitarian*, May 1902, 417. In 1898, the New York County Medical Society had sponsored a bill in the New York Senate to prevent the health department from selling its vaccine and antitoxin. Duffy, *Public Health in New York City*, 241.

76. "Regulation of Serum." "Government Control of Therapeutic Serums, Vaccine, Etc.," *MR*, Mar. 29, 1902, 495. Kondratas, "Biologics Control Act," 17.

77. "Government Control of Therapeutic Serums," 495. "Discussion," *Transactions of the Homeopathic Medical Society of the State of New York for the Year 1902*, vol. 37 (Rochester, 1902), 60.

78. Woodward memorandum dated April 24, 1902, in U.S. Doc. 4407, 57th Congress, 1st Session,

H.R. Reports, Vol. 9, No. 2713, "Sale of Viruses, Etc., in the District of Columbia," June 27, 1902, 4. "Cost of Street Cleaning," *WP*, Apr. 5, 1902, 11. "Regulates Sale of Virus," *WP*, May 3, 1902, 14.

79. Kober memorandum dated April 16, 1902, in H. R., "Sale of Viruses, Etc., in the District of Columbia," 4. See also U.S. Doc 4264, 57th Congress, 1st Session, Senate Reports, vol. 9, no. 1980, "Sale of Viruses, Etc., in the District of Columbia, June 19, 1902. "Virus Sale Licenses," *WP*, Apr. 22, 1902, 12.

80. Walsh to Dr. Joseph McFarland, Dec. 4, 1901, quoted in Liebenau, *Medical Science and Medical Industry*, 85. "Cleveland Experiment," 581. See also, in reference to a memorial from the Cleveland Academy of Medicine calling for U.S. government control of vaccine production, "American Medical Association," *New York State Journal of Medicine*, 2 (July 1902), 194.

81. Robert N. Willson, "Abstract of an Analysis of Fifty-Two Cases of Tetanus Following Vaccinia: with Reference to the Source of Infection," *Proceedings of the Philadelphia County Medical Society*, vol. 23 (Philadelphia, 1902), 157, 162, 165.

82. Untitled item on McFarland's appointment, *MN*, Feb. 9, 1901, 225. The significant changes were matters primarily of tone, as McFarland more resolutely stated his argument that a single make of vaccine, corrupted with tetanus, had caused the outbreaks at Camden and elsewhere.

83. Joseph McFarland, "Tetanus and Vaccination—An Analytical Study of Ninety-Five Cases of This Rare Complication," *Proceedings of the Philadelphia County Medical Society*, vol. 23 (Philadelphia, 1902) [hereafter McFarland, *Proceedings*], 166, 171. Joseph McFarland, "Tetanus and Vaccination: An Analytical Study of 95 Cases of the Complication," *Lancet*, Sept. 13, 1902 [hereafter McFarland, *Lancet*], 730.

84. McFarland, *Proceedings*, 168, 169. See, for example: "Death Follows Vaccination," *NOP*, Dec. 15, 1893, 4; "Vaccination, Lockjaw, and Death," *NYT*, May 29, 1894, 2. McFarland also implied that attempts were made to "suppress" cases "at the present time," and perhaps also in the past. McFarland, *Proceedings*, 168.

85. McFarland, *Proceedings*, 169.

86. McFarland also considered, and rejected, the (plausible) argument that the recent introduction of shields, to cover vaccination wounds, had contributed to the occurrence of tetanus. The argument was that the shields created just the sort of anaerobic environment where tetanus bacilli thrived. But McFarland pointed out that in very few of the reported cases had shields even been used. McFarland, *Proceedings*, 171.

87. McFarland, *Proceedings*, 173, 174. McFarland, *Lancet*, 733.

88. McFarland, *Proceedings*, 174, 175.

89. *USROSENAU*, 6–7. See also John H. Huddleston, "Tetanus and Vaccine Virus," *Pediatrics*, 16 (Feb. 1904), 65–71.

90. William Osler, *The Principles and Practice of Medicine*, 4th ed. (New York: D. Appleton and Company, 1901), 231. McFarland, *Proceedings*, 177. Today, the Centers for Disease Control places the normal incubation period at "3 to 21 days, usually about eight days," adding: "In general the further the site is from the central nervous system, the longer incubation period. The shorter the incubation period, the higher the chance of death." (*Epidemiology and Prevention of Vaccine-Preventable Diseases*, 10th ed. (2008), 72. http://www.cdc.gov/vaccines/pubs/pinkbook/downloads/tetanus -508.pdf, accessed February 23, 2009.)

91. "Virus, Antitoxins, and Serums," *NYT*, Apr. 14, 1902, 8. The *Congressional Record* documents no debate on the legislation. JCSP, General Correspondence, Boxes 51–54.

92. Public Law No. 244, "An act to regulate the sale of viruses, serums, toxins, and analogous products in the District of Columbia, to regulate interstate traffic in said articles, and for other purposes," 32 Stat. L., 728, approved July 1, 1902.

93. Kondratas, "Biologics Control Act," 17.

94. Kondratas, "Biologics Control Act," 18–19. John Parascandola, "The Public Health Service and

the Control of Biologics," *PHR*, 110 (Nov. /Dec. 1995), 774–75. Milstein, "Strengthening the Science Base," 176.

95. "The Best Vaccine," *BG*, Jun. 15, 1903, 6. Barbara Gutman Rosenkrantz, *Public Health and the State: Changing Views in Massachusetts, 1842–1936* (Cambridge: Harvard University Press, 1972), 123–27. "The Bacteriologic Laboratory," *CMJ*, 2 (Jan. 1903), 37–38.

96. Kondratas, "Biologics Control Act," 19–20. Liebenau, *Medical Science and Medical Industry*.

97. Pure Food and Drug Act, 1906, approved June 30, 1906, 34 U.S. Stats. 768.

98. "Statement of Dr. C. T. Sowers, of Washington, D.C.," Hearings Before the Committee on Interstate and Foreign Commerce of the House of Representatives on Bills Relating to Health Activities of the General Government, Part I (Washington, 1910), 385–86.

99. "Smallpox in New Jersey," *PMJ*, 9 (Jan. 11, 1902), 50. "Smallpox in Camden," ibid., 9 (Mar 1, 1902), 466.

SIX: THE POLITICS OF TIGHT SPACES

1. "Doctors Make a Raid: Many Persons in Little Italy Are Forcibly Vaccinated," *NYT*, Feb. 2, 1901, 10. None of the Caballo family members, nor Antoinette Alvena, appeared in the 1900 or 1910 census. I was unable to find any further information about them.

2. "Doctors Make a Raid." See also "Smallpox in Little Italy," *NYT*, Jan. 31, 1901, 2. "The Weather," ibid., Feb. 2, 1901, 3.

3. Blauvelt in "Smallpox Scare Is Unwarranted," *NYT*, Dec. 29, 1900, 8. See also "New York Library's Record," ibid., Jan. 9, 1901, 8; "Smallpox Scare's Hardships," ibid., Dec. 29, 1900, 8; "Over a Thousand Vaccinated," ibid., Jan. 18, 1901, 2; and "Smallpox Rumors Hurt Trade," *NYTRIB*, Jan. 8, 1901, 2.

4. Blauvelt in "Army of Vaccinators," *NYT*, Dec. 25, 1900, 4.

5. On the social and cultural history of Italian Harlem, see Robert A. Orsi, *The Madonna of 115th Street: Faith and Community in Italian Harlem, 1880–1950*, 2d ed. (New Haven: Yale University Press, 2002).

6. "War on Disease Germs," *NYT*, Jul. 7, 1900, 5. Jacob August Riis, *The Children of the Poor* (New York: Charles Scribner's Sons, 1902), 24. John Duffy, *The Sanitarians*, 207.

7. Dillingham quoted in "Small-Pox, Hid, Now Breaks Out," *NYEW*, Jan. 31, 1901, 3. "Smallpox in 'Little Italy,'" *NYTRIB*, Feb. 1, 1901, 3. "Smallpox in Little Italy," *NYT*, Jan. 31, 1901, 2. "Doctors Make a Raid."

8. "Doctors Make a Raid."

9. Ibid.

10. Ibid. Orsi, *Madonna*, esp. 21–24, 35.

11. "Doctors Make a Raid."

12. Ibid.

13. Ibid.

14. *United States Constitution*, Article II, Section 1. For a concise overview of Italian immigration during this period, see Rudolph J. Vecoli, "The Italian Diaspora, 1876–1976," in *The Cambridge History of World Migration*, ed. Robin Cohen (Cambridge: Cambridge University Press, 1995), 114–22.

15. U.S. Treasury Department, *Immigration Laws and Regulations* (Washington, 1900), esp. 12. U.S. Department of Commerce and Labor, Bureau of Immigration, *Immigration Laws and Regulations* (Washington, 1904). Walter T. K. Nugent, *Crossings: The Great Transatlantic Migrations, 1870–1914*, reprint ed. (Bloomington: Indiana University Press, 1995), 27–33.

16. William Pencak, "General Introduction," in *Immigration to New York*, ed. William Pencak et al. (Philadelphia: Balch Institute Press, 1991), xiii. Mary Elizabeth Brown, "'. . . The Adoption of the

Tactics of the Enemy': The Care of Italian Immigrant Youth in the Archdiocese of New York During the Progressive Era," in ibid., 109–10. Alan M. Kraut, *Silent Travelers*, esp. 51–52.

17. Sean Dennis Cashman, *America in the Age of Titans: The Progressive Era and World War I* (New York: NYU Press, 1988), 155–57. See also William J. Rorabaugh et al., *America's Promise: A Concise History of the United States* (Lanham, MD: Rowman & Littlefield Publishers, Inc., 2004), 400. Nugent, *Crossings*, 31–33. On steerage journeys from Asia to San Francisco, see Robert Eric Barde, *Immigration at the Golden Gate: Passenger Ships, Exclusion, and Angel Island* (Westport, CT: Praeger, 2008).

18. Journalist quoted in Nancy Foner, *From Ellis Island to JFK: New York's Two Great Waves of Immigration* (New Haven: Yale University Press, 2000), 31; ibid., 29–32.

19. "Carriers by Water—Their Relations with Passengers," *CLJ*, 52 (Jan. 25, 1901), 66. U.S. Treasury Department, Public Health and Marine-Hospital Service, *Handbook for the Ship's Medicine Chest*, by George W. Stoner, 2d ed. (Washington, 1904), 24. "U.S. Quarantine Laws and Regulations," in *USSGPHMHS 1894*, 242. 29th U.S. Congress, 1st Session, H.R. Doc. No. 182, "Surgeons on Packet Ships," Apr. 6, 1846, 2. See "Smallpox at Sea" [from London *Times*], *NYT*, Aug. 4, 1891; "Pestship in the Offing," ibid., Aug. 29, 1896, 9.

20. Excerpt from *Annual Report of the Commissioners of Immigration, State of New York* (1868), in *Immigration: Select Documents and Case Records*, ed. Edith Abbott (Chicago: University of Chicago Press, 1924), 44, 45, 46. For an earlier (1845) call for a law requiring surgeons aboard immigrant ships, see "Surgeons on Packet Ships," 3.

21. Congressional debate on "A Bill to Regulate the Carriage of Passengers by Sea," in Abbott, ed., *Immigration*, 54, 53. 47th Congress, 1st Session, H.R. Doc. No. 118, "Introduction of Contagious and Infectious Diseases into the United States," Mar. 13, 1882, 2. "Vaccinating Immigrants: A New Move by the National Board of Health," *WP*, Aug. 31, 1881, 4. On the 1878 law, see U.S. Department of State, *Commercial Relations of the United States with Foreign Countries* (Washington, 1887), vol. 2: 1865–1866.

22. "Report of the Health-Officer of the Port of New York," *SCI*, 13 (Apr. 19, 1889), 304. "Vaccination of Immigrants," *MR*, Nov. 11, 1882, 550.

23. F. Scrimshaw to William Tebb, May 7, 1883, in William Tebb, *Compulsory Vaccination in England: With Incidental References to Foreign States* (London: E. W. Allen, 1884), 48. On New York, see "An Act for the Protection of the Public Health," in Department of State, *Commercial Relations of the United States*, vol. 2: 1929–30. On Boston, see *O'Brien v. Cunard Steamship Company*, 154 MA 272 (1891). California had long had such a policy for San Francisco, but it only applied to ships with smallpox aboard or ships arriving from an infected port. See "Health and Quarantine Regulations for the City and Harbor of San Francisco," *CALBOH 1890–92*, 192–98.

24. See Jimmy Casas Klausen, "Room Enough: America, Natural Liberty, and Consent in Locke's *Second Treatise*," *Journal of Politics*, 69 (2007), 760–69.

25. *O'Brien v. Cunard Steamship Company*, 154 MA 272 (1891). This accounts draws upon the records from the case—including the plaintiff's list of exceptions and the briefs from both sides—in Massachusetts Reports, Papers and Briefs, SLL.

26. *O'Brien v. Cunard Steamship Company*, 154 MA 272 (1891).

27. O'Brien also claimed that the vaccination had been negligently performed, causing an eruption of blisters over her body. The Supreme Judicial Court absolved the Cunard Steamship Company from any responsibility, insisting that under the federal law steamship companies had done all that was required when they provided a competent medical practitioner; "[t]he work the physician or surgeon does in such cases is under the control of the passengers themselves." *O'Brien v. Cunard Steamship Company*, 154 MA 272, 276 (1891).

28. "The United States Public Health and Marine-Hospital Service," *JAMA*, 43 (1904): 809–11.

29. "United States Quarantine Laws and Regulations," *USSGPHMHS 1894*, 252, 247, 240–41.

30. Alan M. Kraut, "Plagues and Prejudice: Nativism's Construction of Disease in Nineteenth- and Twentieth-Century New York City," in *Hives of Sickness: Public Health and Epidemics in New York City*, ed. David Rosner (New Brunswick, NJ: Rutgers University Press, 1995), 65–90, esp. 69.

31. "Smallpox on Cunard Liner," *NYT*, June 19, 1900, 7. This practice continued for years. See "Vaccinate 1,045 Immigrants," ibid., Oct. 25, 1909, 4. See Samuel W. Abbott, "Vaccination," in *A Reference Handbook of the Medical Sciences*, vol. 8: 147.

32. Amy L. Fairchild, *Science at the Borders: Immigrant Medical Inspection and the Shaping of the Modern Industrial Labor Force* (Baltimore: The Johns Hopkins University Press, 2003), 125.

33. Alfred C. Reed, "Going Through Ellis Island," *PSM*, Jan. 1913, 5–18. Kraut, "Plagues and Prejudice," 69. Nancy Foner, et al., eds., *Immigration Research for a New Century: Multidisciplinary Perspectives* (New York: Russell Sage Foundation, 2000), 96–99.

34. *USSGPHMHS 1903*, 20. Kraut, "Plagues and Prejudice," 69, 70. Kraut, *Silent Travelers*, 55.

35. *PHR*, 14 (Feb. 24, 1899), 240, 241.

36. *PHR*, 14 (Mar. 3, 1899), 281. Ibid., 14 (Mar. 24, 1899), 390. Ibid., 14 (Feb. 24, 1899), 242. Ibid., 14 (Mar. 10, 1899), 311. Ibid., 14 (Mar. 31, 1899), 423. See Carlos E. Cuéllar, "Laredo Smallpox Riot," *Handbook of Texas Online*, http://www.tshaonline.org/handbook/online/articles/LL/jcl1.html (accessed April 15, 2009). See also John McKiernan, "Fevered Measures: Race, Communicable Disease, and Community Formation in the Texas-Mexico Border" (PhD diss, University of Michigan, 2002). Howard Markel and Alexandra Minna Stern, "The Foreignness of Germs: The Persistent Association of Immigrants and Disease in American Society," *Milbank Quarterly*, 80 (2002), 765.

37. "Copy of letter addressed on October 2 [1905] by the vice-consul of France, at Colon, to the secretary of foreign affairs, Paris (American section)," in 59th Congress, 1st Session, Senate Doc. No. 127, Part 2: *Isthmian Canal. Message from the President of the United States, Transmitting Certain Papers to Accompany His Message of January 8, 1906* (Washington, 1906), 60. "Clubbed by Police," *WP*, Oct. 2, 1905, 1. "No Vaccine for Them They Said," *El Águila de Puerto-Rico*, Oct. 3, 1905, 1. See also "Club Canal Workmen to Force Them to Land," *NYT*, Oct. 2, 1905, 1; "Laborers Who Leaped Overboard Safe," ibid., Oct. 3, 1905, 6. Leon Pepperman, *Who Built the Panama Canal?* (New York: E. P. Dutton & Company, 1915), 273–74. See generally Julie Greene, *The Canal Builders: Making America's Empire at the Panama Canal* (New York: The Penguin Press, 2009), 39–43.

38. Gustave Anguizola, "Negroes in the Building of the Panama Canal," *Phylon*, 29 (1968), 351–59, esp. 355. See James C. Scott, *Weapons of the Weak: Everyday Forms of Peasant Resistance* (New Haven: Yale University Press, 1985); and idem, *Domination and the Arts of Resistance: Hidden Transcripts* (New Haven: Yale University Press, 1990).

39. James Nevins Hyde, "The Late Epidemic of Smallpox in the United States," *PSM*, 59 (Oct. 1901), 567. "School Vaccinations," *American Medicine*, précis in *MR*, Oct. 4, 1902, 547.

40. Dutch Doctor Barnes, "How to Produce a Scar Resembling Vaccination," *Medical Talk*, 5 (1904), 308. This article was reprinted numerous times in journals sympathetic or dedicated to the cause of antivaccinationism, including *The Liberator*. "How to Produce a Scar Resembling Vaccination," *The Liberator*, March 1908, reprinted in *A Stuffed Club: A Journal of Rational Therapeutics*, Part I, ed. John H. Tilden, orig. 1908, reprinted (Whitefish, MT: Kessinger Publishing, 2003), 56. *FBOH 1904*, 69. See Nadav Davidovitch, "Negotiating Dissent: Homeopathy and Anti-Vaccinationism at the Turn of the Twentieth Century," in *The Politics of Healing*, ed. Robert D. Johnston, 24–25.

41. Chapin, *Municipal Sanitation*, 573–80, esp. 579. Abbott, "Vaccination," 120, 126.

42. Freund, *Police Power*, 109, 116.

43. Edwin Grant Dexter, *A History of Education in the United States* (New York: The Macmillan Company 1904), appendices. Chapin, *Municipal Sanitation*, 575–78.

44. Hunter Boyd in *Proceedings of the National Conference of Charities and Correction at the Thirtieth Annual Session Held in the City of Atlanta, May 6–12, 1903* (1903), 110. George M. Kober, "The Progress and Tendency of Hygiene and Sanitary Science in the Nineteenth Century," *JAMA*, Jun. 8, 1901, 1624. "Medical Inspection in the Schools," *NYT*, Sept. 27, 1903, 6. See Judith Sealander, *The Failed Century of the Child: Governing America's Young in the Twentieth Century* (New York: Cambridge University Press, 2003); and David Tyack, "Health and Social Services in Public Schools: Historical Perspectives," *The Future of Children*, 2 (Spring 1992), 19–31.

45. "Vaccination Certificate Frauds," *NYT*, May 9, 1904, 8. "Vaccination," *CT*, reprinted in *NYT*, Jun. 24, 1900, 20. "Led Scarless Kids to School," *AC*, Dec. 5, 1902, 2.

46. Martin Friedrich, "How We Rid Cleveland of Smallpox," *CMJ*, 1 (Feb. 1902), 78. See also "Compulsory Vaccination Upheld," *NYT*, Sept. 1, 1901, 8; "Vaccination Stirs Revolt," ibid., Feb. 5, 1906, 1; "Teacher Must Be Vaccinated," ibid., Nov. 15, 1901, 7. "Teachers Opposed Vaccination Census," *PMJ*, 9 (Mar. 8, 1902), 42.

47. "New Jersey Smallpox Panic," *NYT*, Dec. 8, 1901, 8. "Smallpox Scare's Hardships," ibid., Dec. 29, 1900, 8. "Smallpox in the State," *PMJ*, 9 (Feb. 1, 1902), 195.

48. On labor law during this period, see generally, William E. Forbath, *Law and the Shaping of the American Labor Movement* (Cambridge, MA: Harvard University Press, 1991).

49. "Over a Thousand Vaccinated," *NYT*, Jan. 18, 1901, 2. On railroads' liability, see "Agency—Notice to Agent Is Notice to Principal—Liability of Carrier," in "Recent Decisions," *Columbia Law Review*, 7 (May 1907), 360. For examples of compulsion, see (re: United Traction Company of Albany, New York) "To Vaccinate 500 Street Railway Men," *NYT*, Jan. 17, 1901, 5; and (re: Pennsylvania RR Corp.), "Vaccination," *NYT*, Dec. 18, 1903, 8. "Orders 300,000 Vaccinated," *CT*, Feb. 14, 1903. On the Frick Company, see American Iron and Steel Institute, *Directory to the Iron and Steel Works of the United States* (Philadelphia, 1904), 72–73.

50. "Factory Girls' Resistance," *NYT*, Apr. 12, 1901, 3.

51. Martin Friedrich, "How We Rid Cleveland of Smallpox," *CMJ*, 1 (Feb. 1902): 77–78. "Smallpox at Stockport," *NYT*, June 16, 1900, 10.

52. "Miners Resist Vaccination," *NYT*, Apr. 25, 1902, 1.

53. "Wage War on Smallpox," *CT*, Feb. 4, 1902, 2. "Smallpox in Chicago," *PMJ*, 9 (Feb. 22, 1902), 344. "Roads to Fight Smallpox," *NYT*, Feb. 14, 1902, 2.

54. *MBOH 1899–1901*, 3–4. "Compulsory Vaccination for Rhode Island," *PMJ*, 9 (Mar 1902), 386. "In Senate," *Chicago Medical Recorder*, 20 (June 1901): 604.

55. *JAMA*, Jun. 15, 1901, 1712. *Journal of Proceedings of the Forty-Fifth Session of the Wisconsin Legislature, 1901* (Madison, WI, 1901), 926. "Compulsory Vaccination," *Wasatch Wave* (Utah), Feb. 1, 1901. *General Laws of the State of Minnesota, Passed During the Thirty-Third Session of the State Legislature* (St. Paul, 1903), ch. 299, 530.

56. "Topics of the Times," *NYT*, Jan. 19, 1901, 8. James Colgrove, "Between Persuasion and Compulsion: Smallpox Control in Brooklyn and New York, 1894–1902," *BHM*, 78 (2004), 372. "Compulsory Vaccination," *PMJ*, 9, Mar. 15, 1902, 466. "Smallpox in Hospitals," *NYT*, Mar. 14, 1902, 2.

57. *NYCBOH 1901*, 12.

58. *NYCBOH 1902*, 18. Ernest J. Lederle, "Municipal Suppression of Infection and Contagion," *North American Review*, 174 (June 1902), 769–77.

59. *NYCBOH 1902*, 8, 92. "Physician Badly Scares Trolley Car Passengers," *NYT*, Mar. 28, 1902, 1. "Smallpox Panic in Harlem," *NYT*, Apr. 28, 1902, 2.

60. "Smallpox Patient Taken from Tenement," *NYT*, Nov. 23, 1902, 19.

61. *NYCBOH 1903*, 8–9, 62, 238.

62. "Keeping the Health of a City," *Scientific American*, 89 (Oct. 10, 1903), 254.

63. "Fusion Campaign Cards," *NYT*, Oct. 9, 1903, 2. See also "Citizens' Union Campaign," ibid., Sept. 21, 1903, 2; and "Mayor Low's Superb Administration," ibid., Oct. 12, 1903, 1. "Dr. E. J. Lederle Dies in Sanitarium," ibid., Mar. 15, 1921, 11.

64. "Compulsory Vaccination," *CT*, Mar. 13, 1899, 6; "Wages War on Smallpox," ibid., Jan. 28, 1900, 34. "The Cambridge Smallpox Epidemic," *MN*, June 28, 1902, 1230. "Virus Squad Out," *BG*, Nov. 18, 1901, 7. *BOSHD 1901*, 45.

65. Carl Lorenz, *Tom L. Johnson: Mayor of Cleveland* (New York: A. S. Barnes Company, 1911), 57–58. Friedrich, "How We Rid Cleveland," 78.

66. Friedrich, "How We Rid Cleveland," 88. *Annual Report of the Public Health Division, Department of Police, of the City of Cleveland, Ohio, For the Year Ending December 31st, 1901* (Cleveland, 1902), 5, 16.

67. Belt quoted in Friedrich, "How We Rid Cleveland," 87. Ibid., 89. "Editorial: Smallpox, Vaccination and Disinfection," *CMJ*, 1 (Feb. 1902), 119–20. "How Cleveland Stamped Out Smallpox Without Vaccination," *PMJ*, 10 (Oct. 11, 1902), 486. For examples of antivaccinationists' praising Friedrich's disinfection campaign, see B. O. Flower, "How Cleveland Stamped Out Smallpox," *Arena*, 27 (Apr. 1902), 426–29; C. F. Nichols, *Vaccination: A Blunder in Poisons*, 2d ed. (Boston: Blackwell and Churchill Press,1902), 22–28.

68. Friedrich in *Annual Report of the Department of Public Health of the City of Cleveland, Ohio, For the Year Ending December 31st, 1903* (Cleveland, 1904), 937–42, esp. 937. "Vaccination Is the Only Remedy," *Cleveland Plain Dealer*, Jun. 20, 1902. *Annual Report of the Department of Police, Public Health Division of the City of Cleveland, Ohio, For the Year Ending December 31, 1902* (Cleveland, 1903), 20. "Vaccinate!" *CMJ*, 1 (May 1902): 279–80. "The Smallpox Situation," ibid., 1 (July 1902): 383. "How Cleveland Was Rid of Smallpox?" ibid., 1 (1902): 470–73. "Smallpox Decreasing," ibid., 1 (Dec. 1902): 568. "Vaccination in Cleveland," ibid., 1 (Dec. 1902): 571–72. "The Smallpox Situation in Ohio," ibid., 2 (Feb. 1903): 96–97.

69. "Smallpox in the State," *PMJ*, 9 (Jan. 25, 1902), 155.

70. On Roseto, see Stewart Wolf and John G. Bruhn, *The Power of Clan: The Influence of Human Relationships on Heart Disease* (Piscataway, NJ: Transaction Publishers, 1998), esp. 13–24.

71. Leroy Parker and Robert H. Worthington, *The Law of Public Health and Safety, and the Powers and Duties of Boards of Health* (Albany, NY: Matthew Bender, 1892), 131. See "Many Tricks of the Ignorant Poor to Hide Contagious Diseases from the Health Board," *NYTRIB*, Aug. 2, 1903, 3. See also "Girl Hid from Vaccinators," *NYT*, Mar. 14, 1901, 3; "Smallpox Nest in Brooklyn," ibid., Mar. 20, 1901, 2; "Defies the Health Board," ibid., Jul. 14, 1901, 3.

72. Chapin, *Municipal Sanitation*, 607–8.

73. "New Orleans Pesthouse," *NYT*, Apr. 1, 1900, 2. "Lay All Blame on Pest House," *Salt Lake Herald*, Jun. 2, 1903, 2. "At North Brother Island," *NYT*, Jun. 16, 1901, 20. "Wrong Body Sent Home," ibid., Nov. 25, 1901, 11.

74. *Kirk v. Board of Health*, 83 S.C. 372 (1909), 374, 384, 383. Samuel W. Abbott, "Legislation with Reference to Small-Pox and Vaccination," *MC*, Jan. 1, 1902, 155.

75. "Hospital Spread of Smallpox," *JAMA*, June 16, 1894, reprinted in ibid., June 15, 1994, 1812. "Air-Borne Smallpox," *Scientific American Supplement*, 1422 (Apr. 4, 1903): 22737–38. London *Times* quoted in ibid., 22737.

76. *NCBOH 1903–04*, 16 (recalling Durham episode circa 1899). "North Side Men Indignant," *Omaha Daily Bee*, Jan. 17, 1899, 5; "Object to the Pest House," ibid., Jul. 11, 1899, 7. "Fire Destroys Pest House," ibid., Nov. 9, 1899, 12; "Cause of Action Burned," ibid., Nov. 14, 1899, 7. On Houston, see "City Council Meeting," *Houston Daily Post*, Nov. 21, 1899, 6. On Union County, see "Here and There," *Hopkinsville Kentuckian*, Apr. 17, 1900, 8. On Bradford, see "Pest House Fired by Mob," *AC*, Apr. 12, 1901, 3. On Turtle Creek, see "Quaker Mob Defies Sheriff," *AC*, May 14, 1900, 1.

77. "Tried to Burn a Smallpox Hospital," *NYT*, Mar. 10, 1901, 3. "Police at Orange Hospital," ibid., Mar. 11, 1901, 3. "Smallpox Hospital Razed by Mob," ibid., Mar. 12, 1901, 2. "Hospital Ruins Set on Fire," ibid., Mar. 13, 1901, 2.

78. "The Outrage at Orange," ibid., Mar. 13, 1901, 8. "Orange's Smallpox Hospital," ibid., Mar. 14, 1901, 3. "Plea of an Orange Resident," ibid., Mar. 15, 1901, 8.

79. *Potts v. Breen*, 167 Ill. 67, 76 (1897).

80. Jack London, *War of the Classes* (New York: Macmillan Co., 1905), 276–77.

81. Ibid. Jack London, *The Road* (New York: Macmillan, 1907, 1916), 74–97, esp. 90.

82. London, *The Road*, 90.

SEVEN: THE ANTIVACCINATIONISTS

1. "The Smallpox Versus Dr. Pfeiffer," *MN*, Feb. 22, 1902, 363. "The Case of Dr. Pfeiffer," *BMSJ*, 146 (1902): 201–11.

2. "Quarantine More Rigid," *BG*, Nov. 26, 1901, 4. Durgin repeated his challenge at the annual meeting of the Massachusetts boards of health; "Smallpox Talk," ibid., Jan. 31, 1902, 2.

3. *BOSHD 1901*, 43–45. "Smallpox in Roxbury," *BG*, May 18, 1901, 9. "First Death from Smallpox," ibid., Oct. 27, 1901, 16. "Boston's Weekly Health Report," ibid., Nov. 3, 1901, 16. "Ninety Percent Not Vaccinated," ibid., Nov. 23, 1901, 11. "Eight New Cases," ibid., Nov. 25, 1901, 8. "Virus Squad Out," ibid., Nov. 18, 1901, 7. See Michael Albert et al., "The Last Smallpox Epidemic in Boston and the Vaccination Controversy, 1901–1902," *NEJM*, 344 (Feb. 1, 2001), 375–79; and Michael Albert et al., "Smallpox Manifestations and Survival during the Boston Epidemic of 1901 to 1903," *AIM*, 137 (Dec. 17, 2002): 993–1000. In a study of surviving medical files from the Southampton Street hospital, Albert et al. concluded that "the Boston epidemic was caused by the classic variola major form" of the smallpox virus. Ibid., 993.

4. "Vaccination Is the Curse of Childhood," antivaccination circular distributed during the epidemic of smallpox in Boston, 1901, Countway Library of Medicine, Harvard University, http://pds.lib.harvard.edu/pds/view/5817279, accessed Jul. 8, 2009. Samuel W. Abbott, "Legislation with Reference to Small-Pox and Vaccination," *MC*, 19 (1902), 163.

5. "Retirement of Dr. Samuel H. Durgin from the Boston Board of Health," *AJPH*, 2 (May 1912): 384–95; C. V. Chapin, "Doctor Samuel H. Durgin," ibid., 357–58. "Vaccination Is the Curse."

6. "Pfeiffer Yet Alive," *BG*, Feb. 10, 1902, 1. "Wonderful, But True," advertisement, ibid., Jul. 22, 1900, 22. "His Long Fast Broken," ibid., Mar. 27, 1900, 6. "Dr. Pfeiffer Protests," ibid., Apr. 29, 1901, 8. "Dr. Pfeiffer Has Smallpox," ibid., Feb. 9, 1902, 1. "In the Interest of Science, Boston Physician Fasts a Month," *SFC*, Aug. 24, 1901, 6. Pfeiffer's interest in free speech made him known to the radical Emma Goldman, who nursed him in 1904, when he was stricken with pneumonia. Emma Goldman to Alexander Berkman, Jan. 18, 1904, in *Emma Goldman: A Documentary History of the American Years: Making Speech Free, 1902–1909*, ed. Candace Falk (Urbana: University of Illinois Press, 2008), vol. 2: 129. On *Our Home Rights*, see "Exchanges," *Metaphysical Magazine*, Jan. 1902, 77–78. *Tenth Census of the United States* (1880): Schedule 1—Population: Franklin, Gloucester, New Jersey, Enumeration District No. 92.

7. "Its Big Benefits," *BG*, Dec. 20, 1901, 5. "Dr. John H. McCollom," *NYT*, Jun. 15, 13. Advertisement for Harvard University Medical Department, *BMSJ*, 143 (Nov. 22, 1900), 34. See, e.g., C.-E. A. Winslow, "The Case for Vaccination," *SCI*, new ser., 18 (1903): 101–7.

8. "Its Big Benefits."

9. Pfeiffer to Durgin, quoted in "Smallpox Versus Dr. Pfeiffer," 363.

10. Figures from *BOSHD 1901*, 44–45. Quote from *BOSHD 1902*, 36. "Smallpox Decreasing," *BG*, Dec. 27, 1901, 7.

11. William N. Macartney, *Fifty Years a Country Doctor* (New York: E. P. Dutton & Company, 1938),

245. "Pfeiffer Yet Alive," *BG*, Feb. 10, 1902, 1. "Funeral Friday of Dr. Paul Carson," ibid., Nov. 28, 1923, 6.

12. Commonwealth of Massachusetts, *The Journal of the Senate for the Year 1902* (Boston, 1902), 333. "Dr. Pfeiffer Has Smallpox."

13. "Current Comment," *PMJ*, 9 (Jan. 4, 1902), 5. Macartney, *Fifty Years*, 246. *KBOH 1898–99*, 98. *California State Medical Journal*, January 1905, quoted in *FBOH 1904*, 114. Dr. James Nevins Hyde, "The Late Epidemic of Smallpox in the United States," *PSM*, 59 (Oct. 1901), 565. Michael Specter, "The Fear Factor," *New Yorker*, Oct. 12, 2009, 39.

14. C. F. Nichols, *Vaccination: A Blunder in Poisons,* 61. "Opposed to Vaccination," *NYT*, Mar. 29, 1902, 10. The threat of gunplay was a cliché of manly antivaccinationist speech. "I would stand in my door with a Winchester and a brace of six-shooters and forbid any such outrages upon my family, if it cost me my life. Every other free, brave man would do the same." "Vaccination Tyranny," *The Life* ("A monthly magazine of Christian metaphysics"), November 1905, 222–23.

15. Samuel W. Abbott, *The Past and Present Conditions of Public Hygiene and State Medicine in the United States* (Boston: Wright & Potter, 1900).

16. John Pitcairn, *Vaccination* (Anti-Vaccination League of Pennsylvania, 1907), 8. "John Pitcairn," *NYT*, Jul. 23, 1916, 17. Following historian Steven Hahn, I am employing "a broad understanding of politics and the political that is relational and historical, and that encompasses collective struggles for what might be termed socially meaningful power." *A Nation Under Our Feet*, 3. See James C. Scott, *Domination and the Arts of Resistance.*

17. "Will Ignore Leverson," *NYT*, Aug. 17, 1900, 2. "Defies the Health Board," ibid., Jan. 7, 1901, 2. "To Lead Fight on Vaccination," *CT*, Jan. 6, 1901, A2. For a revealing study of late nineteenth-century libertarian radicalism in America, see David M. Rabban, *Free Speech in Its Forgotten Years,* esp. 23–76. On the transformation of governance in the Progressive Era, see Michael Willrich, *City of Courts.*

18. "An Anti-Vaccination Riot in Montreal," *MR*, 28 (Oct. 3, 1885), 380. Jeffrey D. Needell, "The Revolta Contra Vacina of 1904: The Revolt Against 'Modernization' in Belle-Epoque Rio de Janeiro," *Hispanic American Historical Review*, 60 (1980): 431–49.

19. "The Hon. Frederick Douglass," *Vaccination Inquirer and Health Review* (London), 4 (Mar. 1883), 200. (Excerpt from an 1882 letter.) Paul Finkelman, "Garrison's Constitution: The Covenant of Death and How It Was Made, *Prologue*, 32 (Winter 2000), http://www.archives.gov/publications/prologue/2000/winter/garrisons-constitution-1.html, accessed Jun. 12, 2009. Pfeiffer quoted in "Exchanges," in *Metaphysical Magazine*, Jan. 1902, 77. J. W. Hodge, *The Vaccination Superstition: Prophylaxis to Be Realized Through the Attainment of Health, Not by the Propagation of Disease* (read before the Western New York Homeopathic Medical Society in Buffalo, Apr. 11, 1902), pamphlet held at CHM, 49. "Dr. Jas. M. Peebles Dies, Almost 100," *NYT*, Feb. 16, 1922, 12. On British antivaccinationists and their appropriation of abolitionist rhetoric, see Durbach, *Bodily Matters*, esp. 83–84. The papers of William Lloyd Garrison, Jr., including two boxes of materials on "Anti-Vaccination" (Boxes 176 and 177), are part of GFP.

20. "The Anti-Vaccinationists," *Northwestern Lancet* (Minneapolis), 21 (Feb. 1, 1901), 61. On the groups cited between 1879 and 1900, see Martin Kaufman, "The American Anti-Vaccinationists and Their Arguments," *BHM*, 50 (1976), 465–66. Membership numbers for 1901 from *Brooklyn Daily Eagle Almanac*, 1901 (Brooklyn, 1901), 308. On California: "Question of Compulsory Vaccination," *SFC*, Oct. 16, 1904, 7. On Colorado: "Medical legislation in Colorado." *NYMJ*, Mar. 2, 1901, 378. On Connecticut: "The Anti-Vaccinators of Connecticut," by "One Who Knows Them," *American Medical Journal*, 31 (Jan. 1903), 9–12. On Massachusetts: see the Massachusetts Anti-Compulsory Vaccination Society's 1902 pamphlet, "A Vaccination Crusade and What There Is in It" GFP, Box 177, Folder 8. On Minnesota: "Sanitation and Legislation in Minnesota," *St. Paul Medical Journal*, 5 (June 1903), esp. 456–57. On Missouri: "Vaccination Tyranny," *The Life* ("A

monthly magazine of Christian metaphysics"), November 1905, 222–23. On Pennsylvania: Pitcairn, *Vaccination*. On Utah: "Vaccination War On," *SLH*, Jan. 24, 1901, 8. On Berkeley: "Bitter Fights Against Law," *SFC*, Aug. 12, 1904, 4. On Cleveland: "Medical News," *CMJ*, 2 (Mar. 1903), 164. On Milwaukee: Leavitt, *Healthiest City*, 94, 267. On St. Paul: J. W. Griggs, of the Anti-Vaccination Society of St. Paul, to William Lloyd Garrison, Oct. 26, 1904, GFP, Box 176, Folder 14. On the General Federation of Women's Clubs, see Theda Skocpol, *Protecting Soldiers and Mothers*.

21. Leo Tolstoy to William Tebb, quoted in *Antivaccination News and Sanatorian* (New York), June 1895, 7, GFP, Box 176, Folder 11. [George] Bernard Shaw, *Collected Letters: 1874–1897*, ed. Dan H. Laurence (New York: Viking, 1965), 448. Alfred Russel Wallace, "Vaccination a Delusion—Its Penal Enforcement a Crime," in idem, *The Wonderful Century: Its Successes and Its Failures* (New York: Dodd, Mead and Company, 1898), 232. *Vaccination* was edited by F. D. Blue and published for the Anti-Vaccination Society of America as "a journal of health, justice and liberty, that tells the truth about vaccination." *The Liberator* was the official organ of the Minnesota Health League and billed as "a monthly journal devoted to freedom from medical superstition and tyranny." Its editor, from 1902 to 1907, was Lora C. Little. See William Tebb, *Sanitation, Not Vaccination, the True Protection Against Small-Pox*, A Paper Read Before the Second International Vaccination Congress at Cologne, October 12th, 1881 (London, n.d.), CHM. "Antivaccination Movement," *MN*, Feb. 11, 1899, 178. On Harry Weinberger's career as an antivaccination attorney during the 1910s, see HWP, esp. Box 21, Folders 3–11, Box 48, Folders 4–14.

22. Nadja Durbach, "'They Might as Well Brand Us': Working-Class Resistance to Compulsory Vaccination in Victorian England," *Social History of Medicine*, 13 (2000): 45–62. Durbach, "Class, Gender, and the Conscientious Objector to Vaccination, 1898–1907," *Journal of British Studies*, 41 (2002): 58–83. Durbach, *Bodily Matters*, 197.

23. Martin Kauffman was perhaps the first scholar to point out the connection between antivaccinationism and the licensure issue in the United States. Kauffman mistakenly concluded that this was practically all there was to antivaccinationism, and he saw the licensure debate as largely a professional grievance, rather than a larger struggle for freedom of belief. Kauffman, "American Anti-Vaccinationists."

24. R. Swinburne Clymer, *Vaccination Brought Home to You* (Terre Haute, IN: Frank D. Blue, 1904), 27. On the history of alternative medicine, see esp. John Duffy, *From Humors to Medical Science*, 80–94; Johnston, ed., *Politics of Healing*; and James C. Whorton, *Nature Cures: The History of Alternative Medicine in America* (New York: Oxford University Press, 2004).

25. Massachusetts Sanitary Commission, *Report of a General Plan for the Promotion of Public and Personal Health* (Boston, 1850), 58.

26. Charles E. Rosenberg, *The Cholera Years: The United States in 1832, 1849, and 1866* (Chicago: University of Chicago Press, 1962), 161. Whorton, *Nature Cures*, 9–19.

27. Whorton, *Nature Cures*, 69, 133, esp. 134.

28. John Duffy, *The Sanitarians*, 153. Whorton, *Nature Cures*, 135–39.

29. "American Medical Association Advising Compulsory Vaccination," *Indiana Medical Journal*, 18 (May 1900), 470. See Leslie J. Reagan, "Law and Medicine," in *The Cambridge History of Law in America*, ed. Michael Grossberg and Christopher Tomlins (New York: Cambridge University Press, 2008), vol. 3, 232–67.

30. Davidovitch, "Negotiating Dissent," esp. 13. J. W. Hodge, "The Decline in Smallpox Which Preceded and Accompanied the Introduction of Vaccination—To What Was It Due?," *Medical Visitor*, 19 (June 1903), 269. New England Eclectics quoted in Alexander Wilder, "From 'Vaccination,'" *Health*, Oct. 1901, 340. Clymer, *Vaccination Brought Home to You*. "The Late Dr. T. V. Gifford," *Phrenological Journal*, 116 (Nov. 1903), 164.

31. Whorton, *Nature Cures*, 19. Johnston, "Introduction," in *Politics of Healing*, 1–11.

32. Jenny Franchot, "Spiritualism," in *A Companion to American Thought*, ed. Richard Wightman Fox and James T. Kloppenberg (Cambridge, MA: Wiley, 1995), 650–51. "Smallpox in Zion City," *NYT*, Aug. 12, 1904, 7. Henry Warner Bowden, "Dowie, John Alexander," http://www.anb.org/articles/08/08-00399.html, *American National Biography Online* Feb. 2000, accessed June 9, 2009.

33. *State ex rel. Adams v. Burdge*, 95 Wis. 390 (1897). "Christian Science and Vaccination," *BMJ*, 39 (Dec. 1899), 369. "Dies of Disease He Defied," *NYT*, Jul. 26, 1902, 5. James Colgrove, *State of Immunity*, 57.

34. Whorton, *Nature Cures*, 135. Mary Baker Eddy, "Obey the Law," *Christian Science Journal*, 18 (Mar. 1901), 724. "Christian Scientists' Change of Front," ibid., Nov. 14 ,1902, 2. "Christian Science Did It," *NYT*, Aug. 19, 1903, 1. See John C. Myers, "Christian Science and the Law," *Law Notes*, 12 (April 1908), 5–6.

35. Griggs, introduction to Lora C. Little, *Crimes of the Cowpox Ring: Some Moving Pictures Thrown on the Dead Wall of Official Silence* (Minneapolis: The Liberator Pub. Co., 1906), 3. Clymer, *Vaccination Brought Home to You*, 6. Piehn's story is told in D. D. Palmer and B. J. Palmer, *The Science of Chiropractic: Its Principles and Adjustments* (Davenport, IA: The Palmer School of Chiropractic, 1906), 377–79. On Pitcairn, see Colgrove, *State of Immunity*, 52–53.

36. "Anti-Vaccination League," *NYT*, Jan. 6, 1901, 5. *BOSHD 1902*, 36.

37. Quoted in Andrew Dickson White, "New Chapters in the Warfare of Science: XII. Miracles and Medicine," Part II, *PSM*, June 1891, 161. C. W. Amerige, *Vaccination a Curse* (n.p., 1895).

38. Alfred Milnes, *What About Vaccination? The Vaccination Question Plainly Put and Plainly Answered* (London: The Anti-Vaccination League, 1893), 20.

39. J. W. Hodge, "The Decline in Smallpox Which Preceded and Accompanied the Introduction of Vaccination—To What Was it Due?," *Medical Visitor*, 19 (June 1903), 252–78, esp. 261, 276. See Milnes, *What About Vaccination?*, 14–18; Charles Creighton, "Vaccination," *Encyclopedia Britannica*, 9th ed. (London, 1888); Edgar Crookshank, "Professor Crookshank's Evidence Before the Royal Vaccination Commission," *BRMJ*, 2 (1894), esp. 618.

40. Hodge, "Decline in Smallpox," 258, 276.

41. Pitcairn, *Vaccination*, 4. Wallace, "Vaccination a Delusion," esp. 271–86. Hodge, *Vaccination Superstition*, 10, 29–30.

42. Richard L. McCormick, "The Discovery That Business Corrupts Politics: A Reappraisal of the Origins of Progressivism," *American Historical Review*, 86 (1981): 247–74. Daniel T. Rodgers, "In Search of Progressivism," *Reviews in American History*, 10 (1982), 123–24.

43. Felix Oswald, *Vaccination A Crime; With Comments on Other Sanitary Superstitions* (New York: Physical Culture Publishing Company, 1901), 4, 98. Little, *Crimes of the Cowpox Ring*, 6. "Cope, Porter Farquharson, Publicist, Lecturer," in John W. Jordan, *Encyclopedia of Pennsylvania Biography* (New York: Lewis Historical Publishing Co., 1914), vol. 2: 696–701, esp. 698.

44. "Medical Monopoly," *Metaphysical Magazine*, 8 (1898), 70–77 [From *Boston Evening Transcript*, Mar. 2, 1898]. Twain quoted in Whorton, *Nature Cures*, 137.

45. "Medical Monopoly," 70, 71, 72. "Called Trust Legislation," *BG*, Mar. 3, 1898, 7.

46. "Medical Monopoly," 74, 73, 75. "Against a Medical Trust," *BG*, Mar. 8, 1898, 6. William James, *The Varieties of Religious Experience: A Study in Human Nature* (New York: Longmans, Green, and Co., 1902). Idem, *Pragmatism* (Cambridge, MA, 1975). For a concise introduction to James's thought, see James T. Kloppenberg, "James, William," in *A Companion to American Thought*, ed. Richard Wightman Fox and James T. Kloppenberg, 346–49.

47. "Dr. Pfeiffer Protests," *BG*, Apr. 29, 1901, 8. *Commonwealth of Massachusetts, Revised Laws*, 1901, Ch. 76, Sec. 9.

48. "Plan War on Vaccine," *WP*, Feb. 10, 1910, A2. "Antivaccination," *MN*, May 25, 1895, 586. Editorial, *Health*, 52 (March 1902): 495–96.

49. William M. Welch and Jay F. Schamberg, *Acute Contagious Diseases* (Philadelphia, 1905), 134.

"Antivaccination," *MN*, May 25, 1895, 586. See, e.g., Oswald, *Vaccination A Crime*, and Clymer, *Vaccination Brought Home to You.*

50. Little, *Crimes of the Cowpox Ring*, 5. See Ellen F. Fitzpatrick, ed., *Muckraking: Three Landmark Articles* (Boston, 1994), 1–39.

51. Little, *Crimes of the Cowpox Ring*, 74, 18. The best work to date on Little is Johnston, *Radical Middle Class*, 197–206, esp. 199.

52. Little, *Crimes of the Cowpox Ring*, 6–7.

53. Ibid., 7–8.

54. Ibid., 12–14, 29. "Victims of State Blood Poisoning," *Liberator*, Supplement September 1904, 1, GFP, Box 177, Folder 8. "Vaccination 'Points,'" *CC*, Aug. 16, 1902, 11. See John H. McCollom, "Vaccination: Accidents and Untoward Effects," *MC*, Jan. 1, 1902, 125.

55. James Martin Peebles, *Vaccination, A Curse and a Menace to Personal Liberty* (Battle Creek, MI: Peebles Pub. Co., 1900), 138. Edward Whipple, *A Biography of James M. Peebles, M.D., A.M.* (Battle Creek, MI: published by author, 1901), 506.

56. Mill and Blackstone quoted in Pitcairn, *Vaccination*, 1–2. George E. Macdonald, "The 'Vaccination' Outrage," from *Truth Seeker*, reprinted in *Liberty (Not the Daughter but the Mother of Order)*, May 19, 1894, 10. Curiously, Mill himself did not mention the vaccination question in his treatise. His main principle—that "the sole end of which power can be rightfully exercised over any member of a civilised community, against his will, is to prevent harm to others"—would seem to cut either way. Compulsory vaccination was a measure intended to protect others, but at least from the antivaccinationist perspective, it was not a necessary measure. As many argued at the time, a man who refused to be vaccinated was, by the vaccinationists' own theory, no threat to the members of the population who were vaccinated. The general response from supporters of vaccination was twofold: 1) there would always be some for whom vaccination did not work; the only way to protect them was by immunizing everyone else; and 2) the best way to permanently stamp out an epidemic in a community was to vaccinate everyone, leaving the virus with no one to infect. John Stuart Mill, *On Liberty*, ed. David Spitz (New York: W. W. Norton, 1975), 11.

57. J. W. Hodge, "Is the Compulsory Infliction of the Jennerian Rite by the State, Expedient, Justifiable, or Possible?" *Medical Century*, 14 (Dec. 1906), 360. "To All Who Care for Human Rights!" *Anti-Vaccination News and Sanatorian* (New York), June 1895, 3, GFP, Box 176, Folder 11. Little, *Crimes of the Cowpox Ring*, 62–63.

58. Hodge, "Compulsory Infliction," 359. "Topics of the Times," *NYT*, Dec. 9, 1901, 8.

59. See, generally, Willrich, *City of Courts.*

60. Hodge, "Decline in Smallpox," 276. B. O. Flower, "How Cleveland Stamped Out Smallpox," *Arena*, 27 (Apr. 1902), 429.

61. Robert Johnston has argued with great insight that American antivaccinationism constituted a "middle-class populism of the body"; Johnston, *Radical Middle Class*, 178. My own view is that personal liberty concerns loomed larger than populism in most antivaccinationists' thinking about the politics of public health.

62. Little, *Crimes of the Cowpox Ring*, 61. Nichols, *Vaccination*, 27. Clymer, *Vaccination Brought Home to You*, 78.

63. Michael Willrich, "The Two Percent Solution: Eugenic Jurisprudence and the Socialization of American Law, 1900–1930," *Law and History Review*, 16 (1998): 63–111.

64. Little, *Crimes of the Cowpox Ring*, 62–63.

65. "Anti-Vaccinators of Connecticut," 9–12.

66. State Board of Health data reported in "A Danger Signal," *OSE*, Feb. 5, 1901.

67. "Vaccination War On." "M'Millan Bill Now Law," *OSE*, Feb. 22, 1901. "Smallpox and Vaccination," ibid., Jan. 26, 1900. *State ex rel. Cox v. Board of Ed.*, 9 Utah 401 (1901). "Supreme Court Decision," *OSE*, May 1, 1900. "Vaccination War On," *SLH*, Jan. 24, 1901, 8.

68. The nineteen people I have identified as "activated" members of the Utah league were named in newspaper articles as either having leadership positions in the organization, speaking out against compulsory vaccination at a meeting, or serving on a committee to draft resolutions. Others named as "present" at the meeting I did not assume to be more than passive listeners. I was able to locate eighteen of the nineteen members, unmistakably, in the 1900 U.S. Census. The nineteenth named participant was J. H. Parry, the name of a well-known book publisher in Salt Lake City at the time. I have assumed that if this J. H. Parry was not the same publisher, a responsible newspaper would have identified him otherwise to avoid confusion. "Antis Hold Session," *SLH*, Jan. 14, 1900. "Vaccination War On," ibid., Jan. 24, 1901, 8. *Twelfth Census of the United States* (1900): Schedule 1—Population: Salt Lake City, Salt Lake, Utah.

69. "The Topic of the Hour," *Deseret Evening News*, Jan. 24, 1901, 4. *Denver Post* charge of Mormon involvement reported in "A Danger Signal," *OSE*, Feb. 5, 1901. In a brief account, Thomas G. Alexander has also argued that Mormon church members and leaders were divided on the vaccination question; *Mormonism in Transition: A History of the Latter-day Saints*, esp. 195. See, generally, Sarah Barringer Gordon, *The Mormon Question: Polygamy and Constitutional Conflict in Nineteenth Century America* (Chapel Hill: University of North Carolina Press, NC, 2002).

70. "Antis Hold Session."

71. *Laws of the State of Utah, Passed at the Fourth Regular Session Legislature of the State of Utah Held at Salt Lake City, the State Capital, in January, February, and March, 1901* (Salt Lake City, 1901), 15. "Vaccination War On." "Dr. MacLean's Startling Challenge to Anti-Vaccinationists," *SLH*, Jan. 26, 1901, 1. "Board of Education Defies Board of Health," ibid., Jan. 26, 1901, 1. Thomas Hull, "Events of the Month," *Improvement Era*, Mar. 4, 1901, 397–98.

72. "Governor Wells Vetoes Anti-Vaccination Bill," *SLH*, Feb. 9, 1901, 1. "McMillan Bill Vetoed," *OSE*, Feb. 8, 1901. Hull, "Events of the Month." "From the Editor's Notebook," *Medical Standard*, 24 (March, 1901), 165.

73. "Hearing Over," *BG*, Feb. 5, 1902, 4. "Repeal Wanted," ibid., Jan. 30, 1902, 2. "Vaccination," ibid., Feb. 1, 1902, 4. "All in Favor," ibid., Feb. 4, 1902, 4. "Loss to Boston," ibid., Feb. 3, 1902, 4. "Anti-Vaccination," *Boston Evening Transcript*, Feb. 19, 1902, 1. "Vaccination Bills In," ibid., Feb. 20, 1902, 3.

74. "Hearing Over." "Death From Lockjaw," *CC*, Jan. 4, 1902, 5.

75. "Seven Bills," *BG*, Feb. 20, 1902, 3. "Work Well Ahead," ibid., Feb. 23, 1902, 24. "Brakeman's Bill," ibid., Feb. 27, 1902, 6. "Antis Gain Point," ibid., Mar. 11, 1902, 11. "Long and Busy," ibid., Mar. 5, 1902, 4.

76. "An act to prevent compulsory vaccination and to prevent vaccination being made a condition precedent to school attendance," *General Laws of the State of Minnesota . . . 1903* (St. Paul, 1903), ch. 299. "Sanitation and Legislation in Minnesota," in section entitled, "Hygiene and Public Health," ed. Henry M. Bracken [sec. of state board of health], *St. Paul Medical Journal*, 5 (June 1903), 456. "Anti-Vaccination Law in Minnesota," *Medical Sentinel* (Portland, OR), 11 (June 1903), 331–32. Little (1903) quoted in Johnston, *Radical Middle Class*, 358, n. 8. William J. Mayo, "The Medical Profession and the Issues Which Confront It," *SCI*, new ser. 23 (Jun. 15, 1906), 900.

77. "Anti-Vaccination Crusade," *Pacific Medical Journal*, 47 (Sept. 1904), 535. "Bitter Fights Against Law," *SFC*, Aug. 12, 1904, 4. "Question of Compulsory Vaccination," ibid., Oct. 16, 1904, 7. Governor George C. Pardee's veto message, Mar. 8, 1905, in *The Journal of the Senate During the Twenty-Sixth Session of the Legislature of the State of California, 1905* (Sacramento, 1905), 1445. "Vetoes Anti-Vaccination Bill," *Los Angeles Herald*, Mar. 9, 1905, 2. "May Open a Private School to Evade Law," *SFC*, Jul. 18, 1905, 6.

78. Little quoted in Johnston, *Radical Middle Class*, 201.

79. Albert et al., "Last Smallpox Epidemic," 375.

80. "Dies of Disease He Defied," *NYT*, Jul. 26, 1902, 5. "Anti-Vaccinationist Offered Up," *Medical*

Sentinel, 11 (June 1903), 332. "Topics of the Times," *NYT*, Aug. 13, 1904, 6. "Smallpox in Zion City," ibid., Aug. 12, 1904, 7.

81. "Dr. Pfeiffer Has Smallpox," *BG*, Feb. 9, 1902, 1. "Pfeiffer Yet Alive," ibid., Feb. 10, 1902, 1.

82. "Dr. Pfeiffer Has Smallpox." "Pfeiffer Yet Alive," *BG*, Feb. 10, 1902, 1. Nichols, *Vaccination: A Blunder in Poisons*, 51. See also "Dr. Pfeiffer's Condition Encouraging," *BG*, Feb. 11, 1902, 3; Albert et al., "Last Smallpox Epidemic," 377.

83. "Bedford May Sue," *BG*, Feb. 17, 1902, 1.

EIGHT: SPEAKING LAW TO POWER

1. *Plessy v. Ferguson*, 163 U.S. 537 (1896). *Brown v. Board of Education*, 337 U.S. 483 (1954). *Gideon v. Wainwright*, 372 U.S. 335 (1963).

2. Transcript of Record, *Jacobson v. Massachusetts*, U.S. Supreme Court, October Term, 1904, No. 70-175, filed June 29, 1903, 5, 4 [hereafter "Jacobson USSC Transcript"]. *Twelfth Census of the United States* (1900): Schedule No. 1—Population: Cambridge, Massachusetts, Enumeration District No. 691. Today, Pine Street, which lies just north of Massachusetts Avenue, is not generally considered part of Cambridgeport; but it was in 1902. See "Small Pox Scourge. Alarming Outbreak of the Disease in a Section of Cambridgeport," *Cambridge Chronicle*, Jun. 21, 1902, 4. American wage figure in 1900, from "Responses to Industrialism," Digital History, http://www.digitalhistory.uh.edu/historyonline/us26.cfm, accessed December 17, 2009.

3. *Jacobson v. Massachusetts*, 197 U.S. 11, 13, 26 (1905).

4. Wendy E. Parmet et al., "Individual Rights versus the Public's Health—100 Years after *Jacobson v. Massachusetts*," *NEJM*, 352 (2005), 652–54.

5. Brief for Defendant, *Commonwealth v. Jacobson*, Supreme Judicial Court of Massachusetts, Mar. 1903, 19; in *Massachusetts Reports Papers and Briefs*, vol. 183, SLL (hereafter "Jacobson SJC Brief").

6. Defendant's Bill of Exceptions, *Commonwealth v. Jacobson*, *Massachusetts Reports Papers and Briefs*, vol. 183, 4, SLL (hereafter "Jacobson's SJC Exceptions"). *Twelfth Census of the United States* (1900): Schedule No. 1—Population: Cambridge, Mass., Enumeration Dist. No. 691. Peter Skold, "From Inoculation to Vaccination: Smallpox in Sweden in the Eighteenth and Nineteenth Centuries," *Population Studies*, 50 (1996): 247–62.

7. Obituary of E. Edwin Spencer, *White Family Quarterly*, vol. 1 (Apr. 1903), 38–39. John S. Haller, Jr., *A Profile in Alternative Medicine: The Eclectic Medical College of Cincinnati, 1845–1942* (Kent, OH: Kent State University Press, 1999). George Otis Ward, *Worcester Academy: Its Location and Its Principals, 1834–1882* (Worcester, MA, 1918).

8. "Small Pox History," *CC*, Sept. 20, 1902, 15. City of Cambridge, *Annual Report of the Board of Health for the Year Ending November 30, 1901* (Cambridge, MA, 1902), 20.

9. "Death from Lockjaw," *CC*, Jan. 4, 1902, 5.

10. "Small Pox History." "Smallpox Scourge," *CC*, Jun. 21, 1902, 4. *CAMBOH 1902*, 6–9.

11. *BOSHD 1901*, 45. The Boston compulsory vaccination order is quoted in full in Defendant's Exceptions, *Commonwealth v. Mugford*, 1902, *Massachusetts Reports Papers and Briefs*, vol. 183, 1, SLL (hereafter "Mugford Exceptions").

12. "Fifteen Days in Jail," *BG*, Feb. 21, 1902, 5. "Mugford Exceptions," 3. "To East Boston," *BG*, Jan. 27, 1902, 1. "Mugford Will Appeal," ibid., Mar. 2, 1902, 2. *Twelfth Census of the United States* (1900): Schedule No. 1—Population: Boston, Massachusetts., Enumeration Dist. No. 1162.

13. Cambridge Vaccination Order in "Jacobson USSC Transcript," 10. "Compulsory Vaccination," *CC*, Mar. 8, 1902, 5. "Smallpox History." *CAMBOH 1902*, 8.

14. "Those Who Favor Anti-Compulsory Vaccination Are Not Idle—Organization Being Formed," *CC*, Apr. 5, 1902, 12.

15. "Smallpox Scourge." According to the Cambridge Board of Health, the family had moved to

Cambridge from Boston some time after Cambridge's wholesale vaccination campaign in March. "Smallpox Fully Under Control," *CC*, Jun. 28, 1902, 4.

16. Ibid. "The Cambridge Smallpox Epidemic," *MN*, Jun. 28, 1902, 1230.

17. "Smallpox Fully Under Control."

18. Harlan in *Jacobson v. Massachusetts*, 197 U.S. 11, 30–31 (1905).

19. "In the Brickyards," *CC*, Aug. 2, 1902, 5. "Another Smallpox Case," ibid., Sept. 20, 1902, 6. "Small Pox Is Once More Disappearing," ibid., Jul. 26, 1903, 1.

20. Spencer complaint in "Jacobson USSC Transcript," 2.

21. "Four Prosecutions by Board of Health," *CC*, Jul. 26, 1902, 4. William T. Davis, *Bench and Bar of the Commonwealth of Massachusetts* (Boston: The Boston History Company, 1895), vol. 1, 377. On American inferior courts, see Willrich, *City of Courts*, 3–58.

22. Biographical details on the defendants drawn from *Twelfth Census of the United States* (1900): Schedule 1—Population: Cambridge, Massachusetts, Enumeration District 698 (Cone); District 731 (the Goulds); District 727 (Morse); and District 723 (Pear).

23. "Anti-Vaccinationists Must Go into Court," *CC*, Jul. 19, 1902, 1. "Won't Submit," *BG*, Jul. 18, 1902, 12. "Fined Them $5 Each," ibid., Jul 24, 1902, 12. The *Globe* erroneously reported Pear's age as thirty-three. "Cambridge's Electric Plant," *Boston Globe*, Nov. 20, 1895, 7. Pear also told the press that an aunt of his had been an invalid for much of her life, a condition he attributed to vaccination.

24. "Four Prosecutions."

25. Ibid. "Won't Submit." Davis, *Bench and Bar*, vol. 1, 280.

26. Brief published in full in William F. Davis, *Christian Liberties in Boston: A Sketch of Recent Attempts to Destroy Them Through the Device of a Gag-By-Law for Gospel Preachers* (Chelsea, MA: W. Kellaway, 1887); quotation, 48–49. *Commonwealth v. Davis*, 162 Mass. 510, 511 (1895). "Against Rev. W. F. Davis," *BG*, Jan. 2, 1895, 4. "Man with a Conscience," ibid., Jul. 29, 1894, 32. On Holmes and rights, see Louis Menand, *The Metaphysical Club: A Story of Ideas in America* (New York: Farrar, Straus and Giroux, 2001), esp. 422.

27. "Four Prosecutions."

28. Ibid.

29. "Fined Them $5 Each."

30. On the Pear case as a test case supported by the Massachusetts Anti-Compulsory Vaccination Society, see "Vaccination Test Case," *BG*, Nov. 13, 1902, 4; "Stands by Albert M. Pear," ibid., Dec. 2, 1902, 4; "The Vaccination Question," ibid., Nov. 15, 1902, 2; "Test Vaccination Case," *CC*, Nov. 15, 1902, 12.

31. "Test Vaccination Case." Defendant's Exceptions in *Commonwealth v. Pear*, 1903, *Massachusetts Reports Papers and Briefs*, vol. 183, 2–3, SLL (hereafter "Pear's SJC Exceptions").

32. See Akhil Reed Amar, *The Bill of Rights: Creation and Reconstruction* (New Haven: Yale University Press, 1998).

33. "Test Vaccination Case." "Pear's SJC Exceptions," 2–4.

34. "Stands by Albert M. Pear," *BG*, Dec. 2, 1902, 4. "In the Brickyards."

35. "Discuss Vaccination," *BG*, Nov. 4, 1902, 7.

36. "Jacobson's SJC Exceptions," 4.

37. Ibid., 2–4.

38. Ibid., 4–6.

39. "Smallpox History." "An $18.30 Tax Rate," *CC*, Aug. 23, 1902, 1. "Smallpox Annihilated," ibid., Sept. 6, 1902, 5. *CAMBOH 1902*, 9, 22–26.

40. Brief for the Commonwealth, *Commonwealth v. Pear*, 1903, *Massachusetts Reports Papers and*

Briefs, vol. 183, SLL, 2 (hereafter "Bancroft SJC Pear Brief"). The language is identical to that in Brief for the Commonwealth, *Commonwealth v. Jacobson*, 1903, *Massachusetts Reports Papers and Briefs*, vol. 183, SLL, 4 (hereafter "Bancroft SJC Jacobson Brief").

41. "Jacobson SJC Brief," 18–19.

42. "About the Court," Supreme Judicial Court Web site, http://www.mass.gov/courts/sjc/about-the-court.html, accessed December 21, 2009. Mary Beth Norton, *In the Devil's Snare: The Salem Witchcraft Crisis of 1692* (New York: Knopf, 2002), 290–92. "Ex-Justice Knowlton Dies," *NYT*, May 8, 1918, 11.

43. *Commonwealth v. Alger*, 61 Mass. 53, 84–85 (1851).

44. See generally Ernst Freund, *The Police Power: Public Policy and Constitutional Rights* (Chicago: University of Chicago Press, 1904); William J. Novak, *The People's Welfare*.

45. *Roberts v. Boston*, 59 Mass. 198, 209 (1849).

46. *Barron v. Baltimore*, 7 Pet. 243 (U.S., 1833).

47. *Slaughter-House Cases*, 83 U.S. 36 (1873).

48. United States Constitution, Amendment XIV, Sec. 1.

49. *Slaughter-House Cases*, 83 U.S. 36, 78, 81 (1873).

50. *Slaughter-House Cases*, 83 U.S. 36, 87, 88, 122 (1873).

51. Freund, *Police Power*, v.

52. Thomas M. Cooley, *A Treatise on the Constitutional Limitations Which Rest Upon the Legislative Power of the States of the American Union* (Boston: Little, Brown, and Company, 1868). See David P. Currie, *The Constitution in the Supreme Court: The Second Century, 1888–1986* (Chicago: University of Chicago Press, 1990), 40–50.

53. Christopher G. Tiedeman, *A Treatise on the Limitations of Police Power in the United States* (St. Louis: The F. H. Thomas Law Book Co., 1886), 10. See *In Re Jacobs*, 98 NY 98 (1885); *Ritchie v. People*, 155 Ill. 98 (1895).

54. *Allgeyer v. Louisiana*, 165 U.S. 578, 589 (1897). Currie, *Constitution in the Supreme Court*, 47.

55. See Willrich, *City of Courts*, esp. ch. 4.

56. "Political Temperaments," *Outlook*, Jul. 30, 1904, 728–29. On this crucial point, see also David G. Ritchie, *Natural Rights: A Criticism of Some Political and Ethical Conceptions* (London: Swan Sonnenschein & Co., 1895). Ritchie observed, "Compulsory education, compulsory vaccination, compulsory notification of infectious diseases, etc., are infringements of the family, but in the interest of the liberty—the real, positive liberty—of the individuals who belong to the family, and of others. If an individual has a certain minimum of education and of protection from gross neglect and from infectious diseases secured to him, he is to that extent more 'free' to make what he can of his natural powers and of his opportunities, than if he is entirely at the mercy of ignorant parents, and of dirty, diseased, or fanatical neighbors." Ibid., 218.

57. Later historians and legal scholars would adopt the progressives' perspective, emphasizing that "in the early decades of the twentieth century, substantive due process was by and large confined to the protection of economic liberties from government regulation." See, e.g., "Due Process, Substantive," in *Encyclopedia of American Civil Rights and Liberties*, ed. Otis H. Stephens et al. (Westport, CT: Greenwood, 2006), vol. 1, 281.

58. Freund, *Police Power*, 109, 16.

59. "Compulsory Vaccination and Detention in a Pest House as an Infringement of Personal Liberty," *Central Law Journal*, 54 (1902), 361.

60. The school entry cases took two forms. A parent might ask the court to issue an injunction (to enjoin school officials from excluding an unvaccinated child), as Frank Blue did in *Blue v. Beach*, 155 Ind. 121 (1900). Or a parent might petition the court for a writ of mandamus (to compel

school officials to admit an unvaccinated child), as Michael Breen did in *Potts v. Breen*, 167 Ill. 67 (1897). See also *Mathews v. Kalamazoo Board of Education*, 127 Mich. 530 (1901); *State v. Hay*, 126 N.C. 999 (1900); *Morris v. Columbus*, 102 Ga. 792 (1898); "Teacher Must Be Vaccinated," *NYT*, Nov. 15, 1901, 7.

61. Irving Browne, "Inviolability of the Human Body," *Green Bag*, 9 (1897): 441–51, esp. 450.

62. Freund, *Police Power*, 478.

63. Ballard in "Jacobson SJC Brief," 36.

64. *Abeel v. Clark*, 84 Cal. 226 (1890).

65. *Duffield v. Williamsport School District*, 162 Pa. 476, 482 (1894). "Note," *PABOH 1903*, vol. II, 918.

66. *Duffield v. Williamsport School District*, 162 Pa. 476 (1894). Boyd's *Directory of Williamsport*, 1899 (Reading, PA, 1899), 167, 402. *Historical Sketches of the Bench and Bar of Lycoming County, Pennsylvania* (1961), http://www.lycolaw.org/history/sketches/20.htm, accessed January 5, 2010. Tiedeman's own libertarianism diminished when he contemplated police control of the working class, and he concluded that compulsory vaccination was defensible. Tiedeman, *Limitations*, 32.

67. *Duffield v. Williamsport School District*, 162 Pa. 476, 483, 484 (1894).

68. *Lawton v. Steele*, 152 U.S. 133, 152 (1894).

69. See, e.g., *Abeel v. Clark*, 84 Cal. 226 (1890); *Bissell v. Davison*, 65 Conn. 183 (1894); *Viemeister v. White*, 179 N.Y. 235 (1904). See "Compulsory Vaccination," *Yale Law Journal*, 12 (1903): 504–6; "Public Schools: Conditions of Attendance," ibid., 13 (1904): 261. "Bancroft SJC Jacobson Brief," 8.

70. *Adams v. Burdge*, 95 Wis. 390 (1897).

71. Ibid.

72. *Adams v. Burdge*, 95 Wis. 390, 400, 404, 405 (1897). "Silas U. Pinney (1833–1899)," http://www .wicourts.gov/about/judges/supreme/retired/pinney.htm, accessed January 6, 2010.

73. "Topics of the Times," *NYT*, Feb. 27, 1897, 8. *Adams v. Burdge*, 95 Wis. 390, 399 (1897).

74. *Potts v. Breen*, 167 Ill. 67, 76 (1897). See also *State ex rel. Freeman v. Zimmerman*, 86 Minn. 353 (1902). Freund, *Police Power*, 116. The Kansas Supreme Court went even further, ruling that in the absence of clear legislative authority, a local board of education could not deny admission to an otherwise eligible pupil for failing to be vaccinated. *Osborn v. Russell*, 64 Kan. 507 (1902).

75. *Mathews v. Kalamazoo Board of Education*, 127 Mich. 530, 535, 539 (1901).

76. "Note—Right of Boards of Health to Make Vaccination Compulsory," *Central Law Journal*, 54 (1902), 56. On the doctrine of overruling necessity, see Novak, *People's Welfare*, 72; W. P. Prentice, *Police Powers Arising Under the Law of Overruling Necessity* (New York: Banks & Brothers, 1894).

77. *Godcharles v. Wigeman*, Penn. 1886, *Atlantic Reporter*, 6 (1886), 354–56, esp. 356. "Compulsory Vaccination," *Yaw Law Journal*, 10 (1901), 159.

78. "Vaccination Not Compulsory," *NYT*, May 6, 1894, 16. "Decision on the Vaccinating Raid," ibid., May 4, 1895, 9. *In the Matter of the Application of William H. Smith et all for a Writ of Habeas Corpus*, 146 N.Y. 68, 73, 78 (1895). Smith subsequently sued Brooklyn Health Commissioner Z. Taylor Emery for false imprisonment. The jury rendered a verdict for Smith, but the verdict was reversed on appeal. *Smith v. Emery*, 42 N.Y.S. 258 (1896).

79. "Bancroft SJC Jacobson Brief," 9.

80. *Morris et al. v. City of Columbus*, 102 Ga. 792 (1898). *Wyatt v. Rome*, 105 Ga. 312 (1898).

81. *State v. Hay*, 126 N.C. 999, 1000, 1001 (1900).

82. *Levin v. Town of Burlington*, 129 N.C. 184 (1901).

83. *Levin v. Town of Burlington*, 129 N.C. 184, 187, 188, 189 (1901).

84. "Compulsory Vaccination and Detention," 361. "Jacobson SJC Brief," 12; "Pear SJC Brief," 12.

85. The court set aside the verdict and ordered a new trial. *State v. Hay*, 126 N.C. 999, 103 (1900).

86. *State v. Hay*, 126 N.C. 999, 1005 (1900).

87. *State v. Hay*, 126 N.C. 999, 1004 (1900). "Jacobson SJC Brief," 30, 31. "Those who pose a risk to the community can be required to submit to compulsory measures for the common good," writes Lawrence Gostin of the harm avoidance principle. "The control measure itself, however, should not pose a health risk to its subject." Lawrence O. Gostin, *Public Health Law: Power, Duty, Restraint* (Berkeley and Los Angeles: University of California Press, 2000), 69.

88. *Wong Wai v. Williamson*, 103 F. 1, 7, 10 (1900). Charles J. McLain, *In Search of Equality: The Chinese Struggle Against Discrimination in Nineteenth-Century America* (Berkeley and Los Angeles: University of California Press, 1994), 234–76. Henry Bixby Hemenway, *Legal Principles of Public Health Administration* (Chicago: T. H. Flood & Co., 1914), 633: "Few diseases have been more subjected to judicial inquiry than smallpox." Tobey, *Public Health Law* (1926), 118: "A few decades ago, it seems as if the bulk of court decisions arose out of conditions in which smallpox was the principal factor."

89. "Jacobson SJC Brief," 3, 14, 16, 18. "Pear SJC Brief," 3, 14, 16, 18.

90. "Marcus Perrin Knowlton," memorial, 231 Mass. 615 (1919).

91. *Commonwealth v. Pear; Same v. Jacobson*, 183 Mass. 243, 245 (1903).

92. *Commonwealth v. Pear; Same v. Jacobson*, 183 Mass. 243, 246, 248 (1903).

93. *Commonwealth v. Pear; Same v. Jacobson*, 183 Mass. 243, 248 (1903).

94. "Virus Squad Out," *BG*, Nov. 18, 1901, 7. Antivaccinationist literature after 1903 noted the no-force principle articulated in *Commonwealth v. Pear; Same v. Jacobson*. See, for example, Charles M. Higgins, *Open Your Eyes Wide! Parents, School Officers, Editors, Judges, Legislators, Doctors; And Look at These Facts About Vaccination*, 2d ed. (London: Anti-Vaccination League of America, 1912), 15.

95. *Commonwealth v. Mugford; Same v. Same*, 183 Mass. 249. There was a straightforward reason why the SJC would identify *Jacobson* rather than *Pear* as governing. *Mugford*, like *Jacobson*, had raised two questions: constitutionality of the statute and admissibility of evidence. Like *Jacobson*, *Mugford* had tried to put vaccination itself on trial by presenting medical evidence as to its dangers. *Pear* had made only the constitutional case.

96. "Jacobson USSC Transcript," 21–22.

97. See, e.g., J. C. Henderson, "An Appeal," *Life* (New York), Sept. 24, 1903, 288; Stuart Close, "Drug Diseases and Compulsory Medicine," *Medical Advance and Journal of Homeopathics* (Chicago), 41 (Nov. 1903), 588. On the Court's writ of certiorari, see Currie, *Constitution in the Supreme Court*, vol. 2, 5.

98. Geoffrey T. Blodgett, "The Mind of the Boston Mugwump," *Mississippi Valley Historical Review*, 48 (1962), 614–34. Gordon S. Wood, "The Massachusetts Mugwumps," *New England Quarterly*, 33 (1960), 435–51. "Williams, George Fred," *Who's Who in New England*, ed. Albert Nelson Marquis, (Chicago: A. N. Marquis & Company, 1916), 1160.

99. "George Fred Williams' Platform," in *The Commoner Condensed*, ed. William Jennings Bryan (Lincoln, NE: The Woodruff-Collins Printing Co., 1903), 344. George Fred Williams, "Our Real Masters," *Arena*, Jan. 1903, 7–12. "In the Mirror of the Present," *Arena*, Oct. 1906, 405–10, esp. 408. *Dunbar v. Dunbar*, 190 U.S. 340 (1903).

100. Plaintiff in Error, Brief to the Supreme Court of the United States, *Jacobson v. Massachusetts*, No. 70—October Term, 1904 (hereafter "Jacobson USSC Brief"), esp. 19. See also ibid., 11 (schools) and 26 (no exemptions). "Involves Vaccination Law," *WP*, Dec. 7, 1904, 5. "Final Appeal on Vaccination," *Boston Herald*, Dec. 7, 1904, 16.

101. *Jacobson v. Massachusetts*, 197 U.S. 11, 15, 16 (1905). "Jacobson USSC Brief," esp. 8.

102. "Jacobson USSC Brief," 30–31.

103. Lisa Paddock, "Harlan, John Marshall," American National Biography Online, http://www.anb .org/articles/11/11-00385.html; accessed Jul. 21, 2010. See Linda Przybyszewski, *The Republic According to John Marshall Harlan* (Chapel Hill: University of North Carolina Press, 1999).

104. *Plessy v. Ferguson*, 163 U.S. 537, 559 (1896). *Northern Securities Co. v. U.S.*, 193 U.S. 197, 351 (1904).

105. *Jacobson v. Massachusetts*, 197 U.S. 11, 22–24 (1905).

106.   *Jacobson v. Massachusetts*, 197 U.S. 11, 26 (1905).

107. *Jacobson v. Massachusetts*, 197 U.S. 11, 27–29 (1905).

108. *Jacobson v. Massachusetts*, 197 U.S. 11, 28 (1905).

109. *Jacobson v. Massachusetts*, 197 U.S. 11, 28–39 (1905).

110. *Jacobson v. Massachusetts*, 197 U.S. 11, 39 (1905).

111. "Compulsory Vaccination," editorial, *Wisconsin Medical Journal*, 3 (March 1905), 588. Dr. Hix of Binghamton, New York, in New York State Department of Health, *Proceedings of the Conference of Sanitary Officers of the State of New York* (Albany, 1905), 38. "Compulsory Vaccination," *Boston Journal*, Feb. 22, 1905, 6. Untitled editorial, *NYT*, Feb. 22, 1905, 6. See also "Vaccination Right," *BG*, Feb. 21, 1905, 7; "Vaccination by Law," *WP*, Feb. 21, 1905, 11; "A Test Case," *CC*, Feb. 25, 1905, 12.

112. Untitled editorial item, *Book Notes*, May 6, 1905, 71. "Compulsory Vaccination," *Medical Advance*, March 1905, 166. On antivaccinationism in the 1910s and 1920s, see James Colgrove, *State of Immunity*, 45–80.

113. "The State's Police Power," *NYTRIB*, Feb. 26, 1905, 8.

114. *Lochner v. New York*, 198 U.S. 45 (1905). E. F. [Ernst Freund], "Limitations of Hours of Labor and the Federal Supreme Court," *Green Bag*, 17 (July 1905), 411–17.

115. *Lochner v. New York*, 198 U.S. 45, 72 (1905).

116. *Lochner v. New York*, 198 U.S. 45, 75–76 (1905).

117. Charles Warren, "The Progressiveness of the United States Supreme Court," *Columbia Law Review*, 13 (1913). On the "myth" of *Lochner*, see William J. Novak, "The Myth of the 'Weak' American State," *American Historical Review*, 113 (2008): 752–72. For a fuller discussion of legal progressivism and the police power after Lochner, see Willrich, *City of Courts*, esp. 96–115. See also Morton J. Horwitz, *The Transformation of American Law, 1870–1960: The Crisis of Legal Orthodoxy* (New York: Oxford University Press, 1992).

118. William Howard Taft, *The Anti-Trust Act and the Supreme Court* (New York: Harper & Brothers, 1914), 43–44, 45.

119. Investigation Case Files of the Bureau of Investigation 1908–1922, Old German Files, 1909–1921, National Archives and Record Administration, Case # 17615; Case Title: Sedition; Suspect Name: Lora C. Little. Ibid., Case # 175676; Case Title: Neutrality Matter; Suspect Name: William Heupel. Ibid., Case # 178488; Case Title: General War Matter; Suspect Name: Mrs. Walter B. Henderson. I accessed these files via the online database Footnote.com, Dec. 10, 2007.

120. Holmes to Hand, June 24, 1918, in Gerald Gunther, "Learned Hand and the Origins of Modern First Amendment Doctrine: Some Fragments of History," *Stanford Law Review*, 27 (1975), Appendix, 757.

121. *Schenck v. U.S.*, 249 U.S. 47, 52 (1919). *Abrams v. U.S.*, 250 U.S. 616, 628 (1919), emphasis added. For a fascinating analysis of "Holmes's Transformation in *Abrams*," see David M. Rabban, *Free Speech in Its Forgotten Years*, 346–54.

122. *Buck v. Bell*, 274 U.S. 200, 207 (1927).

123. *Michigan v. Tyler*, 436 U.S. 499, 509 (1977). *Hamdi v. Rumsfeld*, 542 U.S. 508, 592 (2004) (Justice Thomas dissenting opinion).

124. Concurring opinion in *Doe v. Bolton*, 410 U.S. 179, 213–14 (1973). Majority opinion in *Planned Parenthood v. Casey*, 404 U.S. 833, 857 (1992).

125. *Jacobson v. Massachusetts*, 197 U.S. 11, 29.

EPILOGUE

1. *BOSHD 1902*, 36. Michael R. Albert et al., "The Last Smallpox Epidemic in Boston and the Vaccination Controversy, 1901–1903," *NEJM*, 344 (2001), 377. John Duffy, *A History of Public Health in New York City*, 564. Gretchen A. Condran et al., "The Decline in Mortality in Philadelphia from 1870–1930: The Role of Municipal Services," in *Sickness and Health in America*, 3rd ed., ed. Judith Walzer Leavitt and Ronald L. Numbers, 452–66. "Seattle's worst smallpox epidemic was in 1901–02; 642 reported cases, four deaths." "Medicine: Smallpox Epidemic," *Time*, Apr. 8, 1946.

2. C.-E. A. Winslow, "The Untilled Fields of Public Health," *SCI*, 51 (Jan. 9, 1920), 30. On this point, see James A. Tobey, *Public Health Law*, 1–6. Franklin H. Top and Laura E. Peck, "A Small Outbreak of Smallpox in Detroit," *AJPH*, 33 (1943): 490–98, esp. 491, 492.

3. J. P. Leake, "United States Lags in Fight Against Smallpox," *Science News Letter*, 29 (1936), 213. A. W. Hedrich, "Changes in the Incidence and Fatality of Smallpox in Recent Decades," *PHR*, 51 (Apr. 3, 1936): 363–92. Robert D. Johnston, *The Radical Middle Class*, 183.

4. "The Anti-Vaccinationists," *Southern Medical Journal*, 14 (1921), 503. *Zucht v. King*, 260 U.S. 174 (1922).

5. Williams quoted in "Medicine: Smallpox Epidemic."

6. Hedrich, "Changes in the Incidence and Fatality of Smallpox," 366. Judith Walzer Leavitt, "'Be Safe. Be Sure.': New York City's Experience with Epidemic Smallpox," in *Hives of Sickness: Public Health and Epidemics in New York City*, ed. David Rosner (New Brunswick, NJ: Rutgers University Press, 1995), 95–114.

7. Albert et al., "Last Smallpox Epidemic," 378. J. V. Irons et al., "Outbreak of Smallpox in the Lower Rio Grande Valley of Texas in 1949," *AJPH*, 43 (1953): 25–29.

8. Charles L. Jackson, "State Laws on Compulsory Immunization in the United States," *Public Health Reports*, 84 (1969), 787–95, esp. 788, 789. Judith Sealander, *The Failed Century of the Child*, esp. 330, 338, 352.

9. Albert et al., "Last Smallpox Epidemic," 378. C. Henry Kempe, "The End of Routine Smallpox Vaccination in the United States," *Pediatrics*, 49 (1972): 489–92.

10. D. A. Henderson, *Smallpox: The Death of a Disease*, esp. 26, 53. Erez Manela, "A Pox on Your Narrative: Writing Disease Control into Cold War History," *Diplomatic History*, 34 (2010): 299–323.

11. Henderson, *Smallpox*, 14, 90–92. Manela, "Pox on Your Narrative," 316.

12. Stanley Music quoted in Paul Greenough, "Intimidation, Coercion and Resistance in the Final Stages of the South Asian Smallpox Eradication Campaign," *Social Science & Medicine*, 41 (1995): 635–36. Ibid., 643. See also Manela, "Pox on Your Narrative," esp. 316–17.

13. Henderson, *Smallpox*, 239, 245, esp. 249. Edward A. Belongia and Allison L. Naleway, "Smallpox Vaccine: The Good, the Bad, and the Ugly," *Clinical Medicine and Research*, 1 (2003): 88.

14. Henderson, *Smallpox*, 269–86.

15. Ibid., 296–97. Jon Cohen and Martin Enserink, "Rough-and-Tumble Behind Bush's Smallpox Policy," *Science*, Dec. 20, 2002, 2312–16.

16. Massimo Calabresi, "Was Smallpox Overhyped?" *Time*, Jul. 26, 2004, 16. Madeline Drexler, "A Pox on America," *Nation*, Apr. 28, 2003, 7–8. "Fear of Vaccine," *CQ Researcher*, Jan. 13, 2006, 39. Jocelyn Kaiser, "Report Faults Smallpox Vaccination," *Science*, Mar. 11, 2005, 1540. Donald G. McNeil, Jr., "National Programs to Vaccinate for Smallpox Come to a Halt," *NYT*, June 19, 2003. Pamela Sankar et al., "Public Mistrust: The Unrecognized Risk of the CDC Smallpox Vaccination Program," *American Journal of Bioethics*, 3 (2003): W22–W25. "U.S. Smallpox Vaccine Programme Stalls as Volunteers Balk," *Lancet*, May 10, 2003, 1626. Pascale M. Wortley et al., "Healthcare Workers Who Elected Not to Receive Smallpox Vaccination," *American Journal of Preventive Medicine*, 30 (2006): 258–65.

17. Kathleen S. Swendiman, "Mandatory Vaccinations: Precedent and Current Laws," Congressional Research Service, CRS Report for Congress, Oct. 26, 2009. Sealander, *Failed Century of the Child*, 323–25.

18. "Refusing Kids' Vaccine More Common Among Parents," *USA Today*, May 3, 2010. See *Mead v. Secretary of Health and Human Services*, U.S. Court of Federal Claims, Office of Special Masters, E-Filed: March 12, 2010, esp. 164. http://www.uscfc.uscourts.gov/sites/default/files/Campbell -Smith%20Mead%20Autism%20Decision.pdf, accessed July 8, 2010. See "Vaccine Court Finds No Link to Autism," CNN.com, Mar. 12, 2010; Donald G. McNeil, Jr., "3 Rulings Find No Link to Vaccines and Autism," *NYT*, Mar. 12, 2010. See also Gary L. Freed et al., "Parental Vaccine Safety Concerns in 2009," *Pediatrics*, 125 (2010): 654–59; and Saad B. Omer et al., "Vaccine Refusal, Mandatory Immunization, and the Risks of Vaccine-Preventable Diseases," *NEJM*, 360 (2009): 1981–88.

19. Philip J. Smith et al., "Children Who Have Received No Vaccines: Who Are They and Where Do They Live?" *Pediatrics*, 114 (2004): 187–95. For a revealing argument about contemporary anti-vaccination sentiment, see Dan Kahan, "Fixing the Communications Failure," *Nature*, 463 (2010): 296–97.

Index